SCOTTISH MEN OF LETTERS

IN THE

EIGHTEENTH CENTURY

BY

HENRY GREY GRAHAM

AUTHOR OF 'THE SOCIAL LIFE OF SCOTLAND IN THE EIGHTEENTH CENTURY'

CONTAINING THIRTY-TWO PORTRAITS

LONDON
ADAM AND CHARLES BLACK
1908

PREFACE

THE eighteenth century forms a very distinct period of Scottish literary history, for of its men of note not one had begun to write when the century began, and all of them, except Dugald Stewart, had ceased to write when it ended. This volume, however, does not aim so much at giving a history of the literature as at giving an account of the men who made it. Most of the Scots writers had all the characteristics of their country in their speech, their manners, and ways of living, and they preserved their individualities and peculiarities unsuppressed by those social conventions and restraints of fashion which in a later age moulded their countrymen to more ordinary types. It is these personal characteristics, old-fashioned and pronounced, which render them all the more interesting. We are helped very little to a knowledge of them by biographies written by their friends, for these consisted chiefly of brief, colourless memoirs prefixed to their works. Neither can we gain a picture of their times by such diaries and voluminous correspondence as abounded in England, from which we can reconstruct the social life of the age. In Scotland no diaries were written, little correspondence was preserved: the writers themselves did not keep copies for publication, or their friends did not keep the originals for love.

Probably they wrote few letters: being of a frugal mind, they may have grudged the postage. Even the biographies which were written by contemporaries of the men of letters are disappointing. Dugald Stewart, in his Lives of Reid, Robertson, and Adam Smith, would not spoil a fine period by introducing an anecdote or a personal trait, which would have been of far more interest and value than a hundred sonorous pages. That Adam Smith should have said in his lectures on Rhetoric that he was glad to know that Milton wore latchets in his shoes instead of buckles, to him must have seemed a lack of due sense of literary dignity. In two important quartos Lord Woodhouselee gives a history of Lord Kames, which lets us know as little of his Lordship's real characteristics when we close the last page as when we opened the first. It is a curious fact that when in 1811 the relatives of Dr. Carlyle of Inveresk thought of publishing his Autobiography, which is invaluable as a picture of his times and his friends, they were discouraged by those they consulted—Adam Ferguson among the number—on the ground that the incidents and anecdotes were too unimportant to interest the public. Fortunately we learn much about the men of letters who lived in Edinburgh from the traditions and stories remaining in the recollection of those to whom their presence was familiar, which in various ways have been handed down. An apology perhaps should be made for entitling one chapter "Women of Letters," for strictly speaking it describes women who were not literary persons, like their learned sisters in England. Their whole output consisted of one or two songs; yet these have survived the laborious contributions of women of letters south of the Border. An apology is certainly due to the shades of those high-born dames for bringing them into the company of men who wrote for vulgar fame or money; seeing that their life-long anxiety was to conceal from the public the fact that they had ever written a line or composed a verse. Each of these ladies desired, as the erudite Miss Aikin said of Joanna Baillie, " to lie snug in the asylum of her taciturnity."

In giving portraits of the men of letters, the effort has been made to take them when possible from original paintings, and by preference from those which have not before been copied. Thanks are due to General Carlyle Bell for allowing the author the use of unpublished manuscripts of his relative, Dr. Carlyle of Inveresk.

H. G. G.

CONTENTS

CHAPTER I

DAWN OF LITERATURE—ALLAN RAMSAY—HAMILTON OF BANGOUR—ROBERT BLAIR 1

CHAPTER II

EARLY SCOTTISH PHILOSOPHY—HUTCHESON—DAVID HUME . 30

CHAPTER III

JOHN HOME 60

CHAPTER IV

PRINCIPAL ROBERTSON 78

CHAPTER V

ADAM FERGUSON—DR. HUGH BLAIR—WILLIAM WILKIE—DR. BLACKLOCK 104

CHAPTER VI

ADAM SMITH 148

CHAPTER VII

LITERARY JUDGES: LORD KAMES—LORD MONBODDO—LORD HAILES 172

CHAPTER VIII

JAMES BOSWELL 203

CHAPTER IX

JAMES MACPHERSON . . . 226

CHAPTER X

DR. THOMAS REID—DR. JAMES BEATTIE . . 243

CHAPTER XI

SCOTTISH MEN OF LETTERS IN ENGLAND: MALLET—THOMSON—SMOLLETT 273

CHAPTER XII

WOMEN OF LETTERS: LADY WARDLAW—LADY GRISELL BAILLIE—MRS. COCKBURN—JEAN ELLIOT—LADY ANNE BARNARD—LADY NAIRNE 321

CHAPTER XIII

SONG-WRITERS—SKINNER—BRUCE—FERGUSSON . 355

CHAPTER XIV

ROBERT BURNS 382

CHAPTER XV

HENRY MACKENZIE—DUGALD STEWART—CLOSE OF THE CENTURY . . . 417

INDEX 437

LIST OF ILLUSTRATIONS

DAVID HUME	*Frontispiece*	
THOMAS RUDDIMAN	*Facing page*	10
ALLAN RAMSAY	,,	14
WILLIAM HAMILTON OF BANGOUR	,,	22
FRANCIS HUTCHESON	,,	30
JOHN HOME	,,	60
PRINCIPAL ROBERTSON	,,	78
ALEXANDER CARLYLE	,,	92
ADAM FERGUSON	,,	104
HUGH BLAIR	,,	122
THOMAS BLACKLOCK	,,	140
ADAM SMITH	,,	148
LORD KAMES	,,	172
LORD MONBODDO	,,	188
LORD HAILES	,,	198
JAMES BOSWELL	,,	204
JAMES MACPHERSON	,,	226
THOMAS REID	,,	244
JAMES BEATTIE	,,	260
JAMES THOMSON	,,	282
TOBIAS SMOLLETT		298
LADY GRISELL BAILLIE	,,	324

Mrs. Cockburn	*Facing page* 330
Jean Elliot	,, 336
Lady Anne Barnard	,, 340
Lady Nairne	,, 348
John Skinner	,, 360
Robert Fergusson	,, 374
Robert Burns	,, 400
Henry Mackenzie	,, 418
Dugald Stewart	,, 424
Robert Henry	,, 430

SCOTTISH MEN OF LETTERS IN THE EIGHTEENTH CENTURY

CHAPTER I

DAWN OF LITERATURE—ALLAN RAMSAY—HAMILTON OF BANGOUR—ROBERT BLAIR.

THE divisions of history into centuries may be highly convenient, but they are usually very arbitrary and artificial. There is no breach of continuity with the past as a century opens, no breach of continuity with the future as a century closes. It is like the division of a country into counties, which are marked by lines clearly on the map, while there is no visible partition in the landscape: fields join fields, rivers flow on their course, roads run on their way indifferent to the surveyor's marches, and to the outward eye it is impossible to see where or why one province begins and another ends. It is so with centuries—as divisions or periods in history—in most cases. In Scotland, however, it is not always so arbitrary, and certainly the eighteenth century stands out so markedly in all respects apart from other periods as to form no unnatural division in Scottish history in its social, industrial, religious, political, and literary life. It is with its literary aspects we have specially to interest ourselves in this volume. We have to note how throughout the century new intellectual interests were awakened, and fresh forms of literature were begun.

The century opens in Scotland to find the country almost

devoid of literature. Men of letters there were none; of making books there seems to have been an end. For this literary stagnation there were many causes. The country was hotly stirred by political and ecclesiastical questions—by the intrigues of parties about the Union; by the oppositions of Whigs and Tories, of Presbyterians and Jacobites; by jealous commercial grievances and bitter trade quarrels with England. These causes dulled intellectual interest; other circumstances hindered literary productions. There was the depressing poverty of the land, whose nobles, merchants, and farmers were alike in sore straits for money; the people lived humbly, spent sparingly, travelled seldom, and read little. It was enough that in a laird's book-shelves was his ragged array of old school-books—a well-thumbed Cæsar or Horace, or Buchanan's *Latin Psalms*—reminiscent of a flagellated boyhood. There side by side lay a dilapidated *Ovid*, *Samuel Rutherford's Letters*, Despauter's *Grammar*, and a *Confession of Faith*—telling of years when he had been drilled in Latinity at school and harrowed with piety at home. In several old country mansions, and in a few Edinburgh flats, there were, however, libraries which showed that their owners or their ancestors had some taste for polite letters. Gentlemen who had finished their college course by study at Paris or Leyden or Groningen, and returned with a less supply of continental vices and a larger store of scholarly aptitudes than usual, had collections of classics of no mean size or worth. These men, when they went into winter-quarters in Edinburgh, consorted with lawyers and physicians who had learned their law or their physic and improved their Latinity at Utrecht or Leyden, and in maturer years had not forgotten their classics in devotion to drink.

There came from England by smacks to Leith or Bo'ness, occasionally, small supplies of English books—the newest productions of Mr. Addison or Sir Richard Steele, or the ponderous historical tomes of Echard and Rapin, whose bulk filled a large space in their purchasers' cupboards, and whose reading required a large space of their lives. Certainly the Union had a great effect in stimulating Scottish intellectual interest and widening the literary tastes. Scots gentry who went as members of Parliament to Westminster—some giving their self-sacrificing services to their country for a comfortable salary from their constituency—would bring back books from London, and in various ways literature penetrated to remote rural mansions as to city life, conveyed in cadgers' creels. Thus to young ladies were borne the echoes of far-away gay London life, of fashions and follies and intrigues they should never share. By the firesides they would read aloud the adventures of Orindas and Millamants, or of Sir Roger de Coverley, in accents whose broad Scots would have amazed the heroes and heroines of whom they read—an uncouth, incomprehensible tongue, which would have made Will Honeycomb roar with laughter, and Sir Roger utter gentlemanly oaths of exasperation as he listened.

It is clear that there was as yet little encouragement for the home-made literature—no inducement for men to devote their talents to letters either for pleasure or for profit. The political atmosphere was wild and tempestuous; poets were silent, for in a storm no bird sings. The population, consisting of one million, being impoverished, purchasers were rare, and authors depending on them would have starved in Scotland. Nor could they have appealed to a wider and richer public beyond the Tweed, seeing that men who in daily life spoke the broadest of vernacular could not easily write in English, which to them was a foreign tongue in which they might make more blunders than in school-learned Latin. But most depressing of all was the burden of religious tyranny—the gloom with which mirth was checked, the discouragement given to all worldly entertainments—in song, in fiction, or in play—the censures levelled at all who indulged in profane literature, against which ministers inveighed and the pious frowned. It is not surprising that the men who had taste of letters at that early period were Jacobites and Episcopalians, for sentiment and humour were starved in the cold austerity of the Kirk, which seemed unable to smile. Yet what was outwardly the difference between Episcopalian minister and Presbyterian when the century began? Their worship, their forms, their faith were the same. In private one could be known from the other only by the fact that the Episcopalian said grace standing and the Presbyterian sitting. Their differences were as foolish and whimsical as when the aristocratic Ghibellines cut their fruit cross-ways at table, and the democratic Guelphs sliced theirs long-ways. It was only later, when the clouds of dull pietism had drifted away, that genial literature could flourish without opposition, and did so even in the courts of the National Zion.

It is worth notice that, by the fine irony of events, it was the very austerity of the Kirk that led to the production of one of the greatest works of English fiction. There can be no doubt that if it had not been for the disciplinary severity of an obscure Kirk-Session in Fife, there would have been no *Robinson Crusoe*. It happened in this wise. The dull little fishing village of Largo was occasionally enlivened by the misdeeds of a scapegrace lad, Alexander Selkirk. In 1695 he had misconducted himself in church,[1] and was summoned to appear before the Session, of which his father, a shoemaker, was an elder; but the report was brought back by the kirk-officer that he had absconded and "gone away to the seas." Six years after, he returned, and having in a rage shot at his imbecile brother, he was appointed "to stand at the pillar" as penance for his sin; and after being solemnly rebuked, he promised amendment, "in the strength of the Lord." Determined, however, to run risk of such disgrace no more, he ran off "to the seas" again. Thereafter followed his strange adventures, which ended in his lonely residence for four years in Juan Fernandez, his rescue from which stirred widespread interest after he landed at Bristol. It is certain that the shrewd Daniel Defoe founded his immortal *Robinson Crusoe* on those adventures, which never would have come to pass but for the disciplinary terrorism of the minister and elders of Largo over the village ne'er-do-weel.

At this period there was no possibility for a decent livelihood being gained by a professional man of letters. Scots printers were content to pirate English books—glad of a profitable retaliation on their aggressive neighbours in the South. In dark cellars in the Saltmarket of Glasgow, or Morocco Close, Edinburgh, were produced shabby issues in

[1] Largo Session Records.

execrable type of the *Spectator* or the *Tatler*, or of Dryden's works. But as a rule the productions that came from the superannuated wooden presses — bought second-hand from Holland — that wheezed forth their proofs, in dark wynds, were devoted to law-books, Whig or Tory pamphlets, Presbyterian or prelatic treatises in which the abuse was as villainous as the type, and tractates on antiquities and royal pedigrees which antiquaries refuted and the public never read.

If we look for professional men of letters, we find that class in the most ragged type of mortals who ever wrote for bread. A considerable number of needy and thirsty men formed an Edinburgh Grub Street—broken schoolmasters, law-clerks, and students, who had failed of a profession. They hung on the skirts of fortune, poor starvelings, not too reputable or sober, who were ready with pens to indite funeral elegies in English, Scots, or Latin verses, on the "universally lamented" or "deplorable" death of some "incomparable" lord or citizen; or an epithalamium on the wedding of some person of quality. Whenever the news passed through the town that a lord of Session, merchant, or laird was dead, or had lost his wife, they went to their garrets, wrote out panegyrics, often in acrostics, and with them neatly copied out, but abominably spelt, they went up to the door of the house of mourning, at which they "tirled the risp." If a composition met with approval, the poet would receive a few shillings as payment,[1] and it was duly printed on a broadside with an appropriate border of cross-bones, skulls, spades, and hour-glasses, and sent to the friends of the bereaved. The diction of these first Scotsmen of letters is instructive as showing what poetry consoled great folk in time of affliction. The family of Atholl had their griefs assuaged by reading the "Elegy on the never enough to be lamented Death of the illustrious and noble John, Marquis of Tullibardine, in 1709":

> What sighs, what groans are these I hear always?
> What gushing torrents now run down my eyes?
> What wofull news, what killing sound is this
> That fills all hearts with tears and bitterness?

---

[1] So Sir J. Foulis of Ravelston in his *Accompt Books* notes, "To Mungo Murray, £4:16 Scots for elegy on his son's death."

> Ah dolfull news ! but they cannot be fled,
> The noble Marquis Tullibardin's dead.
> That sweet, that noble matchless paragon ;
> Ah ! is he gone ? He's gone ; alas, he's gone.

And the afflicted poet proclaims his incapacity to recount all the virtues of the deceased :

> I'd hold the seas far sooner in my hand,
> And without pen or ink recount the sand.

A learned judge has expired, and the elegy (remunerated with £6 Scots) laments :

> O ! Senators who sable weeds put on,
> Bowhill has scaled the heavens to a throne,
> And trumpets forth the Mediator's praise,
> Where angells flee about delight to gaze ;
> Who did pronounce pointed decreets 'mongst you,
> With open face the Deity doth view.

Yet another scribe pens his woeful lamentation on Lady Anne Elcho, who was burnt to death, in broken accents and metaphors :—

> My lady Elcho we the more lament,
> That she by a malignant flame is sent,
> And early to the charnel-house doth pass,
> Since nothing of malignant in her was.[1]

It was thus that those scribblers in threadbare clothing and shabby old wigs, which had seen better days and had covered better heads, eked out a living with pens ready to write a venomous lampoon or a metrical lie, buzzing like wasps round any rival, and attacking the popular wigmaker with " A Block for Allan Ramsay's Wig," or malicious " Dying Words of Allan Ramsay," which the poet pretended not to feel. The cleverest of the tribe was Alexander Pennecuik, nephew of the laird of Romanno, always in need and generally in liquor, who could toss off a satire as quickly as he tossed off a glass, would sell it for five shillings, or get it sold in a broadside for twopence, and get drunk on the proceeds. It was in the natural course of events that he died in destitution.[2]

[1] *Scottish Elegiac Verses*, 1629-1729, 1842, pp. 112, 178, 208.
[2] *Lives of Scottish Poets*. The chief works of Alexander Pennecuik are *Britannia Triumphans*, 1713 ; *Streams from Helicon*, 1720.

Of a very different stamp were the gentlemen who were addicted to verses, and produced songs which were long favourites in all circles—such as that lover of verse and country sports, William Hamilton, the laird of Gilbertfield, a lieutenant on half-pay, whose "Last Words of Bonnie Heck," his greyhound, which appeared in Watson's *Choice Collection*, 1706-1711, stirred Allan Ramsay's literary ambition. His rhyming epistles to his wig-making, verse-making friend made popular that form of verse which Francis Sempill of Beltrees in the former century had adopted in his "Habbie Simson, the Piper of Kilbarchan." That was to become the favourite style of stanza for Scots verse with Ramsay, Fergusson, and Burns, and their imitative successors.

If we wish to seek for the beginnings of Scottish literature, we shall find it in the clubs of gentlemen that met in dingy taverns, in dark wynds of Edinburgh. There they had their gatherings over ale and claret, where they would discuss politics, books, and ballads; and after a prolonged sitting, and ample regaling, they would go argumentatively home, as the city guards' drum at ten o'clock gave the warning for all citizens to return decently to their families and to sleep. We can see them—wits and literati—in the periodical reunions in Niddry's Close, where the gilded emblems of the Cross Keys betokened that Patrick Steel had his inn, and where guests could get good claret wondrous cheap,[1] and where once a week met the Musical Club, to which all fashion resorted. There gentlemen of taste and culture and joviality met in fine fraternity—antiquaries like Dr. Patrick Abercrombie, noted for his folios on the *Martial Atchievements of the Scots Nation*, who were not so dry in their cups as in their books; Dr. Archibald Pitcairn, with his dangerous wit; and Sir William Scott of Thirlstane, Sir William Bennet of Grubbit, and others with their excellent Latinity. The possessor of a pretty knack in English and Latin verse would take from his pocket his last effusion—humorous or pathetic, classical or amorous—which was recited, handed round, and maybe printed afterwards for presentation. At the Athenian Club, others held their

[1] *Hamilton of Bangour's Life and Poems*, edited by Paterson.

literary Saturnalia; and at Thomas Ranken's hostelry gathered men who (with carnal refreshments) discussed philosophy.[1]

It may indeed be said that in taverns Scots modern literature was born, and the first public it addressed was in a public-house.

One eminent antiquary—James Anderson—whom Scots Parliament had rewarded for upholding the independency of the Scottish crown, tried to live by his pen. In consequence he was obliged to sell his books, and before dying to pledge the plates for his most learned *Diplomata*.

Among the scholars stands conspicuous the figure of Dr. Archibald Pitcairn—famous at the opening of the century as a physician, a wit, a scholar, and a *bon vivant*—who had been born in 1652. He had been professor of medicine at Leyden —a signal honour—where he had the famous Boorhaave and Dr. Mead as his pupils, before he settled as a doctor in Edinburgh, where his practice and his fees were of the largest. Rival physicians mocked at his theories of applying mathematics to the practice of physic—a curious combination of the most exact of sciences with the least exact of arts. The State authorities eyed askance the ardent Jacobite, and threatened him with prosecution for treason after tearing open one of his private letters, which he explained limply he had "written in his cups." And most of all did the pious Presbyterians regard with even horror a man who was reported to be a free-thinker as well as a free-liver—a man who mocked at Scripture, flouted at religion, jeered at ministers of the everlasting Gospel, and entertained his iniquitous friends with profanity. Mr. Robert Wodrow groans forth his soul over these devilries, of which he heard dreadful rumours, fit to bring judgment on the city. He records his pious tattling about the physician who was haunted with "an apparition," who with his friends "doe meet very regularly every Lord's Day and read Scripture in order to lampoon it," who was "drunk twice every day"—and so on with equal veracity.[2] The person of the learned and very able doctor, whose wit was somewhat profane, and his pen rather licentious,[3] is familiar from the painting of Sir John

---

[1] Tytler's *Life of Kames*, i. 60. [2] Wodrow's *Analecta*, i. 323; ii. 255.
[3] Of which his play, *The Assembly*, first published in 1729, affords an instance.

Medina and engravings therefrom—a pleasant, confident, smiling countenance, shrewd, sagacious, humorous, under his flowing periwig. At six o'clock in the morning he was to be found in that cellar room below the level of the street—called from its gloom the "groping office"—ready for a consultation on any case, and during the day borne in his sedan-chair to visit patients of high degree, from whom his fee was a guinea, though the poor he served from kindness. In the evening he was to be found in the tavern with choice spirits and learned cronies, with whom he jested too freely and drank too much, till the night and the liquor were far spent. His Latin and English epigrams and verses which he would print in broadsides for his friends count for nothing to-day, though they were admired and even famous in his time [1]—and some of them John Dryden was pleased to translate and Matthew Prior to turn into nimble English verse. Pitcairn before he died in 1713 did much to revive in his town the taste for classics, which amidst theological strife and fanatical pietism was dead in the universities, dying in schools, and rare in society. "If it had not been for the stupid Presbyterianism," he would grumble, "we should have been as good as the English at longs and shorts."

After the Union there was a growth in antiquarian and classical interests, and this was largely due to Thomas Ruddiman. One day in 1699, Dr. Pitcairn happened to be stayed by stress of weather in the village inn at Laurencekirk in Kincardineshire, and on asking if there was any one of education whom he could have to dine and talk with, he was told that the schoolmaster was a man of learning.[2] The threadbare young dominie was invited, and was found to be a scholar and a Jacobite to boot. At the physician's encouragement, Ruddiman next year quitted his thatched school-house, and his beggarly salary of £5, chiefly paid in meal, and came to Edinburgh, where by his patron's influence he became, with a salary of £8, sub-librarian of the Advocates' Library, then stored in a dismal room in Miln's Court. The needy scholar copied out chartularies, composed theses for aspirants for the

---

[1] *Selecta Poemata Archibaldi Pitcairnii*, 1729.
[2] Chalmers's *Life of Ruddiman*, p. 31.

Bar, whose Latinity and intelligence were weak, revised manuscripts for authors and proofs for booksellers, sold books by auction in the Parliament Close, and kept boarders (£30 Scots each for their chambers for the half-year) in his humble home. While Ruddiman was thus laboriously engaged, there were only two respectable printing-presses, both belonging to keen Jacobites, in the city; the other booksellers were Presbyterians who printed atrociously.[1] It was from the press of James Watson, at the miserable little room called majestically the "King's Printing House," that there issued the *Collection of Scots Songs*, 1706-1711, sold in his booth opposite St. Giles, which marks the dawn of literature in the North. But it was from Robert Freebairn that the best editions began to come after 1712, and the scholarly Jacobite librarian found a congenial friend in this Jacobite printer, who was the son of a nonjuring "disorderly" bishop. In zeal for the Cause, the printer followed the rebels in '15, and printed proclamations for the Pretender at Perth, and yet afterwards was magnanimously allowed to print books for the Whigs and proclamations for the King in Edinburgh.[2] In the grim dusty crypt under the Parliament House to which the library was transferred, Ruddiman pored over dusty manuscripts, exhumed Scots authors, edited Gavin Douglas's *Virgil*, which came out in stately folios, with a glossary, learned and erroneous, and many a book on knotty points of Scottish history over which there were shed much ink, party enthusiasm, and ill temper. On his producing an edition of George Buchanan's works, in which the historian was charged with fraud, forgery, calumny of Queen Mary, the Whig scholars—generally grammar-school masters—rose in their wrath at the "aspertions and animadversions" of the accuser, and wrangled for forty years. No more energetic soul than Ruddiman lived in Edinburgh, and he added to his many callings that of printer—from his press issuing his famous *Latin Rudiments* in 1714, school classics, vended at sixpence a copy, and the Jacobite newspaper the *Caledonian Mercury*, which began in 1718. His time was passed

---

[1] Lee's *Memorials of Bible Society*, p. 150.
[2] *Ibid.* 183.

THOMAS RUDDIMAN
By permission of J. Steuart, Esq., W.S., from the Painting by De Nune, 1749.

in writing historical treatises learnedly, printing classic texts accurately, controverting vituperatively, marrying frequently, becoming prosperous yearly. At last, in 1757, when deaf and almost blind, the old grammarian died, who had done so much to revive learning and excite controversy.[1] Then there disappeared from the High Street the well-known and eminently respectable figure of the old scholar, with his thin, wiry form, erect and active walk, his solemn face, with the bushy eyebrows, and those piercing eyes which daunted any who ventured to question his opinion; clad on "best days" in an orange-coloured coat and a scarlet waistcoat, with cocked hat over the curled, grizzled wig. A sober, sedate man, he knew when at convivial boards he ought to stop, saying, "The liquor will not go down."

Allan Ramsay

While scholars and antiquaries were busy wrangling in dingy pamphlets and treatises over obscure points of Scottish history and Royal claims and pedigrees; while Freebairn was issuing some seemly folios, such as his Sallust, in noble type; while men of fashion with a taste for letters and facility in rhyme were meeting at Coffee-houses (where no coffee seems ever to be drunk), and at concert-rooms, balls, and suppers, there was living in two rooms, in the wooden-fronted tenement in the Canongate, the wigmaker, Allan Ramsay. Outside, over the door, was a figure of a flying Mercury, and inside, in the ill-lighted little apartment, was a collection of periwigs, tiewigs, bobwigs, of dimensions to suit all pates, and of qualities to suit all purses, from fourteen shillings to £10 sterling. There a little "blackavised" man with a friendly smile, a familiar smirk and twinkle of humorous eyes, nightcap on head, tended any customer who came to get flaxen or hair wigs changed, trimmed, and perfumed.

But this man was more than a wigmaker, he was a verse-maker too.[2] No one was more popular than this

---

[1] Chalmers's *Ruddiman*, p. 269.
[2] *Works of Allan Ramsay* (Life, by G. Chalmers), 1806, 2 vols. *Gentle Shepherd, with Illustrations of its Scenery*, 2 vols., 1808.

framer of perukes: his songs were sung at every festive meeting; his verses were hawked about the streets at nights, and the melodious voices of gingerbread women were heard above the plash of household filth from the windows, crying, among their chap-books, "Satan's Invisible World Displayed," and Allan Ramsay's "new piece" at the price of six bodles. He was a boon companion at the Easy Club, where gentlemen and citizens of taste were wont to meet in the tavern to drink, to sing new songs, to hear essays, to discuss literary points, suggested by papers in the weekly *Tatler*. Each member bore some nickname—Allan's was "Isaac Bickerstaff" or "Gavin Douglas"—and the merriment of jocose lawyers and lively Jacobites was tempered by fines for neglected rules, which went to buy more ale. Of this gay fraternity Allan Ramsay was made poet laureate.

It was in 1686 that Allan had been born among the high bleak Leadhills, where his father had been manager of the mines; there he lived after his father was dead and his mother married again, with his stepfather, herding sheep and cattle in that dreary district—a treeless waste in summer, a snowy waste in winter, swept by all the winds that blew. When his mother died, he found his way to Edinburgh, where he became apprentice to a wigmaker—joining the most flourishing of trades in that wig-wearing age. But other tastes and talents were soon roused. In the book-shops in Parliament Close were exposed for sale editions of Pope and Addison, revealing to the apprentice the glories of English poesy in most inglorious type, which he was eager with his earnings to buy, and in leisure hours to read. In 1707 he was master of his own shop, and there came for barberising and for trimming citizens of all sorts, while the little bustling young man was as keen over poetry as over periwigs. He was busy making verses and songs in 1711; his humorous eye saw every foible and characteristic of city life, and his muse did not soar to greater heights in his earliest verses than an alewife and a scold. He was satirical, but he was cautious; he made no enemies, he took no side in Church or State, for he was mindful not to spoil his trade. Sagaciously he made verses as he made wigs, to please the heads of all customers. Printed on broadsides, they were sold in the streets for one penny a piece; and some were pirated by the nefarious Lucky Reid, the printer's widow, and hawked about the Canongate by strenuously-voiced beggars. In time the list of fugitive poems had grown so large, they were so popular with people who had heard no such quaint lively humour in verse before, that Ramsay proudly resolved to publish them in a volume in 1721. Four hundred copies of the little quarto were subscribed for, and advocates and lairds, noblemen and merchants paid down their money without a grudge. So forth to the world the work went with the poet's benediction: "Far spread my fame, and fix me an immortal name." Horace in such confidence had written in his *Ad librum suum*: why should not he? His fame did spread far and wide—it passed even to England. Gay admired the verses; Pope heard of them and condescended to read them; and Hogarth, charmed by a congenial painter of homely manners, inscribed to him his plates for *Hudibras*. Allan was a successful poet, and not less happy was he as a family man. He had married a small lawyer's daughter, who was as prolific in children as he was in verses. Every twelvemonth there would appear in the parish records some contribution to population with the name Allan Ramsay, "weeg-maker" or "periwigo-maker," as father —offspring of whom he was vastly proud.[1] Only a tradesman as he was, he was welcome in all company, even the highest. After all, could he not claim as his great-great-grandfather, Ramsay, the Laird of Cockpen, brother to the Lord Dalhousie? Did not the very best in the land have cousins who were shopkeepers, silversmiths, linen-drapers in Edinburgh, under the vague denomination of "merchants"?

Two of the pleasantest literary resorts in Scotland were at the mansions of Newhall and Pennecuik, where Ramsay was a frequent guest. At the latter place lived Sir John Clerk, distinguished as antiquary, lawyer, and congenial spirit—a kindly rival of the poet, if he did indeed write the song, "O merry may the maid be, that married the miller"—who afterwards showed his esteem for his friend by erecting an obelisk to his memory in his garden. At Newhall, the hospitable

[1] *Gentle Shepherd, with Authentic Life*, i. 98.

home of Mr. Forbes, met a clever set of men with a taste for letters, who gathered in the chamber called the "Club-room," adorned with portraits of its members from the skilful brush of William Aikman, the laird of Cairney. Among them was old Dr. Alexander Pennecuik, laird of Romanno, whose ne'er-do-weel nephew was lampooning everybody and drinking everything—a physician who, from choice rather than need, doctored the people in Tweeddale, over forty miles of bleak country [1]; who loved his carouse in the roadside inn, enjoyed the humours of gypsies and ministers and small lairds of West Linton, of whom there were forty-five—"fourteen of them on the poor box." He could write in verses not decorous, and withal was learned in Latin, Spanish, and French. It was this old gentleman who suggested to Allan Ramsay the plot of *The Gentle Shepherd*, the scenes of which lie round Newhall. A notable humorist in his time, he died in 1727, an old man of eighty-one, leaving poems, some clever, most of them coarse, which we read with a yawn.

To return to the better poet. Old Scots lyrics existed in abundance, and the airs to which they were set were charming —whence these came none can tell—but many of the ancient ditties were deplorably gross and coarse to the ears of a modern age. Many were more suitable for the harvest-field and penny wedding than for ears polite and ladies, who now were singing songs to viol da gamba and virginal. Ramsay therefore saw a task to his taste, though the wigmaker's notions of delicacy were peculiar. He took many a familiar song to change, and to purge of wanton words, for ladies' lips; and in the process he improved some and spoilt not a few; left many hardly cleaner than before, and added others by himself and his friends. These were issued in his *Tea-Table Miscellany*, the first volume of which appeared in 1724. His collection was a valuable boon to society at the time; but not altogether an unmitigated boon to literature, for many poor songs being composed by him for old airs, the originals passed into oblivion, and words familiar to bygone generations, whose preservation, with all their crudity and coarseness, would have been invaluable to students of old manners, were

[1] *Pennecuik's Works*, 1817, including a "Description of Tweeddale."

ALLAN RAMSAY
From the Drawing by Aikman in the Scottish National Portrait Gallery, Edinburgh.

lost for ever. We would rather have the rudest of the rejected songs than many of those mocking-bird verses, that sang notes which were not their own. In the work of emendation and addition he was helped by some "ingenious gentlemen." These were young men of taste and talent who wrote with ease, and often with success, whose presence was frequent at the tavern clubs—sons of lairds like Robert Crauford, whose "Leader Haughs and Yarrow," "Bush aboon Traquair," and "Tweedside" remained popular long after he was drowned in 1733, while returning from France. There was the witty, genial ex-lieutenant, Hamilton of Gilbertfield, represented best by his "Willy was a wanton wag," a favourite in all convivial parties. None was so congenial to Ramsay as he; they exchanged rhyming epistles, jocular and humorous —the young laird the wittier, and destined to receive the compliment, sixty years later, of being imitated by Robert Burns.[1] Still more popularly was Hamilton to be known by his abridgment of Blind Harry's "Wallace," published in 1722, which became a chap-book to be found in every cottage—ill-printed, peat-begrimed, thumb-marked, and in later days to give a patriotic thrill to the Ayrshire ploughman, prompting to "Scots wha hae." He died in 1751.

Less good work did Ramsay achieve in his *Evergreen, being a Collection of Scots Poems wrote before* 1600, in which old Scots pieces were garbled and spoiled in words and versification, and his own "Vision" was audaciously foisted as an ancient poem. In this collection appeared "Hardyknute," which had been issued first in the folio sheets in 1719, as an antique ballad.

---

[1] Hamilton's second Epistle has this as its first stanza:

> When I received thy kind epistle,
> It made me dance and sing and whistle;
> O sic a fike and sic a fistle
>   I had about it!
> That e'er was knight of the Scots thistle
>   Sae fain I doubted.

Burns's "First Epistle to Lapraik" has this as its last stanza:

> And to conclude my lang epistle,
> As my auld pen's worn to a grissle;
> Twa lines frae you wad gar me fissle,
>   Who am, most fervent,
> While I can either sing or whistle,
>   Your humble servant.

None guessed then that it was the work of clever Lady Wardlaw of Pitreavie.

All literary faults which proceeded from Allan's profound conceit of his powers and his taste were to be condoned by his *Gentle Shepherd*, which appeared in 1725, based upon earlier efforts. For this Hamilton of Bangour wrote the dedicatory address to the ever-charming Susanna, Countess of Eglinton—the sweetest patroness a poet could find, then in her matchless beauty and wit, who was the loveliest dowager at the Assembly, the fairest burden borne in a sedan-chair along the High Street; who was to grace the balls in far later years with seven daughters, as lovely as herself, to charm the great Dr. Johnson in 1773, and yet to live till 1791, a dear old woman of ninety-one. In his pastoral play, Ramsay is at his best, for its racy humour, its genuine poetry, its scenes of country life and manners. The characters are human beings, not the shepherds and shepherdesses of conventional, pastoral songs, with crooks adorned by dainty ribbons, and clad in attire no mortal ever wore, with reeds which no lips ever played on, and "pipes" which no sheep ever followed. It was surely providence that interfered to prevent the worthy man from imitating Guarini's *Pastor Fido*, which he read in a translation and desired to emulate. This comedy at least has the freshness of the country; the broad Scots speech is real, the characters have life; yet it is true the town-bred wigmaker idealised rural ways and peasant life, of which he knew nothing very familiarly. It does not present the people as they lived in his day, still less in the time of Cromwell, in which the plot is laid. We smell no dirt, we find no squalor, we touch no rags, we see no hovels, all which were in the common lot of the peasantry. But then we must remember that after all it is a pastoral, which dare not be a squalid picture of real life; it is poetry, and often very good poetry too.[1]

Never had been such success for a Scots poem: it sold edition after edition; it won a fame in England as in Scotland;

---

[1] Some papers in the *Guardian* (1713) first ridiculed the fantastic form of pastoral, and urged that, instead of the conventional Corydon and Phillis, Tityrus and Amaryllis, there should be English rustics and real English scenery. These papers would be read and remembered by Ramsay and his friends of the Easy Club.

Gay was charmed. Pope was pleased, as his friend Dr. Arbuthnot read it to him and explained the Scots—an unknown tongue to the poet of Twickenham.[1]

Now prosperous, in 1726 Ramsay quitted the dingy old shop near the Tron Kirk, and established himself in the Luckenbooths—a row of "lands" standing in the High Street fronting St. Giles', and blocking the street to a narrow entry. Above his door he placed the busts of William Drummond of Hawthornden and Ben Jonson, instead of the dilapidated figure of Mercury which had adorned the door of the wig-shop—for the poet had abandoned the trade in periwigs, razors, and curling-tongs, and become a bookseller, as befitted his dignified literary position. He started the first circulating library in the kingdom, and lent out books at a penny a night, sometimes of a description which made the godly weep. Instead of soul-guiding works like those of the reverend and faithful minister of God, Mr. James Durham, *The Groans of Believers*, or the *Balm of Gilead*, there were the works of Congreve, Wycherley, Dryden, and Matt Prior: yea, the scandalous *Atalantis* of Mrs. Manley, which was found in the hands of young ladies. One knows how the Reverend Robert Wodrow wrote his lamentation that "all the villainous, profane, and obscene books and plays, as printed at London, are got down by Allan Ramsay and lent out, for an easy price, to young boys, servant weemen of the better sort, and gentlemen . . . by these wickedness of all kinds are dreadfully propagat among the youth of all sorts."[2] Magistrates, who were pious elders, examined the shelves to see if ugly rumours which the pious hypocrite Lord Grange had reported were true, but the pawky librarian had hidden the worst before they looked, leaving ministers to moan in vain over the soul-destroying influence of the scurrilous and godless books which were in circulation, for "a villainous obscene thing is no sooner printed at London than it is spread and communicat at Edinburgh."

Thus, in making books, selling them, and lending them, the

---

[1] *Ramsay's Poetical Works and Life*, 1806, p. 80.
[2] Wodrow's *Analecta*, iii. 516. Alexander Pennecuik issued a lampoon entitled "The Flight of Religious Piety from the Land upon account of Ramsay's Lewd Books and the Hell-bred Comedians who debauch all the Faculties of the Soul of our Rising Generations."

little poet was prosperous as well as famous, and how delightful it was in his shop to have little paunchy Mr. Gay, the poet, when on a visit to her capricious grace the Duchess of Queensberry, to hear his talk about the great world of letters, of the great men he knew, and to point out to him from his window all the Edinburgh notables as they passed along the street. He was proud to think that he was known in London, that his songs were sung there, and his "Sodger Laddie" was rapturously received in Marylebone Gardens—though it must be owned it was listened to less for its vapid words than for its music; for Scots tunes had been made fashionable by William Thomson, now musician to Queen Caroline, formerly oboe player in Edinburgh. By 1730 he ceased to write; he felt his Pegasus getting old and stiff, his muse was less inspiring. But he must be busy; he must be an important personage. He loved play-actors, had written prologues for the plays performed surreptitiously "gratis" as part of a concert of music to evade the law, and now he ventured to build a theatre in Carrubber's Close in 1736. To his dismay, under the new licensing Act it was summarily closed by the magistrates, and the proprietor was ruefully left with injured feelings and an empty purse, while the luckless theatre was left to pass through many vicissitudes—to be the meeting-place for nondescript societies and sects, to become a Jacobin club, and a Roman Catholic chapel. Poverty seems even to have come to Ramsay, for he is found writing abject letters to Forbes of Culloden, asking assistance in his sore straits—"Will you not give me something to do?"—a bitter pill for the vain little man to swallow.[1]

The worthy soul in later years was ensconced in his brand-new house—of whimsical form, popularly likened to a "goose pie"—on the brow of the hill overlooking what was then the Nor' Loch, and facing the green fields on which Princes Street stands, looking away to the Fifeshire coast. There he was happy with his family of daughters, while his son Allan had become a famous artist, a fine scholar, a leader of society. His daughters married, and his wife died, passing away without one of those elegies which he wrote so readily, "because,"

[1] Carruthers's *Highland Note-book*, p. 63.

suggests George Chalmers kindly, in his inimitable style, "the loss was too affecting for loquacity to deplore."[1]

He went in and out of his shop, adjourned to tavern suppers, trotted up and down the High Street, with his little squat form, his big paunch, his short legs, his head adorned with fair round wig and cocked hat, surmounting a kindly, smirking, self-complacent face—the best-known and vainest man about town. In 1758, January 8, the little poet ended his prosperous career, at the age of seventy-two.

It is in Scots verse he lives: his English efforts are as forced and feeble and mechanical as his more learned friends' Latin elegiacs, mere echoes at the best of the poets he studied and whose phrases he copied. His songs are not his best work, though "Farewell to Lochaber" and the "Lass o' Patie's Mill" deserve to live. At his best he writes pieces which have sly humour, with touches of racy satire; verses which give graphic pictures of city life and portraits of character, caustic and vigorous, but sometimes only coarse and squalid. But with self-complacency he produces much cleverish commonplace with a too nimble fluency. Old Edinburgh, in those writings of his, is vividly pictured for us. We see the ladies wearing their green and red plaids—for whose continued use he pleaded so well[2]—held with one arm round the waist to keep them tight to the body, and gloved hand holding them close to the face, from which the eyes sparkled brightly—a costume so useful in kirk to hide the modest from the ogler's eye, and to hide the slumbering eyelids from the preacher's sight. We see the archers, eight brigades, marching in blue St. Andrew's bonnets, trimmed with green ribbons on their wigs, to shoot at the butts on Leith or Musselburgh links, while a splendid array of fashion watch as the Duke of Hamilton[3] and his comrades compete for the Silver Arrow amid thunders of applause. Then comes the supper at the tavern, when at the chairman's word toasts are given of ladies fair, and the glass goes round. "My lord, your toast, the preses cries," and in bewildering succession each proposes the lady of his praise. We hear at mid-day the

---

[1] *Poems of A. Ramsay* (Life, by G. Chalmers).
[2] In his *Tartana*.
[3] Oliphant's *Jacobite Lairds of Gask*, p. 101

chimes of St. Giles' playing the gay tunes of Italy and France, and sweet airs of Scotland, over the romantic and dirty capital of the north, and hear the tread of hasty citizens leaving their shops to drink at taverns their "meridians" at the sound of the "gill bells." There are the caddies in their rags and impudence, running their errands from wynd to wynd, and gilt sedan-chairs borne by Gaelic porters trotting on the causeway. In the Meadows, which Mr. Hope of Rankeillor has just reclaimed (in 1727) from morass, and planted and hedged, professors walk when their classes are over, and ladies and gentlemen saunter on the grass beside these trees, as yet too small for shade or shelter. In the afternoon we see the crowd in the grim West Bow, as the Assembly meets at five o'clock—sedan-chairs blocking the narrow lane with their behooped occupants, and gentlemen in silk and satin, gold-laced coat and waistcoat, and clinking-sword, and wavy periwigs, making their entrance up the dark turnpike stair. As night goes on, we hear the roysterers as they reel and sing on their way home from the taverns, when the sound of the drum's tattoo rumbles through the dark streets—

> With tattered wigs, fine shoes, and uncocked hats,
> And all bedaubed with snuff their loose cravats.

And then the hawkers sell and sing their songs with sounds that make hideous the malodorous air. On Saturday the Bruntsfield Links are full of golfers, whose balls smashed the knee of that now wooden-legged scholar Mr. William Lauder—who pretended to prove Milton a plagiarist, and proved himself a forger—and then they adjourn to the little inn at Morningside, where Maggy Johnstone dispenses "tippeny" of rarest quality to her customers who lie sprawling on the grass, drinking damsels' healths and playing "high jinks"—that game of drunken gambling; and the modest toper, whose glass is not yet emptied, at their warning cry of "Pike yer bane!" drinks it to the dregs. Sunday comes, and the throngs go forth to listen in the High Kirk to the Rev. James Webster, who with a leaden cap on head, expounds his texts and pounds the pulpit with rampant vigour; while in the evening, in the silent streets, the Kirk-treasurer's man slinks along to detect any

Sabbath "vaguers," or to report the transgressor to the session, or extort hush-money from their trembling victim. All these scenes live over again in the works of Allan Ramsay.

HAMILTON OF BANGOUR

Among the literary obscurities or celebrities of that age, one of the best known to posterity is William Hamilton, son of the laird of Bangour. When only twenty years old, he wrote a song which made him famous in his country, and has earned for him an attenuated immortality—the "Braes o' Yarrow," composed in 1724. It was sung many a time at the symposia in the Crosskeys, kept by Patrick Steel—no common tapster, but a musician who made violins as well as he played them [1]—where young Hamilton and his friends so often met, and found its way by manuscript copies to town and country houses, where the verses were sung to the fine old Scots melody. Where was there lady with voice or ear who did not sing to virginal or harp "Busk ye, busk ye, my winsome marrow," by Willy Hamilton? This young poet was a man of taste and sentiment. He could write verses in colloquial Scots and fluent lines in English, in which his deftness was considerable, though in that foreign tongue his vocabulary is limited. To his countrymen, who could not be critics of English, his verses seemed admirable, and he certainly deserves the credit of being the first Scotsman in that century to write poetry in good English. He would copy verses in plain hand on folio sheets, gilt-edged, and present ladies with lines adoring their persons, their virtues, and all that were theirs, and much that was not—which they carefully transcribed into their albums, where they lurked for many a day, till 1748, when, without the author's knowledge, they were published.

Hamilton was a man of fashion, and where was life more fashionable than in Edinburgh? Year by year, as winter drew near, and the snows began to tip the Ochils or the Lammermuirs, and the country looked bleak and bare, coaches set forth from mansions and castles laden with families bent

---

[1] Chambers's *Domestic Annals*, ii.

on the gaiety of the capital. Slowly, noisily the vehicles ploughed the roads, and on the leathern straps their huge bodies swung and creaked. It was to Edinburgh, rather than to the foreign and expensive court at London, that the Scots nobility flocked, and society was made brilliant with the presence of the Dukes of Hamilton, Douglas, and Perth, my lords Annandale, Eglinton, and Panmure, Kilmarnock, March, Dundonald, and many more, who, with the ladies, readily exchanged baronial homes for lofty flats, fine avenues for dirty wynds, fresh country air for city smells. On week days they would go to see Signora Violante, the Italian dancer and tumbler, with her mountebanks, in Carrubber's Close, next door to the poor little chapel to which Jacobites went on Sundays. Once a fortnight they went in their silks and brocades, and hoops of vast rotundity, to the "consorts" held in the Steel's Crosskeys, in the close off the Canongate, listening to hautbois, 'cello, and virginal, where musicians with "sweetest sound Corelli's art display"—the laird of Newhall on the viol da gamba, Lord Colville on the harpsichord, and Sir Gilbert Elliot of Minto on the German flute, which he was the first to introduce into Scotland. To the Assembly they would go, where, from five to eleven o'clock, at charge of half-a-crown, with serious grace they danced their minuets in those several sets—the "maiden set," the "married set," the "heartsome set," the "quality set," and the "beauty set" —at which last all eyes were fastened on faces which showed how justly Scotland was famed for beautiful women. Those high-born, country-bred dames and damsels were not richly dressed—the parental incomes were too small for that; they were not powdered or painted—their complexion was too fine for that; they were not noisy, intriguing "misses"—their simplicity was too good for that; their attire displayed no jewels; their hair was simply worn in ringlets; and their modest mien showed forth the freshness of Scottish damsels, whom all travellers from England admired. Nor were they without accomplishments: they learned from the celebrated Lamotte to dance; they learned from foreign masters who came north in winter how to sing, if not to speak Italian; and with a grudge their fathers supplied the fees to learn virginal and harpsichord, to

WILLIAM HAMILTON OF BANGOUR
From the Painting by Gavin Hamilton in the Scottish National Portrait Gallery, Edinburgh.

which their daughters sang so well.¹ There were men of fashion, too, who imitated London modes—from the days when that beau, John Law of Lauriston (before he blossomed into a disastrous financier in France), was known as "Jessamy John," from his assiduous polishing of his shoes with oil of Jessamine,² till modishness attained its height in Beau Forester of later times—known afterwards as the "Polite Philosopher" from his book so-called—who sat in chintz *négligé* to be dressed and powdered by his valet on the open balcony on the High Street. In Edinburgh young men of rank were far from uncouth; and often vain of their "flaxen hair perfumed, their Indian cane, embroidered coat, and stocking silver clocked," as Bangour describes them.

It was in such high society that Hamilton lived—himself a flirt, a philanderer, inflammable as tinder to female attractions. His hospitable, commodious soul could entertain several loves at once, or receive them in quick succession, while he gallantly speeded the parting guest. He loved in facile verse to celebrate the charms of fair daughters of lords and lairds and judges that graced the balls. "Sweet Humcia's lips," "Kinlochia's shape," "Maria's snowy breast," "Dundasia's face"—these were the themes to which he "strikes the golden lyre" with painful alacrity. At tea-parties, to circles of admiring ladies, the polite poet would recite his verses, while "fair Pringle" accompanied them on harpsichord, and lovely Mistress Jane Erskine sang them. Love-lorn strains they were, expressive of tears he never shed, and of passion he never felt. The poetic "laird of a small estate of rural acres" fluttered from one "Cynthia of the minute" to another with the vagrant ease of a butterfly—yet too careful to give to any an exclusive devotion. There was Mistress Jane Stewart, whose beauty the versifier loved to celebrate, who, being vexed what to do with this dangler, in perplexity asked the lank, long advocate, Henry Home (for the Lord Kames of the future was a beau in those days) how she could get rid of his attentions. "Dance with him at the Assembly to-night, show him every mark of your kindness, as if you resolved to favour his suit.

---

¹ *L'Éloge d'Écosse et des Dames Écossaises*, par Mr. Freebairn, 1732.
² Wilson's *Memorials of Edinburgh*, ii. 83.

Take my word for it, you'll hear no more of him." The lady took the shrewd advice, and the cautious poet took his leave.[1] Yet twice did the poet marry—the first time, because he loved the lady; the second time, because the lady loved him. But Hamilton had other companions and more robust delights, and when the concerts and the balls were over he, with his friends, would go to Maclauchlin's tavern to drink deep and recite sentimentally his stanzas, or visit Coutts's cellar, of "Cimmerian darkness"; for he, like Allan Ramsay, despised a "tea-faced generation"—descending as to the bowels of the earth with unequal steps to drink the claret from tin cans.[2]

Facile, good-natured, changeable in his politics as in his affections, though a Whig by training under President Dalrymple, his sympathies were transferred as he was sauntering one day at the Capitol of Rome, and a hand was laid on his shoulder, and a smiling voice said, "Well, Mr. Hamilton, whether do you like this prospect or the one from North Berwick Law?" This—a greeting from Prince Charles—made him a Jacobite to his cost.[3] In the '45 he followed the Prince, and escaping from Culloden in the guise of a serving-man, he was seized in a cave and discovered with love-verses in his pocket addressed characteristically "To the Mysterious Inmate of my Heart," which was fatuously supposed to mean the Pretender. After hiding in the garret of a manse for six weeks, he escaped with impaired health from his martial adventures, and joined that pathetic little colony of Scots fugitives at Rouen which lived frugally in scanty quarters, waiting eagerly for news from the old country many were never to see, and for remittances from their estates that few were ever to get, dreaming of a Restoration which was never to come. Stout Stewart of Threipland was there, and shrewd Andrew Lumsden, afterwards ill-paid secretary to the Prince, who dismissed him because he would not accompany him, when his Highness was drunk, to the Opera. There, too, was Lumsden's brother-in-law, Robert Strange, the engraver—a Jacobite *malgré lui*, all to please his vigorous

---

[1] Tytler's *Kames*, i. 63.
[2] *Hamilton's Life and Poems*, ed. Patterson.
[3] Ramsay's *Scotland and Scotsmen*, i. 29.

spouse, who remained in Edinburgh in a garret trying to
support herself and child working her spinning-wheel while
she rocked the cradle, and would go forth at dusk in threadbare gown to dispose of her work for sixpence.[1] Hunter of
Burnside touched Smollett's heart by telling him how, when
resident at Boulogne, he and his companions used wearily to
pace the beach, to feast their longing eyes with a prospect of
the white cliffs of Albion, which they were never to approach.[2]
Meanwhile at home the songs and poems of the amiable exile
were remembered. At every Tory tea-table was sung his
"Ode to the Battle of Gladsmuir," in which he celebrated
the victory at Prestonpans, to music set by the favourite
M'Gibbon. In 1748 a collection of his poems, edited by
his friend Adam Smith, was published in Glasgow, to forestall a pirated edition, and in this were old pieces reprinted
and verses gathered from private collections and feminine
desks without the exile's knowledge. His land was restored
to the harmless rebel, and he returned to take possession
—only to be forced by ill-health to leave once more and
die of consumption at Lyons in 1754. He left behind him
memories of an amiable soul, of merry nights and literary
days, of gay visits to subterranean cellars, "full many a
fathom deep." Ladies long recalled the kindly, harmless ways
of "Willy Hamilton," and when they were old and grey and
wrinkled, lean or corpulent, they would read over the lines
which he had presented them, describing their "beauteous
form," their "snowy breast," their waists of divine propor-
tions, when they were young; and then giving a furtive
glance at their tell-tale mirrors, would wonder if ever these
glowing words could really have been true of them. But
did not the spinster aunt of Sophia Western boast to her
niece that she—even she—had in her time been called the
"cruel Parthenissa"?

When news of the poet's death was heard, the *Caledonian
Mercury*, kindly to a Jacobite, proclaimed him to be "in language,
sentiment, and numbers a poet little (if at all) inferior to a
Dryden, an Addison, or a Pope"; with which assertion the

[1] J. H. Smith's *Life of Nollekens*, i. 27.
[2] *Peregrine Pickle*, chap. xxxvi.

editor of his works in 1763 was in full accord, for David Rae (afterwards Lord Eskgrove) in his preface shows he was hardly less absurd when he was young and an advocate than when he was old and a judge. There are one or two fine lyrics, there are a few fine lines, but the verses are stone dead, except the "Braes o' Yarrow." Odes, elegiacs bleat forth their grief in melodious tears over people long vanished, and magnify the graces of those long passed from this fleeting world. Dr. Johnson scoffed when Boswell praised this Scots poet, and admiringly quoted from his "Contemplation" unhappy lines, though the great doctor in his *Lives of the Poets* lauded versifiers far worse than he. Boisterously he laughed at a writer who made "wishes" rhyme with "blushes," having evidently been wont to pronounce it "wushes" in society. But Bozzy tells the world (though assuredly he did not dare to tell his revered friend) that "I comforted myself with thinking that the beauties were too delicate for his robust perception."[1]

Robert Blair

Allan Ramsay had ceased to write, and was spending a complacent old age trotting up and down the High Street to his shop, and meeting old friends in familiar taverns. Hamilton of Bangour was penning sentimental nothings, and handing them round for the delectation of his many friends. William Meston, the Jacobite, and ex-professor of Latin of Aberdeen, was writing clever Latin verses and Scots satires; living as a dependent on kindly Jacobite dames—the Countess Mareschal and Lady Erroll, who gave him food and clothing; drunken when in funds, destitute when he was out of them, the merriest, wittiest, most learned of companions over a bottle; till, forlorn and broken in constitution and character, he died in 1745.[2] Meanwhile, at the manse of Athelstaneford, a grave, stately minister of the Gospel was trying to get a bookseller in London to publish a poem of solemn import—as unlike the light verses of his contemporaries as the toll of a funeral bell to the merry "gill bells" of St. Giles'.

[1] Boswell's *Life of Johnson* (edit. Croker, 1848, p. 544).
[2] *Poems*, by W. Meston, 1765.

At last, in 1743, there appeared a tiny volume *The Grave*, by Robert Blair. The author was a member of a distinguished clerical family — grandson of the Rev. Robert Blair who had been appointed to treat between Charles I. and Oliver Cromwell. A reserved man he was, known intimately to few even in his neighbourhood—keeping himself much to the precincts of the manse garden, except when he wandered among the glens and moorland botanising; yet full of scientific interest, corresponding with authorities on optics and microscopic science in England. He was a courtly, dignified friend with county families, but not intimate with his clerical brethren, who little frequented his house, in spite of his wife being "frank and open and uncommonly handsome." Young folk, like Alexander Carlyle when he was a lad, avoided that manse, with its minister "austere and void of urbanity."[1] For several years Mr. Blair had been busy in his book-room, which long after his death was known as "The grave," with his science, his books, and also in writing poetry, though he had as yet only published an elegy on Professor Law, his father-in-law. Anxiously he sought a publisher for the poem on which he had long been engaged. But booksellers knew that the public cared only for something light and lively—epigrams that glittered, or satires that stung—and such literary wares the Presbyterian minister did not offer them. Not far from his parish were living the soldier-saint Colonel Gardiner and his wife Lady Frances; they were intimate with Mr. Blair, who was pious and preached sermons "serious and warm," and through Lady Frances, who loved saintly dissenters,[2] acquaintance was made with nonconforming lights.[3] Dr. Watts on his behalf tried the booksellers; but they doubted if "a person living 300 miles from London could write so as to be acceptable to the fashionable and the polite." Doddridge next exerted his interest, and the poem was finally accepted. But not yet were his troubles over. Society did not care for poetry of the charnel-house, the bookseller insisted that he should relieve the gloom of his poem; and the disconsolate author was obliged to sit down in his book-room

---

[1] Carlyle's *Autobiography*, p. 94; Blair's *Grave* (with Life by Anderson), 1797.
[2] Fergusson's *Henry Erskine*, p. 40.   [3] *Ibid.* p. 40.

—as he says bitterly to Dr. Doddridge—"to use proper arts to make such a piece go down with a licentious age which cares for none of these things." If the piece was more lugubrious before he began to alter it "to suit the licentious age," it is difficult to imagine how he had ever managed to make it so, for it treats sombrely enough of "skulls and coffins, epitaphs and worms." The work met with unexpected success. It appeared at a period when there was in many quarters a reaction from the frivolous tastes of society, when Wesley and Whitfield were beginning to touch the more earnest hearts of the age, when Watts and Doddridge were leaders in dissenting communities. To such sober circles *The Grave*, like Young's *Night Thoughts* and Hervey's *Meditations among the Tombs*, was grateful, if not exhilarating. It says much for Blair that, treating of a subject where there is but the one perilous step between the sublime and the ridiculous, he never makes the fatal step. Unequal as it is, with intervals of solemn commonplace, there is a striking impressiveness and sombre power which raise *The Grave* to a high level of poetry. That the poet carried in his mind, and imbedded in his lines, thoughts and phrases from other writers need not much diminish his claim to originality.[1] Little known to the

---

[1] Reminiscences of his reading of English poets recur here and there. Nat Lee's lines—

> While foulest fiends shun thy society,
> And thou shalt walk alone, forsaken fury
> 			(*Alexander the Great*, Act i. sc. 1)

are reproduced in

> The common damned shun their society,
> And look upon themselves as fiends less foul.

Dryden's

> Whistling to keep myself from being afraid
> 			(*Amphitryon*, Act i. sc. 1)

suggests his schoolboy

> Whistling to keep his courage up.

Norris's

> Like angels' visits, short and bright,

suggested his

> Like those of angels few and far between.

(Compare Campbell's

> Angels visits few and far between.)

world while he lived, and leaving few memories behind when he died, at the age of forty-seven, in 1746,[1] he has left one poem which merits an honourable place in literature, and has earned continued distinction from the designs, instinct with genius, which come from the pencil of William Blake, whose weird fancy revelled over these grim pictures of mortality.

And Norris's lines

> Some courteous ghost, tell this great secrecy,
> What 'tis thou art and we must be
> (*Meditation*, 1697)

are copied in

> O that some courteous ghost would blab it out,
> What 'tis you are and we must shortly be.

[1] His third son, a distinguished advocate, became Lord President of the Court of Session.

CHAPTER II

EARLY SCOTTISH PHILOSOPHY—HUTCHESON—DAVID HUME

WHILE there were signs of a growth of literary interest in Scotland in poetry, history, and antiquarianism, there were also in the Universities signs of fresh intellectual life. In the first years of the century, the Universities were centres of dulness, the regents carrying their pupils through their three years' curriculum of learning with antiquated methods and scholastic authorities of past ages; but there gradually came into those chairs teachers of a new type. Aristotle was superseded by Locke, Descartes gave way to Newton as the authorities. Colin Maclaurin leaving Aberdeen in 1725, where since he was nineteen he had been teaching a few students, came to Edinburgh to begin his brilliant career in the chair of mathematics, as colleague to James Gregory, who kept the salary and left him the fees, which Sir Isaac Newton, in compassion for his disciple, supplemented by £20; in 1727 Alexander Monro was installed as the first professor of anatomy, and with other teachers began to form a great medical school, gathering students to his class-room from all quarters. In Glasgow, in 1712, Robert Simson became the first professor of mathematics, soon to attain fame as a brilliant reviver of Greek geometry. And in 1730 there began to lecture on philosophy Francis Hutcheson, who was to quicken philosophic interest in Scotland, and to influence deeply and widely the thought and tone of a new generation.

For thirty years the chief teacher in philosophy in the West had been Mr. Gershom Carmichael, a laborious and

FRANCIS HUTCHESON
From the Painting by John Foulis in Glasgow University.

conscientious man, the son of an old covenanting minister, who had named his offspring "Gershom" because, having been born in London, he was, as the Hebrew name signifies, a "sojourner in a strange land." He had been appointed to that chair when he was young and knew little of modern philosophy, and died when he was old without knowing much, although he was the best commentator on the great text-book of Puffendorf.[1] He was, however, as Mr. Robert Wodrow relates, "singularly religious," and "under great depths of soul exercise,"[2] which is not a common exercise for professors to indulge in. His successor was of a calmer temperament.

Born in 1694, Francis Hutcheson was the son of a Presbyterian minister in County Down, grandson of a minister who had come from Ayrshire. Like most Irish Presbyterian youths preparing for the ministry, he was sent to Glasgow College, and there he studied under Mr. Gershom Carmichael, who then as regent taught to his pupils in successive years Greek, logic, philosophy, and physics. From the "soul-exercised" Carmichael he passed to study divinity under Professor John Simson, whose alleged Arianism and hopes for the salvation of the heathen agitated for years the whole church, till he was suspended from his chair, though not before he had instilled more liberal thinking than Calvinistic professors had ever encouraged in students.

In 1716 Hutcheson was licensed to preach, but his tone and teaching were not of the evangelical, soul-searching order that Irish Presbyterians loved. One Sunday being rainy, his father did not like to venture out, so Francis for the first time took his place in the pulpit. As the weather cleared, Mr. Hutcheson went out of doors, and met the congregation going home, dissatisfaction marked on their countenances. An elder, a Scotsman, accosted the anxious father and said, "We a' feel wae for your mishap, reverend sir, but it canna be concealed, your silly loon Frank has fashed a' the congregation wi' his idle cackle; for he has been babbling this 'oor about a gude

---

[1] It is curious that Sir William Hamilton should say that "Carmichael may be regarded as the real founder of the Scottish School of Philosophy" (*Reid's Works*, p. 30, edit. Hamilton).

[2] *Analecta*, iii. 440; iv. 95.

benevolent God, and that the souls o' the heathens themsels will gang to heaven, if they follow the licht o' their ain conscience. No a word did the daft lad ken, speer, nor say aboot the gude auld comfortable doctrine o' election, reprobation, original sin, and faith. Hoot, mon, awa' wi' sic a fellow!"[1] Here surely were forbidden fruits plucked from Mr. Simson's doctrine.

The premature moderate did, indeed, find a congregation to appoint him their minister; but he soon gave it up, and for eight years he kept a private academy in Dublin, and pursued his philosophical studies. A treatise on the *Original of Beauty and Virtue* in 1725, and an *Essay on the Passions and Affections*, established his literary reputation, won him the friendship of men of high position, and resulted in his appointment to the Chair of Moral Philosophy in Glasgow when good Carmichael died. When entered on his post in 1730, his name and his success attracted dissenting students from England and Ireland, who with the others soon filled those benches, before which Carmichael had lectured to about thirty pupils. He was the first professor to give up lecturing in Latin—to the joy of the students—and his lectures were full of animation, as he discoursed, walking backwards and forwards in the room, with his clear persuasive voice. A pleasant man to look at, with a kindly expression on his florid face, with a genial dignity in his presence as he stood in his gown and ample wig. In his teaching he discarded the old arid scholasticism, though he had no fancy for new abstract speculation.[2] He set himself rather to study the mind, with its faculties and passions, as a botanist examines a plant and separates it into component parts. According to his theory of virtue there is in man a "moral sense" (adopting Lord Shaftesbury's phrase) by which he discriminates virtuous and vicious actions, just as the physical senses discern colours, sounds, and taste. What is the quality that this sense approves in any act? Hutcheson replies it is Benevolence—"all the kind affections which incline us to make others happy, and all the actions which

---

[1] Reid's *History of Presbyterian Church in Ireland*, iii. 408.
[2] Leechman's *Life of Hutcheson*, prefixed to *System of Moral Philosophy*, 1754.

flow from such affections." Using a phrase which Bentham afterwards created into a moral creed, he maintains "that that action is best which procures the greatest happiness of the greatest numbers."[1] As he discoursed on the beauty of virtue, on the moral affections, on the regulation of passions, he impressed his scholars with an enthusiasm akin to his own. "When enforcing moral virtues," says Carlyle, one of his students in 1743, "he displayed a fervent and persuasive eloquence which was irresistible."[2] There was a fine optimism in his theological creed, born like his moral theory of his genial nature. There was a teaching very different from that prevalent in the Church. The philosopher taught that by morality man can serve a benevolent God; evangelical ministers taught that by faith alone God can be pleased, and by moral works no man be saved. Insensibly he was revolutionising religious thought—especially in the west, where clergy and people were the sternest of Calvinists, the keenest of evangelicals. Now, youths who were to form the new generation in church or society were inoculated with the new thought—hard dogmas lost their hold over them, the doctrine of total corruption grew unreal as he depicted the beauty of human nature. A remorseless creed was shaken by the doctrine of a benign Universal Parent—"whose world shows happiness, whose chastisements are tender admonitions." To his influence was added that of Dr. Leechman—professor of Divinity, afterwards the Principal of the University—who put morality as the essential of religion to the front and theological doctrines in the background. Hutcheson prophesied that "this man would put a new face on theology in Scotland," and he was right.[3] The saintliness of the divine, with quiet, earnest face, thin and pale like an ascetic, gave him power which few students could resist, and which not even zealots that opposed him could gainsay. As for Professor Hutcheson, he was not only affecting a class-room, but, by his Sunday evening discourses on Christian truth and evidences in the College Kirk,

---

[1] *Inquiry Concerning Moral Good and Evil*, sect. 3.
[2] Carlyle's *Autobiography*, p. 70.
[3] M'Cosh's *Scottish Philosophy*, p. 64; Leechman's *Sermons*, with Life by Wodrow, vol. i.

he influenced men of all classes in the town. His works and speculations do not mark an era in philosophy, neither did they greatly mould future thought; but they certainly gave a stimulus to thinking, influenced theological opinion in the Church, and increased the ranks of the moderate clergy. It is true his disciples were not always wise. With youthful crudeness preachers would sometimes bring the style of the class-room into the pulpit, and speak of the "harmony of the passions," of the "balance of the affections," quote Shaftesbury and cite Socrates to bewildered rustics who could not comprehend their phrases and loathed their "heathen morality." While the evangelical fathers spoke of "sanctification," their sons spoke of "virtues"; the old school preached about "graces of the spirit," the new school discoursed on "moral qualities"; and while the old held forth about "holiness," the young talked of a "high pitch of virtue." In ability they were fit to fill a pulpit; in indiscretion they were fit to empty a church. As they grew older, however, they became wiser, and the hope which David Hume expressed to Hutcheson, "that such instructive morals will get into the world and then into the churches,"[1] was amply fulfilled.

As years went by, the popularity of Hutcheson increased. His range of subjects was vast — ethics, natural religion, jurisprudence, government — in all of which his insistence on religious and civil liberty was keen and eloquent; and young Adam Smith caught not a little stimulus in his moral and political opinions from the master he loved — "the never to be forgotten Hutcheson." In the quadrangle of the college the professor's closest friends were the congenial Professors Leechman and Robert Simson — the quaint mathematician, who, when Hutcheson left him at his tavern at ten o'clock, was ready to remain talking and moderately drinking till three in the morning with Professor Moor, renowned for his Greek, for his jests, and as an adept in geometry. In 1746, when on a visit to Ireland, the philosopher died — a man whose character was intensely admired while he lived, and whose memory was cherished with singular fondness after his death.

[1] M'Cosh's *Scot. Phil.* p. 86.

David Hume

While thus was proceeding the awakening of intellectual life in Scotland, while lawyers, lairds, and some clergy had emancipated themselves from kirk austerity, and in Thomas Rankin's tavern, the club known as the "Rankinian" was discussing the *Characteristics* of Shaftesbury and the theological metaphysics of Dr. Samuel Clarke and the idealism of Berkeley, a lank lad was attending the college class-room, taking listless notes of Latin lectures which gave light to none. The worthy professors of philosophy were prelecting drowsily on Puffendorf and Grotius, while David Hume was studying literature, reading classics, interested in Berkeley's *Principles of Human Knowledge*, and thinking boldly for himself.

It was in 1711 that he had been born in his father's town house, but it was at the mansion-house of Ninewells in Berwickshire that he passed his childhood—that quaint plain house with its thick walls, narrow passages, creaking staircases, and low-ceiled rooms, ill lighted by little windows. It stood on a slight acclivity, from the sides of which rose the nine small springs from which the place took its name—making their way down to the Whitadder in front. There lived John Home, the laird, with his wife, daughter, and two sons. After education at home under the simple-minded minister, David was sent when eleven years old to Edinburgh College, with its 300 students, where he studied Greek—the only classical learning he got there—and heard cumbrous Latin lectures on half-obsolete philosophy which made as little impression on his ear as the rumbling of carts outside the college walls. Ancient moralists, "polite letters," and poetry were the delight of the tall, spare youth—for the obese philosopher of after years was then lank and meagre. His health breaking when he was about eighteen, a strange depression came over him, for which he asked advice from the able but ponderous physician of 30 stone, Dr. Cheyne of London. The calm philosophy of his favourite Cicero failed to cheer him, and for his broken spirits and weakened constitution physicians could only suggest long rides on the rough country roads, and prescribe a daily pint of claret and anti-hysterical pills. In time came a change. The lean, raw-boned youth became robust, his complexion ruddy, his face cheerful, all symptomatic of that physical exuberance which was in after years to pass into unwieldy corpulence. The choice of profession for a gentleman in those days was very limited. He thought of the law, but the weary subtleties of Cujacius and Heineccius had no allurements for a mind that loved poetry and mild philosophy; yet he went to an occupation even less congenial—a merchant's office in Bristol —which he soon quitted. His father was now dead, and on the slender patrimony of £50 a year he departed for France at the age of twenty-three, "exercising rigid economy," he tells us, and "regarding every object contemptible except the improvement of his talents in literature."[1] Here the young man, still becoming fatter, in spite of his frugality, visited Paris, Rheims, and made his way to La Flèche, which had something to stir his mind. Two years before the miracles wrought at the tomb of Abbé Paris, the Jansenist, at St. Medard had given triumph to his party, and filled society and the church with excitement, and the practical insight into the mode in which belief in miracles is formed was not wasted on the young Scotsman, and bore fruit afterwards in his famous Essay on Miracles. He discussed such questions with Jesuits in their cloisters, and ruminated over philosophic doubts in the very seminary in which Descartes had meditated on his system, which began in scepticism and ended in dogmatism.

Returning to Ninewells after three years, he devoted himself to study, and to completing a treatise which he felt sanguine would startle the world. It is a curious picture we can form of the old-fashioned frugal Scots household at Ninewells: the good prosaic mother busy with her stores and her maids, looking with maternal compassion on her younger son poring over his books and papers, and making ineffectual efforts at poetry,—"Davy's a fine good-natured crater, but uncommon wake-minded," she is reported to have said of her portly offspring—while the sister was busy with her work and her spinning-wheel, and the young laird was absorbed in planting trees and rearing turnips. A visit

[1] *Memoirs of my Life.*

to London resulted in finding in Mr. John Noone a bookseller bold enough to give £50 and twelve bound copies of an edition of 1000 copies of the work which the Scotsman submitted to him. The *Treatise on Human Nature* was published anonymously in 1739. The author knew that his views must cause surprise, for they were subversive of all established philosophy; though in his desire to win the good opinion of Dr. Joseph Butler, whose famous *Analogy of Religion* had been published the year before, he " cut off the nobler part "—which probably included that Essay on Miracles which one day was to explode like a shell in the camps of orthodoxy. Anxiously he awaited the effect on the world; he listened eagerly for the explosion his theories were to create. Alas! "it fell," as he says, "still-born from the press." Instead of a storm, it raised not a ripple. A few obscure reviews noticed its arrival; that was all, for the English mind was utterly indifferent to philosophy.

In this little treatise it is easy to trace the origin of Hume's speculations. In 1710 Berkeley, then only twenty-six years old, propounded his subtle idealism, in that style which is so charming to read and so easy to misunderstand. Starting from the accepted view of Locke, that we have no immediate perception of an external world, that we are conscious only of sensations, which we refer to outward objects, he maintained that there is no material world to know. The sole objects of knowledge are ideas, and these exist only as they are perceived [1]; though when these pass from our mind, they do not cease to exist, for they are perceived by the infinite mind of God. In this way by Berkeley matter is disposed of, materialists are silenced; and at the same time mind or spirit is shown to be all that exists. Hume, with the same courage of a man of twenty-five, carries this theory to its utmost conclusion. With Locke he agrees we have only knowledge of our sensations and ideas; with Berkeley he agrees that there is no evidence for a material world; but he further argues we have as little knowledge of the existence of mind, for all that we know is merely a series of ideas or impressions. Whence they come, wherein they exist, whither they go, we cannot tell. Away then vanish body and soul, mind and matter, the world

---

[1] *Esse* is *percipi* is his dictum.

outside, and personal identity within—for of the reality of these what evidence exists? We can no more go beyond our ideas than we can jump off our shadows. "I am at first affrighted and confounded," said the author, "at the solitude in which I am placed by my philosophy." But fortunately, while reason could not dispel his gloom, Nature, which snaps its fingers at reasoning, soon gave him relief. "I dine, I play a game at backgammon, or am merry with my friends, and when, after three or four hours' amusement, I would return to these speculations, they appear so cold, and strained, and ridiculous, that I cannot find it in my heart to enter into them any further."[1] In fact, he felt of his own theory what he said of Berkeley's, that it allows of no confutation, and produces no conviction. Hardly less memorable, and almost as fruitful of philosophic debate, were his views on causation. Denying that we know of the existence of such a relation as cause and effect, he holds that we only learn from experience that certain objects are invariably conjoined; that when certain things occur, certain other things will follow in uniform sequence; but of power in one thing to produce another we are ignorant. Though this treatise, full of daring and original speculation, seemed still-born, it had a vigorous life before it. It was destined to incite philosophers, who felt that the weak points in accepted philosophy had been fatally exposed, to endeavour to reconstruct philosophy and establish convictions on a new and firmer basis.

Disappointment David Hume bore fairly well, but there was chagrin that the work to which he had devoted his young energies and brilliant thought should pass unnoticed. He went on with his studies, which in 1741 and 1742 bore fruit in two other little anonymous volumes entitled *Essays Moral and Political*. These met with a reception which consoled him for his former failure. The subjects were more popular, the style was fresh, the acumen was admirable, and they were warmly welcomed. The most whimsical result of the new literary importance he had won was his appointment in 1745 as companion, governor, or keeper—it is difficult to fix on the proper term—to the Marquis of Annandale. This nobleman was half-

[1] Book I. part iv. sect. 7.

mad, but sane enough to have read and admired Hume's *Essays*, and the young impecunious philosopher, allured by a salary of £300 a year, attended on his charge at St. Alban's—walked with him, talked with him, humoured him. A year ended the engagement.[1] Disputes, intrigues, in which his lordship's friends played a shabby part, resulted in the governor's dismissal from the service of the crazy peer (who three years after was declared a lunatic), and then followed petty squabbles about arrears of salary which, on Hume's part, show a spirit not quite philosophical. He next appears in a new character —as secretary to General St. Clair, who was sent on a foolish expedition to Canada, which ended in a feeble attack on the French coast—a rare piece of bungling, neither the general nor the admiral knowing anything of their parts, the troops being without guides, the ships without pilots, the captains supplied by the Admiralty with charts for the sea, when they had asked for maps of the coast.[2] Could any position be more unsuitable for this philosopher, who loathed the sea, than to be kept on a squalid ship which, he would have agreed with Johnson, was but a prison, with the added chance of being drowned? The poor man owned he was "mortally sick at sea," and soon he was heartily sick of it. Verily ten shillings a day, even with perquisites, was not enough recompense for this. More congenially he served on shore with St. Clair, as part of his staff, when his friend was on a military embassy at Turin. There he was gorgeous in scarlet and gold lace, "with his broad fat face and wide mouth void of all expression except good-nature, his eye meaningless, his corpulence vast—looking like a grocer of the trained bands," as he masqueraded in the garb of an aide-de-camp.[3] Here at least he had good company, good fare, and good pay; and he quitted the service £1000 richer.

All these incongruous occupations did not divert him from his literary pursuits. He busied himself in recasting his unlucky treatise, and a volume, modestly priced three shillings, and entitled *Essays Concerning Human Understanding*,

---

[1] Burton, i. 180; Walpole's *Letters*, i. 185.
[2] Burton's *Life*, i. 213.
[3] *Memoirs of Charlemont*, i. p. 15.

appeared anonymously in 1748. In this he had rewritten his
youthful work, omitting some of the most daring speculations,
which he desired should be thenceforth forgotten. This was
a vain desire, for they were to prove the most memorable and
fruitful in controversy of all his writings. Others, however,
were added, including the famous essay on Miracles, which
was to bring him a troublesome notoriety, for invalidating all
evidence for the miraculous, and an essay on necessity which
denied free will and pronounced the reign of invariable law in
mind as in nature. At first the book was ignored, but afterwards
he had no reason to complain of neglect. "Answers, from
reverends and right reverends, came out by twos and threes,"[1]
and Bishop Warburton, the swashbuckler of the Episcopal
bench, railed in his most truculent fashion. Two more volumes
in 1752 continued his contributions to philosophy; a new
version of his *Principles of Morals*, in which he makes utility
the criterion of moral action, and his *Political Discourses*, which
received the warm welcome in England and in France that
they deserved—possessed as they are of singularly acute understanding, practical suggestiveness, and fulness of knowledge,
whether discoursing on "the populousness of nations" or the
balance of trade; giving studies in sociology and economics,
which anticipated and suggested much of Adam Smith's
doctrine.

In 1751 the laird of Ninewells married, and in Riddell's
Close, near the head of the West Bow, and afterwards in a
flat in Jack's Land in the Canongate, David Hume settled.
"I have £50 a year, £100 worth of books, great store of linens
and fine clothes, and near £100 in my pocket, along with
order, frugality, a strong spirit of independency, good health, a
contented humour, and an unabating love of study."[2] With
such modest possessions he was content. His sister took up
house with him, contributing a further £30 a year to the
little household, a cat, and a servant-maid. It was well for him
that he had this easy nature, for patrons were chary of offering
posts to an infidel, even though he was most amiable. In
vain he applied for the Chair of Moral Philosophy which Sir
John Pringle vacated—that physician, naturalist, philosopher,

[1] *Memoirs of my Life*. [2] Burton's *Hume*, i. 342.

whom Samuel Johnson hated as Macaulay hated Croker and cold boiled mutton—that versatile man who, as President of the Royal Society, at last

> sat on Newton's chair,
> And wondered how the Devil he got there.

Professor Hutcheson had refused the post, and Hume, in the simplicity of his heart, was surprised that neither he nor Principal Leechman—his own friends—supported his claims as an instructor of youth in ethics and natural theology. A little comfort came to him when he was elected Librarian to the Advocates' Library on the retirement of old Ruddiman. Ladies loved the benignant freethinker; they became his enthusiastic partisans, and pestered advocates to surrender their scruples. When news came to the playhouse that "the Christians were defeated," the caddies in a body proceeded with flaming torches and crowded Riddell's Close, where the tattered admirers serenaded him with drums and discordant music—proud at his becoming "a great man."[1]

The last work on philosophy and religion that he published—*Four Dissertations*—appeared in 1757, containing the famous *Natural History of Religion*,[2] in which he discusses the origin and evolution of religion, final causes, miracles, providence, with rare lucidity and brilliant dialectics—coming to the conclusion: "The whole is a riddle, an enigma, an inexplicable mystery. Doubt, uncertainty, suspense of judgment appear the only result of our most accurate scrutiny concerning this subject." In his desk were essays on Suicide, the Immortality of the Soul, and Dialogues concerning natural religion, which he left to be published after his death. Hume's writings were the armoury which should furnish weapons for agnostics of the future, and afford subjects of debate in universities for a century. They contained arguments which were to impel thinkers to reconsider the whole basis of philosophy. As a reaction from their destructive criticism

---

[1] Burton, i. 372.
[2] To this he put a dedication to John Home: "You possess the true theatrical genius of Shakespeare and Otway, reformed from the barbarisms of the one and the licentiousness of the other."

were soon to come the philosophy of Reid and Kantian speculation. Hume's attitude was that of an agnostic—feeling too much to deny, knowing too little to believe. Yet the believing side of him was often uppermost; and in his essays the last word is usually in favour of theism. In a brilliant discussion the arguments seem to shatter every evidence for that belief, with keen dialectics to confute every reason in its support; but it implies that as the most likely solution of the problems of the world. Whether this was due to his caution or to conviction is not very clear. It is not surprising, however, from the halting way he puts the positive side of a question, that his conclusions do not feel conclusive. One clear, beautiful night, as Adam Ferguson and he were walking home, Hume suddenly stopped, looked up to the starlit sky, and exclaimed: "Oh, Adam, can any one contemplate the wonders of the firmament and not believe in a God!"

When he was busy in his study, he was also delighting in society—known to everybody and liked by every one. He gained friends among the young moderate clergy, on whom he never obtruded his views. Carlyle, Robertson, Home, and Ferguson, younger men than he, were among his chosen companions—not from sympathy with his opinions, for they had none, but from common literary tastes, and the comradeship of ability. No more honest divine could be found than Dr. Jardine of the Tron Kirk; yet no more attached friend did Hume possess. They might argue about the necessity of revealed religion, but always in good humour. One night Hume, having declined to be lighted down the turnpike stair from his friend's lodging, fell in the darkness. Jardine rushed for a candle, and as he lifted the bulky body of his guest, slyly said: "Davie, I have often tell't ye that 'natural licht' is no sufficient."

The post of librarian yielded only an income of about £40, and that salary he gave to the blind poet Blacklock, in his indignation at the curators—including Lord Hailes and Lord Monboddo—who had censured him for polluting the immaculate shelves with such immoral authors as Crébillon and La Fontaine. His post, however, he retained, for the library of 30,000 volumes gave him command of books which he could turn to good purpose. He had almost abandoned philosophy, and now turned to history as an unoccupied field for his energies. A history of the reigns of James I. and Charles I. was the project he set before him, and to this he turned with a vigour that astonished his unwieldy and indolent self. He, who could not endure the trouble of answering a letter in two years, could despatch a quarto of history in eighteen months. "I am," he owned, "industrious in keeping up a correspondence with posterity whom I know nothing about, and who will probably concern themselves nothing about me, while I allow myself to be forgetful of friends whom I value." The spur of literary ambition, which was his ruling passion, urged him on. No history worthy of the name as yet existed. Men with the spirit of pamphleteers had written; hacks with the prospect of guineas had compiled; chroniclers like the dull Rapin had been translated; but for a man with power of grasping facts, and style to record them, the field was open for an historian of England. When the volume was written, Millar in London published it in 1754, but the reception in England was frigid —only forty-five copies in a twelvemonth, their author asserts, were sold in London, and with an emphasis which we must discount he tells us: "It met with reproach and even detestation. English, Scots, and Irish, Whig and Tory, Churchman and Sectary, freethinker and religionist, patriot and courtier united in their rage against a man who shed a generous tear for the fall of Charles and the Earl of Strafford."[1] How such widespread animosity could be felt towards a book of which only forty-five copies had been bought and read it is difficult to understand; but then for a philosopher Hume was amazingly sensitive, and sadly addicted to exaggerating his grievances. Certain it is that in his vexation he threatened his friends to abandon his country and settle in France. In time he calmed down, and proceeded with his *History of England*, and issued in 1756 a continuation up to the Revolution, which Tories asserted was too whiggish, and Whigs complained was too tory. All this dissatisfaction was due to the author's indifference to either side, which pleased neither. How could he sympathise with Puritans or Covenanters who staked their lives

[1] *Memoirs of my Life.*

and their country on questions he laughed at? As little as Gibbon, who sneered both at Arian and at Trinitarian, and wondered how churches and states should madly quarrel over the difference of a diphthong.

In spite of adverse criticism, the History made its way into popularity, and the historian was encouraged to continue his work. Two volumes on the house of Tudor appeared in 1759; and the last part, which should have been the first, treating of the period from Julius Cæsar to Henry VII., was published in 1761. Sagacious Andrew Millar offered Hume any price to continue the history to a later date, but he was tired of the work. He was now famous, and even "opulent."[1] With perfect complacency the historian remarks on his account of the Stuarts, "I fancy I shall be able to put my account of that period of English history beyond controversy." Happy delusion of any man who imagines his words or his works are final! Gibbon spoke rightly of the "inimitable beauties" of Hume's style (which others condemned as not English, but French); and the shrewd insight into the purpose underlying political movements, which later research has often confirmed, the admirable clearness of narrative, the vigorous portraiture of character, and the keen perception of social movements going on silently amid wars and political strife, made the History, in spite of all defects, a fine literary achievement. As the author had proceeded with his work, his sympathies with the aristocratic as opposed to the democratic, with the Tory rather than the Whig parties, had increased, partly from his distaste to enthusiasm and bigotry either in church or state, and as he corrected his editions he was as unwilling as Samuel Johnson "to let the Whig dogs get the best of it." What pains he took to write good English! How he tried to avoid Scotticisms and solecisms, having "the misfortune to write in the language of the most stupid and factious barbarians in the world"! It is pathetic to see this great Scotsman begging that upstart David Mallet to revise his work and correct his vocabulary and his grammar —an appeal the great little man did not deign to answer; at another time asking a worthy linen-draper in Bristol to correct

---

[1] Altogether he seems to have been paid £2500. Hume's *Letters to Strahan* (ed. Hill), p. 15; Burton's *Hume*, ii. 61.

his style [1]; and in 1775 submitting the text of a new edition to two Scots lads fresh from an English school.[2]

His great work finished, a change comes over his life again —a strange one for an easy, slumbrous, portly man of letters who loved his fireside. Lord Hertford was appointed in 1763 ambassador to France—a faithful churchman with a pious and orthodox wife. Yet to him Hume was appointed to act as secretary with an alluring £1000 a year of salary. "I am now a person clean and white as the driven snow: were I to be proposed for the See of Lambeth no objection could henceforth be made to me," the amiable infidel chuckled to a friend. A few months later he was in Paris, where his fame had preceded him, for his Essays having been translated, were read by all the *esprits forts*. In intellectual circles that knew literature, and aristocratic circles that prattled about it, he was the fashion, and ladies who prided themselves on their emancipation from "prejudice"—that meant religion—found him adorable. Society abounded in women who boasted of being intellectual, to whom philosophers paid court. They discussed freely everything with vivacity and brilliant inaccuracy—the last scandal from Versailles about the Pompadour, the last quarrel of Rousseau with his friends, the last pamphlet of Voltaire against providence. They dabbled in science, as in philosophy, and rustled into lecture-rooms where Abbé Nollet discoursed on chemistry, and fancied they were scientific because they enjoyed an "experiment"; and greeting every explosion of fetid gas with pretty little screams and terror-stricken "ahs," with dainty handkerchiefs at their noses, they pronounced the whole thing charming. Such were fashionable amusements of society, from the farmer-general's wife to the scion of royalty for whom the courtier-physician prefaced his performances: "The oxygen and hydrogen will now have the honour of amalgamating before your Royal Highness." David Hume found it delightful to be petted in the bright salons. What mattered it to him that his hostesses did anything except their duties, loved anybody except their husbands, attended to everything but their children, and went everywhere but to

---

[1] Hannah More's *Memoirs*, i. 16.
[2] *Caldwell Papers*, ii. 89.

mass? Everything English was then *bon ton*—English sentiment, frocks, and literature; and David Hume, having the further charm of being a freethinker, was now their idol. It is true he had no graces, no wit, and spoke only a little French atrociously. Yet "no lady's toilette was perfect without his attendance"—his ponderous person resplendent in bag-wig and laced coat and waistcoat of "bright yellow, spotted with black."[1] He sat at the opera (without understanding a word of the libretto or a note of the music), with adoring dames on either side, to whom he distributed fat, amiable smiles. "The more I resiled from their civilities, the more I was loaded with them," he avowed with complacency. Yet, if we may believe Lord Charlemont's description, there was nothing in his appearance to fascinate them. "Nature, I believe, never formed any man more unlike his real character. The powers of physiognomy were baffled by his countenance; neither could the most skilful in the science pretend to discover the smallest trace of the faculties of his mind in the unmeaning features of his visage. His face was broad and fat; his mouth wide and without any other expression than that of imbecility. His eyes vacant and spiritless, and the corpulence of his person was far better fitted to communicate the idea of a turtle-eating alderman than of a refined philosopher. His speech in English was rendered ridiculous by the broadest Scotch accent, and his French if possible still more laughable. So that wisdom most certainly never disguised herself before in so uncouth a garb."[2] Here is an admirable little scene of comedy. Ladies at this time made the fashion of giving tableaux vivants. In one of these Hume was made to take a part, and there he is seen seated, dressed like a sultan, between two obdurate beauties, to whom he was supposed to make love, and thus he plays his part.[3] Placed on a sofa between two of the loveliest women in Paris, he looks at them attentively, and strokes his stomach and his knees again and again, but nothing else can he find to say than "*Eh bien, mes demoiselles. Eh bien! voilà donc, eh bien, vous voilà! vous voilà ici!*" At last, these phrases having

---

[1] *Caldwell Papers*, i. 38; Hardy's *Memoirs of Lord Charlemont*, i. p. 8.
[2] *Memoirs of Lord Charlemont*, i. p. 122.
[3] Madame d'Epinay's *Mémoires*, iii. 284.

continued for a quarter of an hour, the ladies rise in impatience, and exclaim with indignation, "That man is only fit to eat veal!" Not the less, in spite of epigramless stupidity, was he fêted, and the worthy man enjoyed it all. He was to be found at Madame Geoffrin's, when the glass manufacturer's widow gave her famous dinners to artists, men of science, and philosophers—the best hostess to manage men of hostile opinions, and make gesticulating Frenchmen calm. He visited Madame du Boccage, rich, beautiful, and learned, whose guests shivered at the necessary ordeal of praising her *Amazons* and *Columbiade*, which they could not read. He appeared at the splendid rooms of Madame de Boufflers, and the brilliant salon of blind old Madame du Deffand, where he went through the usual ordeal for new guests, of having his broad face patted all over by the hostess to spell out his features, producing probably on her as much surprise as when she felt the baggy cheeks and button mouth of Mr. Gibbon. At the table of the wealthy Mæcenas of philosophers, Baron d'Holbach, he was a constant guest, and there it happened one day that as the company, Diderot, Hélvetius, d'Alembert, and others, talked freely against religion, Hume interjected, "As for atheists, I do not believe that any one ever existed. I have never seen one." "You have been very unlucky," his host answered: "you see yourself at table with seventeen for the first time."[1] The Scots philosopher, who was so superstitious as still to believe in a deity, was treated with courteous compassion. Elsewhere Hume was overwhelmed with adulation. Did not Madame de Pompadour show herself more gracious to him than she had been to any other? Were not the little princes, afterwards Louis XVI., Louis XVIII., and Charles X., aged respectively nine, eight, and six, set up to deliver to him prepared addresses on his philosophy at Versailles? The effect was somewhat spoiled by the youngest forgetting his speech, and being only able to mumble some words to the smiling recipient. So he wrote to his friend Dr. Robertson, "I eat nothing but ambrosia, drink nothing but nectar, breathe nothing but incense, tread on nothing but flowers."[2]

---

[1] Romilly's *Memoirs*, i. 179.
[2] Stewart's "Life of Robertson," *Works*, x. 363.

All, however, was not merely pleasure at Paris. Hume proved himself a capable man of affairs, writing despatches with skill, getting up details with industry, and giving interviews always with bland good-humour. It is not surprising that Lord Hertford, when called off to be Lord-Lieutenant of Ireland, left him behind as *chargé d'affaires*, and would have taken him as secretary to Dublin, if the outcry against promoting a Scotsman (which was more objectionable than promoting a deist) had not been too great.

At the close of his Parisian career occurred an episode which was a source of perplexity to himself, and of vast amusement to society. When Jean-Jacques Rousseau was driven from place to place, less by the machinations of his enemies than the delusions of his half-mad brain, he had come to Paris under risk of arrest of Parliament. In a soft, unguarded hour, Hume offered to seek a shelter for the persecuted writer of the *Contrat Social* in that land where bigots cease from troubling and heretics are at rest. So together the philosophers crossed the channel—which neither enjoyed —and as they landed, the exile leaped on his ponderous friend's neck and covered his ample cheeks with tears and kisses, to his modest embarrassment. In a lodging in Fulham, Rousseau got the quietness he professed to seek, and in London streets the public notice he loved to find, for his Armenian dress was a rare sight for Londoners, and the recluse, in spite of his protestations, loved notoriety dearly. Assiduously his friend guarded the distinguished exile; and to add to his burden, Thérèse la Vasseur, Jean-Jacques' irregular spouse, was brought over under the fussy charge of James Boswell, who was delighted, even through this coarse quondam servant, to be associated with a man of distinction. A pension of £100 a year was got from George III.; a home was found for him in the country seat of Wootton in the Peak of Derby, where he could write and botanise and grumble at his will. In the delightful guilelessness of his heart, Hume asserted, " I think I could live with him all my life in mutual friendship and esteem. I am sorry that the matter is not likely to be put to trial." That "trial," unwarily longed for, came soon enough. In that retreat, without books or companions, with no occupation except writing his morbid *Confessions*, no amusements except gathering and arranging his herbs, with no interests except listening to Thérèse squabbling over coals and a kettle with their host's housekeeper, while the snow lay deep on the dreary uplands, Rousseau's mind, always morose and perverse, began to turn every favour into a grievance, every kindness into an insult, every friend into a foe. In June a letter was written from the solitudes of Wootton to Hume, breaking off all friendship, raising marvellous accusations, which were the offspring of a diseased brain. David Hume he denounces as a "traitor." Had he not lodged with a son of Dr. Tronchin, his bitterest enemy? Had not Hume one evening, as they sat at supper, gazed at him with a steadfast, jeering look, which had agitated him—Jean-Jacques—almost to fainting? "Presently I was seized with the most violent remorse, till in a transport I sprang on his neck and embraced him eagerly. Almost choked with sobbing, and bathed in tears, I cried in broken accents, 'No! no! David Hume cannot be treacherous; if he is not the best of men, he must be the basest!' David Hume politely returned my embraces, and gently tapping me on the cheek, repeated several times in a placid tone, 'Why, what, my dear sir! Nay, my dear sir! Oh, my dear sir!'" (One recalls the limited vocabulary at the tableaux vivants in Paris.) And did not Hume in his sleep, coming across in the vessel, utter the significant words, "*Je tiens, Jean-Jacques Rousseau!*" (Poor Hume, who had not sufficient French for his waking hours, had not enough to expend during his sleep.) Further charges he hurled against his old friend: of tattling with Thérèse behind his back; of opening his letters; of writing a mock letter in his name to Frederick the Great (which was a mischievous trick of Horace Walpole). Never was there such a quarrel. In Paris society was in wild excitement. Men of letters, who disliked the querulous egotism of their countryman, made merry over the row—"just what they expected"; and ladies, who adored him, vehemently espoused his cause. In England discussion was not so keen, though one peeress, from excitement of her defence of Hume, gave premature birth to a son.[1] Unluckily

---
[1] *Caldwell Papers*, ii.

Hume, over-persuaded, published a vindication,[1] and the war proceeded furiously, while poor Jean-Jacques felt and acted like a man distraught. For a year Rousseau lived in Wootton in his misery; and one day, in April 1767, he and Thérèse suddenly disappeared, leaving their baggage and money behind them, and found their way back to France. Hume, kindliest, most placid of souls, for once in his life regretted that he had done a good-natured action. Now he saw "ingratitude, ferocity, and lying"[2] in the fugitive he had trusted so simply.

In a short time Hume was installed in a post which showed that he had earned a reputation for capacity in business. General Conway, brother of Lord Hertford, being Secretary of State, appointed him Under Secretary, an office which he held till his chief's resignation in 1768. Among his various duties it is interesting to think that one of these would be the composition of the King's annual letter to the General Assembly of the Church of Scotland—that venerable assembly which, some years before, issued solemn resolutions against his writings, and its abhorrence "of the impious and infidel principles in books published of late."[3] We may picture the corpulent pagan sitting down to concoct the royal epistle to the "right reverend and honourable" body; but we could not venture to picture the horror of elders and ministers had they known that these majestic counsels, these august hopes for their good behaviour, and the pious commendation to the blessing of providence (all which gracious message was received standing) had been written with a copious smile by the arch heretic whom they had banned some years before.[4]

In Paris we have seen Hume lionised, and he admired the noblesse for the honour they paid to philosophers; but he found men of letters ignored by high society in London, where "a man who plays no part in public affairs becomes altogether insignificant." There no bevies of high-born dames

---

[1] *Concise and Genuine Account of the Dispute between Mr. Hume and Mr. Rousseau*, 1765.
[2] Burton, ii. 378.
[3] Morren's *Annals of General Assembly*, ii. 54, 86.
[4] Burton, ii. 382.

fluttered round him; although General Fitzpatrick—a man of wit and fashion—pronounced him "a delicious creature."[1] If he spoke, they might sneer at his Scots accents and Scots phrases; while in Paris ladies would listen with courteous gravity to his most abominable mistakes. When Dr. John Moore—author of *Zeluco*—expressed a fear that some word he used was not correct French, a marquis replied with exquisite courtesy, "It is not actually so, but it quite deserves to be."[2] There was no such tact in England. We hear of Hume very little in literary sets; and Dr. Johnson, who disliked him as freethinker and sneered at him for a Scot, refused to meet him, as he had refused to greet Abbé Raynal, keeping his hands behind his back. Yet this austere moralist and Christian could be proud of his intimacy with Topham Beauclerc, most rakish of gentlemen, and be vastly entertained by John Wilkes, rake, infidel, and demagogue. To no sittings in Sir Joshua's studio was he invited, although Allan Ramsay painted a portrait of him in scarlet and gold lace. On George III. suggesting that the dress was too fine, the privileged Court painter replied[3] that "he wished posterity to see that one philosopher in His Majesty's reign had a good coat to his back." It was with Scotsmen he fraternised chiefly; and these were to be found at the favourite resort, the British Coffee-House, which so swarmed with men of the North that Gibbon used to speak of it as the *Breetish* Coffee-House.[4] There John Hume, Dr. Armstrong, Wedderburn and Elliot, the Hunters and Smollett, were constantly meeting. Hume felt little at home with Englishmen, whom he never wearied of stigmatising as "stupid, factious, barbarous," because he was convinced "they had conspired against himself and his History"—all which, his friends told him, was "melancholy nonsense." Certainly the serenity of the philosopher could be ruffled if his literary work was disparaged, and his spleen against English critics extended to Englishmen in general. Yet fair opposition to his views he bore with fine good-humour. Dr. Campbell controverted his theory of miracles, and he was

---

[1] *Table-Talk of Sam. Rogers*, p. 106.
[2] Moore's *View of Society and Manners in France*, 1779.
[3] *Boswelliana*, p. 255.   [4] Gibbon's *Letters*, i. 201.

amiable; Dr. Wallace controverted his views, and he corrected the press for his opponent; Reid attacked his philosophy, and he revised his manuscript; Dr. Gerard disputed his opinions, and he was friendly—for these wrote with the manners of gentlemen; but when Dr. Beattie assailed him with spiteful piety, he flew into a rage. One time, at his request, Cadell the bookseller invited to meet him as many persons as he could collect who had written against him, and they proved a goodly gathering.[1] Dr. Adams, Dr. Price, Dr. Douglas were there, and they were charmed with him and he was charmed with them.

Once again, and finally, David Hume settled in Edinburgh, in 1769, and he was glad to be at home. "Very opulent," he says, "for I have £1000 a year; healthy, and, though somewhat stricken in years, with the prospect of enjoying my ease, and of seeing the increase of my reputation." He was comfortable and fat, and had all the good-nature which accompanies corpulence. And of his fatness he liked to make a jest. When coming across the Forth—probably from visiting Adam Smith at Kirkcaldy—during a violent storm, he expressed fear to the lively Lady Wallace that they would soon be food for fishes. "And pray, my dear friend," she asked, "which do you think they will eat first?" "Those that are gluttons," replied Hume, "will undoubtedly fall foul of me; but the epicures will attack your ladyship."

Truly the world, in spite of his grumbling, had used the obese historian kindly; and he was happy in his flat in James' Court, which, during his residence in London, he had lent to Dr. Blair, having recommended it to him as possessing the singular merit of "being free of vermin." The Court was a fashionable quarter; it was inhabited by "most genteel families," who had their little balls and suppers among themselves, and they boasted of having a scavenger of their own. In Hume's spacious parlour was to be met everybody of note in the city—judges, ministers, advocates, doctors, professors: Lord Kames with his sarcasm, his coarse jokes, his cackling laugh; John Home—"dear Johnnie" with his many friends—with his radiant presence, which was genial if not brilliant as the

[1] *Table-Talk of Sam. Rogers*, p. 106.

sun; Carlyle of Inveresk, stately, handsome, full of life and good talk; Dr. Blair, prim, precise, and pompous; Dr. Robertson, and Adam Ferguson. His bosom friend, Adam Smith, had a chamber ready for him whenever he came across from Kirkcaldy. But David Hume himself was the most delightful of all. "He had the greatest simplicity of mind and manners, with the utmost facility and benevolence of temper, I ever knew,"[1] says his friend, Dr. Carlyle. All such qualities made him loved by everybody. He was so loyal to his friends, so patriotically admiring of his countrymen. With him blind Blacklock, mildest of poetasters, was a Pindar; Wilkie, dullest of versifiers and most grotesque of mortals, was a Homer; Home was a Shakespeare "without his barbarisms."

It was a kindly, genial, friendly life which was to be found in Edinburgh in those days—with a familiarity of social intercourse found nowhere else. When Home, Carlyle, and Dr. Jardine of the Tron Kirk resolved to have a supper in a tavern, the caddies were sent out to mount the several stairs to ask Mr. Adam Ferguson, Mr. David Hume, and Dr. Blair to meet at nine o'clock at John Dowie's or at Fortune's tavern; and thither David Hume was sure to come, the huge door-key lying beside him on the table, which his servant Peggy had given him, that she might not be kept out of bed till one o'clock in the morning. Every Tuesday at Nicholson's tavern there dined, at a shilling a head, the Poker Club—a club ostensibly formed to "poke up" the national spirit against English oppression and insolence, but practically for the consumption of that beverage which was a favourite in Scotland—a wine which came into vogue from the old intercourse with France, and was popular from its cheapness till the English government enforced the duty and raised its price. The philosopher affected the generous port wine, while John Home stood up for the long-established drink of which the taxes of tyrannical England sought to deprive them. And his epigram uttered his scorn:

> Firm and erect the Caledonian stood;
> Old was his mutton, and his claret good.
> Let him drink port! the English cried.
> He drank the poison, and his spirit died.

---

[1] Mackenzie's *Life of Home*; Carlyle's *Autobiography*, p. 278.

But still more genial were the suppers at Hume's own house, for he gave and enjoyed good fare. He would copy out carefully his recipe for making *soupe à la reine*; and as for his sheep's-head broth, it was made by Peggy in a manner that made his friends rave about it for days. He boasts of his beef and cabbage—a "charming dish" he succulently remarks; and for old mutton and old claret " nobody," he avows, "excels me." He was somewhat of an epicure, and he owned to be even something more of a glutton. James Boswell tells of his presence at a dinner at the house in company with Lord Kames and Dr. Robertson; but he only remembers the excellent supper, with three sorts of ices. "I can recollect nothing of the conversation,"[1] he remarks; but the loss of memory was probably due to the partaking of something else than the ices.

Though living a contented bachelor life, Hume had not always looked forward to that as his fate. In his earlier and poorer days he had proposed to and been rejected by a lady of position and beauty. When he was rich and famous it was intimated to him that the lady, no longer young and fastidious, had "changed her mind." "So have I," he bluntly rejoined.[2] Now he was the favourite of all ladies; whose attentions and intentions were not matrimonial. Ladies of the sourest orthodoxy could not resist the sweet-tempered deist. Never was there so good-humoured a man—playful, almost infantine, in his ways and speech. Rigid women, shocked at reports of his works which they had never read, were won by his good-nature. The mother of Robert Adam, the architect, had a horror at the "atheist"—a term which women vaguely supposed was the synonym for "deist"—and she vowed that never should that man darken her doors. One evening, without telling his mother his identity, Adam had Hume at supper, and when the company had left, the old lady said, "I must confess, Robert, that you bring very agreeable companions about you, but the large jolly man who sat next me was the most agreeable of them all." When he revealed that this was her monster of impiety, she replied, "Well, you may bring him as much as you like, for he is the most innocent, agreeable, and facetious man

[1] *Letters to Temple*, p. 203. [2] *Caldwell Papers*, ii. 190.

I ever met." [1] The good man's appearance at any tea-table was a family delight; children clambered on his knees, though to maintain their position was no easy task—the huge paunch projecting so far, that to keep on their perch they held on by the buttons of his coat. There was a delicious amount of childlike simplicity side by side with his intellectual shrewdness. Theoretically he denied the evidence of his senses for the existence of the physical world, and practically he trusted everything and everybody in equal defiance of his senses. "David, maun, you'll believe onything except the Bible!" exclaimed Lord Saltoun, who had crammed his friend with incredible tales, to see how far his credulity would go. Careful to avoid uttering one word in private intercourse which would give offence,[2] he never could understand why exception should be taken to his works. That the world should condemn him for such trifles as doubts on miracles, revelation, and providence seemed to his simple heart extremely unjust. When Dr. Blair sent to him Dr. George Campbell's reply to his Essay on Miracles, he wrote in an injured tone, "I wish your friend had not denominated me an infidel writer on account of ten or twelve pages which seem to have that tendency, while I have wrote as many volumes on history, literature, politics, trade, morals, which in that particular are entirely inoffensive. Is a man to be called a drunkard who has been fuddled once in his lifetime?" A similar complaint of his once met with a retort which pleased his sense of humour. "You put me in mind," said one of the company in which he was speaking, "of an acquaintance of mine, a notary-public, who, after having been condemned to be hanged for perjury, lamented the hardship of his case, that, after having written many thousand inoffensive sheets, he should be hanged for one line."[3] Probably there were more articles in his creed than his speculations logically allowed. The ghost of the old faith which he had killed seemed to haunt him, and he did not like to vex that ghost. His presence in Greyfriars' Church when Principal Robertson preached, and his careful provision of church seats for his

---

[1] Carlyle's *Autobiography*, p. 272.
[2] Mackenzie's *Life of Home*, p. 20.
[3] *Memoirs of Charlemont*, i. 121.

servants, were not merely due to conventional decorum.
"Though I throw out my speculations to entertain and employ
the learned and metaphysical world, yet in other things I do
not think as differently from the rest of mankind as you
suppose," he said to a friend.[1] So far true at any rate,
that the philosopher, who had said there was no evidence
for an external world, enjoyed that world as much as ever
mortal did. One day Hume was telling his orthodox friend,
Dr. John Gregory, that he could reckon many of the female
sex among his disciples.[2] "Now tell me," said the doctor,
"whether, if you had a wife or daughter, you would wish them
to be your disciples?" With a hesitation and a smile he
replied, "No; I believe scepticism may be too sturdy a virtue
for a woman."

In Edinburgh, however, of female disciples there were very
few, and they were certainly not due to any proselytising of
his. Other women only thought he was too good a man to be
damned, and tried to save him from the everlasting fires. It
was in his last days that a member of the Berean congregation
came to his door, pressing for admission as she had received a
message from on High. The philosopher received her and
heard her graciously and gravely. "This is an important
matter, madam. We must take it with deliberation—perhaps
you had better get a little temporal refreshment before you
begin—(Lassie, bring this good lady a glass of wine)." As
she partook of the preliminary refreshment, Hume discovered
that her husband was a tallow-chandler, and cunningly stating
that he was in need of temporal lights, he entrusted his visitor
with such a large commission for candles, that the worthy
woman, in the joy of her heart, forgot the order from Above,
and hastened home to give her order for the "moulds."[3]
One dark night, as he walked along a footpath over a boggy
ground behind the Castle, his ponderous frame fell and stuck
fast in the mud. His calls brought a woman to the spot,
who unsympathetically asked, "Are ye Hume the infidel?"
"Well, well, my good woman, but Christian charity bids us

[1] Carlyle's *Autobiography*, p. 273.
[2] Forbes's *Life of Beattie*, ii. 54.
[3] Burton, ii. 436, 457.

help our enemies," he pleaded. "I'll dae naething for ye if ye dinna say the Lord's Prayer and the Belief, but leave ye where I fand ye." The philosopher readily obeyed, and the body of the Deist was laboriously extricated from the mire by the Christian.

In 1770 he quitted the old town, with its endless stairs, so wearying to his panting body, for the new town, which was rapidly being built on fields and meadows. He removed his household gods to a corner house in St. Andrew Square, with the door entering from a little street as yet unnamed. One morning the servant lass beheld in flagrant white letters the words "St. David Street" chalked up on the house, and in dismay reported what she had seen: his very name turned into a saint. "Never mind, lassie, many a better man has been made a saint o' before," replied her master. So the frolic of a young lady amused the town, and gave a permanent name and memory to the street where the historian died. There he grew older, frailer, though not less cheerful, not less lovable. He set forth to Bath to try its helpful waters, accompanied by his true friend John Home; but he got little benefit in that town where, according to Mrs. Montague, the topics were "How d'ye does?" all day, and "What's trumps?" all night. The two friends returned, beguiling the tedious journey in the chaise with piquet and lively talk; going over their old disputes on the merits of port *versus* claret, of the spelling of their name, Hume *versus* Home. The valorous dramatist kept a huge pistol by his side, ever on the outlook for highwaymen in his usual heroic manner. "Frighten as many highwaymen as you please, John," said the invalid, "for I have little life left to be an object worth saving."

With shaky hand he indited to Dr. Hugh Blair the last note he was ever to write to his old friend:

DONCASTER, *27th June* 1776.

John Hume, *alias* the Home, *alias* Lord Conservator, *alias* the late minister of the gospel at Athelstaneford, has contrived matters so as to arrive infallibly with his friend at St. David Street on Wednesday evening. He has asked the favour of the doctor to make up the number.

He returned to die. But death's approach brought no

dismay to the man who, Lord Monboddo went about saying, confessed on his dying bed not his sins but his Scotticisms,[1] and chatted humorously over Lucian's *Dialogues of the Dead*, wondering what excuses he could give to Charon to plead for delay before being rowed across the Styx.[2]

One pleasant scene in the sick-room we find when the widow of Baron Hume came to take farewell of him. On parting he gave her a copy of his History. "Oh, David!" the good lady said, "that's a book ye may weel be proud o'; but before you dee, you should burn a' your wee bookies." Raising himself in bed, he answered with playful vehemence, "What for should I burn a' my wee bookies?" He was too feeble to say more, so the old friends shook hands, never to meet again. When he lay on his deathbed, a little girl, a relation of his own, used to come to see him; and every morning and evening he would make the child kneel by his side and say her prayers aloud—often desiring her to repeat the Lord's Prayer, which came touchingly from the young lips to the ears of the dying philosopher.[3] Dr. Cullen and Dr. Black attended him as doctors, and Adam Smith sat with him day by day—the two philosophers talking more, doubtless, of things seen than of things unseen. Hume was anxious that essays which he had written many years before, but, in deference to the wish of his friends, had been reluctant to publish, especially the Dialogues on Religion, should be edited after his death by his friend; but this Smith refused to do, thinking that they would raise clamour and increase odium against his friend. The end came with "tranquillity and pleasantry,"[4] said Dr. Cullen; and on 25th August 1776, David Hume was dead, and there was mourning in many a home in Edinburgh. The historian

---

[1] Sinclair's *Old Scenes and Distant Places*, p. 170; Burton, ii. 611; *Caldwell Papers*, i. 40.

[2] With the jocularity that never deserted him, he wrote a codicil to his will twelve days before his death. "I leave my friend, Mr. John Home of Kilduff, twelve dozen of my old claret at his choice, and a single bottle of that other liquor called port. I also leave him six dozen of port, provided that he attests under his hand, signed John *Hume*, that he has himself finished the bottle in two sittings. By this concession he will terminate the only two differences that ever came between us concerning temporal matters" (Mackenzie's *Life of Home*).

[3] Chambers's *Walks in Edinburgh*, p. 183.

[4] Thomson's *Life of Cullen*, i. 607.

was the most popular man in the city, and as he lay dying his condition was the universal subject of inquiry and interest with high and low Every one spoke of him with the anxiety of an intimate friend. The crowd that gathered round the door on the day of the funeral was drawn there as much from affection as from curiosity. Among the lowest of the rabble one was heard to say, " Ah, he was an atheist." " No matter," rejoined another, "he was an honest man." On that pouring day of rain, as the burial took place, it was witnessed by great throngs, and for days people came to see the place where rested the body of the philosopher whose huge, corpulent form, with kindly, good-humoured face, had been so long familiar in the streets.[1] Next year Adam Smith's account of the last days of his friend was published with his verdict: that " he was as nearly to the idea of a perfectly wise and virtuous man as perhaps the nature of human frailty will permit." Addison called his stepson, Lord Warwick, to his bedside, " to see how a Christian can die." Religious circles were scandalised when Adam Smith called the world to witness how a sceptic could die.[2]

---

[1] *Curious Particulars and Genuine Anecdotes respecting David Hume, etc.*, 1788. "After his interment two trusty persons watched the grave for about eight nights [was this from fear of fanatical outrage?]. The watch was set by eight at night, at which time a pistol was fired. Candles in a lanthorn were placed on the grave, where they burned all night " (p. 16).

[2] With regard to Hume's private religious views, it is not easy to discover what they were from his books. In his works often occur passages which are curiously and inconsistently orthodox. Were these merely sops to the Cerberus of orthodoxy, or were they sincere? He himself approved of the policy of accommodation, for he defended it in his cynical advice to an English clergyman who was troubled with religious doubts: "It is putting too great a respect on the vulgar and to their superstitions to pique oneself on sincerity with regard to them. Did one ever make it a point of honour to speak truth to children or madmen?" (Burton's *Hume*, ii. 188.)

CHAPTER III

JOHN HOME

THE first public appearance of John Home, the author of *Douglas, a Tragedy*, was in the '45, when he played a part suited to his fine heroic vein. Edinburgh was full of excitement; the rebels were at hand, and a wonderful band of 400 or 500 volunteers was raised to defend the city—an awkward squad of students, law-clerks, domestically-minded citizens, possessed of fluctuating courage, to whom the firing of a musket with closed eyes with aim into space was an agitating effort. As the fire-bell rang for the brave guardians of hearth and home to march forth, supported by two regiments of dragoons, they mustered with trembling hearts—their wives and mothers protesting with tears that their husbands and sons, to whose necks they clung, were too precious to be slaughtered by Highland villains. When the order to march to the West Bow was given, officers complained that the men would not follow, and the men murmured that the officers would not lead. The dauntless spirit of those doughty patriots is exemplified in the legend of the writing-master who protected his manly breast by two quires of paper, whereon was written: "This is the body of John Maxwell; pray give it Christian burial"; but even he slunk into his lodging as the feeble forces passed his door in the Lawnmarket, and remained in the bosom of his family. Among the more ardent set was John Home, divinity student. Convivial tradition was wont to tell of the adventures of him and his comrades on their way to join Sir John Cope; of their calling at every ale-house to drink in a chopin of "twopenny" or

JOHN HOME

From the Painting by Raeburn in the National Portrait Gallery, London.

mutchkin of brandy confusion to the Pretender; of their sleeping comfortably the night before the battle in a manse, only to wake up and discover that the fight was over: that the volunteers had fled before a violent charge of Highland cavalry, consisting of three or four gentlemen with their servants, in full pursuit.[1] More effective was John Home as lieutenant in the Glasgow volunteers, when he was present at the battle of Falkirk, and his warlike career was closed by his being cooped up in Doune Castle, whence he and some comrades escaped by making their bed-clothes into ropes. He was a susceptible youth, full of fine romantic sentiments, and addicted to very heroic utterances, which afterwards he expended chiefly in his plays.

He had been born in Leith in 1722, where his father was town-clerk, and he had been educated in Edinburgh College. It was not a military career that lay before him, but, as with many of his brilliant associates, the peaceful profession of the church. The old fanaticism was dying out in Scotland; a new order of clergy, taught by a more rational philosophy in the universities, and moulded by the tone of society, were preaching a religion in which there was less dogma and more morality than of old; and if their sermons lacked unction, they had no fanaticism and much sanctified good sense.

In 1746 John Home was ordained minister of Athelstaneford, as successor to the Rev. Robert Blair, whose poem of *The Grave* had earned no little fame for the parish. Poetical taste seemed to be infectious, for the young minister was full of literary ardour. As he angled in the East Lothian streams, he thought more about his poems than about his trout; when he returned to his home he wrote down his verses, and even on the backs of sermons scribbled his lines. Though his presbytery had once to censure him for being out of his parish for months,[2] he proved a good minister, popular with his people. He had his friends near him—Carlyle at Inveresk, full of life and social interest; Robertson at Gladsmuir, busy with his History; and at his lodging in the village—for he never lived in the manse—there often met a merry, clever

---

[1] *Scott's Works, Periodical Criticisms,* xix. 309; Carlyle's *Autobiography.*
[2] *New Stat. Acct. Scot.* "Athelstaneford."

set of moderate ministers, to take the dulness from country life with talk of the doings of Edinburgh and jokes at the "high-flyers." As he was reading Plutarch one day, Home, who loved the romantic, was stirred by the stimulating pages to set about the composition of a tragedy; for it was an age when heroic plays were in vogue; when playwrights poured forth their preposterous Cleones, Zangas, Barbarossas, and Mahomets; and when actors in grotesque costumes played them in appropriate fashion. When the play was being written, many were the consultations with his friends over it. At Minto House, Lord Kames, Oswald of Dunnikier, and Sir Gilbert Elliot would sit after dinner revising it with the author; for to them the production of a drama was a strange and great experience. At last it was finished, and the sanguine minister set forth to London on horseback with pistols in his holsters, to defend from highwaymen the precious manuscript in his saddle-bags at the cost of his life.

He interviewed Mr. Garrick, manager of Drury Lane, and submitted his production, entitled *Agis*, all the more confidently that Mr. Pitt, to whom he had got an introduction, had given it praise. The little manager, from his height of five feet three inches, surveyed this Scotsman, nearly six feet high, who explained his errand in northern accents, and with his affable manner Mr. Garrick bade him leave the manuscript for perusal, and sent it back regretfully declined.[1] To the tomb of Shakespeare in Westminster Abbey the disappointed dramatist resorted, and with swelling breast wrote some mighty lines:—

> Image of Shakespeare! To this place I come,
> To ease my bursting bosom at thy tomb.

And informing the "image"

> That day and night revolving still thy page,
> I hoped like thee to shake the British stage,

he concluded with the insane desire—

> Let petrification stop my falling tear,
> And fix my form for ever marble here.

---

[1] Mackenzie's *Life of Home*.

Having thus eased his "bursting bosom," disappointed but not despairing, Home retraced his steps to the North, to find boundless sympathy from his friends, solace in his fishing-rod, and occupation in his parochial visits, his sermons, and his poetry. In spite of his unlucky experiences, his ambition to produce a great drama was not crushed, and he found another subject for a tragedy as one evening he heard a young lady sing the old ballad of "Gil Morrice" to its tender music. For four years he laboured at a play based on the ballad. He was ever consulting friends, who heard his reading without a murmur, while ladies listened with tears and admiration. He would often ride to town to get the advice of Blair or Robertson or Lord Elibank. Carlyle copied part of the manuscript from his friend's execrable handwriting, and law-clerks transcribed the rest. When it was finished, his friends were delighted; David Hume was in raptures, pronouncing that it surpassed Shakespeare and Otway at their best; while Lady Hervey (Pope's "Molly Leppell") wept over it like a child. To London friends looked for a fitting introduction of such a treasure. Dr. Alexander Carlyle describes the eventful journey: how on a cold February day in 1755, when the snow covered the ground, he and some friends escorted the budding dramatist on his way to submit his great work to Garrick; how Home, always slovenly, started on his horse with the bulky manuscript stuffed in one pocket of his greatcoat, his shirt and nightcap in the other. The companions, more thoughtful than the author, stopped at a manse and secured a valise, in which the minister as synod-clerk kept his records, to carry the wardrobe and the play. At Wooler they parted company with valedictory cheers and wishes for his success, and Home trotted off on "Piercy," his favourite galloway, which was to bear him on his journeys for many a year.[1]

The great manager was seen; but again the mortifying verdict was given that the play was not suitable for the stage. With swelling breast, once more the discomfited playwright ambled home, to gain renewed sympathy from his friends, who denounced loudly English stupidity, barbarity,

[1] Carlyle's *Autobiography*, p. 303; Mackenzie's *Home*, p. 36.

and jealousy.[1] With unbroken admiration, they declared that such a work should not be lost to the world. At that time there was a theatre in the Canongate—admittance from 2s. 6d. to 1s.—in which there was an ill-paid English company, which contained two or three good actors. There was Mrs. Ward, charming and beautiful; Mr. Love, who had changed his name from Dance, not to disgrace his father, the city architect of London; and there was West Digges, a gentleman by birth, a bankrupt ex-officer in the army, a reprobate by repute, an actor by profession. Rehearsals took place in a tavern attended by Carlyle, Home, Ferguson, and Lord Elibank, after partaking of a supper of pork griskins. News of the meetings of what the town called the "Griskin Club" spread about, and whetted curiosity; and on 14th December 1756 the theatre was thronged, the Canongate was crowded with sedan-chairs—for *Douglas*, by the minister of Athelstaneford, was to be performed. Mrs. Ward appeared as Lady Barnet, the name not being yet changed to Lady Randolph; and Digges personated Forman—not yet changed to Norval—in his harsh voice and pompous tone, and doubtless adorned with the huge, ponderous periwig in which he enacted Cato.[2]

The curtain rose, and the national sympathies of the audience were touched by the appeal:

> This night, our scenes no common tears demand :
> He comes, the hero of your native land !
> Douglas, a name thro' all the world renowned—
> A name that rouses like a trumpet sound.

Never was there such success; men were in raptures and women in tears; the town rang with applause over the Caledonian Shakespeare; citizens and judges never before in a play-house went shamefacedly there. When all fashionable

---

[1] Carlyle's *Autobiography*, 304. A ballad at the time appeared in Edinburgh—a parody of "Gil Morrice":

> When Garrick had a' Douglas read,
> He glowered with baith his een ;
> And stamping with his foot, he said,
> Sic damned stuff ne'er was seen.
> *Notes and Queries*, Jan. 1866.

[2] *Colman's Recollections*, i. 257.

society had seen the play, and the seats and the treasury were becoming emptier, there was hawked through the streets "A Full and True History of the Bloody Tragedy of Douglas, as it is now being enacted in the Theatre in the Canongate," and the seats were filled with denizens of dirty wynds and closes, attracted by this catchpenny which Dr. Carlyle had concocted.[1]

Soon there were ominous mutterings of a coming storm. The pious, the sedate, and the clergy were scandalised. A play was bad enough, but that a minister of the gospel should write it, that ministers should go to see it, and should consort with stage players "no better than they should be," was past all bearing. Certainly the respectable Messrs. Carlyle, Home, and Ferguson were in strange company with Gentleman Digges—a bankrupt and libertine, who lived down to his reputation by afterwards allying himself with Mistress Bellamy by a mock marriage, while his own wife was living, and by finally running off with an Edinburgh merchant's wife! The presbytery issued a solemn admonition—with a preamble about the growing irreligion of the day, as evidenced by neglect of the Sabbath—warning old and young against the soul-ensnaring performances of the stage. This was greeted by lampoons by wits and wags; but several presbyteries proceeded against offending ministers within their bounds. One chicken-hearted offender got off with suspension for a month after his plea that he had attended only once, and had endeavoured to conceal himself in a corner "to avoid giving offence"; while Carlyle of Inveresk encountered a libel by his presbytery, in that he did keep company and familiarly converse with West Digges, also with Sarah Ward, in the house of Henry Thomson, vintner in the Abbey, persons of bad fame; and that he did appear in an unlicensed theatre, did behave disorderly, and did witness a tragedy in which the name of God was profaned and taken in vain by mock prayers and tremendous oaths, such as "by the blood of the cross" and "the wounds of Him who died for us on the accursed tree"—words which were taken from the old ballad "Gil Morrice."[2] The chief culprit

---

[1] Carlyle's *Autobiography*, 314; Arnot's *History of Edinburgh*.
[2] In his defence to his presbytery, Carlyle states: "I have once or twice dined in a tavern with gentlemen of good reputation, when Mr. Digges was of

soon saw that his sin was past all redemption, and ultimately resigned his charge, having two days before delivered his last sermon, which drew tears from the congregation.

Success came at last in England. The play was accepted by Rich, the manager of Covent Garden Theatre. It was no preternatural discernment on the part of that illiterate worthy, who had been the most famous harlequin and pantomimist on the stage, but whose finest leap was from being an acrobat to a theatrical manager, in which capacity he arranged dresses and scenery admirably, and ventured to "*larn*" young men to act, though unable to speak two lines with decent pronunciation, or one sentence with decent grammar.[1] He had sense enough to listen to advice from high quarters. The voice of the Duke of Argyle—Home's friend—was powerful with his nephew, Lord Bute, whose influence in turn, through the Prince of Wales, could move Mr. Rich to take the worst play ever concocted. Sir Gilbert Elliot spoke everywhere of this new drama, and soon Lady Hester Pitt and Lady Mary Coke were busy disposing of tickets with irresistible blandishments.[2]

One night in March 1757 the house was full, and as "silver-tongued" Barry acted young Norval, the audience saw nothing ridiculous in that man, over six feet in stature, gorgeous in lace, white puckered satin, and capacious powdered wig,[3] personating a poor stripling shepherd lad, who should have been in Caledonian rags when he announced—

> My name is Norval. On the Grampian hills
> My father feeds his flock, a frugal swain.

---

the company. I have heard great part of the tragedy of *Douglas* read or repeated at Mr. Digges's house, where Mrs. Ward and some others of the actors were present. I have two or three times called on Mr. Digges along with the author of *Douglas*, and was witness to some conversation about the performance; but neither on these nor on any other occasion did I converse with Mrs. Ward farther than in assenting or not to any remarks that were made on the tragedy. Nor did I eat or drink in her company, as some articles in the charge seem to imply. I was present at the theatre with ten or twelve gentlemen during one rehearsal of *Douglas*. I afterwards saw that performance once represented; places being engaged by a company of my acquaintance, I was admitted to a seat with them—as is very common in a crowd, with some difficulty and pressing" (from Dr. Carlyle's Papers).

[1] Davies's *Life of Garrick*; Tate Wilkinson's *Memoirs*, i. 119, iii. 72.
[2] *Elliots, and the Family of Minto*, p. 340 (for private circulation).
[3] *Account of English Stage*, iv. 495.

Peg Woffington, who in her harsh voice and Irish brogue was Lady Randolph, was then emaciated, worn, and ill on that stage from which she was to vanish tragically a few weeks later. When, acting as Rosalind, she spoke the epilogue, " If I were among you, I would kiss as many of you as had beards that pleased me," her tongue became paralysed, and with a loud scream she tottered from the stage—to linger for three weary years a palsied woman.

Douglas was successful—though it only ran a usual nine nights at first. On the third night the Duke of Cumberland handed twenty guineas to the elated author, his pride not objecting to take what an author out-at-elbows would blush now to have offered.[1] Society found a charm about the play which struck a finer note than the turgid dramas which were fashionable at that time; there were true touches of nature, a chord of human tragedy, a vein of poetry, which, though the play does not appeal strongly to us to-day, made it, by contrast with the bombast and fustian then in vogue, deserving of the honour it won. The fastidious Mr. Gray wrote to his friend Horace Walpole that the author of *Douglas* " seems to have retrieved the true language of the stage, which has been lost for a hundred years, and there is one scene (between Lady Randolph and the stranger) so masterly that it strikes one blind to all its defects." It was played with success in Ireland; and Thomas Sheridan, the manager, munificently sent from Dublin a gold medal—worth £10—as a mark of admiration of the author. This Dr. Johnson stigmatised in his sweeping way not merely as a piece of impudence, but as an act of folly in rewarding a play " without ten good lines." English praise was high, but the enthusiasm of Scotsmen was boundless. The drama was proclaimed " the first of English tragedies "—though really and chronologically it was only the first of Scottish tragedies. The delighted dramatist absorbed the flattery and believed it all. He had not that modest self-estimate shown by Dr. Samuel Johnson, who, when he was informed that young Mr. Pott, the poet, had pronounced *Irene* " the finest tragedy of modern days," growled out, " If Pott says so, Pott lies."

[1] *Family of Minto*, p. 340.

When Home, anticipating prosecution, prudently resigned his living, he was taken up by Lord Bute. His lordship was not yet known as a statesman, but as a favourite of the Prince of Wales, and especially of the Dowager Princess Augusta. Reserved, proud, and cold to his equals, he could condescend to charming affability to men of lower estate. A man of scholarly tastes, his library was magnificent; a patron of letters and science, he was ready to get pensions and distribute favours to literary protégés. There was a magnificence in his person; and in that picture by Allan Ramsay which portrays him to posterity there is a distinction in his robes, drawn aside to display his leg well posed, which Sir Joshua Reynolds copied with envy in his portrait of the Marquis of Rockingham. The world might deny the strength of his brains; none could deny the beauty of his limbs. Meanwhile, cold and haughty as he might be to others, to John Home he was the most affable of patrons and friends; he had nothing but kindly words for "dear John" or "dear Johnnie," who had a gushing admiration which satisfied his lordly vanity, and who served him as secretary and factotum with boundless assiduity.

Garrick soon saw he had blundered in not taking *Douglas*, though the world was sure he had rejected it because there was no part of sufficient prominence for himself. He began to court the favourite of the powerful courtier, and they became intimate friends — none could resist the charm of Home's genial manner and nature — and he was ready to receive from the popular dramatist the very piece which a few years before he had summarily refused. He read *Agis* now in quite a new light, was impressed by its beauties, avowed there were acts written more like Shakespeare than any author ever did,[1] and mentioned that Mrs. Garrick had wept over it. *Agis* was performed: the house was crowded, the Prince of Wales was present three times, and Scotsmen wrote home jubilantly of its success. But there were others who spoke with abominable frankness—not merely the snarlers who lampooned every Scot and sneered at any favourite of Lord Bute. "I cry to think it should be by the author of *Douglas*," wrote the well-disposed Mr. Gray, not moved even by the best acting of

---

[1] Fitzgerald's *Life of Garrick*, i. 376.

Garrick in Lysander, clad like a Venetian gondolier to represent a Spartan chief. It ran eleven nights and then dropped exhausted. All the same, the author made £500 or £600. Truly, with its dull scenes, its Spartan politics, its tedious declamations, the play is intolerable. No doubt Henry Mackenzie says the more he read *Agis* "the more he liked it"; posterity has not tried to acquire the taste by reading it once. Another drama, the *Siege of Aquileia*, in which Garrick and Mrs. Cibber did their best, won for its author more money and fresh fame.

No mortal now can go over any of Home's laborious tragedies except *Douglas;* and one may apply to them the verdict which the Marquis of Wellesley passed on Dr. Johnson's Latin verses —"All of them are bad, but some of them are worse than others." We need not, however, superciliously laugh at Home's defunct tragedies, for they admirably suited the taste of the age. All dramatists gave the same sort of produce for the stage, and society, strange to say, admired it. They must have had a very vague sense of the ludicrous, else the bombast of Zangas, Zenobias and Zaras, Cleones and Tancreds would have moved them not to tears but to laughter. That age saw nothing grotesque even in the garments their actors wore—in Mrs. Yates as Boadicea wearing not the rudimentary garments of the Britons, but farthingales, vast hoops, and high nests of powdered hair. They never smiled at seeing Othello played by Spranger Barry in a complete suit of English regimentals and gold-laced, cocked hat; or at seeing Garrick as Macbeth resplendent in a court suit of scarlet and gold, sometimes with a tail-wig like an attorney, at other times with a periwig fit for a Lord Chancellor. Thomas Sheridan was thought appropriately apparelled as Macbeth in the uniform of an English general. In the enthusiasm of his youth, Jackson of the Edinburgh stage determined to make his début in London as young Norval, and provided himself with a kilt, and dirk, shield, and broadsword taken from the field of Culloden; but his manager, Garrick, afraid of the rancour prevailing against Caledonian ways and men, and probably thinking the guise supremely absurd, forced the aspirant to relinquish either his garb or his part. It was in 1774 that old Macklin, playing the part of Macbeth, first introduced the adoption of supposed contemporary costume, dressing his com-

pany in the fancied garb of old Gaul, and he himself appearing
—as the orchestra played the march of the Coldstream Guards
—in a "Caledonian habit." Unfortunately the veteran, with
his huge ungainly figure, stumping on the stage, was said more
to resemble a Scotch piper than a prince of the blood.[1]

Home was now a prosperous man and a successful writer,
a useful friend of the great Lord Bute, at whose bidding
he was pleased to be, and possessed of a comfortable income.
But though living in London, he consorted chiefly with Scotsmen, for the feeling was keen against the North Britons.
Lampooners, pamphleteers, men of fashion laughed and sneered
at them; and Lord Bute's ascendency with the King intensified
the animosity, owing to his patronage of his countrymen, and
his flattery by patriotic parasites. Scotsmen in London
retaliated contempt for contempt. Yet in spite of these
international sentiments they would meet on quite pleasant
terms. At the British Coffee-House—which was kept by
Mrs. Anderson, a clever, pleasant Scotswoman, sister of Dr.
Douglas, who became Bishop of Salisbury—all true Scotsmen
foregathered. Thither gentlemen from Edinburgh were sure
to find their way, for in national dialect they could talk of
their people and their grievances to their patriotic hearts'
content. So much was this tavern the recognised resort of
men from the North, that it is said that when the Duke of
Bedford[2] was soliciting the votes of the Scottish peers in
1750, he put all the letters in one enclosure, addressed
to the British Coffee-House. A Scotsman was ever loyal to
his countrymen in London. If he wanted a publisher for his
book, it was to a Scots printer or bookseller he took it—to
Strahan, Andrew Millar, or John Murray; if he needed a
physician, it was to a Scots doctor he carried his complaints—
—to William Hunter, or Pitcairn, or Gusthard, to Sir John
Pringle, or Fordyce, or Armstrong. Garrick asserted that
the Adams, though liberal-minded architects, employed only
Scottish workmen; and bantered James Boswell, saying, "You
are, to be sure, wonderfully free from nationality, but it so

---

[1] O'Keefe's *Recollections*; J. Taylor's *Records*, ii. 12; Jackson's *Hist. of Scot. Stage*; Davies's *Dram. Miscellanies*.
[2] Gibbon's *Letters*, i. 201.

happens that you employ the only Scotch shoe-black in London."¹ John Home shared the national prejudices, and expressed his opinion of the Southrons with freedom on his first visit. He wrote to Carlyle, that though the chop-houses were good, the people were "execrably stupid, and their men of learning are such shallow monsters that I am obliged to be on my guard lest I should seem to insult them." Really the author of *Douglas* was too fastidious. As to the poor Londoners, their very appearance in the eyes of John Home—then smarting under the rejection of his *Agis*—was despicable. "The mien of the English, even in the resorts of fashion, I think but poor. I observed it to Smollett after walking at High Mall, who agreed with me."² This bland feeling of superiority was comforting to the despised Scots, who grumbled over the English, and made pleasant little fortunes out of them. Home eventually had no cause to rail at them: they went to his tragedies when they were played, and bought them when they were published. In 1760 he collected his three great dramas and published them, with a dedication to George III., who settled on Lord Bute's secretary a pension of £300 a year, and three years later the post of Conservator of the privileges of Campvere was given him, with no duties to perform and a further salary of £300 to receive.

What and where is Campvere (or Kampenveer)?

In Holland, on the banks of the Scheldt, are the remains of a town which centuries ago was a centre of life and trade. In those days ships filled its port laden with merchandise; the streets were alive with busy crowds, vocal with the hum of tongues of many lands; men of wealth lived in stately houses, with old Burgundian architecture, furnished with splendour. Amid the voices of the Dutch population were heard the tones of the Scots folk, who had formed a colony there, ever since in the sixteenth century special "privileges" were granted to Scotsmen to trade with Campvere in wool, which was the staple, and all Scottish traders were required, under penalty of confiscation of goods and ships, to load and discharge at that port. There Scots settlers

---

[1] Boswell's *Johnson* (ed. Hill), ii. 325.
[2] Mackenzie's *Life of Home*, p. 134.

formed an important community, sending officials to Court, and represented by elders to the General Assembly. How changed is that once thriving town to-day! On its old ramparts the cattle graze; in its empty streets the grass is growing; where once were rows of stately homes are trees, with a ruined house standing here and there marking where once rich Scots and Dutch merchants had their mansions. There is the Stadt-house, with dormer windows, quaint façades, and rich woodwork; and within are the benches, covered with the old dark red cushions whereon once grave councillors sat. There are the majestic church, which could hold twenty times the present population of the deserted city, and the empty Scots Haus, with arched windows and decorated gables, as it stood 300 years ago. The commerce has gone; the people have vanished; the port, spoiled by encroachments of water and sand, is empty—a silence, impressive and oppressive, reigns over that dead town, which seems haunted by the ghost of a buried past. Such is Campvere to-day.[1] It was not more flourishing when John Home received the sinecure office of Conservator of its Scots privileges, for there were no longer Scots or privileges or commerce to conserve. The Conservator, however, had the privilege of being a representative elder for Campvere in the General Assembly of the Kirk of Scotland, though of Scots Presbyterians not one remained; and even to this day the place has the right (which there is nobody to exercise) of sending an elder annually to the mother kirk. Year by year, when the Assembly met, John Home would come, as member for Campvere, and take his fluent, though not brilliant, part in its debates, supporting his moderate party, while the "Highfliers" sneered at the man who, ousted as a minister, returned as an elder.

Great was the delight of old friends when he came from London and for a while gave his cheery presence at their suppers. Greater still when he gave up the sunshine of Court, and the operation of dancing attendance on his affable but exacting lordship, and bought the little property of Kilduff, near his old parish in East Lothian. The affection

[1] Havard's *Heart of Holland*, pp. 167-184.

of his old parishioners showed itself when he set about building his new house, for they insisted on carting stone and wood and lime to help their old minister. He was eager in his youth for military affairs; now we find him joining the Fencibles, and scandalising grave elders and brethren by appearing in the sombrely-attired General Assembly in the brilliant scarlet uniform of a lieutenant. "This," sneered one of the members, "is only the farce after the play."[1]

Now he became part of Edinburgh society. A welcome addition he proved, with his hearty laugh, his unfailing good-humour; and he was happy once more in the company of his old friends Hume and Blair, Ferguson and Robertson. He and Hume enjoyed a banter, and a favourite subject was their names, which were pronounced alike, and had been spelt the same till the historian changed his paternal surname of Home to "Hume." When jocularly he proposed to end the dispute by drawing lots, "Nay," quoth John, "that is an extraordinary proposal, for if you lose you take your own name, and if I lose I take another man's name." The literati dearly loved a gentle pleasantry. When they were discussing the case of a young man of high character who had lapsed into crime, John Home interposed: "I can easily account for it, by the kind of books he was reading; for in his pocket were found Boston's *Fourfold State* and Hume's *Essays.*" At which jest, however, the philosopher looked sore displeased. Home's exuberant praise of everybody and everything was not empty flattery, but sheer good-heartedness; and even his vanity over his achievements was likeable. Carlyle tells how "he came into a company like a sunbeam into a darkened room; his excellent temper, unaffected cheerfulness, his absence of everything like reserve or formality, giving light to every eye, and colour to every cheek"[2]; and "when he left the room, the company grew dull and soon dissolved." His hospitality was unbounded; "his purse had no strings," and he was the resource of all who needed help[3]; always believing the best, he would allow in a friend neither a fault nor an ailment. "He never," Dr.

[1] Ramsay's *Scotland and Scotsmen*, ii. 555.
[2] Carlyle's *Autobiography*, pp. 232, 268.
[3] Mackenzie's *Life of Home*, pp. 7, 14.

Robertson used to say, " would allow that a friend was sick till he heard of his death." Many poor plays may surely be pardoned to one who himself played so fine a part in life as he. But it must be owned there were a good many to pardon, and there were more yet to come. There was *Rivine*—a name taken from *Ossian*, then in full fame—which Garrick pronounced an "original and a noble performance," and put on the stage with the title of *The Fatal Discovery*. Owing to the popular feeling against Scotsmen at that time, it was thought prudent to avoid all prejudice by having it ascribed to a young Oxford student, who attended the rehearsals, and surprised the actors by the philosophical calmness with which he allowed the piece to be cut and carved. It was successful; the theatre was filled from pit to gallery, to see Garrick at his best; but unluckily Home grudged the success in which he got no glory, and avowed himself the writer. Whereupon, at this "fatal discovery," Garrick and Home had the mortification to see the audience dwindle and the exchequer empty. After all, the fate of the play was worthy of its merits. There is a repetition of the sonorous sentiments, even of the scenes and plot, which had done duty in *Douglas*. Walpole laughed cynically, as was his wont. " Somebody asked me what prose Home had ever written; I said I knew of none but his poetry." Two more plays Home was still to produce. The Barrys gave life in 1773 to the now forgotten *Alonzo*, and the dramatic career ended in 1778 with *Alfred*, which no actors could galvanise to semblance of life.

In Edinburgh Home settled in 1779, and there was no companion so cheerful as he. David Hume, his dearest friend, had been the first of that brilliant coterie to die, and make a blank that was never filled. In time the famous clubs of his youth expired, with their bright talk, their buoyant patriotism, their copious claret; and a new generation gradually sprang up, amid which the old men—Carlyle, Robertson, Ferguson—continued in vigorous age. As year by year, on the Edinburgh stage, was enacted the favourite *Douglas*, the public looked with respect on the white-headed man with the kindly face, who never failed to be present in the box reserved for him, listening to the plaintive air of " Gil

Morrice" which was for generations played as the curtain rose—and ladies wept before the play began.¹ Every great actress felt that in that piece she must display her powers and excel her rivals. Old play-goers—the most reminiscent and garrulous of beings—loved to talk of actresses whom they had seen as Lady Randolph—the grandeur of Mrs. Barry, the splendour of Mrs. Yates, the cleverness of that "pretty baggage" Mrs. Bellamy, and the majesty of Mrs. Siddons in her sable body and train and white ruffs. They would recall how, when old Norval (Henderson in wig and knee-breeches) described that he found the babe in the basket on the river (" nestled curious the infant lay"), the Barry uttered the cry, " Is he alive ? " with piercing maternal shriek, and the audience caught their breath, while the Siddons spoke the words with soft, low tones, and thrilled them to their bones. It was as Lady Randolph that Mrs. Barry, forgetting her age and discordant voice, challenged the rising fame of Sarah Siddons in London; and it was in that character Mrs. Siddons chose to make her last appearance on the stage in 1819—no longer handsome and shapely, but unwieldy, infirm, and seventy years old. Yet when young Norval exclaims, " As you excel all women," the audience, applying the lines to herself, burst into thunders of applause.² Sir Walter Scott has avowed that the cliff scene between Lady Randolph and old Norval, in which the preservation of Douglas is discovered, " has no equal in modern, and scarcely a superior in ancient drama." With that the shade of John Home may be content.³

What changes had the venerable dramatist seen! In 1756 his first play had been condemned as godless by the kirk, and ministers punished for witnessing it; in 1784 the same play was lauded by the clergy, and the General Assembly was almost deserted when Mrs. Siddons played Lady Randolph—for the pit of the theatre was black with ministers, like a corn-field with crows.

In 1778 Home had begun to gather materials for a

¹ Wilson's *Memorials of Old Edinburgh*, i. 128.
² Fitzgerald's *Lives of the Kembles*, i. 157 ; ii. 1, 191 ; Boaden's *Life of Siddons*, i. 50, 76.
³ Only one phrase lives as a quotation : " As women wish to be who love their lords."

History of the Rebellion, of which much was expected; but it did not appear till 1802, when, being dedicated to the King, all reflections on the Duke of Cumberland, and much that might be piquant, was courtier-wise omitted. All were disappointed with the work; some were angry, but others kindly remembered that the author was old. Years ago, when acting as officer of the Fencibles, he fell from his horse, and got concussion of the brain, and he never was the same again. His mind became duller and feebler year by year.[1] Still there were many gatherings at his house in Hanover Street, where the old gentleman was full of kindly garrulity and gentle pleasantry. One day especially was remembered, when there sat down seven guests at the table—five of them nearly as venerable as the host himself, who was eighty-four—and the least ancient of them, as in bachelor parties, acted as "boots" to ring the bell when required during the repast. There were the national dishes which had long gone out of fashion, and the claret served in the tankards; and as they talked of times and comrades long ago dead, "the subjects of conversation might be compared to that held by ghosts, who, sitting at the midnight table, talk over the deeds they had done and witnessed in the body."[2] How changed all this from those bright earlier days when, as his friend Carlyle says, "he was truly irresistible; his entry into a company was like opening a window and letting the sun into a dark room." John Home and his wife were getting very old. Never had worthy Mrs. Home been a brilliant companion at her best; yet is it really true that when David Hume asked Home why he had married Miss Logan, with atrocious naïveté he replied, "Ah, David, if I had not, who else would have taken her?"[3] The last glimpse of the household we get is at a visit Sir Adam Ferguson paid to them. He told the aged couple of the Peace of Amiens just made, and the frugal old lady thoughtfully propounded this question of domestic economy, "Will it mak' onie difference in the price o' nitmugs (nutmegs)?"[4]

[1] Mackenzie's *Home*, p. 67.
[2] Sir W. Scott's Prose *Works*, xix. 391.
[3] *Caldwell Papers*, ii. 179.
[4] *Chambers's Journal*, 1855, Reminiscences of Sir Adam Ferguson.

On 5th September 1808, at the age of eighty-six, Home died, having survived his friends and his intellect. One likes to think of him as he is pictured in one of Raeburn's portraits, sitting in his arm-chair, with the pleasant face, the comfortable figure, the far-away look, becoming to a poet's pose, as he appeared when in his younger years he was the life of all good company.

CHAPTER IV

PRINCIPAL ROBERTSON

"Tom Birch," said Dr. Johnson, "is a dead hand at a life." What was said of the biographical efforts of the Rev. Thomas Birch may, we fear, be said with equal justice of Professor Dugald Stewart's Lives of his friends, Robertson, Reid, and Adam Smith. The sentences flow on from this "elegant exponent of Scottish philosophy" with rhetorical fluency, the sonorous periods are well poised, the pompous paragraphs finely rounded, but they utterly fail to present the personality of the men. To condescend to anecdote was beneath his professorial dignity—an indecorous concession to trivial taste. We get, therefore, colourless sketches, instead of living portraits.[1] Dr. Robertson deserved a little more than this, and the world would have liked something else about a man who fills such a prominent place in the literary and ecclesiastical life of his time. With his suave manners, his dignified air, his punctilious ways (his own sisters were careful to address him respectfully as "Sir"[2]), he had all the qualities which constitute an admirable man—an important though not a vivacious personage, a divine who seldom made a joke and never made a blunder. Everything he did had an air of propriety; everybody spoke respectfully of him—not with the affection they bore to David Hume, not with the pride they showed in Adam Smith, not with the kindliness they felt for John Home and Dr. Blair, with their guileless vanities; but with an esteem

---

[1] "I hate biography, and scarcely know whose Life I would not rather have written than Robertson's," he writes to Alison (Stewart's *Works*, x. p. 75).

[2] *Life and Times of Lord Brougham*, i. p. 35.

PRINCIPAL ROBERTSON
From the Painting by Raeburn in Edinburgh University.

they felt it a duty to pay. His character was as well composed as any page of his Histories.

Born in 1721 in the manse of Borthwick, in Midlothian, he belonged, like so many of the ministers of that time, to families of good lineage and position. In 1733 the Rev. William Robertson, his father, became minister of Lady Yester's in Edinburgh, and three years later of Greyfriars'. He was a man of learning, of refined tastes and some poetical gifts, as some paraphrases by him, sung still in the churches of Scotland, serve to prove.[1] His son was only eleven years old when he entered College, after having attended the famous Grammar School of Dalkeith. As class-mates he had John Home, John Erskine, William Wilkie, in the rooms where the famous Colin Maclaurin lectured on natural philosophy, the versatile Sir John Pringle taught not too profoundly moral philosophy, and Dr. Stevenson expounded with stimulating spirit logic and rhetoric. In 1743 he was licensed to preach, and two years afterwards succeeded his uncle as minister of Gladsmuir. During that year his father died, and in a few days later his mother was buried beside her husband, and the family was left in poverty. But in his manse Robertson gave a welcome home to his brother and six sisters—bringing them up, educating them, and maintaining them till they were settled in the world—with fine devotion postponing his marriage for eight years for their sakes.

When the rebellion of '45 broke out he cast off his gown and shouldered his musket, to join with other loyal friends the ranks of Edinburgh volunteers, who enlisted with quivering courage to defend the city from the rebels. To cool the dauntless ardour of the students, a body of professors and clergy appealed to them with deep, but quite unnecessary emotion, that they should not endanger their precious lives and deprive by their rashness the country of the flower of its youth.[2] When the pusillanimous bands of citizens withdrew

---

[1] Paraphrases beginning—
    1. You now must hear my voice no more.
    2. How few receive with cordial faith.
    3. Let not your hearts with anxious thoughts.
                           Julian's *Dict. of Hymnology*, p. 968.

[2] Carlyle's *Autobiography*, p. 118.

to the security of their wynds, and a stalwart few boldly advanced to the West Port—and stayed there—Robertson and some comrades set forth to join Sir John Cope's forces, only to find that their gallant services were declined, evidently as being more likely to help the rebels than the loyalists.

He was more successfully employed in his parish. Busy with his pastoral work, visiting the sick, catechising the young, he was beloved by his people, and his whole conduct falsified the charges of persons who, knowing little and vilifying much, proclaim that a "moderate" was a man without earnestness, a minister who preached moral duties, while lamentably lacking in piety. Up early in the morning,[1] he devoted himself to classics and the study of literature, which had engaged him since his student days, when he filled commonplace books inscribed with their grave motto *Vita sine literis mors est.* He had good society around him in country mansions, and congenial companionships in country manses—especially with easy-humoured John Home at Athelstaneford, keen-witted Alexander Carlyle at Inveresk, and many a scholarly clergymen in neighbouring parishes. He was within an easy ride of Edinburgh, where he could see Blair and Wilkie, Hume and Lord Elibank; and after 1755 he would turn up at the meetings of the Select Society and Poker Club, where he took a prominent part in their debates and a modest share in their festivities.

It was in Church courts, however, that he was first to make himself distinguished, especially in the General Assembly.

The ecclesiastical parliament was an affair of importance in those days—the centre of interest, and often the scene of excitement. Proceedings in the House of Commons were little thought of and little known in Scotland. Two or three pages of the *Scots Magazine* gave a bald outline of the debates, which had lost their interest long before they were printed, and, after all, concerned English or foreign affairs that few persons north of the Tweed cared anything about. In the Assembly, however, Church questions were discussed which concerned Scotsmen far more than any matters of State, and in them men of light and leading in Scotland took part.

In the dark, dirty aisle of the High Kirk this Assembly

[1] Brougham's *Men of Letters*, 1845, p. 262.

met. There were the high box-pews, above which the heads of the reverend occupants could hardly be seen; there were the dusty galleries, in which the audience sat listening intently to harangues and "cases"; on a gilt throne upon a platform, with dingy velvet hangings, sat the Lord High Commissioner with two or three courtly satellites around him, having made his appearance thither from Fortune's tavern, heading a modest walking procession consisting of some magistrates, with city guards bearing halberds in front, and a bevy of ladies in hoops and newest gowns behind. Just below the throne, in a square pew—in which the elders sat on Sunday listening to Dr. Blair's placid eloquence—were the Moderator and clerks in their robes and ruffles and best curled wigs, round the green table. The whole scene was more quaint than splendid, for St. Giles', though a State church, was not a church of state.

In those days appeared strange contrasts of clerical types at that meeting. There were Gaelic ministers, speaking with high nasal tones, dressed in home-spun coats, coarse brown wigs, plaid stockings, and latchet shoes, who had come from distant straths and storm-swept isles of the Hebrides to attend the annual gathering and to see the wonders of the capital. There were rough-clad ministers from remote Galloway or Caithness, who had travelled for days on vile roads, over which their poor nags staggered, putting up at wretched ale-houses by the way, and finally to be not better sheltered in stabling-houses in the Grassmarket. There came men of birth and good breeding, living on their stipends of £70 or less, who then abounded in the church, making the Assembly distinguished for culture and learning.[1] Beside them were clerical magnates —city ministers and professors—with wigs well-powdered and many-curled, in blue English broadcloth, silk stockings, and buckled shoes, who, as they walked with gold-headed canes, exchanged greetings with my Lord Galloway or ventured on a seemly joke with the Lord President.

Men of great ability sat in that reverend court—many

---

[1] Mackenzie's *Life of Home*, p. 8; Carlyle's *Autobiography*, chap. vi.; Somerville's *Memoirs*, p. 96; Pennant's *Tour*; Cockburn's *Memorials*, p. 236, all testify to the high social standing and ability of the clergy at that time.

then great whose fame has vanished long since. People used to speak in awe of Principal Tullidelph of St. Andrews, who had once been an officer in the Swedish army, as he stood with his gaunt form, his haughty presence, possessed of commanding eloquence rarely equalled in any senate, and likened to that of the elder Pitt. Among the ranks of the party called "Evangelical" or "popular" by their friends (but styled "high-fliers," the "wild," or "fanatical party" by their opponents) was the tall, handsome person of Dr. Alexander Webster, with the fluent tongue, persuasive, unctuous speech, which was so fervid in the pulpit and so genial in society, where he drank portentously and remained erect when the strongest brothers of the bottle were recumbent beneath the table. Contrasting with this convivial man of business and piety was Dr. John Erskine, with a tiny form and benign face, a saint in jet-black wig, zealous for the faith to his finger-tips. In pews facing the Evangelical party sat the Moderates—most of whom were young. Prominent was Professor Patrick Cuming, courtly, plausible, and pliant, the henchman of Lord Islay, who was ruling the political affairs of Scotland, and who trusted this ecclesiastic, whom his own party were apt to doubt. Dr. Jardine sat near him, towering in his height of six feet two, orthodox in doctrine, yet most tolerant by nature, a caustic wit, a pious pastor, though the beloved companion of David Hume. Among the young men were Carlyle of Inveresk, whose presence would be notable anywhere with his tall form, finely-chiselled features, keen, shrewd eyes, and brown hair, then untarnished by powder—a sagacious speaker, a wise pacifier of strife; and John Home, young, good-humoured, facile of speech, but more able to follow than to lead. Dr. Hugh Blair, who was seldom in church courts, occasionally contributed to debates sensible utterances, which were feeble compared with the speeches of Dr. Robert Wallace of the Old Kirk — a man of the world, a brilliant mathematician and statistician of rare capacity, distinguished for learning, whom frequenters of the dancing assemblies consulted in his notes to *Gallini on Dancing*, which he wrote at the age of seventy-three, and whom scholars studied in his *Dissertation on the Numbers of Mankind*, which supplied in after years ideas and facts to Malthus for his famous work on Population. Soon above them all was to rise Dr. Robertson of Gladsmuir.

These ministers, and others whose names now are no more than names, were able to hold their own in ability with the many brilliant elders who sat beside them—judges, advocates, lairds, and lords. Old President Dundas, with querulous face, keen ferret-like eyes, and croaking voice, in that assembly spoke with the authority he showed on the Bench. Lord Islay, afterwards Duke of Argyle, all-powerful with the Court, and dispenser of posts to a thousand obsequious countrymen, sat with Lord Milton, the Judge, who then as agent for his Grace, and afterwards as friend of Lord Bute, was a political power in the North. There, too, was Lord Marchmont, the admired of Alexander Pope, supercilious in manner, and graceful in speech which contrasted, like Lord Hailes's tones, learned at Eton, with the rough, uncouth, coarse Scots harangues of Lord Auchinleck. Among the members were young men who afterwards rose to high position—budding politicians, who were practising their oratory for Parliament, and lawyers preening their forensic wings for the Bar. Gilbert Elliot was acquiring over such questions as "moderation of calls" and "disputed settlements" a skill in debate which was to serve him in good stead when he sat on the Treasury Bench; and with high-set, mincing tones, Alexander Wedderburn—a douce elder at twenty-three—pronounced nimble speeches in those accents to which Mr. Love, the actor in the Canongate, was tutoring him, which in later years were to be heard from the Woolsack, when he sat as Lord Loughborough. Keen in support of the popular party was Andrew Crosbie ("Councillor Pleydell" of *Guy Mannering*), copious and declamatory, possessed of wit and humour, in spite of the solemnity of a countenance which grew more red by indulgence in "high jinks" which did not regard "elders' hours." The younger lay ecclesiastical bloods and convivial old elders were wont to seek relaxation from their dry functions by adjourning to the "Diversorium,"[1] as they nicknamed the Carrier's Inn in the West Bow; and after exchanging the centre of gravity for that centre of levity, would resume their duties with fresh energy and flushed

[1] Carlyle's *Autobiography*, p. 309.

faces. While the debates proceeded, the rank and file of country ministers would bend their wigged heads over the tops of the high pews, discussing the arguments *sotto voce*, and exchanging confidential opinions and snuff-boxes, as that brilliant speaker, Mr. Andrew Pringle (afterwards Lord Alemore), giving up for the occasion his part as an elder for that of an advocate at the bar, defended some ministerial culprit.

Into this ecclesiastical company in 1745 Robertson of Gladsmuir entered—in a few years to make his power felt, and to shape the policy of the Church for thirty years. It was not yet the time that any young man had a chance of being listened to, for it had been long the custom for the moderator to call chiefly on judges and professors round the green table to address the house. When Dr. Webster, however, became moderator, he broke through the old practice; and younger men then had opportunities of acquiring distinction,[1] while venerable guides of the Church looked on with disgust at the forwardness and audacity of "these young sparks." It was in 1751 Robertson made his first appearance in debate. A minister had been presented to the parish of Torphichen; only six persons out of the whole population had signed the "call," and the presbytery therefore refused to induct the minister to a parish which was opposed to him. John Home, then a young man of twenty-nine, moved that the members of presbytery should be suspended from the ministry for their disobedience to the law, and Robertson seconded this motion in a speech of marked ability. They were able to muster only eleven supporters, and a milder motion, merely to censure, was carried by over 200. This was an age when the people were trying to domineer over the Church; year after year the time of the Assembly was occupied by disputed settlements, for the minister appointed by the patron was constantly opposed by the parishioners. They would have rejected St. Paul, if a patron had presented him, and certainly they would have refused to have St. James, because his was the doctrine of a "moderate," and they would have nailed up the kirk door and assaulted the presbytery that dared to

[1] Carlyle's *Autobiography*, p. 271.

induct him. Many of the clergy would not ordain an unpopular presentee: some because they did not like to go against their conscience, others because they were afraid to go against the people. In consequence, years of weary vexatious litigation often ensued before a man was installed in his parish — during which time the heritors were extremely patient, for they calmly pocketed the stipends.

But it was now becoming too much a scandal, that evangelical and "high-flying" ministers, who would have enforced the extreme penalty of law against any one who deviated by a hair's-breadth from the legal standard of orthodoxy, should themselves violate laws which they were equally bound to obey. After the Erskines and others of the popular party finally seceded in 1739, clergy became bolder in maintaining the law against the dictation of the people. Meanwhile the "moderate party" was getting stronger—consisting of men who preached the moral law in the pulpit, and maintained ecclesiastical law in the courts—and their influence became more marked year by year. Robertson showed himself and his friends more powerful on his second appearance. A minister who had been appointed to Inverkeithing, was opposed by the people.[1] Thereupon the presbytery refused to induct him, and next year—1752—the case came before the General Assembly, who ordered the contumacious presbytery to carry out the law on a set day. The day for the induction came, but not the presbytery. Only three ministers appeared at the church of Inverkeithing, and these were not sufficient, for by a quite arbitrary command the Assembly had required six to be present. Robertson made a strong appeal to punish the offenders, and it was agreed that one of the six members who had not obeyed the order should be deposed "to encourage the others." They fixed on Mr. Thomas Gillespie of Carnock as scapegoat, a man of singular piety and amiability, and straightway deposed him from the ministry; his words as he left the house ringing in their ears: "Moderator, I rejoice that to me is given in behalf of Christ not only to believe in Him, but to suffer for His sake." There was nothing of the rebel or the seceder in

[1] Morren's *Annals of General Assembly*, ii. 222.

this man—the fanaticism of the Erskines he abhorred, and though in time he with others formed the Relief Kirk, his heart yearned to his dying day after the Church that had thrust him forth. If the law had to be vindicated, one would wish that a more offensive victim had been chosen. The young men being flushed with success, Carlyle next day proposed that more of the contumacious members should be deposed; but the party had won the day, and rested content with their victory.

From that date the influence of Robertson increased, and his principle was rigorously to enforce the law. He and his friends began a new and thorough policy. They would meet in a tavern at night—young ministers like himself and Carlyle and Home, and young elders like Gilbert Elliot of Minto and Wedderburn—to concert measures and tactics for the next day.

While the new rule was being firmly enforced, it is true discontent did not die out. Many became seceders, because their power to coerce patrons being gone, they could not reject the young moderates coming into the Church, who did not give the people the strain of preaching their souls yearned for—the fervid Calvinism, the favourite doctrines of election, reprobation, assurance, and free grace; the evangelical appeals to their fears and emotions. In the alarm at the widespread spirit of dissent, in 1765 a "Schism Act" was proposed by the popular party for the abatement of schism by a modification of the Act of Patronage, which had caused such dissatisfaction that there were 120 dissenting chapels, with 100,000 adherents—a number which struck dismay. There was perhaps wisdom in this proposal; but Robertson and his party would have none of it, and successfully opposed it with all their vigour. Robertson pleaded that the Act of Patronage of 1712 was the safeguard of the Church against bigotry,[1]

[1] Cunningham's *Church History of Scotland*, vol. ii. p. 528; Stewart's *Works*, x. p. 108. "At the Revolution the churches had been most filled with vulgar and illiterate men, Presbytery having been depressed and sometimes persecuted for twenty-eight years. From the Revolution to the year 1712, popular elections continued to debase the ministerial character. From that period to 1740 the certainty of opposition to every presentation unless the presentee accommodated himself to the humours of the people and the remaining ungentlemanly character of the clergy, deterred the liberal and ingenuous youth from entering into

dulness, and fanaticism; he maintained that before that time the clergy had been of mean abilities, of low breeding, and gross fanaticism; but since Patronage was established, men of higher culture and tolerance had been coming into the Church. Dr. Robertson spoke truly when he attributed to the system of Patronage the advent of men of learning and talent into the Church—especially after it was upheld by the Assembly fearless of popular clamour. Had they depended on the suffrages of the people, there would have been little chance of a living for Blair or Robertson, for Principals Campbell and Leechman, or Professor Reid; yet more pious men than these moderates were nowhere to be found. There would have been no place for Carlyle and Home, afterwards beloved by their parishioners. Professor Matthew Stewart, Professor Playfair, and Dr. Wallace, if they had only the vulgar choice of the people to depend on, would never have entered the ministry and brought science into the Church. It was after hot debate on this Schism overture, as the votes were being taken, that Dr. Jardine—Hume's dear friend—fell dead in the Assembly.

The speeches of Dr. Robertson, though delivered in broad accents, with stiff ungraceful action, were admirably effective in debate, while his firm, yet politic policy, and mild persuasive manners were irresistible. He could win over the dourest country opponent to his side, and soothe the most ruffled judge to acquiescent smiles. During what was called "Robertson's administration," of thirty years, when, by adroit diplomacy, he carried any measure he pleased, he maintained the independence and dignity of the General Assembly: no dictation by the Crown, no menace of the Government's displeasure would have a weight, or ever was attempted, after he

the Church. But after the secession [of 1739] the fear of the people gradually abated, and a set of young men entered into orders who had no need to put on the mask of hypocrisy. They added some degree of politeness and knowledge of the world to their superior learning, and from slaves or demagogues of a bigotted populace they became companions and friends of the superior orders. No change was more rapid and complete, and at the same time less in the extreme. Unreasonable restraints only were removed. Innocent amusements were no longer looked on as indecorums, nor indecorums considered as crimes; while the discipline of the Church prevented or checked all improper freedoms in the manners of the clergy, and manly and liberal behaviour was now sufficiently encouraged."—From an able MS. "Memorial about State of the Church, 1784," by Dr. A. Carlyle, to William Pitt.

directed the affairs of the Church. Perhaps his suave, tactful style as "party manager" made his friends less enthusiastic in his praise. At table they would have preferred less of the speech-maker and more of the conversationalist; in private they would have liked less of the diplomatist, greedy of praise, and more of the cheerful *abandon* of the companion.

When Robertson was beginning to make his position as an ecclesiastic in Church courts, at home he was busy with literary studies, and intent in his little book-room at Gladsmuir since 1752, writing a History of Mary and James I. There was at this time a bent given to Scotsmen towards historical study. Scots antiquaries for many years had been producing treatises on Scottish historical questions. Ruddiman and other erudite Tories had been belabouring George Buchanan for his pestilent heresies regarding Queen Mary, and his fraudulent perversion of facts, while Whigs joined in the fray and lauded his pious memory in pamphlets and octavos in which the composition was vile and the vituperation was villainous. Tractates on chartularies and pedigrees occupied the leisure and exercised the temper of scholars, who always become irascible when they deal with antiquities. Hume was engaged on his *History of England;* and Robertson now began his *History of Scotland,* choosing a period which fascinated Scotsmen, Whig and Tory alike. Many a time he rode to Edinburgh to consult at the Advocates' Library, in which David Hume had succeeded the redoubtable old Thomas Ruddiman in the post of keeper, and where Walter Goodall, the learned, erratic, and fiery controversalist, was assistant. Many a point the suave minister would debate with that keen Maryite and Jacobite—if he happened to be sober, for the red-faced " Wattie " was constantly intoxicated, and controversially stood up for the maligned queen when physically he could hardly stand up himself.[1]

The intervals of study and work were spent by Robertson with his favourite friends, visits to Lord Elibank, walks and discussions on historical points with Hume—for "David," as he called him, was one of his closest companions. He was full of interest in John Home's *Douglas,* which all his confidants were reading in manuscript, and the public were waiting to see

[1] Chalmers's *Life of Ruddiman,* p. 132.

on the stage. It is certain that he did not—as a story alleged[1] —act in any rehearsal, taking the part of Lord Randolph; neither did he ever go to see it performed. That, however, was not owing to cowardice or caution; it was to conform to the wish of his dead father that he should never enter a play-house—for he had been austerely trained in a household where cards, play-acting, and dancing were regarded as vices.[2] Even when in London, and in close intimacy with Garrick, he resisted loyally the temptation to visit Drury Lane Theatre, to see the great actor as Lysander in his friend Home's *Agis*, though in private Henderson, the actor, would give him specimens of his art, and Garrick would personate King Lear and Abel Drugger. His very aloofness from the audacities of his brother clergymen, and his dignified attitude, gave him more power and influence in defending their conduct and the stage in church courts.

In 1758 the *History of Scotland* was ready for the press, and it was necessary to seek a publisher. So on horseback he set forth to London, on his arrival feeling strange and awkward in the unknown capital. There his friend Carlyle found him, showed him the sights, introduced him to the famous Scotsmen in town, took him, of course, to the British Coffee-House and Forest's Tavern, where his countrymen most did congregrate, and where he met Smollett and Armstrong, the Hunters, the famous surgeons, Sir Gilbert Elliot, now Lord of the Admiralty, and Wedderburn, now rising at the bar, who, he was gratified to learn from the door-keeper of the House of Commons, spoke "devilish good English." John Home, who since his resignation of the Church was secretary to Lord Bute, was entirely at his lordship's command, and dared not be away an hour lest he should be summoned from his lodging in South Audley Street. When my lord dined out, however, he was free, and then he bounded forth like a lamb frisking in the meadows, to join in exuberant spirits his old friends, full of his *Agis*, which was being acted

---

[1] *Edinburgh Weekly Chronicle*, 21st January 1829. Though possibly present when *Douglas* was read at the tavern, for against Carlyle the Presbytery cited Robertson and Blair, among witnesses ranging from Lord Elibank to the theatre "candle-snuffer."

[2] Stewart's *Works*, x. p. 110; Carlyle's *Autobiography*, p. 292; Brougham's *Men of Letters*, p. 257, 1845.

in Drury Lane. There was an excursion to Garrick's house at Hampton Court,[1] where Home was often an intimate guest with the lively actor and his charming wife. They played golf, drank tea in the temple of Shakespeare, and came back delighted—Carlyle with tact refraining from reminding the hostess that he remembered coming over from Holland with her when she was only Mddle. Violetti, the dancer. Publishers having been found in Millar and Cadell, and a printer in William Strahan, Carlyle, Robertson, and Home (who was returning to the North) rode merrily and adventurously back to Scotland.

In 1759, in two quarto volumes, the *History* came out. In less than a month the first edition was exhausted, and Robertson's praises were in all circles. Historical writing was a forgotten art; a good history of England was unknown till Hume wrote his volumes on James I. and Charles I., and Smollett issued his facile narrative, which had appeared the year before. Here was another work by a Scotsman, and fascinating too in spite of its subject being Scottish. It did not stir up rampant rage of either Whig or Tory, as Hume's had done. It gave little offence by its tone, and though it was adverse to Queen Mary, "it cut like a razor dipped in oil" some one said. As became the leader of the moderates, it was written with moderation. The age was too much accustomed to formal diction to carp at the style as being stiff and pompous, and it welcomed a narrative animated and vigorous. David Hume, who was then in London, transmitted joyously every word of praise he heard, and wrote with friendly banter, "A plague take you! Here I sat on the historical summit of Parnassus, immediately under Dr. Smollett, and you have the impudence to squeeze past me and place yourself directly under his feet!"[2] He wrote to his friend that Lord Mansfield did not know whether to esteem more the matter or the style; that Mr. George Grenville remarked that "had the author lived all his life in London, and in the best company, he could not have expressed himself with greater elegance and purity"; that the Prince and

---

[1] Carlyle's *Autobiography*, p. 344.
[2] Burton's *Life of Hume*, ii. 51.

Princess of Wales were reading it. For once Horace Walpole was sincere when he spoke his eulogies. When in London Robertson had modestly called on him. "How could I suspect," wrote Walpole,[1] in one of his letters, "that a man whose dialect I scarce understood, and who came to me with all the diffidence and modesty of a very middling author, and who, I was told, had passed all his life in a small living near Edinburgh—could I suspect that he had not only written what all the world now allows the best modern history, but that he had written it in the purest English, and with as much seeming knowledge of men and courts as if he had passed all his life in important embassies." All this was pleasant. Hume had written pages crawling with Scotticisms, notwithstanding his acquaintance with the English world, and yet Robertson, who spoke Scots, and had never been out of Scotland, wrote English almost without reproach. It is true, he had submitted his manuscript to Sir Gilbert Elliot and William Strahan to revise and to remove what Johnson called "colloquial barbarisms," but it was his careful study of literature that had guided his style.[2] For this History the author got £600, and by it Millar and Cadell cleared £6000. Naturally Bishops thought such a man was far too good to be a Presbyterian, and kindly recommended Robertson, as they did Blair and Beattie, to enter their Church. This generous invitation was very firmly declined.

Honours now fell thick upon the historian. He became minister of the Greyfriars' the year on which his History appeared. Three years later, 1762, at the age of forty-one, he was appointed Principal of the University, and in the following year he was chosen Moderator of the General Assembly, of which he was the distinguished leader. The office of Historiographer of Scotland was also given him, with a salary of £200 a year—a preferment which a little hurt the feelings, though it did not excite the jealousy, of his friend and rival historian, David Hume. From the obscurity of a country parish, with a

[1] Walpole's *Letters*, iii. p. 202.
[2] Macaulay, in his slap-dash style, asks a question on Robertson's last work, which there are no readers to answer: "Are there not in the *Dissertation on India* Scotticisms at which a London apprentice would laugh?" (*Essay on Addison*).

stipend of about £80, he had now become a man of wealth—
as clerical wealth was reckoned in those poor days—and he
was noted as the first minister in Scotland who kept a carriage.

Dr. Robertson lived till he became Principal in a house
at the head of the Cowgate, now the most squalid of Edinburgh squalid districts. There he kept boarders, like most
city ministers and professors in those impecunious days, for
English noblemen were in the habit of sending their sons to
Edinburgh for the efficient and sedate college training they
could not get at Oxford or Cambridge. In society he was
prominent, as befitted his position of importance. Courteous
and pleasing, with his bland and intelligent face and keen
eyes, his presence gave an air of propriety to any company, as
he sat in his well-fitting garments, his prim clerical bands, his
legs crossed, displaying the neatest of silver-buckled shoes.
His talk, agreeable but rather too instructive, came forth in
strong Scots tongue, with a fluency which at times was too
flowing for those who wished to speak as well as he. Friends
rather resented his propensity, which increased with years, to
lead the talk, and they murmured that whenever the cloth
was removed after dinner and the wine appeared on the
shining mahogany, the doctor would settle himself with
deliberation in his chair, introduce some topic, and discourse
thereon till general talk ceased. He would take the opinions
and thoughts that his friends uttered yesterday and present them
in elegant paraphrase—" the greatest plagiary in conversation
that I ever knew," says "Jupiter" Carlyle. His admiring
biographer, Dugald Stewart, hints delicately at such colloquial
defects, speaking of "his formal and artificial periods, the language of a strong and superior mind, which embellished every
subject."[1] One day Adam Ferguson and Carlyle determined in
malicious sportiveness to forestall the inevitable monologue. It
was arranged that Carlyle should begin a long panegyric on a
much-puffed patent mustard, and Ferguson privately told the
Principal in a tone of deep concern that poor Carlyle was clearly
going off his head, for he would speak of nothing but this
wretched mustard, whereupon Robertson felt responsive concern for their friend. When the dinner was over, the good

[1] Carlyle's *Autobiography*, p. 287 ; Stewart's *Works*, x. p. 187.

DR. ALEXANDER CARLYLE

From a Painting by A. Skirving in the Scottish National Portrait Gallery, Edinburgh.

doctor settled himself to take his wonted lead, when the minister of Inveresk, in a manner à la Robertson, broke in,[1] "This is an age most notable for its momentous discoveries. Human ingenuity is exerted on the noblest things, and often with the most admirable effects on the meanest things. There is, for instance, an article of the humblest kind which has lately been wonderfully improved by a particular mode of preparation; and he, for his part, was inclined to say that patent mustard was the thing above all others which gave a distinguishing glory to the age. In the first place"—and so on the rigmarole proceeded—a good parody of his host's best manner. Robertson was dumfounded, saddened at his friend's mental state, while the confederates were delighted at having for one day stemmed the flow of their friend's harangue. There was something in the sententiousness and pomp of his manner in public which it was not difficult to imitate. One day, when the High Kirk was more than usually dark during the meeting of the General Assembly, that incorrigible mimic, Francis Cullen—afterwards Lord Cullen—when the Principal was absent, rose in the obscurity of the corner he usually occupied, and made a speech in voice, accent, argument, and style so exactly like the leader's, that every one thought that it was he who was speaking. Later in the debate Dr. Robertson came in and

---

[1] Recollections by Sir Adam Ferguson, in *Chambers's Journal*, 1855. "Robertson's deficiencies were only observed by his friends, for his sagacity, his power of colloquial eloquence, and his admirable talents of translation and making other men's thoughts his own, not only concealed the scantiness of his learning, but gave him an air of superiority that was very imposing. . . . At no time did Blair ever betray any sentiment that was unworthy of his profession or character, though he was perfectly open and unreserved. But Robertson's great love of dissertation made him not only sometimes tedious to his friends, who knew all his topics, but sometimes ensnared him into too free communications with young people, and raised in them a false idea that his principles were not so sound as they expected. As for instance when he used to expatiate on the folly of public men who did not make sure of something good for themselves, while they were serving their country. Such notions amazed the youths, who expected from him a splendid blazonry of a high standard of public virtue. Strange it was that so wise a man should have ever indulged himself in such intemperate talk. But the *cacoethes docendi* is as difficult to restrain as of *scribendi*. . . . Robertson was warped by the spirit of party, and was so much dazzled by the splendour of the French Revolution, that even his sagacity was imposed on, and he could not listen to the 'ravings' of Burke, as he called them."—From Dr. Carlyle's MSS. Mackenzie expresses a higher opinion of Robertson's conversation, *Life of Home*, p. 56.

rose to make his speech, which proved so close a reproduction of Cullen's that every one was amazed, till it dawned on the House that a hoax had been perpetrated, and the reverend members roared with merriment, while the unconscious victim stared in mute wonderment. But all these things were done in good-humour, and the historian was one of the finest-tempered of men. No one, not even the boarders in his house,[1] had ever seen him ruffled. It was characteristic of the man that he objected to the over-display of feeling alike in sorrow and in mirth—censuring levity as unbecoming, and grief as ill-timed, for people should keep their troubles to themselves.[2]

Genial and natural with intimate friends, it was in larger companies that he tried to shine most, but shone least successfully, with a manner awkward and fashion too formal. Dugald Stewart, in his usual style, which painfully resembles the historian's own, takes care to say that on "no occasion did he forget the dignity of his character or the decorum of his profession; nor did he ever lose sight of that classical taste which adorned his compositions."[3] Now, a conversational style which shows "classical taste" and is modelled after a history cannot be exactly considered exhilarating, but it had a sobering effect on company. Sitting at the Principal's well-plenished dinner-table, Lord Kames would subdue his coarse wit and reduce his language to propriety. Dr. Webster, who could discourse on the terrific woes of Hell and the seraphic joys of Heaven one day, and empty a "tappit hen" of its contents in hilarious joys on earth the next, kept both his unctuous fervour and his jovial qualities under control in his presence, and none could guess that this sedate divine was he whom society irreverently called "Dr. Bonum Magnum." Certainly the host could take no exception on the score of frivolity to Adam Smith, who was always instructive, or to Dr. Blair, to whom it was as difficult to see a joke as it was for himself to make one. It was with bland, kindly tolerance he bore the levity of those mirthful friends Ferguson and John Home, and the playfulness, which he called "infantine," of David Hume. Carlyle of Inver-

[1] Brougham's *Men of Letters*, p. 266.   [2] *Ibid.* p. 313.
[3] Stewart's *Works*, x. pp. 138, 157.

esk, with his vivacity and intellectual alertness, would keep the talk at its best, and Lord Elibank, the Jacobite, would utter quaint paradoxes in the squeakiest of voices. By the way, it may be remarked, his lordship and his friend Carlyle belong to those lucky mortals who live in tradition with the reputation of being able to write as well as anybody if they chose, and die without having risked the loss of it by writing anything at all.[1] There was preserved by the historian a quaint, old-fashioned formality of manner, as he addressed every lady as "Madam," and with stately bow would say, "My humble service to you," as he drank her health. The Principal was a dignified presence, both as he sat at table and as he walked down the High Street with his clerical bands fluttering in front, in cocked hat and bushy wig, and gold-headed stick in his hand.

Ten years passed by before he followed up his first literary success. Yet during that time he had not been idle. At first his design was to write a History of England. His friends at home, as well as Lord Chesterfield, who likened his style to Livy's, and King George—pronounced this a fit subject for his pen, and Lord Bute promised that the Government would put every source of information at his disposal. He himself felt that the post of Historiographer had been given to him on condition that he should undertake the work.[2] However, the project was abandoned, chiefly from reluctance to encroach on his friend Hume's special field. After hesitation and listening to conflicting counsels, he chose the History of Charles V. as his subject. Years of labour were devoted to reading and composition, though few Spanish sources of information were within his reach. In 1769, in three volumes quarto, appeared the *History of the Reign of Charles V., with a View of the Progress of Society from the Subversion of the Roman Empire to the Commencement of the Sixteenth Century.* The author reaped £4000—a sum for a history hitherto unknown in the annals of publishing, and the price shows the estimation in which the writer was held. Again the success was brilliant; again the

---

[1] "Dr. Carlyle wants nothing but inclination to figure with the rest of them on paper" (*Humphrey Clinker*). He only published pamphlets and wrote some verses; but left behind him his *Autobiography*, full of vivid pictures of his times and contemporaries.
[2] *Caldwell Papers,* ii. p. 234.

praise was almost unanimous. Suard produced an admirable translation into French; Voltaire wrote flattering compliments in return for a copy; Catherine II. of Russia sent him a gold box set in diamonds in token of her admiration. It is true, Dr. Johnson protested to Boswell that the History was "a romance, cumbrous and tedious," and not to be compared in merit to poor Goldsmith's compilations. But no man uttered from sheer perversity more worthless colloquial verdicts than this autocrat of letters, whom, as Robertson complained at Sir Joshua Reynold's, his admirers were "spoiling" by grovelling worship. Sterne was pooh-poohed by him, Churchill and Fielding were called "blockheads," and Gray was dubbed "a barren rascal." No wonder Scotsmen like Hume, Robertson, Home, and Adam Smith came under his indiscriminate flail.

When Robertson was in London, he was shy of meeting the literary despot, knowing how Adam Smith had fared at his hands; yet when they met, Johnson took to this sensible Scotsman, who did not assert himself too much. "Sir, I love Robertson," he was pleased to say, "though I won't speak of his books." Boswell represents the Principal as always in awe of the dictator. When at his invitation Johnson met Blair and Robertson, with others, at the "Crown and Anchor," the party he asserts "hardly opened their mouths except to say something which they were certain would not expose them to the sword of Goliath."[1] When Johnson met the historian in Edinburgh, he praised him to Bozzy for his caution in "not exposing himself by argument to his own superior opinions"; and when the divine ventured at Boswell's lodging to discuss some point, Johnson chuckled to his friend that he had "downed upon him." Yet the dogmatist, whose conceit in his own powers Boswell fanned with his adulation, meant to be pleasant to the Principal all the while.

The work on Charles V. had brought the historian in touch with the Spanish main, with the conquerors of the New World, and he now chose as his subject for study the discovery and conquest of America. Information that was original could not be found in Edinburgh or in London, and there were few Spanish authorities to consult; though the Ambassador

[1] *Life of Johnson*, edited by Hill, ii. 63; iii. 335; v. 371.

at Madrid helped him with books and papers, of which he made admirable use. The *History of America* was published in 1777.[1] His clear, vigorous, and often picturesque narration, his shrewd grasp of facts, made the work worthy of his reputation. This was the last of his eminent historical works, although in 1783 he began a continuation with an account of the American colonies, which he stopped when the revolt of the States made the interest in these provinces more political than literary.[2]

In estimating the worth of historical productions of former generations, we are apt to show authors scant justice. Later investigations bring old documents to view, fresh facts come to light to modify our opinions, rendering obsolete what seemed a pretty piece of immortality. And yet the work itself, from a literary point of view, may remain admirable. To such reverses Gibbon alone seems superior: the assaults of criticism cannot prevail against him. There stands his work on the decline and fall of the Roman Empire—the marvellous history of centuries, the record of the strife of diverse races and rival creeds which were unconsciously forming out of barbaric chaos a new civilisation on the ruins of the old—the author marshalling multitudinous facts in splendid array, searching out the elements of social force with admirable insight, and producing a work whose accuracy stands unassailable, leaving future editors only the humble task of putting a diffident footnote to correct a date or amend a reference. Such is the triumph of only one historian—of the plump and placid author who, in his study at Lausanne, plans out his works so evenly, tapping his snuff-box and putting a pinch to his nose, as he reads over with special zest some particular passage of subtle irony or majestic pomp.

Robertson had no such genius, "master artist" though Gibbon kindly called him, and he achieved no such glory. The treasures of Simancas were not open to him, state papers of Spain were unknown to him, and much that he wrote is

---

[1] The reading of this History suggested to Keats his well-known lines in his sonnet on Chapman's *Homer* on "Stout Cortez," "silent on a peak in Darien."

[2] His last work, *Dissertation on India*, counts for nothing as literature.

necessarily superseded to-day. One sees him as a philosophical historian in his introduction to Charles V.—a survey of European history which shows him at his best. The style seems pompous and stilted to us now, for it belongs to a formal age of cocked hats, knee-breeches, and bag-wigs. Possessed of a profound sense of the Majesty of History, the author approaches her in court costume, and addresses her with profound ceremony. The reflections may be too obvious, and the phrases too high-sounding, for though Robertson recommended *Gulliver's Travels* and *Robinson Crusoe* as the best of models for narrative style, one finds, unluckily, more of Dr. Johnson than Dean Swift in his pages. "Sir," said Johnson, in a pleasant humour one day to Bozzy, "if Robertson's style be faulty, he owes it to me; that is, having too many words, and those big ones."[1] Sir James Mackintosh, who speaks of the style as having a demureness of manner, primness, and stiffness like the politeness of an old maid standing on formalities of propriety, read a volume through to give a composed dignity to his style in his address to a Grand Jury.

It was in 1780, when only fifty-nine years old, that Principal Robertson retired from his leadership of the Church, abandoning public life, as his hero Charles V. abdicated his throne. His last appearance was consistent in its liberal policy, and its caution with his whole career. Scotsmen were agitated at the proposal to extend to Scotland the Act carried out for England and Ireland, repealing the penal statutes against the Roman Catholics. In 1775 the General Assembly under Robertson carried a motion approving of this measure of justice; but soon the people were in a furore—civil, social, religious bodies agitated against it. The Corporation of Cordiners in Potterrow, the porters of Edinburgh, journeymen staymakers, guilds of gardeners, societies of coal-heavers, masons, butchers, and weavers piously joined with town councils and Church courts in opposing the Bill. "No popery" mobs attacked popish chapels, assailed the supporters of the threatened repeal, while soldiery guarded Robertson's house at the College. The Principal felt it prudent to bend before the storm of fanaticism, and when the Assembly met

[1] Boswell's *Life of Johnson* (Hill's ed.); Mackintosh's *Memoirs*, ii. 110.

next year, while he avowed his sympathy with the Repeal, he pronounced it unwise to pass laws which would cause general disorder in order to relieve a "handful of Roman Catholics in Scotland," and stated that he had advised the Government to relinquish their Bill. It was not a very heroic ending to a distinguished ecclesiastical career.[1]

His work for the Church was not ended, for he remained prominent as a preacher in Greyfriars' Church, discoursing with vigour, if not with inspiration, on fine moral principles and practice—the moderate divine preaching alternately in the pulpit with his evangelical colleague, Dr. John Erskine, a Calvinist whose spirituality took the grimness out of the creed, one of the most gentle of beings, with the blood of a long race of country gentlemen in his veins, and the spirit of stout Covenanters in his heart. These two men, opposed in policy and in teaching, were united by the respect and friendship which draw good men together.

Not the least important part of Robertson's career was his work as a Principal of the University. Great changes had come over the University since, in 1735, he sat in its class-rooms. At that time, amid a number of dull men teaching obsolete science and philosophy, were Colin Maclaurin, in the fulness of his fame, one of the most brilliant disciples of Newton; Sir

---

[1] Cunningham's *Church History of Scotland*, vol. ii. 543. According to Dr. Carlyle in 1780 the palmy days of the Church were gone—less interest was now shown by the laity, and an inferior class were entering the ministry. "The General Assembly was deserted by the most respectable part of the land-lords, in whose place men of an inferior station and narrow and bigotted principles have been allowed to fill that court. A remarkable instance of this was observed in the Assemblies of 1778 and 1779, when the Bill for the Relief of Roman Catholics was the subject which agitated the country to the greatest degree. In neither of which Assemblies were any of the supreme judges present, nor any of the officers of the Crown (being attending their duty in Parliament), nor so much as one landed gentleman worth £300 a year. . . . Through the indifference of the laity and the inattention of Government, the wild party have been gradually gaining ground, while many of the wisest and most experienced of the moderate party have been disgusted with neglect, and have discontinued their attendance in the Supreme Court. Young men of low birth and mean education have discovered that livings may infallibly be obtained by a connection with the most insignificant voter for a member of Parliament, and superior spirits perceiving that the most distinguished among the moderate clergy had not for many years power of recommendation to beneficies, have generally betaken themselves to other professions."—Carlyle MSS.; see Cockburn's *Memorials*, p. 238, on declension of the clergy.

John Pringle, now President of the Royal Society, then lecturing on moral philosophy, and prelecting on Puffendorf and Grotius; Alexander Monro, the first Professor of Anatomy, attracting students from all quarters. When in 1763 the historian became Principal, only one of the old staff remained—good Dr. John Stevenson, Professor of Logic, of whom all his famous pupils spoke with reverence. Now he was an old man, lingering on in an age which had outgrown his methods, though he bravely abandoned Locke for the new "common-sense" of Reid. When the new Principal was going his rounds to visit the classes, as was then his duty, he entered the shabby little class-room which he had left as a boy. There was the learned veteran, whom every one esteemed, going through the same lectures, doubtless yellow with age, thumb-marked by thirty years' wear and tear. At the close of the lecture Dr. Robertson rose and addressed the students in Latin—which we may trust they understood. He told them how he, too, had as a boy from these benches listened to their venerable teacher, and what gratitude he felt for the stimulus towards literature he himself had gained from his prelections on Aristotle's *Politics* and Longinus. As he spoke tears came to the old man's eyes, and when the class was over he fell on the Principal's neck and kissed him.[1] A touching scene worth remembering! Men of a new school and new generation were now teaching in that shabby college building—Adam Ferguson on moral philosophy, Blair on rhetoric, Matthew Stewart on mathematics, Cullen and John Gregory on physic, Joseph Black on chemistry, and Alexander Monro *secundus*, as brilliant as his father, on anatomy. The fame for ability which the university had acquired had drawn students from England who formerly would have gone to Utrecht or Groningen or Paris. Noblemen were eager to entrust the care and education of their sons to Scots professors, who were as eager to get them to increase their meagre salaries. The students had increased from 300 at the beginning of the century to 600 about 1770. The staff of eight regents had enlarged to eighteen professors. But though classes, scholars, and teachers had vastly grown in numbers, there was the same deplorable accommodation in the wretched

---

[1] Grant's *Hist. of Edin. University*, ii. 330; *Scots Magazine*, 1802.

collection of buildings—two half-formed quadrangles of shabby edifices, which had in olden days been dwelling-houses, with the addition of low dark class-rooms and a few chambers for students who had long since deserted them, making squalid way for some printers, tradesmen, and washerwomen. After weary years of effort, it was the joy of Dr. Robertson's heart in 1789 to see the foundation-stone laid of a university worthier of a great seat of learning than those miserable buildings, which he bitterly said were "more fit for almshouses," on which he for years had gazed with sad eyes from his study windows. He did not live to see the work completed, and, from lack of funds, the splendid design of Adam was never fully carried out. After thirty years of appealing and begging, £32,000 were collected; but when he died, there were still standing parts of old dilapidated buildings side by side with portions of the new edifice which were unfinished and going to ruin, in which crows built their nests undisturbed, while beggars set up their huts unchallenged at the college gate.[1]

Time went by, and the year before his death Dr. Robertson removed from the paltry Principal's house in the College, with its mean surroundings, to Grange House, a mile from town, with its gardens enclosed by high walls, in which the old man loved to walk, inspecting his flowers and his fruit. When visitors came they found in him a model of serenity and dignified kindliness. He was deaf and required an ear-trumpet, but this infirmity was not too great a trial for a man who loved more to talk than to listen. Lord Cockburn remembered when a boy visiting the venerable historian [2]—a pleasant-looking old man, with an eye of great vivacity and intelligence, a projecting chin, a small ear-trumpet fastened by a black ribbon to the button-hole of his coat, a large wig powdered and curled. "He struck us boys over the wide table as evidently fond of a good dinner, at which he eat with his chin near his plate, intent upon the real business of the occasion. This appearance, however, must have been produced partly by his deafness, because when his eye told him that there was something interesting, it was delightful to observe the animation with which he instantly

---

[1] Grant's *Old and New Edinburgh*, ii. 23.
[2] *Memorials*, p. 48

applied his trumpet, and when he caught up the scent he followed it up and was the leader of the pack." Devotedly loved by his family, his nature was genial and kindly to his friends. "His home for three weeks before his death was really an anticipation of heaven," says Carlyle. Almost to the last he was full of his little interests, with tottering frame superintending his gardener; placid, even gay, on his death-bed.[1] After a life of almost unbroken prosperity, he died on the 4th of June 1793. He had reached the age of seventy-one—an age, however, which was almost juvenile when so many of his contemporaries bore lightly their weight of years till they were past eighty.

If men lived long in those days, they were fortunate in the fact that their fame and works did not die before them. Yet time in the end plays cruel havoc with literary reputations and "classics." Books that once no gentleman's library could do without, become books that no gentleman's library can do with, and standard works at last lie like their authors prone in the dust. It is not surprising that even Robertson should to some extent share the fate of his fellows. More researches, fresh discoveries, make good works obsolete; as new lights come, old lights grow dim, and once-esteemed books retreat to upper shelves, respected by all who do not know them. It may happen sometimes that visitors at a country house where new books are scanty will read old volumes when the rain is pelting or the snow is falling, to while the hours away, and at dinner they may remark, with the air of discoverers, that they have been looking over Robertson's *History*, and "it is really very well written." But follow these volumes from the library to the sale-room; see them, as we have so often done, put up in handsome sets of fourteen volumes octavo, "bound in full tree calf, gilt extra." After a few half-hearted bids they are knocked down for one shilling a volume—"not a fifth of the price of the binding," mutters in querulous aside the auctioneer, who at least knows the value of the exterior.

Yet, if Dr. Robertson's works have fallen into disuse, he has not fallen into disrepute as a writer. Unfortunately, the sole consolation for eminent but superannuated authors

[1] Stewart's *Works*, x. p. 198; Carlyle's *Autobiography*, p. 549.

such as he, is that they have instructed and pleased the age in which they lived, that they form stages in the evolution of literature, that on stepping-stones of their dead selves successors rise to higher things. Whether defunct writers, great in their day, would have considered this a sufficient consolation for being ignored by posterity is quite another question.

CHAPTER V

ADAM FERGUSON—DR. HUGH BLAIR—DR. WILLIAM WILKIE—
DR. BLACKLOCK

THE remarkable feature of literary society in Scotland in the second half of the century was the familiar fraternity in which these men lived. They all knew one another—most of them since boyhood, for they were all about the same age. They met one another almost every day of their lives; they belonged to the same set of society, sat at the same tables in the dingy old flats, copiously partaking of claret and punch without a headache, and of indigestible national dishes without a nightmare, with all the zest of epicures over the most delicious novelties. They could not go out of their wynds without being sure to see friends they had met last night at Mrs. Cockburn's merry parties, over a light tea and cakes; or at the Lord President's, over a heavy supper and drink. David Hume, when he left his house in James' Court, before he had gone for two minutes up the High Street, might meet the dapper and prim Dr. Hugh Blair, or rub shoulders with Lord Elibank, to whom he would give a stiff bow, as he was not on good terms with his lordship. Principal Robertson, proceeding in his stately gait, would meet Dr. Carlyle arrived from Inveresk, who had just put up his horse in the stabling in the Grassmarket, equipped in jack-boots and spurs and whip, accoutrements which were slightly discordant with his clerical coat and bands. Probably there had ridden into town from Kilduff Mr. John Home—radiant in smiles and a scarlet coat—on his now aged steed. Lord Kames would pass by in wig and gown from his house in the Canongate on his way to court, and as his tall, gaunt

ADAM FERGUSON
From the Painting by Raeburn in Edinburgh University.

figure disappeared round the corner, who should come but Lord Monboddo, who always kept his distance from a man who had the bad taste to ridicule his profound speculations. At his door at the Luckenbooths, standing on the steps leading to his book-shop, Mr. William Creech would be seen, attired in silk breeches and black coat, with carefully-powdered hair, for it was twelve o'clock, the hour that the bibliophile had his levées of literary friends, and he would intimate to Lord Hailes and rubicund James Boswell that in the back room were little Mr. William Tytler of Woodhouselee, turning over some antiquarian books, and Mr. Adam Ferguson, with his young friend Dugald Stewart, who was then professor of Mathematics. Then there might come in to make arrangements for the press, Mr. William Smellie, the printer, also naturalist and natural philosopher, who was the correspondent and translator of Buffon, the editor and compiler of all the principal articles in the first edition of the *Encyclopædia Britannica*, which began to appear in 1771, in three modest volumes, edited for a modest £200. This lumbering, slouching figure, with uncombed hair, unshaven face, clad in a grey coat far too big, all sprinkled with snuff, and a rusty cocked hat, was he of caustic tongue and rude humour, who talked philosophy at Lord Monboddo's suppers, and headed the revelries of the Crochallan Club, in Douglas's tavern, with jocose and roystering comrades. It was there Robert Burns met him on too festive evenings in 1787—

> His bristling beard just rising in its might—
> 'Twas four long nights and days to shaving night;
> His uncombed, grizzly locks, wild staring, thatched
> A head for thought profound and clear unmatched.

Such were the men, notable for learning and letters, who met every day; while there were lawyers like Henry Erskine, the most delightful of jesters, most able of pleaders; the mighty Robert MacQueen, famous as Lord Braxfield; Andrew Crosbie; Lord Cullen, the incomparable mimic; and men of science like Drs. Cullen and Black, Gregory and Robison. Smollett enthusiastically said Edinburgh was a "hotbed of genius."[1]

[1] *Humphrey Clinker.*

When Amyat, the king's chemist, was in town, he said to Smellie: "Here I stand at what is called the Cross of Edinburgh, and can in a few minutes take fifty men of genius by the hand."[1] Allowing for some courteous exaggeration, it certainly was a remarkable time. It was in 1773—the year in which Dr. Johnson arrived in Edinburgh to overawe the Scottish capital with his literary magnitude — that David Hume wrote to his friend Strahan, the printer, alleging that "England is so sunk in stupidity and barbarism and faction that you may as well think of Lapland for an author."[2] This is, of course, in his whimsical way of girding at the Southrons; but it must be owned that there were very few English men of letters when he wrote—singularly few in London. Who were they? Johnson, and Sir William Blackstone, the jurist. Add to these Colman, Murphy, and Richard Cumberland, the playwrights; but who else besides? Gray, Churchill, and Sterne were gone. Burke and Goldsmith were Irishmen. The great writers were dead; their successors had not yet come to literary life. It was much, then, to boast that while London, with about 700,000 inhabitants (and Hume conjectured "there is a kind of impossibility that any city could ever rise much beyond this proportion"[3]), had not half a dozen authors of mark, Edinburgh, with only 70,000, possessed so many. Within a few years, the English, who sneered at the Scots, were obliged to buy and to read their books. They read Ferguson for Roman history; Hume, Smollett, Henry for English history; Robertson and Watson for foreign history. In philosophy little had been produced in England since Bishop Berkeley wrote, and they therefore resorted to Hume and Reid, even to Beattie and Monboddo. They got criticism from Blair and Lord Kames; learned political economy from Smith; and docilely accepted poetry from the piping of the *Minstrel.*

[1] Kerr's *Life of Smellie*, ii. 252.
[2] *Letters to Strahan* (ed. by Hill).
[3] "Essay on the Populousness of Ancient Nations." "I believe this is an historical age—this is an historical nation; and I know of no less than eight histories upon the stocks in this country." (*i.e.* Scotland) wrote Hume to Strahan in 1773 (*Letters of D. Hume* (ed. Hill), p. 155). Even Dr. Carlyle had intended to join the band of historians, for his friend Dr. Dickson writes to him in 1765 from London: "I most ardently wish you to set about your History, and you must procrastinate no longer" (Carlyle MSS.).

All this shows a remarkable contrast in literary activity between north and south of the Tweed.

Few men added more vivacity and freshness to the literary band than Adam Ferguson. He was the only one who was not a Lowlander; and coming from Perthshire, with Gaelic accents on his lips, with Highland blood in his veins, and extremely Celtic temper in his spirit, he brought a refreshingly new, but by no means disturbing, element into the society of Edinburgh.

He was born in the little Manse of Logierait in 1723. His father was an estimable clergyman, who had been brought up in the straitest sect of the evangelicals. This we gather from the simple reminiscences in which the old minister relates how, on one occasion, the regent at the university of St. Andrews, where he boarded, ordered him on the Sabbath to go to the kitchen to dry some tobacco and grind it into snuff; at which the pious student had been grievously offended, for he had seen his father frequently refuse to take a "sneeze" from a person who, he suspected, had prepared it on the Lord's Day.[1] To the same college his son Adam was sent at the age of sixteen, and thence passed to Edinburgh to complete his studies for the church. When he had completed two out of six portentous years of divinity lectures, required then from all preparing for the ministry, he was, by favour of the General Assembly, licensed, in order to accept the post of Deputy Chaplain of the Black Watch. There were special reasons why he should seek such an appointment. The Duke of Atholl was his father's patron, and his Grace's son, Lord John Murray, was colonel of the regiment—a youth of twenty-three—over whose conduct it was thought an advantage that a watchful, though youthful, ministerial eye should be kept. No one was better fitted for the delicate task than the young Highland chaplain, whose knowledge of Gaelic also enabled him to preach and minister to the Highland soldiers. The story is told, to show his impetuous nature, that on the

[1] *Edin. Review*, 1867. It was the custom in pious households to have children baptized as soon as possible. Adam Ferguson and two of his brothers were baptized the day after their birth—the rest of the family a few days after (*Records of Clan Ferguson*, p. 123; see also *Memoirs of Thomas Boston*).

luckless field of Fontenoy he was seen in the front of his regiment, broadsword in hand, and when the commanding officer bade him remember that his commission did not warrant his taking such a position, "Damn my commission!" was his reply, and he flung that document at his head.[1] A good story; but was it usual for chaplains to carry their commissions about their persons, ready to fling as missiles at their superior officers, with appropriate but unclerical expletives? More credible and more creditable is the account that, in answer to a remonstrance at his being in the front of his regiment, he replied that he was there not to fight, but to tend the wounded and the dying.[2] In truth, he was the idol of his men, from his courage and his tenderness; while the dignity of his bearing rendered him able to restrain the conduct and the speech of both officers and men by a word or a look. His military career lasted for ten years, during which he was through the campaign in Flanders, and we have Uncle Toby's authority for saying that, formerly at any rate, "they swore terribly in Flanders." Disgusted at the Duke of Atholl refusing to give him a living—which the chaplain had confidently expected—he, with his pride on edge, gave up his clerical calling. From Groningen, in 1754, he wrote to his friend Adam Smith, bidding him no longer address him by any reverend title, for "I am a downright layman." At this time and place he was governor to a Mr. Gordon, who was studying law, and accompanied him to Leipzic University, where he passed the time conversing in "bad Latin and bad French," the only languages he could muster. From Leipzic he wrote pleasant gossip to his friend Adam Smith, with stories of foreign celebrities. How the nonogenarian Fontenelle, travelling with a lady who happened to drop her fan, put himself in motion to pick it up; but as she prevented him (for he is nearly a hundred years old), he said, "*Plût à Dieu que je n'avais que quatre-vingt ans.*" Another lady, coming into his neighbourhood, paid him a visit, and told him she expected to see him often for that reason. He replied, "That won't be my reason, it will be only

---

[1] Scott's *Works*, xix. 313.
[2] Stewart's *Sketches of Highlands*, ii. Appen. iii.

my pretext." He then relates that "A lady tells me she saw Voltaire on his way from Berlin, and that he caressed one of her children, and said he would be fond of him even if he had been begotten by Maupertuis"—his special antipathy.[1]

In 1757 Ferguson settled in Edinburgh. His tall, handsome person, his air of high-breeding and easy grace, his vivacious talk, were a charm to his friends. They knew he was choleric and would fire up on the smallest provocation in an instant, for he was explosive at a very low flash-point. But then his heart was as warm as his temper. Having renounced his clerical profession, sometimes he would lend an old sermon to a friend, who astonished his hearers by a profound discourse on the "Superiority of personal over physical circumstances" or on "Moral perfections" to which they were quite unused. Merrily he entered into Edinburgh life—its clubs, its dinners, its talk, and its friendships. Most of that literary society consisted of clergymen, all about the same age, all liberal-minded, all good-humoured. They were not witty—no *bon mot* survives from their lips—but they were vivacious. They formed a fine brotherhood, and though they had their tiffs, and might fall out of friendship, they soon fell in again, and when one died they mourned as over a brother's death. To use the words of Dr. Carlyle, one of the ablest of that company: "The whole circle of learned and ingenious men who had sprung up together at this time was remarkable for the unbroken union which prevailed in it. There were circumstances relating to the capital at this time which contributed much to this fraternal concord; such as the small size of the city, though containing a great population, and the social and hospitable manners which then prevailed. It was peculiar to the city and to the period that there could arrive from the country in the afternoon and be almost certain of assembling such men as David Hume, and Adam Smith, and Robertson, and John Home, and Adam Ferguson, and others, in a tavern at nine, which was the hour of supper in those days, and the chief time of convivial entertainment till about the year 1760. These circumstances conduced not a little to that harmony which then reigned among an order of men said

[1] From unpublished letter to Adam Smith.

proverbially to be irritable minds."[1] To this fraternity Ferguson brought humour, dignity, a graceful presence, and the manners of a man of the world. He was full of interest, like all the town, in Home's *Douglas*, and, with Carlyle and Elibank, present at the meetings with Digges and Mrs. Sarah Ward at Thomson's Tavern, partaking of historic "pork griskins" and punch in dubious company. While scandalised ministers were denouncing the iniquitous performance, he freshened the air with a breath of common-sense by a pamphlet, "The Morality of Stage Plays seriously considered." He at least could speak with perfect freedom: the Church could not cast him out, as he had already cast it off. While Ferguson made some money by acting as tutor to the sons of Lord Bute, and from the post of librarian at the Advocates' Library, in which he succeeded Hume, he aimed at a professor's chair. There was a talk of his buying out the professor of Civil Law; for as no professor could then afford to retire, he usually bargained that a round sum of some £800 should be paid down by any one who wanted his place, who was obliged to borrow the money and hamper himself with debt, or to give up the salary and live only on the meagre fees.[2] In those days the point which was considered was not how to get a chair which a man was qualified to teach, but how to secure any chair—Greek or natural philosophy or logic—whose subject he might afterwards learn. It so happened that the chair of Natural Philosophy now fell vacant, and to this post the ex-chaplain was appointed by the town council, "after consultation with the ministers of the city." What did it matter to Mr. Ferguson that he knew nothing about science, and had never opened a book upon it since he had worked at Euclid and hydrostatics in St. Salvator's College when a boy? The appointment was made in July, and the classes began in October, so at once he began working up mechanics, optics, astronomy, and Newton's *Principia*—learning in haste what he had to teach at leisure. The result was admirable. Students never had had so lucid a teacher, so patient a master. He never was too profound for them; in truth, he managed always to be a few days ahead of them in knowledge. "You are a greater genius than any of

[1] From Dr. Carlyle's MSS. [2] Burton's *Hume*, ii. 47.

us,"[1] bantered David Hume, "seeing that you have learned such a science in three months." At which Adam gave a pleasant smile. It must be owned that what he gave was quite worth what he got.

The active minds in the town were keen over the Select Society which was being formed in 1754, for philosophical inquiry and improvement in the art of speaking. The moving spirit was Mr. Allan Ramsay, the poet's son. Besides being an admirable and popular portrait-painter, he was a man of fashion, living in the best society, which did not think less of him for coming from a wig-maker's family. He was also an admirable classical scholar, and the professor of Humanity would have hesitated to contend in learning with the lively, petulant artist with the pugnacious nose and erudite tongue. The Society, which met in the Advocates' Library, consisted at first of only fifteen members, but it became so fashionable that in a few years it numbered 300, including all the literati, many nobility, gentry, lawyers, clergy, and physicians, who met every Friday evening. Trade, politics, social economy, historic questions were debated; such as "Should Bounties on Corn be allowed?" "Should the Repentance Stool be removed?" "Was Paper Credit a Benefit to the Country?" "Was Brutus right in killing Cæsar?" Robertson, Kames, Lord Alemore, Sir Gilbert Elliot, and Wedderburn were frequent speakers. Lord Elibank, William Wilkie, and Lord Monboddo added liveliness by their whims, their cleverness, and their humour. David Hume and Adam Smith gave only their silent presence.[2] In course of time the Society took up the encouragement of trade and agriculture and art in Scotland with excellent results; but as years wore on the ardour fell off, and it was transformed finally into a society for improvement in the English tongue, and died away.

A more convivial Society was formed, in which Ferguson took a leading part. Scotsmen were indignant at the neglect of their interests by the English Government, and were irate at the Militia Act, which excluded Scotland from the power of raising a military force, because it was deemed unfit to be trusted

---

[1] Carlyle's *Autobiography*, p. 283.
[2] D. Stewart's *Works*, x. 204; Tytler's *Life of Kames*, vol. ii. Appen.

with arms after the '45. Accordingly, a society of aggrieved Scotsmen was formed in 1762 — Hume, Elibank, Carlyle, Home, Kames, Sir William Pulteney were of the number. What should the name of the club be? it was asked. "Why not call it the 'Poker Club'?" said Ferguson, who is said to have been standing at the fire with the poker in his hand; for it was to stir up an inert country to a sense of its atrocious wrongs, and "to poke" the fire of patriotic zeal in demand for its defrauded rights. What they did after all we cannot tell, what impression they made on a callous ministry we cannot see; but they spent many happy nights, talked a great deal of brilliant nonsense, consumed a great deal of very cheap claret. They met at the Carrier's Inn, which was known as the Diversorium, near the Cross, where they had dinner at two o'clock, at one shilling a head, wine to be confined to sherry and claret, and the reckoning to be called at six o'clock. With gentle humour Alexander Crosbie was chosen *Assassin*, and to neutralise his severity placid David Hume was added as assessor.[1] They were immensely delighted with a pamphlet squib by Ferguson in 1761, entitled "The Proceedings in the Case of Margaret, called Peg, Only Sister of John Bull." Of course they equalled it to the best work of Swift and Arbuthnot; yet it is not so brilliant that we require to read it with blue spectacles, which Gautier said were necessary when reading the dazzling pages of one of his friends.

Societies like the "Select" and the "Poker" brought men of intelligence together of all classes — nobles and gentry, ministers and lawyers — and fostered a friendliness of intercourse which was peculiar to those days.[2] The Poker, after continuing many years, died at last. It is told how, after

[1] Carlyle's *Autobiograhy*, p. 420; Mackenzie's *Life of Home*, p. 27.
[2] "The club they instituted in 1762, called the Militia or the Poker Club, not only included the lit-rati, but many noblemen and gentlemen of fortune, and the liberal professions, who mixed together with all the freedom of convivial meetings once a week during six months in the year, which contributed much to strengthen the bond of union among them. Although the great object of these meetings was national, of which they never lost sight, they had also happy effects on private character by forming and polishing the manners which are suitable to civilised society, for they banished pedantry from the conversation of scholars, and exalted the ideas and enlarged the views of the gentry, and created in the several orders a new interest in each other which had not taken place before in the country" (from Dr. Carlyle's MSS.).

the famous Club had expired, some of the members, when stricken in years, tried to revive it. They met in the familiar tavern, in the same dingy old room; they sat looking at each other with sunken eyes, and wrinkled faces, as they munched the old-fashioned dishes, with reminiscent talk of departed days and dead friends. These aged gentlemen, who had lost their teeth and kept their friendships, never met again as a Poker Club.[1] It was a melancholy resurrection for a night.

Ferguson remained at his task of teaching a science of which he knew little to pupils who fortunately knew less, till seven years later a vacancy occurred in the chair of Moral Philosophy. He secured this post, for which he was excellently fitted, and began a brilliant course in 1764. Students were attracted to Edinburgh to attend his lectures, always stimulating, often eloquent if not very original. Men of fashion and culture in the city sat down beside raw lads to hear him day by day. Now he could boast of an income from fees and salary of no less than three hundred a year, which was wealth beyond the dreams of the most avaricious professor. Still wider spread his reputation when his *Essay on the History of Civil Society* appeared in 1766—a treatise on the laws affecting the origin and growth of society and government; on the effects of climate and physical conditions on commerce, polity, and thought; the evolution of the race from savagism to civilisation; the influence of political institutions on countries. It is a study in sociology following very closely on the lines of Montesquieu. From London, Hume, though he did not think much of it, sent news about its warm reception: how highly Shelburne and Townshend thought of it; how Lord Bute had read it eight times over; how Lord Mansfield had said "it was extremely well wrote"—we are sure his lordship said "written"; while the Archbishop of York asserted "it surpasssed Montesquieu, and had not a Scots idiom in the whole book.[2] All this was very pleasant, though very extravagant praise of a superficial book, and the news was heard at every supper-table, where friends rejoiced at their

---

[1] Scott's *Works*—" Periodical Criticism," xix.
[2] Burton's *Hume*, ii. 386.

friend's success, and gloried at fresh lustre being thrown on their country.

A greater triumph came when in 1772 Ferguson's now quite forgotten *Institutes of Moral Philosophy* appeared, and made his name known far and wide, being translated into several European languages, and used as a text-book in the Empress Catherine's Universities in Russia.

It was, as we have seen, usual for professors to enlarge their income by taking boarders into their families: Blair had the sons of the Duke of Northumberland and other noble youths packed in his abode in Riddell's Court; Robertson had a son of Lord Warwick's in his salubrious house in the Cowgate; and Ferguson had two younger members of the same family.[1] As tutor he had a huge divinity student standing six feet three on his stocking soles—the warm-hearted, genial son of the minister of Sleat, who was to prove by acts of generosity the loved and lovable friend of his master, when he rose to rank and power as Sir John Macpherson, Governor-General of Bengal. One day there was a curious scene. Dr. Percy, afterwards Bishop of Dromore, of *Reliques* fame, was in Edinburgh in 1765, and after having one Sunday evening visited Dr. Blair, from whom he had in the forenoon heard a most eloquent sermon, he set forth with his young charge Lord Algernon Percy to take tea with Mr. Ferguson. They discussed the merits of Ossian, in which Ferguson had taken much interest and given some faith. Dr. Percy afterwards stated, and with much irritation at being hoaxed, that the professor called on the student to recite ballads from the so-called epic in Gaelic in proof of its genuineness. "Being Sunday," the Bishop relates, "Mr. Ferguson could not decently sing the tune, which I had a great curiosity to hear, and as I was obliged to leave him again, he, as we were going away, took me aside, and in a low voice hummed a few notes to me as a specimen of the old Highland tune."[2] Now it is curious to learn that this story Ferguson denied point-blank; yet we would rather trust the veracity of the Bishop than the memory of the Professor. The amusing thing in the scene is the felt impropriety of a secular tune

---

[1] *Caldwell Papers*, ii.
[2] Small's *Life of Ferguson*, p. 37; Nichol's *Illust. of Lit. Hist.* vi. 567.

coming from the lips on the Lord's Day, and the furtive "humming" of it "in a low voice" by the Scotsman in an aside as he shows his visitor out. Evidently a sin that was "hummed" was less heinous than a sin that was sung.

A break occurred in the professorial life by a new occupation. The free-and-easy way in which Scots professors deserted their chairs without leave of absence when they liked, and for as long as they liked, is a peculiar characteristic of those old days. When Sir John Pringle was appointed to act as army surgeon in Flanders, he calmly left his chair of Moral Philosophy for years, and put a cheap young man to teach in his place. The smallness of their incomes made professors ready to snatch at temporary and more lucrative employment, and become tutors to young gentlemen. There now came a tempting proposal to Ferguson that he should travel as companion to young Lord Chesterfield, and he bargained shrewdly that he should have a salary of £400 a year, and a pension afterwards of £200. Now his lordship was not a man after Ferguson's own heart; unlike his polite godfather, "he had as little good breeding as any man I ever met with," records Madame D'Arblay. Some years before he had had as tutor the famous Dr. Dodd; and when that unctuous divine, after his audacious attempt to bribe the Lord Chancellor Apsley's wife to gain a living (for which Foote gibbeted her on the stage as "Mrs. Simony)," prudently sought seclusion abroad, Lord Chesterfield received him with open arms and presented his tutor and bottle companion to a comfortable living. A few years later, however (in 1777), Dr. Dodd forged his patron's bond for over £4000, and though he might probably have saved from death his old friend (who had paid back the money), he left him to swing on Tyburn tree. His lordship was long known afterwards as the "man who hung a parson."[1]

With this not too distinguished nobleman Ferguson set forth in 1773; saw the world, its gay towns, its brilliant society, its great men—not, of course, excepting Voltaire—and found his fame had gone before him to Paris, at whose salons he was welcome. When he came back he found that the town council, in their wrath, had passed a strong resolution

[1] Fitzgerald's *A Famous Forgery*; D'Arblay's *Diary*, v. 92.

against "professors strolling through the country as governors," and were unwilling to let him resume his post. However, he did return to his class, and even quitted it again a few years later, when in 1778 he was appointed secretary to the commission sent to Philadelphia to negotiate peace with the rebel States—an errand which proved utterly futile, and rather ignominious. Dugald Stewart undertook during his absence to lecture for him on ethics at three days' notice, as well as to carry on his own class of mathematics. It is not surprising that at the end of the session the exhausted young man required to be lifted into a carriage.[1]

It was after his return, when busy with his Roman History, that Ferguson was struck with paralysis, said to have been occasioned by free living. By the grace of a good constitution and the aid of his friend, Dr. Joseph Black, he recovered, and for thirty-six years enjoyed unbroken health. But no more "free living"; no more alluring dishes, such as "crabbie claw" and "friar's chicken"; no longer enlivening magnums of claret and bowls of punch. Henceforth he was condemned to feed on such messes as milk and vegetables. Often on such painfully wholesome fare would he sup with his abstemious crony Dr. Black, whose niece he had married; and his son, Sir Adam, used to say it was delightful to see the two philosophers "rioting over a boiled turnip."[2]

In 1783 the *History of the Roman Republic* appeared, and earned for the author well-merited fame. To say that this History was the best which had yet appeared in England on the subject is to say very little, for who except Nathaniel Hooke had written respectably upon it, yet this work, too, had in time to join the long, pathetic procession of Roman Histories on their way of oblivion—histories great in their day, which successors always fatally supersede. "It was Ferguson's former experiences," says Dr. Carlyle, "which turned his mind to the study of War in his History, where many of the battles are better described than by any historian but Polybius, who was an eye-witness of so many."[3] Carlyle was always

---

[1] Stewart's *Works*, x. (Life by Veitch).
[2] Cockburn's *Memorials*, p. 50.
[3] Carlyle's *Autobiography*, p. 283. Ferguson, whose admiration for the

under the belief that his friend's works were not sufficiently appreciated.

Two years later Ferguson retired from the chair of Moral Philosophy, for he found "its duties pressed upon his health and spirits"; and now Dugald Stewart, giving up his uncongenial mathematics, took the chair which his friend resigned, and soon became the most distinguished expositor of Scottish philosophy. Strange academic manœuvres were common in those days, and indeed necessary in times when, there being no retiring pensions, old men must either retire and starve or linger on in senile incapacity till their death. By an ingenious device, Ferguson was transferred to the vacant chair of Mathematics, of which he got the salary, while young John Playfair, as his colleague, did all the work and only drew the students' fees. It must have required all the geniality of that amiable natural philosopher to see this literary patriarch with irritating vitality retaining the salary of a chair which he did not teach for thirty long years.

Dr. Ferguson, at least, had no reason to complain. He had abundant leisure to enjoy society, and to pursue his favourite studies. It is true, his temper was keen, his spirit was peppery, and his blood was hot; and in one of these moods there arose a quarrel with his old friend Adam Smith—the only serious estrangement that severed any of those brothers of the pen. Years after, however, when tidings reached him that his former friend was dying, forgetting all old sores, he took his sedan-chair and went to visit the companion of bright days, and sat by the sick-bed—the two as peaceful, as companionable as if they had never passed each other by in the High Street.[1] Now Ferguson lived without a burden to bear or an old lecture to repeat. In the social life of the town he had only one cause for chagrin: his diet could no more be the succulent dishes that loaded the boards and highly flavoured the dining-rooms. For him there was now only Spartan fare of "mashed turnips" and cauliflower, while

Roman people was great, as a disciple of Montesquieu marks the effects of political institutions on the national character, and the steps by which a republican government gave way to a despotism.

[1] Rae's *Life of A. Smith*, p. 433.

he watched his friends, with appetites provokingly vigorous, enjoying the fragrant fare of his youth, and quaffing gloriously the genial claret and emptying the "tappit hen," while he sipped his cold milk. The choleric professor taught a fine stoicism in his books, but he found it terribly hard to practise in his daily life. Woe to that member of the household who ventured into his study, which he usually kept locked, and who dared to remove the dust and rubbish which had for months accumulated on the books and papers. His temper was in a state of incandescence for days.

He was a septuagenarian when he set about the retrospect of his past teaching on moral philosophy, which appeared in 1792 under the title of *Principles of Moral and Political Science*. The philosopher contributes one more infallible theory on moral judgment to the many that the age was propounding. Man is said to acquire his notions of duty from his conception of perfection—the ideal which he forms in his mind of what is highest and best. A buoyant optimism pervades Ferguson's teaching: in the keen love of political as well as religious and social liberty, which made him expect much from the French Revolution, till its excesses blighted the hopes of enthusiasts. His philosophical works—able in argument and elegant in style—are now completely forgotten, and as Johnson has said, "There is no need to criticise what nobody reads."

At the age of seventy-two[1] he set out for Germany and Italy, attended by his servant-man, James, to inspect the famous historic scenes; for he was preparing a new edition of his History. The old man rode along the banks of the Adige, visited Verona, viewed old battlefields with the eye of an amateur master of strategy. He was glad, however, to get back once more to his house at Sciennes (called "Sheens"), within a mile of Edinburgh Town—which was known by friends, from its remoteness and the chilly, fur-clad frame of its fiery occupant, by the name of "Kamtschatka." There he could regulate his temperature by Fahrenheit, putting the family into commotion if he found he was a degree too hot or too cold. His house was the resort of the brightest and the merriest companies at tea or supper.

[1] Small's *Life of Ferguson*; Carlyle's *Autobiography*, p. 57.

It was at one of these brilliant gatherings that the boy Walter Scott saw Robert Burns. He was proud to be the only one able to tell the poet who was the author of the lines written below the picture of a soldier dead in the snow which moved him to tears[1]. Who in that company could have imagined that the fragile, shivering host would last for nearly thirty years longer, when most of that bright gathering were in their graves! What a vitality there was in that good old philosopher, in spite of the old shock of paralysis; in spite of milk and turnip diet; in spite of his fragile frame and his bloodless body, which shivered at every whiff of air beneath his furs! A man he was of "cheerful yesterdays and confident to-morrows."

It is as a veteran of over seventy years, possessed of benignant face and choleric temper, that he is pictured in Cockburn's vivid pen-portrait — with his hair silky and white, his animated light-blue eyes, his cheeks mottled with broken red, like autumnal apples, fresh and healthy; his thin lips—the under one with a touch of acidity in the curl; his face of sweet dignity. His frail frame was clad in garments, even to his hat, of Quaker grey. With single-breasted coat, long waistcoat with capacious pockets, fur greatcoat, worn out of doors and within his house, and half-boots lined with fur, he presented a curious, venerable appearance as he walked along the streets, with a tall staff held at arm's length, his two coats, each held only by the upper button, displaying the whole of his handsome old form. "His gait and air were noble, his gestures slow, his look full of dignity and composed fire. He looked like a philosopher from Lapland." "Truly," as Lord Cockburn says, "a spectacle worth beholding"; and as he sits with folded hands and benign, thoughtful gaze, as if no earthly trouble could ever ruffle his irritable soul, he is worth looking at in Raeburn's noble portrait.

We see the old gentleman leaving his Edinburgh home when over eighty years of age, settling for a while in the gaunt, grim, half-ruined fortalice house of Neidpath Castle at Peebles[2]—a fitter haunt for owls and bats than for a frail

---

[1] Lockhart's *Life of Scott*, i. 185.
[2] Small's *Life of Ferguson*, pp. 61, 62.

philosopher. Charming it was, no doubt, when the bright sunshine glittered on the silvery Tweed, that runs beneath; but dreary in winter, when the light came feebly through the little iron-barred windows that pierced the walls six feet thick. After a hot quarrel between the fiery tenant and his cynical landlord, the disreputable "Old Q," the old man removed to the more genial mansion of Hallyards in the Vale of Manor, which he described to one of his friends as having in view a most delightful kirkyard, retired and green, on the bank of a running water. "To me it gives the idea of silence and solitude away from the noise of folly." And the old man pictures himself laid in Manor Kirkyard, with a tombstone bearing this inscription in Greek: "I have seen the works of God; it is now your turn. Do you behold and rejoice." It was not there, however, that his thin body was to lie, or a Greek epitaph was to puzzle wayfaring posterity; for the old gentleman was full of vitality, looking after his turnip-fields with all the energy of a young farmer. It was when staying in 1797 with the philosopher and his son that Walter Scott first saw the Black Dwarf, whose name he was to make immortal. After the visitor entered, the creature locked the door of the hut, smiled with horrid grin, and seizing him by the wrist, weirdly asked: "Man, hae ye ony poo'er?" All magical power was earnestly disclaimed by the young advocate, who, pale and trembling, quitted the hut of Davie Ritchie.[1]

Age made its presence felt at last in the old man, who—feeling need of more companionship, for his soul was gregarious, and finding need of more comforts, for his body was frail—took up his residence in the then slumbrous city of St. Andrews. There he found cultivated company among the professors; peace in the grass-grown South Street; and quiet morning walks on the links, which were not the crowded turf of to-day, crawling with golfers and hurtling with balls. There in the city, where so often, as round the Cave of Spleen, "the dreaded east is all the wind that blows," his furs and wraps kept the acrid air at bay. At ninety-three there was still wondrous freshness in the venerable face, with the ribstone-pippin complexion, the mild blue eyes, the soft,

[1] Chambers's *Life of Sir W. Scott*, p. 35.

humorous mouth, the silvery hair. There was the old mental alertness about everything that was new, and the aged philosopher listened eagerly when the divinity student who attended him read out to him the newspapers. He who was a young man when the Rebellion of '45 broke out, lived to read the bulletins of the battle of Waterloo. At last, in 1816, he died, his final words as he turned to his daughters by the bedside being the exclamation of bright assurance: "There *is* another world,"[1] and in a few minutes he was gone to see it. One of the best of a brilliant company of literary comrades, he was the last to die. He had seen his old friends pass away one by one, in fame, honour, and old age. After having lived in the bright old days of Scottish literature, he survived to see with unjealous eyes another brilliant day dawn which should rival the past.

Dr. Hugh Blair

It is not easy to understand at times the reputation borne by many men of the past, and the deference they met with, the flattery they incited, the ceaseless applause that attended their course. We read their books and we are not impressed; we turn to their finest passages and we see no beauty; we extract their best thoughts and they seem woefully commonplace. There are fashions in literature, as there are in art, costume, and furniture, but a bygone literary fashion rarely returns. "Queen Anne patterns" may again come into vogue, Chippendale chairs may be recovered from the dusty garrets to adorn rooms and to torture backs, but a Johnson's *Rambler*, a Beattie's *Minstrel*, and Blair's *Sermons* come back to our bookshelves no more. The authors themselves, however, have an interest for us. We are curious as to what manner of men these were who were so celebrated in their day, when their names were on every lip, and their books were in every hand.

In Edinburgh none was more famous in the latter half of the eighteenth century than Dr. Hugh Blair. His dingy church was attended by the most fashionable when he preached; his little, dark class-room at college was full of the most cultured

[1] *Edin. Review*, Feb. 1868.

when he lectured; every tea-table was silent when he spoke; every supper-party was deferential as he conversed. An uneventful life of unbroken health and prosperity was the fortune of the preacher-critic of Scotland. Born in 1718, the son of a merchant of good position and connected with clerical families of great note, Blair passed through the usual classes at the University with unusual distinction, and when he was in the Divinity Hall, with a cousin he wrote a poem on the "Resurrection," which, after being handed round in manuscript to admiring readers, at last, to the author's amazement, made its appearance in a handsome folio, dedicated to the Prince of Wales—a Dr. Douglas having claimed it as his own and bartered his conscience for a living, though when he was about it he might have done it for a better production. After being tutor to Simon Fraser, the son of Lord Lovat, Blair was licensed to preach, and soon won the good opinion of all moderates and the respect of all unemotional patrons by sermons distinguished for the qualities "correctness of design and chastity of composition," which were then immensely admired. Men of the world and of taste felt that the common duties of life preached by moderate clergy were quite enough for them, and that what evangelicals or "High-fliers" denounced as "filthy rags of self-righteousness" formed a very good costume for a Christian's daily wear. After a few months in the parish of Collessie in Fife, the popular minister was appointed to the Canongate parish, then the centre of all that was notable for rank and wealth and fashion, as it is now the centre of dirt and poverty and squalor. The hideous kirk, with its deep gallery and box pews, was thronged with ladies in their brocades and hoops and powdered hair, and with gentlemen in their satin coats and powdered wigs. Patrons wooed and congregations yearned for this preacher, so he passed on to Lady Yester's Church, endowed by a pious lady of evangelical propensity (which, it is to be feared, Mr. Blair would not have satisfied), and thence to the High Kirk in St. Giles', the summit of clerical ambition.

At that period St. Giles' Cathedral was deformed to its utmost capacity.[1] Attached to its walls outside were little wooden-

[1] Chambers's *Traditions of Edinburgh*, ii. 212; *Peter's Letters to his Kinsfolk*, ii. 9; Arnot's *History of Edinburgh*.

DR. HUGH BLAIR
From the Painting by David Martin in Edinburgh University.

fronted shops in niches of the building, fixed like barnacles to a ship, occupied by jewellers, booksellers, glovers. Only one of these was two storeys high, and in that a goldsmith had his shop and dwelling, his large family living in the flat above, while a cellar beneath, lighted by an iron grating in the pavement of Parliament Square, served as nursery. This merchant was Mr. Ker, member for the city, who had married the daughter of the Marquis of Lothian. It was thus people dwelt in those simple, frugal days. The interior of the building was divided into four places of worship, each of which had its minister of different type and doctrine, and its congregation of different type and class. At the door of a Sabbath day rival throngs of worshippers would meet on their way to "sit under" their favourite pastor—evangelical or moderate. If they were "high-flying," they entered the door which led to the Tolbooth Kirk, where Dr. Alexander Webster entranced the "Tolbooth saints," as they were called, thrilling them by his fervid appeals, gratifying them by his Calvinistic doctrines, and edifying them by those unctuous prayers which he uttered as he stood with black-mittened hands fervently clasped. If they enjoyed a solid, sound, yet intellectual discourse, they went into the Little Kirk, otherwise called lugubriously "Haddo's Hole," where Dr. Wallace, the most accomplished of all the clergy, might be heard discoursing elegant morality with a wholesome blend of doctrine, quoting Gray's *Elegy*, just published, and comparing it with the finest specimens of classic poetry. But most of those pertaining to the fashionable world went in by the left door opening into the High Kirk, where Mr. Hugh Blair preached in the forenoon. They took care not to go at the "diet" when his colleague, Mr. Robert Walker, did duty; for that estimable man was as evangelical as his partner was moderate, one who preached Calvinism and denounced worldly dissipation, and indeed had boldly preached powerful discourses before the Magistrates and Lords of Session on the iniquity of patronising the stage, to which Mr. Blair was addicted. To his ministrations the poorer classes came, and the Church plate was then conspicuous for the number of halfpence; an observant elder remarking that it took twenty-four of Mr. Walker's hearers to equal in contribution one of Mr. Blair's.

So it happened that on one part of the day there went the *élite* to worship, on the other there went the elect. When Mr. Blair was to conduct the service the church was full of all the great folks of Edinburgh flats, in their most brilliant attire. Lords of Session were there, who may have been drunk as lords the night before, but were as sober as judges when the ten o'clock bells were sounding; magistrates came gorgeous in their scarlet robes from the Exchange, preceded by the city guards bearing their halberds, eagerly watched by the crowd, on whom the display of civic splendour never palls. To please the taste of a throng so fashionable,[1] a precentor had been brought from York Cathedral, and the psalmody lost its weary drawl, while varied tunes charmed the most fastidious Presbyterian ears. All listened with rapt attention as the great preacher read closely from the pulpit cushion his well-rounded, sonorous sentences, his indisputable truths of morality, expressed with elegance and taste. They soon forgot the pompous, inanimate manner, the irritating burr of the orator's voice. Judges and bailies, lords and writers would remark with great satisfaction as they walked home, "That was a truly admirable discourse we have had to-day." In their wynds and turnpike stairs, to which they returned, they never were accustomed to cleanliness; they did not, therefore, observe that St. Giles' was deplorably grimy, that there were cobwebs on the pillars, dust thick on unswept pews and passages, that the dingy windows had not been cleaned for ages. When Dr. Samuel Johnson in 1773 looked in—not on Sunday, for he would not attend a worship fit for Presbyterian dogs—St. Giles', as Boswell confesses, was "shamefully dirty." At the time the distinguished traveller said nothing; but when he came to the Royal Infirmary, and saw a board with the inscription, "Clean your feet," he turned slyly to his friend and said, "There is no occasion for putting this on the door of your churches."[2]

Year by year the reputation of the preacher was increased by his sermons, to each of which he devoted a whole week's labour. He had an art in composition which pleased men of taste, a common-sense which satisfied men of the world, a vein

---

[1] Kay's *Edinburgh Portraits*, i. 348.
[2] Boswell's *Life of Johnson* (edit. Hill), v. 42.

of mild sentiment which touched women of emotion. But he was also a man of literary judgment, a man well read in literature, which more and more was being considered in Scotland. The *Edinburgh Review*, even if it had not died six months after it was born, would have given little scope for his skill; but a chance occurred for his establishing a new reputation. Adam Smith, in the winter months of 1750-51, had given a course of lectures on Literature in a class-room at the College before his departure for Glasgow. These were successful, as were also those of his successor, Dr. Watson, who soon after left for a chair in St. Andrews, where he earned a reputation by a *History of Philip II.*, which had the distinction of being praised both by Dr. Johnson and Voltaire, and of being quoted by Charles Fox in the House of Commons. Dr. Blair now took their place and continued their work with enormous favour. Persons possessed of good memories and ill natures said that the minister, who had studied Adam Smith's manuscript lectures, had got all his best matter from his friend; but people will say anything, and this time they were wrong.[1] The small dingy room in the old buildings of the College was filled by the best society; the lawyers, the *literati*—to use the favourite term—and the ministers attended, and all the pronouncements of the critic were received with profound respect. So great was the success that the town council was moved to found in 1761 a chair of "Rhetoric and Belles Lettres," and Dr. Blair was appointed to the post, with a modest salary of £70. All this was a sign of the interest in "polite letters" in Scotland which had been increasing year by year. Of old it had shown itself in discussions in tavern clubs, and later in the effort of people of rank and fashion to discard Scots provincialism and acquire an English polish; in the cultivation of literary taste, which had sprung up all around, and was now bearing excellent fruit in the works of Hume and Robertson and Ferguson. So keen was the interest excited by the lectures on literature and rhetoric, that impecunious students wrote out their notes to sell them to booksellers, who exposed the manuscript reports for sale in their windows in Parliament Close.[2]

[1] Rae's *Life of Adam Smith*, p. 32.
[2] Chambers's *Lives of Eminent Scotsmen*.

Great was the excitement in Edinburgh when, in 1760, the little volume *Fragments of Ancient Poetry* appeared, with a preface by Dr. Blair, in which remains of a great poem of Ossian, "discovered and translated from the Erse" by the big Highland tutor James Macpherson, were brought before the world. It was believed to reveal a work by a Gaelic poet of the fourth century, in which Homer was rivalled, all modern epics excelled, and Scottish national genius nobly vindicated in the eyes of the English. The poetry was regarded by Blair —the pre-eminent judge—as undoubtedly genuine, as undoubtedly ancient work of rarest beauty, and to large audiences he delivered a course of lectures on the antiquity, the value, and the sublimity of the songs of the son of Fingal. The professor's name was spread far and wide by his *Critical Dissertation on the Poems of Ossian* in 1763, which were ingenious and acute, and as good as could possibly be written by a gentleman lecturing on a language he did not know, of a past he had not studied, of a poem on whose origin he was utterly mistaken. But in all his mistakes he erred with Hume, Ferguson, and Home, Kames and Monboddo; and the very fact that he maintained the authenticity and vast genius of a Caledonian Ossian only made him the more admired by a patriotic country.

He was accepted as the arbiter of taste. Poems and treatises were submitted for his judgment, and his opinion was considered infallible. Home brought to him his *Douglas*, Blacklock his poems, Hume his essays, and we know how in later years his verdict on Burns' poems was awaited with anxiety. He was the literary accoucheur of Scotland. At the same time patrons conferred with him on suitable moderate "presentees" for parishes, and town councils consulted him on candidates for professorial chairs. Is it surprising that the popular preacher, the respected critic, the deferred-to guide, had his constitutional vanity strengthened, and that all this homage made him more pompous and certain of his infallibility, especially as he was utterly devoid of any sense of humour?

It was pleasant to see the good Doctor in his unbending moods mingling with heartiness but dignified propriety with his friends, Carlyle and Home and Ferguson, in their genial suppers.

He could make himself agreeable to Mrs. Sarah Ward, the handsome actress, over whose beauty all the Edinburgh bucks were raving, and be the intimate friend of David Hume, over whose infidelity all the religious world was moaning. We find him at the many gatherings of people of society and letters, with suave manners and imperturbable courtesy, yet without one touch of wit or one grain of humour. Quite impervious to the keen jests that passed, and the jokes that flew about, making the table roar, he would sit blandly, vaguely smiling at their mysterious hilarity.[1] But all respectfully listened as he passed his opinions with shrewdness and weight on less frivolous matters. Many of the moderate ministers had come out of rigid or evangelical homes, to which the austerity of gloomier days still clung. They had learned no pastime, indulged in no worldly entertainment. To play at golf or bowls was a doubtful practice; to play at cards or to dance was a forbidden act. Even the most liberal clergy could not easily throw off traditional shackles, and would only play hazard with doors carefully locked—whereat the laity did not fail to taunt them. Carlyle of Inveresk had cast off these restraints and excelled in dancing, a performance which his worthy father shrank from; and he pressed his friends, Blair and Robertson, the most sedate of that set of men, to learn whist to while dull weather and long nights away. They at last yielded, and began laboriously to learn whist with twinges of conscience and with very poor results,[2] Robertson succeeding in playing decently, and Blair miserably. Still it was a significant symptom of transition from the past, that these middle-aged divines should play, even with incessant revokes, the cards which their fathers had denounced as Devil's devices.[3]

[1] Carlyle's *Autobiography*, p. 114; Mackenzie's *Life of Home*.
[2] Carlyle's *Autobiography*, p. 298.
[3] In "A Comparison between Robertson and Blair," Carlyle remarks: "Robertson was bred in the strictness of an ecclesiastical family at that period, the members of which were not only denied the amusements of the theatre, but likewise of the dancing-school, and prohibited to play at cards or almost any domestic pastime, which favoured his recluse and studious bent when at college. But this induced a personal awkwardness that could never be shaken off. Blair was bred with less austerity, but not being of an opulent house more than the other, he was equally unacquainted with those country sports and amusements which not only strengthen the body but give grace and ease to its motions" (from the Carlyle MSS.).

One of Dr. Blair's hearers in the High Kirk was Lord Kames[1]; and he was so struck by the literary merit of his friend's sermons that he urged him to publish them, feeling sure that they would bring him fame. The judge was not the man one would fix upon as most likely to admire pulpit oratory in any form, but with all his coarseness he was a man of letters, and his opinion was worth much. The result was that the manuscripts were despatched by mail-coach to Mr. William Strahan, the eminent printer, a shrewd critic and a Scotsman, who would naturally be disposed to think well of his countryman's productions. Yet he gave no encouragement, and Blair's hopes seemed shattered. Fortunately, however, the cautious printer, who evidently thought well of the sermons, though sermons were a "drug in the market," showed the manuscripts to his friend Dr. Johnson, and on Christmas Eve a note reached him by the hands of Francis Barber, the black servant, saying: "I have read Dr. Blair's first sermon with more than approbation, to say it is good is to say too little." Such authority dispelled all doubts. The preacher was offered, to his modest surprise, 100 guineas for a volume of the sermons, and Cadell published it in 1777.[2] All the world knows of its success—how the sermons made the Presbyterian minister famous; how Episcopal dignitaries admired them and Episcopal clergy preached them; how ladies in their boudoirs settled down to them; how men not addicted to church-going perused with satisfaction these elegant discourses on "censoriousness," "gentleness," and "dissipation." Lord Mansfield, the "silver-tongued Murray," read them with his fine elocution to King George and his consort in the Royal closet, and His Majesty expressed his wish that every youth in the kingdom might possess a copy of the Bible and of Blair. They were the favourite discourses to read aloud in family circles on Sunday night in mansions and castles; they were translated into most languages in Europe; and, finally, they procured a pension of £300 a year for the author. Success attended each volume as it came

---

[1] Tytler's *Life of Lord Kames*, i. 198.
[2] On the success of the first volume Strahan gave another £100, paid £300 for the second volume, and for the third and fourth volumes £600 each. In those days there was a partnership between printers and booksellers who acted as publishers.

from the press. There was a pomp and sententiousness in them kindred to Johnson's own *Rambler* and the great literary autocrat never lost his admiration for the sermons whose merits he was first in England to recognise. "I love Blair's sermons, though the dog is a Scotsman and a Presbyterian and everything he should not be. I was the first to praise them," he would say. When Dr. Blair made occasional visits to London, he was received with honour in literary circles, and would sit blandly listening to Dr. Johnson's boisterous assertions, careful not to provoke an assault. He saw the best of society, too, in the houses of Scots peers and members of Parliament, and in the company of Anglican dignitaries, who greeted respectfully the well-dressed, dapper, carefully-wigged Presbyterian divine. He condescended even to go to the theatre with that fascinating feather-head, James Boswell; but it must have been an agony to his dignified soul to hear that irrepressible young man beguiling the time between the acts by imitating the lowing of a cow, and, as Bozzy boasted, "entertaining the audience prodigiously," amid unbounded applause of the groundlings in the pit and the footmen in the gallery. Cries of "Encore the cow," "Encore the cow," stimulated the youth next to imitate the cackling of hens, the crowing of cocks, the braying of asses—efforts which met with imperfect success. Whereupon "my reverend friend, anxious for my fame," relates the unabashed Boswell, "with an air of the utmost gravity and earnestness addressed me thus: 'My dear sir, I would confine myself to the cow.'"[1]

The world went well with Dr. Hugh Blair, and his position as a critic was improved by the publication in 1783 of his *Lectures on Rhetoric and Belles Lettres*, which made him the literary pope of Scotland. We can well imagine how he received Robert Burns on his visit in 1787—the dignity, the courteous condescension of his manner toward the remarkable ploughman; how at his table he would give the soundest advice to the "estimable young man," how paternally he would show him how to devote his "really excellent talents," and

---

[1] *Life of Johnson* (ed. Hill), v. 296. The words "Stick to the coo," which are ascribed to the divine by Scott, are not at all in Dr. Blair's manner.

recommend improvement in his style. Burns had approached the great man with modesty and trepidation—for his reputation had made him a being to bow before—but in his presence the poet took the measure—and it was not a large one—of the critic. Sitting in his dingy garret in Baxter's Wynd at night, he wrote down his impressions of the professor. "Truly," recorded the poet, "a worthy and most respectable character. Natural parts like his are frequently to be met with; his vanity is proverbially known among his acquaintances; but he is justly at the head of what might be called fine writing, and might be called in the first rank in prose, even in poetry a bard of Nature's making can only take the *pas* of him." This is all very well, but he goes on to show that he himself had vanity as well as his patron. "My heart overflows with liking when the good man descends from his pinnacle and meets me on equal ground in conversation. When he neglects me for the mere carcase of greatness, and when his eye measures the difference of elevation, I say to myself, with scarcely any emotion, 'What care I for him or his pomp either?'" One sees it all—the farmer ignored when his host converses with my lord; the poet wincing while the Doctor ceases to address him, and turns away to talk with frisky grace or deference to a more important guest across the table.[1]

Vain the worthy man undoubtedly was. Friends would tell how an omitted deference would make him wince, and an imagined slight would cost him sleep. It was at his table Robert Burns blunderingly mentioned that one of the places at which he had found most gratification was the High Church, and in listening to the preaching of—Dr. Greenfield. An awkward stillness fell over the company at the gauche remark of the rustic poet, for well they knew their host's weak point, though the Doctor tried to pass it off by courteously agreeing with his malaprop guest. Long afterwards Burns thought of that awkward moment, and the pained look that came over the face of his reverend friend, who was proud above all things of being the preacher of the age. One day at dinner at Dr. Blair's an English clergyman was asked

---

[1] Chambers's *Life and Works of Burns*, 1851, ii. 61, 68.

by one of the company what was thought of their host's sermons by his professional brethren in the south. "Why," he replied, "they are not partial to them at all." A cloud passed over the divine's face, and dismay over the disconcerted inquirer, who faltered out, "Why?" "Why," answered the clergyman, "because they are so much read, so generally known, that none dare borrow from them." Thereupon the company breathed once more, and Blair's countenance beamed with pleasure. He dearly enjoyed all praise of his sermons, was so delighted to hear that Lady This or Lady That had read them three times over. "He bore the trowel with fortitude and resignation," said Sir Gilbert Elliot, who often witnessed the operation.

Friends laughed over his foibles: his relish for flattery, his angling for compliments, his purring over homage, his puerile curiosity over small things, his equal excitement over a new wig and an epic.[1] Gossip would tell of his anxiety about the perfection of his garments: how the old gentleman would make the tailor place a mirror on the floor, and, standing on tiptoe, would peer over his shoulder to see how his skirts were hanging. But while they laughed at him, with his "infantine disposition," his friends liked him not the less, as a generous, unobtrusive, amiable man without a touch of malignity; an author without jealousy, a critic without an enemy. Where else could such be found? Characteristically he asked the painter to make his portrait have a "pleasing smile."

Dr. Carlyle speaks of him when seventy-eight as "frisking more about the world than ever he did in his younger days, no symptoms of frailty about him, preaching every Sunday with increasing applause, and though he is huffed at not being offered the Principality (on Robertson's retirement), he is happy at being resorted to as head of the University." In fact, he was "irritated far beyond the usual pitch of his temper" at being passed over. Owing to his diffidence, which hindered him in public speaking, he declined to be Moderator of the General Assembly.

[1] Kay's *Edinburgh Portraits*, i. 83; Carlyle's *Autobiography*, 295; *Life of Sir Gilbert Elliot*, i. 84.

With precise and formal air the divine would sally forth, as St. Giles' bells began to chime, each Sunday morning on his way to church from Argyll Square;[1] his neat cocked hat poised with fine exactitude, his frizzled, powdered wig curled to a nicety, his pulpit gown flowing gracefully behind, his bands fluttering neatly in front—the whole presence ceremonious, blandly self-conscious, as he wafted in his well-known burr "good mornings" right and left to acquaintances in the street. At the age of eighty he preached vigorously a sermon on "A Life of Pleasure and Dissipation," which appeared in a posthumous volume of discourses. Thus the old man lived on, diverting himself with reading *Don Quixote* and the blood-curdling romances of Mrs. Radcliffe. One by one his old friends dropped off, and he would say with a sigh that "he was left the last of all his contemporaries." Yet when he died in December 1800 there still survived John Home, with a mind that had lost its vigour, but with the old kindly smile and unruffled good-nature; Adam Ferguson, with the warm heart and choleric temper of olden days; and Dr. Carlyle, busy corresponding with great dames and politicians, composing verses (though "no more a poet than his precentor," said Scott), and writing his delightful memoirs of his times.[2]

Professor William Wilkie

The world has long forgotten William Wilkie, "The Scottish Homer," who in his day was regarded as almost

---

[1] Chambers's *Traditions of Edinburgh*, ii. 96; Kay's *Edinburgh Portraits*, i. 122.

[2] Among Dr. Carlyle of Inveresk's papers there is an interesting "Comparison of Principal Robertson and Dr. Blair." "It is observable that neither of them had wit, and Robertson only a relish for humour, of which he had a small portion, while his rival Blair had none, nor even a taste for it. In colloquial intercourse there is no doubt Robertson far surpassed Blair, with this difference, however, that the conversation of the last was in general most acceptable to his friends and that of the first to strangers. Blair had no desire to shine in company, and his conversation was simple and plain even to puerility. But when the subject called his knowledge and judgment into exertion nothing could excel his clearness and decision. Robertson's constant desire to shine seemed his ruling passion, insomuch that even when he had strangers of eminence to show off to his friends convened for the purpose, he could hardly bear them with patience. Blair, on the contrary, when he had distinguished persons to exhibit to his guests, gave himself up entirely to that duty, and was never

the greatest of that brilliant band of Scotsmen—a startling contrast in appearance and character to the punctilious and precise Dr. Blair. It is strange to notice about the middle of the century the unanimous chorus of admiration of this now unknown man. Hume, Carlyle, Mackenzie, Sir Robert Liston, who became ambassador at Vienna, all speak of his marvellous ability. In the intercourse of young men who afterwards became famous he was all-powerful. Yet a figure so uncouth—in dress deplorably shabby and dirty, with hair unkempt, manners preposterous, and gestures grotesque—never before was seen in society. Born in 1721, Wilkie was the son of a poor farmer in the neighbourhood of Edinburgh, the descendant of an ancient Midlothian family.[1] The death of his father, almost in destitution, obliged him to support his mother and sister when he was but a boy. By break of day his dirty, ragged little person was seen following the plough with its team of oxen, or sowing the seed on the furrows from the canvas-bag; and then, after a hasty dish of porridge, he would trudge for miles along the road from Farmers' Tryste to the eight o'clock class at college. At nights, by the glimmering light of a hardly-bought candle, the lad would pore over his classics, philosophy, and mathematics. At the University none was more loved for goodness of heart, none more admired for ability, none more laughed at for eccentricity.

When licensed to preach, to this strange clownish creature preferment did not readily come, and for ten years he had to continue his rustic life—wretchedly poor, ill-fed, and ill-clad. Sometimes he preached for neighbouring ministers and got a trifling fee; but it was by his little farm he lived, and on it he worked, changing energetically the nettle-covered rigs and marshy ground to fertile soil with fruitful harvests. One day Dr. Roebuck, the founder of the Carron iron-works, then

happier than when in so doing he gratified his friends. Blair's vanity was satisfied with the admiration of the ladies and other persons of taste of his appearances in the pulpit. But Robertson's appetite for praise was truly unsatiable, for in the pulpit or the General Assembly, at table or in the drawing-room, he swallowed large draughts of it from high or low, learned or unlearned, from wise or foolish."

[1] Carlyle's *Autobiography*, p. 394; Burton's *Life of Hume*, ii. 40; Southey's *Life of Dr. Bell*, i. 29. "Of Wilkie all the party spoke as superior in original genius to any man of his time" (Mackenzie's *Life of Home*, p. 15).

travelling in Scotland, passed along the road, near the field where the scholar was sowing corn with a sheet before him, all covered with dirt, clad in ragged coat and breeches, and a dilapidated bonnet. To trick the Englishman, the friend with whom he was riding, who knew Wilkie, cried out, "Here is a peasant; let us call him." They conversed; the talk passed on from manure and turnips to Greek literature. To an observation about husbandry the seeming peasant, in broadest Scots, remarked: "Yes, sir, but in Sicily there is a different method," and he quoted Theocritus to confirm his statement. As he rode off with his friend, Roebuck asked with amazement, "Is it usual for your peasants to read the Greek poets?" "Oh yes," his companion replied; "we have long winter evenings, and how can they better employ themselves than in reading Greek poets?" The doctor went on his way, astonished that the poorest herds in Scotland devoted their nights to Euripides and Homer.

In those days the dove-cots of the lairds were nurseries for thousands of marauders that fed on the sparse crops of the farmers; and poor Wilkie wasted his time in chasing off the crowds of pigeons that devastated his fields. As he set off to his rigs in the morning he had an old gun over his shoulder to frighten the "doos," and paper bulging his pocket whereon to indite his verses, for he was busy composing no less than an epic. As he sat down to pen lines on Agamemnon, the fowls of the air would settle at his expense to their morning meal, which he himself had not had, and incessantly he would be forced to rise from his mood of Homeric inspiration and fire his futile musket—shots and rhymes alternating in disconcerting succession.[1] Poetical though he was, with minute economy he would pick up dead cats and dogs, which were to be found near Edinburgh, and carefully inter them in his ground to enrich his soil.[2]

At length Lord Lauderdale, admiring his abilities and overlooking his oddities, appointed him assistant and successor to the minister of Ratho, where he felt himself in opulence on £30 a year, especially as he remained still on his farm four miles off. Even when he became sole minister of the parish

[1] Burton's *Hume*, ii. 25.　　[2] Southey's *Life of Dr. A. Bell*, i. 11.

he farmed land with a success which astonished his neighbours, who found that the new enclosing, and draining, and manuring adopted by the minister gave good crops while their antiquated methods kept them in poverty. "Potato Wilkie," as he was called from his culture of the then little known vegetable, interested his people perhaps more by his peculiarities than by his pulpit powers, for sometimes he would preach obliviously with his hat on, or omit to pronounce the blessing at the close of the service, and in dispensing the communion perhaps forget himself to communicate. Often he would set off for Edinburgh to meet his friends, Carlyle, Home, or Blair, at a tavern supper, or to debate at the Select Club. Overwhelming in argument, copious in learning, he feared not the best of them. "Shall I, who have kept company with Agamemnon, the king of men—shall I shrink from contest with a puny race?"[1] he would say when praised for his courage in combating Dr. Robertson and Lord Elibank. When at table the company were talking, he kept silence; when all were silent something would tickle his humour, and he would burst into a wild torrent of wit and argument, "in which," said Dr. Wallace, "none could cope with him." Ungainly, erratic, and brilliant, when Charles Townshend met him at Inveresk Manse, he pronounced him a man who approached nearer the extremes of a god and a brute than any one he had ever met. From combats of wit Wilkie would return to classics, and his turnips, to mathematics and his fiddle, which he would play far into the night.[2] His poems he read to an old woman, whose criticism he meekly accepted.

In 1757 there appeared the *Epigoniad, an Epic Poem in Nine Books.* "This poem," says the author, "is called the Epigoniad, because the heroes it celebrates have got the name of the Epigoni (or Descendants), being the sons of those who attempted the conquest of Thebes in a former expedition." Here, with simple-hearted audacity, he tries to imitate and to continue Homer in an account of the second siege of Thebes.

---

[1] Clayden's *Early Life of Sam. Rogers,* p. 166.
[2] "I fancy there has seldom been so much wit, poetry, and philosophy blended together in the conversation of any individual."—*Travels* by Rev. James Hall [William Thomson], 1801, i. 129.

Great expectations had been entertained of his work by his admiring friends, who believed that in him a new Homer would arise, one who would shed fresh lustre on Scotland. David Hume, of course, was the first to applaud.[1] "I suppose," he wrote to his friends, "you have read and admired the wonderful production of the *Epigoniad*, and that you have so much love for art and for your native country as to be very industrious in propagating the fame of it." "It is a most singular production, full of sublimity and genius."[2] And from the Lord Advocate Dundas and a hundred important lips similar praise came forth. London critics were severely just; though it was all "sheer jealousy" Edinburgh admirers protested. The *Critical Review*[3] was contemptuous, but Smollett, its editor, patriotically regretted that such a notice of his countryman's work had appeared by an oversight. The other leading magazine, the *Monthly Review*,[4] was equally caustic in a article written by Oliver Goldsmith, who at that time was the drudge and slave of Ralph Griffiths, who kept his poor hack at work from morning till night in his back shop in return for bed and board, while Mrs. Griffiths, the learned harridan, tampered with the proofs and interpolated the manuscripts. By his laborious review Oliver had well earned his dinner that day. The anachronisms in this second Siege of Thebes, the wearily reiterated phrases, the bad rhymes, the dulness of the story were all brought against the author, whose nationality seemed flagrantly declared by his using the word "hing" for "hang." Any page affords a fair sample of the forgotten epic:

> Now tow'ring in the midst Atrides stood
> And called his warriors to the fight aloud.
> As mariners with joy the sun descry
> Ascending in his course the eastern sky,
> Who all night long by angry tempests tossed,
> Shunned with incessant toil the faithless coast;
> So to his wishing friends Atrides came,
> Their danger such before, their joy the same.
> Again the rigour of the shock returns,
> The slaughter rages and the combat burns.

---

[1] Burton's *Hume*, ii. 29. [2] Burton's *Hume*, ii. 40.
[3] *Critical Review*, June 1757.
[4] *Monthly Review*, July 1757; Gray's *Ode* was reviewed in same number.

And so on—with a succession of Homeric speeches, fights, prophecies, and similes, which form a respectable, though dull, parody of the great original. Ignored in England, Scotland had a monopoly of enthusiasm for the Caledonian epic. His country and his friends exhausted Wilkie's first edition; eternity could not exhaust the second.

Promotion came to reward this most learned prodigy. In 1759 he was appointed Professor of Natural Philosophy in St. Andrews. The salary and fees, amounting to about £80, seemed to this poor man, who had starved during so much of his life, as opulence beyond the dreams of avarice; for "what," said he simply, "could a man want in life which was not to be bought with such a fortune?" In his class-room he was in his element. His ability was immense, his scientific attainments were great, his style of lecturing was attractive, in spite of strange fits of absence of mind, and the affection between him and his students was singularly deep. In his class he had as pupils Playfair and Leslie, who were in after years to add scientific reputation to their country. When the class hours were over, he would be seen slouching along the streets in shapeless clothing, bearing a hoe over his shoulder to weed his turnips and potatoes in fields which he had hired near the town.[1] Sometimes a thin, poverty-stricken lad attended him to his farm, with face of docile, admiring affection. This was his pupil, Robert Fergusson—the luckless poet of later years, who copied out his master's lectures for the class and his *Fables* for the press.[2]

Wilkie, undaunted by the failure of his first literary venture, published *Moral Fables in Verse* in 1769, with engravings by Samuel Wale. His fame was not enhanced. There is some ingenuity in the fables; but the airy gaiety and deftness of La Fontaine and Gay were far beyond this son of the soil.

What stories his pupils were wont to tell of their professor, to whom they were devoted—of his amazing disregard of decorum and the dignity of society! One sees him, when visiting dormitories of St. Leonard's College in his capacity of "hebdomader'

---

[1] Hall's *Travels*, i. 127-40.
[2] Grossart's *Robert Fergusson*, 1899, p. 56.

(as the professor who inspected students' rooms for the week was termed), entering the chamber where young Lord Buchan and his volatile brother Henry Erskine lodged. There he tried to amuse Harry, who was ill, by giving a lesson in astronomy, and the earth's revolution on its axis he described by thrusting his leg between the bars of the chair and making gyrations which resulted in his illustrating the law of gravity instead, as his big form was projected under the bed, to the unspeakable delight of his appreciative audience.[1]

His early life of poverty and exposure to wind and wet and marshy soil had brought on ague fits, from which he was rarely free, and to relieve his trouble he would wear a mass of old garments, piled on till his original form was untraceable, and in his bed he was undiscoverable beneath twenty-four pairs of Scotch blankets. It is difficult to credit that this strange, slovenly, absent-minded mortal, simple as Parson Adams, who passed along in wig awry, old cocked hat, dirty flannel dress, surmounted by an aged greatcoat—one pocket protruding with turnip seed, and the other with a copy of Homer or Sophocles,—on his shoulder a rusty gun to frighten crows from his grain, could really be the man whom Hume, Carlyle, Wallace, Robertson, and Henry Mackenzie, and indeed all the illustrious company, proclaimed a great genius. It is true he was the first poet who ever knew the fluxionary calculus. He lived meagrely not because he was mean, but because he dreaded a return to the old penury whose bitter memories never ceased to haunt him. "I have shaken hands with poverty up to the elbow, and I wish to see him no more," he would say.

In 1772 he died, leaving memories behind him of perfect simplicity and goodness of heart, of clumsy genius, of dirty slovenliness, and amusing eccentricity. Up to the end of the century there were Scotsmen who still spoke with undiminished admiration of the *Epigoniad*[2]; lauding "the splendour of its descriptions," "its mastery of the times of which he writes," as possessing "the very soul of Homer," and containing passages "sufficient to entitle the poet to undying fame."

---

[1] Fergusson's *Henry Erskine*, p. 64.
[2] Mackenzie's *Life of Home*, p. 16; *Stat. Acct. Scot.* i. 339.

Speaking from the painful experience of reading it, we refuse to echo one of these wild encomiums. In a loving Eclogue his favourite pupil Robert Fergusson lamented his dead master:

> Whase sangs will ay in Scotland be revered,
> While slow gaun onsen turn the flowery swaird,
> While bonnie lambies lick the dews o' spring,
> While gaidsmen whistle and while birdies sing.[1]

In part this prophecy was fulfilled, for in a few years the "slow-going oxen" ceased to drag the lumbering plough, in a few years gadsmen were required no more by their whistle to entice the weary team, and in a few years Wilkie's works passed into oblivion.

THOMAS BLACKLOCK

It was in 1773 that Dr. Johnson made his ever memorable raid into Scotland, and in August he was visiting all the sights and objurgating all the smells of Edinburgh. He looked into the churches and pronounced them dirty; he visited the buildings of the University, and found them contemptible; he inspected the wynds and panted up the dark turnpike stairs, and called them squalid; he met the literati, and, hectoring them into silence, declared they had nothing to say. He had, however, a good word to speak of Dr. Blacklock, and it was noted by Boswell as an act of remarkable grace, that when the blind poet was introduced to the great lexicographer in James' Court, he was received with "humane complacency," and greeted with the words, "Dear Dr. Blacklock, I am glad to see you," as the oracle raised his huge frame from the easy-chair and grasped him by the hand. A few days later Dr. Johnson, with his friend, went to visit the blind man, for, we are told, he had "beheld him with reverence." He made himself vastly agreeable, and during the conversation absorbed, to good Mrs. Blacklock's consternation, nineteen dishes of tea.[2]

Through the genial society of Edinburgh, with its vigorous

---

[1] Hall's *Travels*, 1801, i. 128; Fergusson's *Poems*, 1807, p. 228.
[2] Boswell's *Johnson* (Hill's edit.), v. 47; Mackenzie's *Life of Blacklock*.

speaking and drinking, its stalwart race of men of letters, law, and fashion, flits the somewhat pathetic figure of the gentle and helpless Dr. Blacklock. He was to be seen led along the crowded High Street, every one making way respectfully for the blind man, and led carefully up the slippery staircases, whose dirt and darkness could not vex his sight, though the odours might afflict his acuter sense of smell. In the best company he was welcomed, and all forgot the plainness of that pock-pitted face in the amiable expression that gave it charm. In the Meadows friends would find him in the forenoon, leaning on the arm of Robert Heron, the discarded assistant to Dr. Blair—a versatile literary hack, a threadbare toper, who, after an evening's debauch on a meagre supply of potatoes and green peas, with large potations of whiskey, had risen from his garret bed to take his venerated friend out for a stroll.[1] Blacklock's reputation was considerable for genius and for fine literary judgment. To-day we must deny him genius, but may allow him taste.

His story is one of misfortune in youth, strangely guided by kindly fortune in later years. He was born in 1721 in Annan, where his father was a bricklayer. When six months old he lost his eyesight owing to smallpox, which in those pre-inoculating days worked devastation in every class. His calamity was softened by the tenderness and teaching of parents who must for their time and station have been singularly refined; and schoolmates read to him as he grew older the works of English poets. Soon he became familiar with the works of Addison and Pope, of Shenstone and Thomson. His mind became full of the rhymes and images of the authors he loved best, and, strange to say, these were descriptive poets like Thomson, who delighted him with their pictures of Nature which he was never to see with the bodily eye. When he was nineteen his father was killed by falling into a malt-kiln, and he was left to the charge of relations who were too poor to support him. Poems he wrote, and these

[1] MS. "Journal of my Conduct," by Robert Heron, in Edinburgh University. After a career of drinking and of writing, during which he produced plays, pamphlets, travels, biographies, and translations, he died in 1807, a debtor in Newgate, where he wrote a volume entitled, with unconscious irony, *The Comforts of Life* (Disraeli's *Calamities of Authors*, p. 83).

THOMAS BLACKLOCK

From the Painting by W. Bonnar, R.S.A., in the Scottish National Portrait Gallery, Edinburgh.

were handed round to patrons and friends, who gave their
admiration and their wonderment at his genius, but extremely
little money to prevent it from starving. In his despair he
even thought of earning a living as an itinerant musician, for
he had fine skill in playing the flute. His austere conscience,
however, withheld him, and he "drew back in horror at the
notion of prostituting his talents to the forwarding of loose
mirth and riot" at rustic gatherings and penny weddings.[1]

By good fortune Dr. Stevenson, an eminent Edinburgh
physician, saw one of his productions while visiting Dumfries,
and through him the blind lad got means to gain a classical
education, first at school and afterwards at college in
Edinburgh. Class-fellows were glad of his company, and he
was helpful in teaching them in exchange for their kindness
in leading him through the crowded streets and tortuous wynds.
It was thought that the ministry, to which his taste led him,
would afford him a career, so in 1741 he became student of
Divinity, and began that long, dreary course of six years'
training in theology which was then exacted from prospective
ministers. In 1745 a tiny volume of his poems was published
in Glasgow, by the aid of his never-failing patron, that good,
staunch whig Dr. Stevenson, who, when the town was
threatened by the Highlanders, sat day by day as guard at the
Nether Bow, with a musket over his shoulder, all swathed in
flannel, because of the gout which was torturing his limbs.[2]
This volume came in obscurity and in obscurity it remained.
But eight years after a mature collection was issued. Being
printed for himself, the only way in which it could be disposed
of was by friends taking copies or persuading their acquaintances
to buy them. He was a student of twenty-three when David
Hume first saw him at a friend's house, and was struck
by his literary taste, his utter simplicity of nature, and the
strangely acute emotion which agitated his whole frame on
hearing fine poetry. None was more active now than David
Hume in helping the blind poet, for that fat philosopher and
most indolent of beings was always energetic when there was
a kind action to be done. "Take a cargo of these poems," he

---

[1] Mackenzie's *Life of Blacklock*; Chambers's *Eminent Scotsmen*.
[2] *Land of Burns*, ii. 61.

wrote to friends, "which, if I have the minutest judgment, are many of them extremely beautiful, and all of them remarkable for correctness and propriety." The poor man's whole fortune consisted of 100 guineas gained by this volume, and his whole income was a bursary of £6 to prosecute his studies at college. However, Hume got friends to guarantee another £12 for the remaining five years at classes, and when he was in high dudgeon at the curators' objecting to his putting La Fontaine and Crébillon on the innocent shelves of the Advocates' Library, he presented the £40 salary of his librarianship to the impecunious poet.[1] In 1756 appeared a new edition of the poems, and an essay on Immortality, with "An Account of the Life, Character, and Writings of Mr. Thomas Blacklock," from the pen of the "ingenious" Mr. Joseph Spence, Professor of Poetry in Oxford.[2] The editor had prudently prevailed on the author to omit an ode to his heretical friend, lest it should damage his name. Mr. Spence's word carried vast weight in England, where he was the friend of all men of letters, and the story of the "Student of Philosophy" was soon known everywhere—though it was rather his blindness that awakened interest than his poems, which contained such effusions as odes "On a Young Gentleman bound for Guinea"; "On the death of a promising infant"; a "Soliloquy on the author's escape from falling into a deep well by the sound of a favourite lap-dog's feet." In Scotland he was regarded as a "fine poet" —which is the less surprising when we remember that at the time there was not another poet living north of Tweed.

Blacklock at last was licensed to preach; interest was stirred in the poet's career, blind and poor and helpless; and in 1762 he was presented to the parish of Kirkcudbright— a gift to bring bitter vexation. The dour south-country people, with keen covenanting instincts and bitter hatred of patronage which ignored their Christian rights, abhorred the idea of a blind man becoming their minister, even though they might have gained some satisfaction in the certainty that he could never read his sermons. Two years of weary disputation ensued; and the luckless presentee—the most sensitive of

[1] Burton's *Life of Hume*, i. 390.
[2] Spence's *Anecdotes* (Singer's edit.), p. 24.

mortals—was half mad with anguish. He had married in prospect of a comfortable manse, and now there lay the painful alternatives before him—misery if he remained, and poverty if he left. No wonder his letters were wild against the "vindictive people"; but in prudence and despair he resigned the charge, receiving a small part of the stipend, which, if it did not give him luxury, at least brought him peace.[1]

His future life was to be spent in Edinburgh, in a small house in the outskirts of the town, and he gained a livelihood by keeping boarders and taking pupils. He might have been professor of Greek in Aberdeen had it not been evident that, with his blindness and simple nature, he could never have kept unruly lads in order. But now, with a devoted wife to tend and lead him about, with occupation in teaching and writing, and with troops of friends in the liveliest circles in the town, he had a pleasant life. He published sermons which he never preached, and wrote some treatises which it is to be feared the public never read; though to his literary judgment all deferred with devoted homage.

In producing verses he had a most painful facility. "I have known him," says Henry Mackenzie, who was one of his pupils, "dictate thirty or forty verses, and by no means bad ones, as fast as I could write them; but the moment he would be at a loss for a rhyme or a verse to his liking, he stopped altogether."[2] This interruption was merciful. It was a curious, pathetic thing to see the poet in those moods of fluency which he mistook for inspiration—the face all rapt with enthusiasm, the sightless eyes vaguely rolling, the whole body swaying to and fro as he stood upright, dictating to his devoted boarder, whose pen galloped and panted over the paper to keep pace with the utterance. "A strange creature to look at"—John Home[3] described him—"a small, weakly thing, a chill, bloodless animal that shivers at every breeze. But if Nature has cheated him in one respect by assigning to his share forceless sinews and a rugged form,

---

[1] Burton's *Hume*, ii. 164; Mackenzie's *Life of Blacklock*.
[2] Mackenzie's *Life of Blacklock*.
[3] Mackenzie's *Life of John Home*, p. 131.

she has made ample compensation on the other hand by giving him a mind endowed with the most exquisite feelings and the most ardent, kindled-up affection, a soul—to use a poet's phrase—that is tremblingly alive all over; in short, he is the most flagrant enthusiast I ever saw. When he repeats his verses he is not able to keep his seat, but springs to his feet and shows his rage by the most animated motions." The bard was ever ready to respond to the wish that he should recite, and many would go to his house less, it is to be suspected, from reverence than from idle curiosity to see the little, excited man declaim his lines with Sibylline contortions, his body oscillating from side to side, and hand outstretched in the ardour of his feelings—gestures of whose oddness he was serenely unconscious. Morbidly sensitive, he was subject to fits of dire depression. An affront, a trouble, or some untraceable cause would throw the worthy man into abject melancholy. It was then he found comfort in playing on his flageolet tunes sweet and pathetic, whose melody floated through the house and greeted the ears of visitors as the front door was opened. On taking out the little flute, which he always carried in his pocket, the evil spirits departed from him when the old Scots tunes came forth, as they departed from Saul at the sound of David's harp.

His fame as a poet had spread to England, and the circumstances of his life gave an interest to his poems which they certainly did not deserve from their intrinsic merits. At the instigation of his friend, Professor Spence, he even wrote, though with trepidation of conscience, a tragedy, which he committed to the hands of Andrew Crosbie. The carelessness of that bibulous lawyer in losing it the world will cheerfully pardon. After he ceased to publish poetry, he remained a recognised authority in literary taste. Macpherson's *Ossian* was submitted for his opinion; Beattie laid before him the manuscripts of his once immortal *Essay on the Immutability of Truth*, levelled at the heresies of his good friend Hume, from whom he now kept aloof for some unknown reason.[1] The most important production of his pen was certainly his enthusiastic letter to Dr. George Laurie of

[1] Forbes's *Life of Beattie*.

London, who had sent him a copy of Burns's poems for his judgment. This was at a crisis of the greater, though almost unknown, poet's life in 1786. He had resolved to sail for the West Indies, and his chest was on its way to Greenock harbour, " when," as he tells, " a letter from Dr. Blacklock to a friend of mine [Dr. Laurie] overset all my schemes by opening new prospects to my poetic ambition. His opinion that I should meet with encouragement in Edinburgh for a second edition fired me so much that I posted for that city."[1] Burns considered the opinion of so eminent a critic as the blind minister as of vast importance. To everybody Blacklock endeared himself; for he was a very good man, though a very poor poet. Young men he drew from obscurity, educated, and started in life, who never forgot the unhumorous, guileless man, who knew nothing of the world except its goodness. With a temper which nothing could ruffle, he worked with his boarders over Greek and Latin, and entered into all their entertainments with childlike pleasure, while the keenest pleasure of his boarders was to do kindly services for him.[2] In his placid home there would meet at breakfast or in the evening all who had any pretence to wit and culture. There were heard the chatter of Mrs. Cockburn, the lively tongue of the Duchess of Gordon, with the voices of Adam Ferguson, Lord Monboddo, and Dr. Robertson, as they sat at tea; while the boarders handed scones and cookies to the company, and listened eagerly as great men and bright women discussed and jested, making the little room noisy with their talk and merry with their laughter.

When in 1791 the old verse-writer died, an interesting figure passed away from Scottish society. That a good poet had gone no one could say, but certainly a good man who had surmounted physical disadvantages with rare patience and ability. To use Mr. Spence's words, "There is great perspicuity, neatness, and elegance of style" in his pieces—mild elegiacs, and amiable odes and songs. Their only interest lies in the blind man's art in painting external objects with appropriateness of colour and form. Sometimes the art is

---

[1] Chambers's *Life and Works of Burns*, i. 303.
[2] Mackenzie's *Life of Blacklock*.

apparent enough. It consists simply in putting correct names and epithets together from memory of what he had read and heard:

> Yet long-lived pansies here their scents bestow,
> The violets languish and the roses blow.
> In purple glory let the crocus shine,
> Narcissus here his love-sick head recline.
> Here hyacinths in purple sweetness rise,
> And tulips tinged with beauty's fairest dyes.

Here all is accurate and detailed as in a seedsman's catalogue.

He explained the humble secret of his art. Locke tells of a blind man who said that he knew what scarlet was like: "it was like the sound of a trumpet." When Johnson asked Blacklock if he had formed any associations of that kind, and associated colour and sound together, he answered that he so often met in books and conversation with the terms expressing colours, that he formed certain associations which supported him when he wrote or talked about them. These associations, however, were intellectual: the light of the sun, for example, he supposed to represent the presence of a friend; the cheerful colour of green to be like amiable sympathy.[1] In an interesting article on the Blind in the second edition of the *Encyclopædia Britannica*, he says, "that it is possible for the blind, by a retentive memory, to tell you that the sky is azure, that the sun, moon, and stars are bright, that the rose is red, the lily white or yellow, and the tulip variegated. By continually hearing these substantives and adjectives joined together, he may mechanically join them in the same manner; but as he never had a sensation of colour, however accurately he may speak of coloured objects, his language must be that of a parrot—without meaning, without ideas." This is a modest explanation of his art—or rather artifice—which it is too absurd to foist on the world as poetry. But why did he persist so often in trying to be a descriptive poet? "That foolish fellow Spence," growled Dr. Johnson, "has laboured to explain philosophically how Blacklock may have done by means of his own faculties what it is impossible he should do. The solution, as I have given it, is plain. Suppose I know a

---

[1] Burton's *Life of Hume*, i. 389; Boswell's *Johnson* (Hill's edit.), i. 446.

man to be so lame that he is absolutely incapable to move himself, and I find him in a different room from that in which I left him, shall I puzzle myself with idle conjectures that perhaps his nerves have by some unknown change all at once become effective? No, sir; it is clear how he got into a different room—he was carried."[1] Very properly the sage of Bolt Court felt that he had clenched the matter.

[1] Boswell's *Johnson* (Hill's edit.), i. 466.

CHAPTER VI

ADAM SMITH

IN the early part of the eighteenth century, Kirkcaldy, once a prosperous fishing town, had become a mean village. Only a few small vessels with Norway deals and Swedish iron came to its pier, and only a few boats set forth to the deep-sea fishing; for they were burdened by the Salt Tax, imposed since the Union, and Dutch herring busses caught their shoals in sight of their shore and bore their cargoes triumphantly to Holland. The shipping consisted of one coaster of fifty tons and two ferry-boats. There was a little traffic with coal, a little occupation in weaving "Dutch ticks" and "striped Holland" in that cluster of thatched houses with their 1500 inhabitants [1]—among whom the most prosperous was some merchant who, in his little room, sold everything from tobacco plug to anchors. However, there was work for the Customs officers, who had to deal with smugglers who ran their brandy, wine, and lace on the coast. One of the few slated houses was the residence of Mr. Adam Smith, writer to the signet, Comptroller of Customs from Aberdour to Largo, at a salary of £30, supplemented by perquisites. He died a few months before his son, the author of the *Wealth of Nations*, was born in June 1723. The mother nearly lost her child for ever, for whilst she was staying with her father, the Laird of Strathendry, he was kidnapped by tinkers. At the grammar school of the decayed borough the boy had as classmates the sons of Mr. William Adam, King's mason, who lived in the town, whose

---

[1] *Stat. Acct. of Scotland*, 1793 · "Kirkcaldy."

ADAM SMITH
From the Portrait by Kay.

architectural skill was to be far surpassed by his four sons, grinding at their Ruddiman's *Rudiments* and Eutropius in the thatched school.

After four years' training there, Adam Smith was sent to Glasgow College, to which many lads were attracted by teachers who were stirring the old dry bones of scholastic philosophy into intellectual life. Robert Simson was in his chair of mathematics, sustaining a brilliant reputation. Francis Hutcheson was lecturing on moral philosophy to devoted students. Adam Smith imbibed much of his taste for philosophy from that teacher, and he was only a lad of seventeen when Hutcheson recommended David Hume to send him a copy of his *Treatise on Human Nature*.[1]

His gaining the Snell Exhibition—a prize of £40 a year—carried him in 1740 to fresh fields of study. Mr. John Snell in the previous century had left money for the purpose of training students for the Church of Scotland when it was Episcopal; but since the disestablishment of prelacy the funds were devoted to teaching Scots youths of any denomination at Balliol College. It was not a pleasant ordeal for the home-bred lads from north of the border to enter into that foreign society. Their poverty, their unpolished manners, their tongue, and their kirk were objects of ridicule to English undergraduates, who had no hesitation in lacerating their Caledonian feelings with all the brutal frankness characteristic of youth. Eight Scots lads found themselves living in painful isolation amongst eighty English students; and bitterly they complained of the ignominious treatment they suffered, and sometimes plaintively they begged to be transferred to some less arrogant college. Of the Snell scholars' bursary of £40, wages and board absorbed £30, fees took another £5, and little was left for decent clothing and for comforts.[2] After all, what was the benefit of being educated in those days at English Universities? Learning was stagnant in them, their dulness was a byword, ignorance and idleness were characteristics of those "rotten boroughs of the arts." Scraps of antiquated philosophy, tags of forgotten scholarship were given by professors and tutors who taught as little as students

[1] Burton's *Hume*, i. 116.   [2] Rae's *Life of Adam Smith*, p. 19.

cared to learn.[1] They knew Bishop Berkeley more by his praises of the medicinal virtues of tar water in his memorable treatise than by the subtle philosophy he distilled from it. During a great part of the century, though great men were trained there, they regarded the time spent as the most wasted of their lives. Thither Adam Smith rode in June 1740. In the lack of good teachers he taught himself. He browsed in the deserted libraries, devoted himself to Greek and Latin, read with avidity French and Italian literature. Six years he remained at Oxford, and returned to Kirkcaldy well read in classics, well informed in English letters, and able to speak with fairly English tones.

In those days, for a man of literary habits, there were few means of employment in Scotland. There was the Church, but for that Smith had no "call"; there was the Law, but for that he had no gifts. We find him staying with his mother in the house in the Main Street, with its garden, that ran down towards the shore, studying hard in his room, and sauntering meditatively along the beach; and often taking the ferry to Edinburgh, to see David Hume, the most congenial and suggestive of his companions, and Carlyle, Ferguson, and Robertson, at their houses and in taverns. Occupation came at last. Men of leisure and culture were then awakening to a sense of their provincialism; they were desirous of knowing more of literature, ambitious to read English and to speak it; and there were many men of high accomplishments and scholarship among the Scottish gentry. A happy plan was carried out that Smith should give lectures on literature in a class-room at the College, and on these benches sat about a hundred of the best-fashioned and best-brained men in the city—young lawyers and divines, clever merchants, and lairds and noblemen who were spending the winter in town. In this way he earned £100 and a widening reputation with it. One does not usually think of the great economist in the light of a lover of "polite letters," yet none was more alert than he in literary interests, and in later years friends were surprised at his wide acquaintance with poetry, which he could copiously quote.

[1] Gibbon's *Memoirs* (edit. Hill), p. 60; *Wealth of Nations*, iii. 168; *Life of Sir G. Elliot*, i. 39; Lady Minto's *Memoir of Hugh Elliot*, p. 12.

But a poet he himself could never be. As Samuel Rogers said that though he never went to church, he had religious aspirations; so, though this lecturer on Belles Lettres had poetical aspirations, he never worshipped the muses. Blank verse he despised, even in a drama—an opinion for which Dr. Johnson, who vastly disliked him, alleged he could have hugged him—yet he confessed he "never could find a rhyme in his life," while "he could make blank verse as fast as he could speak."[1] The literary critics of that age—are they different now?—were provokingly fallible, and were wont to indulge in criticisms which the calm vision of posterity regards with amazement. So Racine's *Phèdre* was, according to this critic, the greatest tragedy ever written, while Shakespeare had written only "some good scenes, but never a good play." When Wordsworth said "he was the worst critic—David Hume not excepted—that Scotland, a soil to which this sort of weed seems natural, has produced,"[2] he did not yet know all the feats of which Scotland was capable under the reigns of Francis Jeffrey and Christopher North.

In time there came to Adam Smith an occupation which suited him. In 1751 he got the chair of Logic in Glasgow University, which in a year he quitted for the more congenial professorship of Moral Philosophy, in that class-room where he had as a boy sat listening to Francis Hutcheson. Fain would David Hume have succeeded him in the chair of Logic; fain, too, would he have had his friend as a comrade. But, alas! an infidel as an instructor of youth was an unheard-of thing, an atrocity impossible in the pious city of Glasgow, which had of late prospered exceedingly—of course "under providence" —through rum, tobacco, and sugar, and had as its esteemed motto, "Let Glasgow flourish by the preaching of the Word."

To a house in the grim, sombre Professors' Court, Smith brought his mother and his spinster cousin, and there he entered the quaint-fashioned society where professors and their families lived in harmony and severe frugality. Their incomes were meagre—about £70 as salary, and probably another £70 for fees. They could not compete with the rich merchants of the Saltmarket, or the Tobacco Lords who paced

[1] *The Bee*, 1791, pp. 3, 5.   [2] Wordsworth's *Works*, 1858, vol. vi. 356.

the plainstones of the Trongate in pomp and scarlet cloaks. Several of them had got their posts by bribing with slump sums their predecessors to retire, thereby getting into debt, which hung round their neck for years; or they had got the old teachers to retire on their salaries, while they taught and lived only on the fees.[1] Every shilling was therefore of consequence to them. No wonder Professor Black sat at his desk when the students were paying their fees with a brass pair of scales beside him, on which he, with exact nicety, weighed the coins, to sift the light guineas from the good.[2] To increase their income the masters kept boarders, or rather the boarders kept them. They had as inmates sons of lairds or noblemen, whom they treated with respect, to whom they gave of their best, and before whom they displayed their best company manners.

Since the days that Adam Smith had been a student in the College many things had changed. The old austerity had begun to relax. On Sundays the youths no longer assembled to prayer in the early morning, and marched meekly to kirk twice a day; yet they were still expected to go with their professors to Blackfriars Kirk, to sit in the loft, and there to sing melodiously the songs of Zion. It would sometimes happen that at these diets of worship over Mr. Smith's face there would steal a soft smile,[3] and his lips would move strangely during prayers, thereby confirming the devout in their worst suspicions regarding the religious laxity of the friend of David Hume. Yet it was no act of irreverence; it was only the man's thoughts, lulled by a twenty minutes' prayer or a fifty minutes' soporific discourse, wandering away to realms where Calvin was unknown and where evangelical preachers were inaudible. No longer did he assemble his

---

[1] Professor Simson agrees to demit his chair to Mr. James Williamson on condition of retaining the whole of the salary and a sum of money agreeable to arbitration (*Caldwell Papers*, i. 174).

[2] Brougham's *Men of Letters and Science*, p. 352. In 1766 Dr. Reid writes: "The salary of Dr. Black's place is £50 as Professor of the Theory and Practice of Medicine. . . . Dr. Black, and Dr. Cullen before him, had £20 yearly from the College for teaching chemistry. . . . The chemical class this session might bring £50 or £60 of fees; so that the whole salary and fees will be between £140 and £160."—*Works* (edit. by Hamilton), p. 43.

[3] Ramsey's *Scotland and Scotsmen*, i. 468.

students on Sabbath evenings and give a suitable discourse, as Professor Hutcheson had done: he even desired to discontinue the opening prayer in his class-room. This godless omission, however, the Faculty would not permit, so he continued to offer prayers, savouring, it was sadly noted, of "natural religion."

In his class-room the range of subjects was enormous—ethics, natural theology, and jurisprudence, commerce and political institutions. Nor was this all. The energetic professor discoursed on the history of philosophy and on rhetoric. A curious miscellaneous company of students filled his class-room—raw Lowland and Highland students from farm and croft, from manse and mansion; Irish students with the richest of brogues and the poorest of clothing; boarders in laced coats and powdered hair; youths in their teens and ministers in their sixties. Speaking almost extempore, and sensitive as to the impression he made, Smith never was satisfied till the dullest face was moved to interest. He used to tell how, during a whole session, one student served him as a measure of success.[1] "If he leant forward to listen, all was right and I knew that I had the ear of my class; but if he leant back in an attitude of listlessness, I felt at once all was wrong and that I must either change the subject or the style of my address." It was not often he had to complain of inattention.

So early as 1753 Smith laid down in his class those principles of free trade and economy which he was to enforce and illustrate in his *Wealth of Nations;*[2] and his priority to the French economists, Quesnai and Turgot, he jealously asserted, his usually equable temper being roused when his claims were disputed. In Glasgow his doctrines fell on grateful soil. It was a period in Scotland when attention was being directed to economic questions—to the encouragement of trade, agriculture, and the industrial development of the country. Men of intelligence and rank were inciting practical men to energy. In 1752 David Hume had published his essay on the Balance of Trade; in 1754 the

---

[1] Sinclair's *Old Times and Distant Places*, p. 9.
[2] *Lectures in Glasgow* by Adam Smith (edit. by Cannan).

Select Society, which soon numbered 300 members, began to promote the improvement of land, linen manufacture, shipping, and art. In Glasgow there was a Political Economy Club, presided over by the public-spirited provost, to further the trade of the town with its 20,000 people, whose prosperity and commerce were increasing year by year. Young men even were eagerly discussing the duties on iron, the relative merits of £1 and £5 notes, at meetings in taverns which finished up the evening with inevitable suppers and rum punch. Among such a community, Adam Smith's opinions could not lie barren. But if Glasgow learned much from him, he learned no less from it: a mercantile city was the best study for an economist to live in.

In other directions appeared signs of intellectual and scientific progress in Glasgow. Behind the college lay the pleasant gardens, where professors and their families strolled in the evening, on the gravelled walks and grass under shady trees. Within these the University built a humble structure, to which the type-founder, Alexander Wilson, formerly an apothecary's apprentice in St. Andrews, removed his machinery. Munificently the college expended £60 for its erection, and usuriously charged six and a half per cent for its use. Science also began to excite interest, and Wilson, the type-founder, in 1761, became the first Professor of Astronomy, and made a name by his discovery that the solar spots were depressions in the luminous matter surrounding the sun. In a part of the college quadrangle, James Watt, whom the exclusive corporation of Hammermen prevented plying his trade in the city, was allowed to set up his workshop and sale-room, there mending, making, and selling spectacles, flutes, and guitars (though without the slightest ear), as well as quadrants and mathematical instruments. His shop was the resort of professors, pleased with his talk and interested in his models. Young Robison, the student, would linger there, discussing physics and science with the mechanic, and forming a friendship that was to be as close when James Watt was the great engineer and Professor John Robison was one of the first of Scottish natural philosophers. Dr. Black, whose discoveries on latent heat and fixed air were to be potent in the evolution of steam engineering, often came to discuss problems with his young friend, whistling gently as he explored the strange contents of the room, while Watt was busy making a barrel-organ for him—in which he was helped by a book on "Harmonics."[1] In another part of the quadrangle, Robert and Andrew Foulis had been given rooms by the hospitable college for their bookshop and for their printing-press, from which had come, on Wilson's fine types, their magnificent Homer and the supposed immaculate text of their Horace. In yet another big chamber assigned to them the worthy brothers had their Academy of Design for the furtherance of art, being guilelessly proud of their poor " bustoes " and bad "masterpieces," which students were copying. Never were two mortals more congenial than these Foulises—equally enthusiastic over books, of which they knew much, and about pictures, of which they knew nothing. In winter evenings they held their auction sale of books, when Robert, on the rostrum, would with delicious simplicity carefully point out every flaw in the volumes. "How was this book presented for sale?" one night he asked severely, as he took up *Tom Jones.* "It is most improper for young persons," and he flung it indignantly aside. A poor threadbare student one day was bidding tremulously for an Antoninus, and the good man, asking him if he was really anxious for it, gave it to him for nothing. Practical and paunchy Andrew soon dislodged his brother from the post, for which his honesty and humanity totally unfitted him: "Robin, come down, that place is not for you."[2]

When Smith was in Glasgow there were congenial companions in these College homes. Besides others who are less known to fame were Dr. Cullen, till he left for Edinburgh; Dr. Joseph Black, who succeeded him in the chair of Chemistry; Moor, the fine scholar, professor of Greek, who corrected the press for his brothers-in-law, the Foulises. Then there was Dr. Robert Simson, the renowned professor of Mathematics, who was learned in theology—having studied for the Church— in classics, in philosophy, and in botany, who had got from St.

---

[1] Smiles's *Lives of Boulton and Watt*, 1878, p. 32.
[2] Duncan's *Lit. Hist. of Glasgow*, p. 43.

Andrews the degree of M.D., though he knew nothing of drugs except those he tried to swallow. Few were admitted into his learned and dusty abode in the court, which was under the care of a housekeeper who managed the house and its master. For forty years the great geometer's habits continued unchanged like his costume. His tall, benignant person was clad in white cloth coat, waistcoat, and breeches; he took his daily walk in the grounds, and made his stated visits to the alehouse, at the college gate in the High Street, where he ate his frugal meal, and where on the Friday evenings he entertained his friends with supper and whist. There were the visits every Saturday to the Club, which met at a little tavern in the village of Anderston, then remote from the city, but now part of its most peopled and squalid quarters. Thither a little band of professors made their way every week—Dr. Simson whimsically counting each step he took, and from his lips would come softly the successive numbers "1760-1761-1762," and so on, as he continued his reckoning and his walk. At the board, over which the old professor presided, the members were happy over their national fare—their hen soup, sheep's head, collops, and haggis—and when the cloth was removed, the table was prepared for whist and rum punch. Simson, who loved "the rigour of the game" as dearly as Mrs. Battle, was hard pressed to keep his equable temper when Adam Smith, all absent-minded, shamefully revoked or trumped his partner's best card. When the game ended, good talk followed on books, politics, and philosophy, and there were story and song—the chairman, with voice still mellow, singing Greek odes set to modern music, or chanting a Latin hymn "to the Divine Geometer," with emotion that dimmed his venerable eyes.[1] Dr. Joseph Black, who was brilliantly teaching Chemistry in the College, and practising as beloved physician in the city, at that frugal friendly board gave his clear vivid talk, and his sweet benignity of presence, which was a convivial benediction. Professor James Moor added mirth by his jests and his puns, and brought into the learned company an air of fashion, with his smart dress and carefully powdered wig, which one day caused an officer to remark to another, as he passed

[1] *Envy. Brit.* 1797, *sub voce* (article by Robison).

them in the street, "He smells strongly of powder." "Don't be alarmed, gentlemen," said the dapper professor, turning round; "it is not gunpowder."[1] James Watt often joined the party, for though but a young mechanic, he was as alert at talking on science and letters as any of his seniors. To that fraternity Adam Smith added more solidity than humour. At a seemly hour the learned band would wend their way homewards, in the dusk or the dark, in perfect sobriety, although Dr. Simson may not have been quite so careful and exact in counting his steps on the return journey.

In 1759 Smith published his *Theory of Moral Sentiments*, from the shop of the inevitable Andrew Millar of London. Here was another of the many theories started to find an explanation of the origin of moral feelings and judgments. A pleasant optimism caught from the teaching of his master Hutcheson pervades the treatise. "This is a world where everything is for the best, under a great benevolent Being, who seeks to give the greatest possible amount of happiness here and hereafter." It is through sympathy we form moral judgments of our actions. We put ourselves in another's place, and estimate how the impartial witness would sympathise or not with our conduct. We in this way became spectators of ourselves. "This is the only looking-glass by which we can in some measure, with the eyes of others, scrutinise the propriety of our own conduct."[2] This theory is worked out in its complexity with ingenuity, with great felicity of illustration, and keen analytic skill. It was a success as a piece of literature, though a failure as a piece of philosophy.

David Hume now as ever was the first to tell news of his friend's success, though it upheld a view which was utterly opposed to his own utilitarian theory, according to which, said Smith, we approve a moral action for the same reason that we praise "a chest of drawers." He wrote from London: "The mob of literati are beginning to be loud with praise"[3]; "three bishops called at Millar's shop in order to buy copies

---

[1] Strang's *Clubs of Glasgow*, 2nd edit. p. 313.
[2] *Theory of Moral Sentiments*, i. 230.
[3] Burton's *Life of Hume*, ii. 57.

and ask questions about its author"; "the Duke of Argyll was strongly in its favour"; and much more to the same gratifying effect. Moreover, so charmed was the Hon. Charles Townshend—step-father to the Duke of Buccleugh—that he resolved to put his distinguished relative under the governorship of a man who knew human nature so well, and enforced virtue so finely. Three years later, when the Duke was old enough to travel, it was a matter of surprise that "Weather-cock" Townshend, the most changeable of mortals, was still of the same mind, and offered Adam Smith terms which were handsome to a poor professor—a salary of £400, and a pension for life of £300. He even asked the professor to name his own terms, and these were exceeded by the offer of Townshend. In January 1764 the professor relinquished his post, for he was too conscientious to hold his chair, retain his salary, and desert his duties, as other professors who became tutors were in the habit of doing—getting a cheap substitute to teach for three or four years till their return. We see him at the close of his last lecture bidding farewell to his class, and drawing from his pocket the fees, each neatly wrapped in paper. Beginning to call the students one by one, he handed one of the little parcels to the first youth he summoned. It was at once stoutly refused, the lad protesting that the instruction he had already received from his master were more than he could repay; an answer which evoked a responsive cheer from his fellows. Thereupon the professor seized him by the coat, exclaiming, "You must not refuse me this satisfaction. Nay, by heaven, gentlemen, you shall not!" And forcing the money in his pocket, he shoved him off. The others saw his bidding must be done, and reluctantly gave way. Thus by a pretty scene ended a brilliant university career, which won affection for the man, and reputation for his work.

In those days it was considered essential for a youth of rank and fortune to travel abroad, under charge of a governor, and over the Continent were passing many young noblemen and gentlemen, guided by Scottish professors and physicians. It seemed better to send them to the Continent to study men and manners, to see towns and countries, than to send them to Oxford and Cambridge—drowsy halls haunted by the ghosts of dead languages and defunct philosophies, where was absorbed more port than knowledge. The experiment, it is true, was not always successful in polishing a gentleman and cultivating an embryo statesman.[1] They often came back from the Grand Tour, having only vivid memories of its theatres, its gambling hells, and its frail beauties; with as few intellectual results as Sir Timothy Shelley, the poet's father, who returned with a smattering of erroneous French and two bad pictures of an eruption of Mount Vesuvius. A youth went forth a hobbledehoy of nineteen, and came back a coxcomb of twenty-three, having "spoiled his own language and acquired no more." These sons of leisure sauntered Europe round, travelled from city to city, extracted its pleasures, yawned over its art, and passed over the Alps and the Apennines on osier baskets borne perilously and ignobly on porters' backs, and to their dying day would declaim against "the horrors" of the terrific mountains, having in trepidation for their life observed none of their glories. Tutors had not always a comfortable berth with their noble charges, whom they needed to hold in like a leash of dogs—and often "sad dogs" they were—all the time afraid to offend or thwart their future patrons for a living or an office. They had to sit on the back seat of a calêche, to follow their pupil into a room, to address him deferentially as "My Lord," and to be casually introduced—with an explanation—to his friends. Fortunately Adam Smith had a pupil worth leading, and the young Duke had a governor worth following. Who could have supposed that this least practical of men, this most absent-minded of thinkers, this most guileless wayfarer in the world, would be fit to conduct a youth? Yet the probity, the honourableness, the brilliant intelligence of this tutor counted for much, and Townshend was vain of securing so eminent a man for the post.

Three years passed by. Pupil and governor, with their servants, visited all the chief towns of France—Toulouse, with its leisurely colony of English, who could not speak French; Montpellier, with its crowds of fashion and sicklings and *malades imaginaires*, who sauntered in the shady avenues and resorted to physicians, who prescribed to please

[1] *Wealth of Nations*, bk. v. chap. i.

their patients' fancy and sent in bills to please their own. Smith visited Ferney, the literary Mecca, near Geneva, to see Voltaire; and that patriarch of a pagan dispensation, aged, wrinkled, and weazened, with eyes glittering like carbuncles, showed a wit, malice, and penetration that dazzled the slow-speaking Scot. Then Paris was visited, where every salon, and the Court itself, was open to receive both a Duke and a philosopher. In fashionable circles which doted on "sensibility," after *La Nouvelle Héloïse* and *Clarissa Harlowe* had touched the organs which their owners mistook for hearts, a writer like the author of the *Theory of Moral Sentiments* (already known by a bad translation) was sure of a welcome, especially from emotional dames, who fancied that when he had derived moral sentiments from sympathy, he had reduced morality to sentiment, so that one could be moral without the trouble of being virtuous. The philosophic tutor spoke little French, and that little very poorly, like his friend Hume; but that did not prevent a marquise falling rapturously in love with him, or impulsive Madame Riccoboni (who had given up acting romance badly on the stage for writing it still worse for the press) from raving over "this most lovable and most distrait of creatures."[1] More congenial society than these poor social butterflies he found in Quesnai, physician to Madame de Pompadour, who, with his friends, was full of theories on trade and commerce, and debated in his rooms at Versailles "immediate taxes" and *net produit*, with extravagant gesture and vocal animation. Quesnai was as ready to doctor the State as the King, and had as many remedies for the body politic as for the body royal.[2] Amid these discussions in the *entresol* Adam Smith learned much—so much, indeed, that those who knew not what he had been teaching in Glasgow for years, believed that he derived all his doctrines from Quesnai and Turgot.

He witnessed the miseries of the people, on whom the State was, as Turgot said, trying the experiment of plucking the fowl without making it cry. He saw the shameless extravagance of the Court; the light hearts of the noblesse, and the heavy hearts of the peasantry; yet, deceived by the

---

[1] Rae's *Life of A. Smith*, p. 212.
[2] Marmontel's *Memoirs* (Eng. trans.), 1895, i. 213.

optimism of Quesnai, Turgot, and Necker, with their sanguine projects, he did not foresee the inevitable downfall of the corrupt old régime. The surface of society was deceptively calm as he gazed at it from hotel windows. "Everything is quiet," said a complacent official in a silent, sulky district of India, to Sir John Malcolm on one occasion. "Yes," he answered, with more discernment, "quiet as gunpowder."

Society in France had some charm for Adam Smith who, in spite of his bad French, enjoyed the brilliant talk of Helvétius, D'Alembert, and Morellet; the gatherings at Madame du Deffand's—that Voltaire in petticoats—and at Madame Geoffrin's, whom young Lord Carlisle irreverently called "an impertinent old brimstone." But it palled on him, as it did on Hume. "I am happy here; yet I long to rejoin my old friends. If I once got fairly to your side of the water, I think I should never cross it again"—so he wrote to good Andrew Millar, the bookseller. A melancholy accident hastened the fulfilment of his wish. Lord Hugh Scott, the Duke's brother, who was now also under his charge, was murdered in the streets of Paris, and with his body the party returned to England.

It is certain that the experience and observation of these three years of travel were an immense advantage to Adam Smith. The pages of his great work are filled with references to the laws and customs of France. If the sure way of learning to cure disease is to study it, he had abundant scope in that distressful country, which afforded a fine study in social pathology. Many a lesson in political economy he gained from the study of political prodigality in France.

The scene now changes, for his tutorship is over and his pension has begun, and he can live in study and leisure. He is once more back in the old house with his mother in the Main Street of Kirkcaldy, which was to be his home for eleven busy years. It was a startling change from the brilliant and polished society of France to the plodding, provincial folk of the little borough, with their talk about the price of fish and coals; their news about the freight of the last smack arrived at the little harbour; and the petty gossip at the weekly meetings of the club of local quidnuncs which Smith attended. As he looked out of the windows he saw Edinburgh at the other side of the firth, and he often was induced to cross the ferry to have rational conversation with his friends, for he knew that David Hume had a special chamber ready for him in James' Court. Years passed by, and he was absorbed in writing his *Wealth of Nations.* In his little study he would dictate to his amanuensis, his body swaying to and fro, and smearing the wall over the mantelpiece with the pomatum on his powdered head.[1] Engrossed in his work, he would become strangely oblivious. One Sunday morning, all engrossed in his thoughts, he began to walk in the garden in his dressing-gown, and vacantly wandered through the gate to the high-road, till he nearly reached Dumfermline, sixteen miles away, where he was roused from his reverie by the sound of the tolling bells and the sight of folk staring at the strange apparition as they went decently Sabbath-clad to kirk.[2]

The years from 1772 to 1775 seem to have been spent chiefly in London, where he was busy completing his work. During former years he had visited the capital, and it was probably in 1761 that he had his famous inverview with Dr. Johnson, when, as the lexicographer put it mildly, "they did not take to each other," or, to put it correctly, they fiercely quarrelled. At Mr. William Strahan's a keen altercation arose; and the economist bounced from the presence of "the brute," as he called him, who had compactly said to him, "That is a lie." The retort, more pungent than proper, traditionally ascribed to the outraged economist may be regarded as apocryphal.[3] The oracle could be rude with little provocation (except, of course, to a bishop or a lord), and he ventured to be so with Adam Smith more than once — probably trusting to the mild temper of the philosopher. When the Scotsman was one day expatiating to him on the beauty of Glasgow — "Have you ever seen Brentford?" was the re-

---

[1] Chambers's *Picture of Scotland.*
[2] Rogers's *Social Life of Scotland,* iii. 118.
[3] When Adam Smith was asked what he replied to Johnson, he said he called him "the son of a b—— -h." This story, however, as told by Sir Walter Scott on the authority of Professor Millar of Glasgow, is so inconsistent in the details that we cannot accept it. Sir Walter had a taste for colouring with graphic touches most anecdotes that passed through his hands (Boswell's *Johnson,* iii. 331, v. 367; Rae's *Life of Smith,* pp. 38, 154).

joinder of the sage of Bolt Court—a retort meant as sheer impertinence, for that place was noted for dulness and dirt— the "town of mud" in the *Castle of Indolence*. No love was lost between the two men. "I have seen the creature" —thus irreverently did Mr. Smith speak of the great man— "stand bolt upright in the midst of a mixed company, and without previous notice fall upon his knees, behind a chair, and repeat the Lord's Prayer, and then resume his seat at table—and this several times of an evening."[1] Time must, however, have soothed Johnson's animosity or brought him to penitence, for in 1775 Adam Smith was admitted a member of the Literary Club, in which the moralist's voice was all-powerful. Boswell was disgusted at the choice of his old professor to sit at the august board. Gibbon's entrance was bad enough—"a disgusting creature," said Bozzy—and here was another to spoil his pleasure. "Smith, too, is a member," he wrote in chagrin to his friend Temple; "it has lost its select merit."[2] This is very fine. Evidently Mr. Smith was not the most vivacious of table-talkers. Instructive, well-informed he certainly was, but London diners-out did not care for too substantial colloquial fare. It was after listening to the economist's rather heavy harangues, delivered in decisive professorial manner, that Garrick one day whispered to his friend—"What do you say to this, eh? —flabby, eh?" His voice was harsh, his utterance thick and almost stammering, which did not help to captivate the wits and men of the world.[3] It is useless for a man in society to have a "wealth of conversation" if he has no small change.

It was in 1776 that the work to which so many years had been devoted saw the light. For years his friends had been looking for it. Great things were expected of it, and when the *Enquiry into the Wealth of Nations* appeared, interest in Edinburgh literary circles was keen. It does not say much for the critical acumen of his friend "Jupiter" Carlyle, that he can only say of this epoch-making book that "it is full of repetitions, and that the second volume consists of essays

---

[1] *The Bee*, 1791, iii. 2.   [2] *Letters to Temple*, p. 233.
[3] Carlyle's *Autobiography*, p. 279; Stewart's *Works*, p. 117.

like occasional pamphlets, without force or determination."[1]
Almost unnoticed by reviews, though it soon passed into a
second edition, its effect was in a few years marked in
legislation; and, curious to say, it was the Tories under Pitt
that first recognised its great principles, and the Whigs under
Fox that flouted them.[2] Political economy was at once raised
by Adam Smith from vagrant theories into a science. The
views he enforced were not all new— free-trade had had its
advocates before him. His theories were not all true—future
economists had to correct them after him. But his keen
insight into the social laws which regulate commerce and
trade, his power of illustrating large principles by the simplest
facts of life, his vast stores of observation, which he would use
to confirm a statement or to burst a fallacy—these were
remarkable in a man who in private life seemed the most
absent-minded of mortals. Friends laughed at his obliviousness to what was going on around him, yet he would see in small
affairs great economic laws at work which were beyond their
vision. Nothing escaped him: the making of pins illustrated
the doctrine on the division of labour; the practice of nailers
at Pathhead exchanging nails for goods, illustrated the principles of barter. The ingenuity of his conclusions, it has been
said, comes often with the pleasant unexpectedness of a
witticism.[3] The whole subject becomes in his hands no
"dismal science," and the illustrative facts which he gives
from his observation at home and abroad even make it, Bagehot
characteristically said, "a most amusing book about old
times."[4] It is not in that light, however, the world is inclined
to regard it. Much has been said about the inconsistency of
the author of the *Theory of Moral Sentiments*, who had derived
moral feeling from sympathy, in his *Wealth of Nations* treating
selfishness as the all-prevailing motive in conduct. But what
else could he do? He took the strongest impulse which undoubtedly works in trade, in commerce, and business—namely,
"the natural effort of the individual to better his condition"

---

[1] *Carlyle's Autobiography*, p. 281.
[2] Fox owned he never read the book and could not understand the subject.
[3] Leslie Stephen's *English Thought in the Eighteenth Century*, ii. 318.
[4] Bagehot's *Biographical Studies*, p. 273.

(which conduces, he holds, to the well-being of the race). Whenever human nature ceases to act in the struggle for prosperity, individual or national, mainly on that self-regarding principle, it will be time to complain of Adam Smith treating it as the main factor in political economy.

Among those who hailed his success with loving praise, no voice was so grateful to him, none so earnest, none so valuable, as that of David Hume, to whose own economical theories he was not a little indebted. The friendship of long years, the intimacy of congenial natures, bound these two men together with an attachment stronger than united any others of that distinguished band. One day in 1775, as Adam Smith and John Home were on their way to Scotland, their chaise stopped at Morpeth Inn, and there they found David Hume travelling alone, weary and ill, to London, to consult Sir John Pringle about his health. In his boundless good-nature John Home at once turned back, accompanied his old friend first to London and thence to Bath, while Smith was obliged to go on his way to Kirkcaldy, where his mother was ill.[1] When next they met, it was at that dinner in July to which the dying philosopher had summoned his old comrades on his return from Bath, and often he visited him in his sick-room. Hume was anxious that he should publish for him after death his Dialogues on Religion and Essay on Suicide, but with his usual caution and timidity he declined the commission. He was afraid of the " clamour," he was afraid of the odium: a tremor which turned out to be quite unnecessary, for when they did appear they caused no commotion whatever. But "clamour" against him did arise where he least expected it. When Hume's brief autobiography was published, he appended a letter to Strahan, the printer, giving an account of the historian's last days, and an estimate of his character, which concluded with the words: " Upon the whole, I have always considered him, both in his lifetime and since his death, as approaching as nearly to the idea of a perfectly wise and virtuous man as perhaps the nature of human frailty will permit." Here were words which created a furore among the pious and the

[1] Mackenzie's *Life of Home*, p. 169.

orthodox. An atheist yet "perfectly virtuous," an infidel yet a "good man," a denier of revelation yet "perfectly wise." There indeed was blasphemy! It was useless to protest that Hume was no atheist; for excited orthodoxy does not stickle about the accuracy of an epithet or a fact. The vigorous *Letter to Adam Smith, LL.D., by one of the People called Christians,* from Bishop Horne's pen, ran through several editions, showing that a man could not be wise and good who was "guilty of the atrocious wickedness of diffusing atheism throughout the land," and denouncing poor Adam Smith as upholding the criminal opinions of the pagan saint.

After all, Adam Smith suffered no damage in his prospects, for two years later he was appointed Commissioner of Customs, with a salary of £600; and as the Duke of Buccleugh would not accept his offer to resign the pension of £300, he had a comfortable fortune for a homely bachelor. Mr. Commissioner Smith conveyed his goods and chattels, his ample library, his old mother, and spinster cousin, Miss Jean Douglas, to Edinburgh, where he chose as his residence Panmure House at the end of a narrow wynd off the Canongate, which seemed a palatial residence in those days.[1] There he had all that could make him happy: his mother whom he adored; old friends around him; his library of 3000 volumes, with binding in which he took pride, saying to Smellie, the learned printer, who was looking over them, "I am a beau in nothing but my books." He was employed at his office in the Royal Exchange over plans for a lighthouse, reports on smuggling, the suppression of illicit stills, the appointment of excisemen. This was no very appropriate occupation for a man of his intellectual power; yet the insight he gained into details about taxes and revenue was of no small service to him in successive editions of his great work.

Edinburgh was full of interest for his idle hours. It was impossible to go out of his office without seeing some acquaintance to speak to, or some bore to avoid. He engaged with Principal Robertson and Dr. Ferguson in forming the Royal

---

[1] Yet not too spacious, for in 1790, when a friend is going to stay with him, he writes to his nephew: "By putting a bed in our drawing-room we can easily accommodate him" (unpublished letter).

Society of Edinburgh, at whose scientific meetings he was to be seen in placid slumber[1]; and he acted as captain of the trained bands of the town, decked out in their quaint garb. There was the Oyster Club, which in a tavern at two o'clock sat down to a simple repast. Adam Smith, Drs. Robertson and Blair, Dr. Cullen, Dugald Stewart, Henry Mackenzie were there; and the abstemious cronies, Dr. James Hutton and Dr. Joseph Black, whose diet consisted of a few prunes and milk and water. Black and Hutton were the men Smith loved best—two companions strangely unlike, yet closely attached to each other. Dr. Black, in his modish costume, with his nicely-balanced judgments and apt phrases, uttered in always purest English, was a curious contrast to Dr. Hutton, in drab, Quaker-like dress and broad-brimmed hat, loquaciously eager on every possible and impossible scheme, which he discussed in the broadest of Scots. It was said that "every eye brightened when Hutton came into the room"—a physician who never practised, a farming laird intent on every improvement, a distinguished mineralogist, the founder of modern Geology.[2] "Dr. Black hated nothing so much as error, Dr. Hutton hated nothing so much as ignorance," remarked Professor Playfair. Edinburgh, like all small towns, where every one knew, or thought he knew, everybody else, abounded in gossip, tinctured, however, more with good-humour than ill-nature; and it told stories of the two humorists. They had argued themselves above all popular prejudices on diet, and resolved to carry their opinions into practice. Since the ancient world partook of testaceous creatures of the sea as delicacies, why turn up the modern nose in abhorrence of those that crawl on dry land? Why not eat snails? They were wholesome; they were nutritious; and did not epicures of old prize the molluscs fed in the marble quarries of Lucca? The two emancipated philosophers determined, therefore, to have snails for supper. They sat down to the feast. Silently they looked at the dish; shyly they refrained from looking at each other; slowly each took a mouthful—their gorges rising in flat rebellion as they did so. At length Dr. Black, in slow, delicate, tentative voice, remarked in his gentlest manner, "Doctor, don't you think they taste a

[1] Clayden's *Early Life of Rogers*, p. 96.   [2] Kay's *Edinburgh Portraits*, i. 57.

little—a *very* little queer?" "Queer!—dawmned queer! Tak' them awa'! Tak' them awa'!" vociferated Dr. Hutton, rising in loathing. So began and ended their feast "after the manner of the ancients."[1]

Adam Smith was appreciated in Edinburgh society though not in London. He might "convey his ideas in the form of a lecture," his voice might be harsh and his articulation thick, but there was that smile which Carlyle describes as "captivating"; those manners which were gracious; that full knowledge of things and affairs. His frequent obliviousness to what was going on around him led him into vagaries which delighted his friends, though they occasionally led him into scrapes. At dinner one day he was declaiming loudly against the conduct of a public man, when suddenly it flashed across him that the son of the person he was condemning was sitting beside him, and he was heard ejaculating to himself, "Deil care—deil care, it's a' true!" Placid as he was, at times his feelings could be keenly roused, and when a gentleman at Dalkeith Palace left the room, where he had been speaking of some vicious action with cynical tolerance, Adam Smith broke out: "We can breathe more freely now; that man has no indignation in him!"[2]

Among his many friends in old Edinburgh, life was pleasant in those days. The Sunday suppers at Panmure House were events to remember. About eight o'clock there came the tread of well-known steps and the sound of familiar voices in the narrow wynd, and successive knocks at the door, which betokened the arrival of intimates, who came without the formality of an invitation—all being certain of a welcome at the hospitable board, with its fish and collops and roasted fowls, its punch and claret. During talk, as Blair and Hutton and Carlyle were in eager discussion, the mind of the host might wander far away to dreamland, till recalled by some loud discussion he had not followed, or uproarious mirth over a joke he could not see. Tales flitted around of the good man's abstractedness, and were retailed with unfailing zest. The familiar story was told of his walking round and round the tea-table, engrossed in talk,

---

[1] Sir Walter Scott's *Works*, xix., "Periodical Criticism."
[2] D. Stewart's *Works*, x. 187.

each time as he approached the tray unconsciously abstracting the lumps of sugar, which he munched as he took his rounds, till his spinster cousin, in agony at the "wastry," hid the bowl on her lap below the table. The company in Lady Mary Coke's drawing-room in 1767 were entertained one day by the story of Mr. Damer visiting the philosopher as he was sitting down to breakfast. As they talked Mr. Smith took a piece of bread and butter, which he rolled round and round with his fingers, and then put into the tea-pot and poured water over it. When he poured the stuff out into a cup and tasted it, he said, "it was the worst tea he had ever met with."[1] One day he entered the Customs Office, where the portly porter in his scarlet gown gave him the usual salute with his ponderous staff. Completely forgetful that morning of a form which he had seen gone through day after day, and reminiscent of the drill of the City Train Band, of which he was captain, he fancied this was the drill-sergeant before him, and obediently raised his cane with both hands in the middle, like a musket, to return the salute, and when the porter lowered his staff and turned to the left to make way for his master, the Commissioner drew to the right, and lowered his cane to the same angle. The porter leading the way upstairs, the distrait philosopher marched formally step by step, and as the bewildered official opened the door and lowered again his staff in salute, Mr. Smith copied every motion with his cane, and bowed with equal ceremony—entering the office utterly unconscious that he had done anything unusual.[2] Another day he was observed absently producing an exact copy of the signature of another witness to a document, instead of writing his own name.

His figure was one of the most familiar in the High Street[3]—dressed in a light-coloured coat, in cocked hat or broad-brimmed beaver, white silk stockings, and silver-buckled shoes, a bamboo cane held over his shoulder, as a soldier carries his musket, with one hand, while the other might hold a bunch of flowers from his garden. Thus he walked, with eyes gazing vacantly, and lips moving

[1] Lady Mary Coke's *Journal*, i. 141 (printed for private circulation).
[2] Sir Walter Scott's *Works*, xix.
[3] Kay's *Edinburgh Portraits*, i. 75.

as if in inaudible converse, a placid smile occasionally wreathing his countenance, his body swaying, as an acquaintance describes it, "vermicularly, as if at every step he meant to alter his direction or to turn back."[1] No wonder the Musselburgh fishwife, as she watched the punctiliously attired, vacant-eyed, amiable man pass along the street, mistook him for a demented but harmless old gentleman, and sighed to her sister vender of haddocks, "Hech! and he is weel put on tae!" His very unpracticalness in little affairs of life only endeared him the more to friends, who were comforted at feeling they were at least in some things superior to a genius. In political matters he was, like most of his Scots brethren, on the side of liberalism; in religion he did not pronounce his opinions, and his friends did not question him, though they knew his convictions were deep. Doubtless he was of that religion "to which all sensible men belong," and "which all sensible men keep to themselves." Like Dr. Hutton, he was no great church-goer, and was addicted to going out in his sedan-chair for an airing on Sundays, while the church bells were ringing.[2] Yet he may have agreed with his old friend, when he said it was sometimes worth while going to the kirk merely to enjoy the pleasure of coming out.[3]

Time brought many infirmities to a life so placidly spent. In 1787 he was sixty-four years old, but no longer the sturdy, strong-built man of yore. "Worn to skin and bone," he resolved to visit London to consult his friend, Dr. William Hunter. He was able to enter society, however, where his reputation was so established, that he was as honoured by statesmen as by men of letters. A pleasant story is told how, when at a country house he met Addington, Grenville, and William Pitt, the company rose as the great Scotsman entered the room. "Be seated, gentlemen," said he. "No," rejoined Pitt, "we will stand till you are seated first, for we are all your scholars."[4] The old man had the gratification of finding that his teaching had got apt and brilliant pupils, and posterity were to become his disciples.

---
[1] Smellie's *Lives of A. Smith, etc.*, p. 293.
[2] Clayden's *Early Life of Rogers*, p. 97.
[3] Scott's *Familiar Letters*, i. 301. [4] Kay's *Edinburgh Portraits*, i. 47.

The great economist's last days were spent in revising his *Theory of Moral Sentiments*—a favourite, but not an epoch-making book. His physical strength, however, was spent; his body wasted to a shadow; his spirits had become dull and lethargic, and his friends feared that he was dying. It was then that the lovable, choleric old Dr. Adam Ferguson, hearing that the friend from whom he had been long estranged was ill, came, with his shivering frame clad in furs, in his chair, to wait by his bedside. Dr. Cullen attended him, and the inseparable companions, Black and Hutton, at his urgent request, a week before his death burnt a host of manuscripts which he was anxious should be destroyed. His work was done, yet he said sadly, "I meant to have done more." A curious picture of stoical philosophy and, Scots stolidity is to be found at a supper the Sunday before he died. The board was spread as usual; the usual friends had come; the host received them with cheerful welcome, and the hospitable smile on his wan, sunken face. After they had supped and talked, they saw that he was wearied, and pressed him to retire; and as he left the room he paused with his hand on the door handle, and quietly said, "My friends, I fear I must leave this happy meeting, and that I shall never meet you again. But I trust we shall meet in another and a better world."[1] This was indeed the last meeting, and it is a good instance of unemotional Scottish temperament that the genial company saw the old man withdraw, soon to die, while they remained at his table, discussing his books, his character, his wine, and the prospects of his death, when he went off to bed. Next Saturday (17th June 1790) Adam Smith was dead, and a few days after the merry guests at his supper were mourners at his grave.[2]

[1] Sinclair's *Old Times and Distant Places*, p. 12, on authority of Rev. A. Alison.

[2] Of Smith's religious opinions little is definitely known, but a passage in his *Theory of Moral Sentiments* gives some indication of them. Referring to the cruel fate of the Calas family: "Religion can alone afford them every effectual comfort. She also can tell them that it is of little importance what men may think of their conduct, while the all-seeing Judge of the world approves of it. She alone can present to them a view of another world—a world of more candour, humanity, and justice than the present, where their innocence is in due time to be declared, and their virtue to be finally rewarded."

CHAPTER VII

LITERARY JUDGES: LORD KAMES—LORD MONBODDO—LORD HAILES

THREE judges were distingushed contributors to the literature of Scotland; but it cannot be said that letters owe as much to the Law as to the Church, though the Bar was the "preserve" of men of rank and fortune, fashion and leisure, with whom culture and taste might be expected to abound. Those who had the brains, however, devoted them to the complexities of feudal law and the establishment of a good practice. The clergy had culture and leisure, though we need not credit the accusation of the censorious, that the "moderate" ministers devoted time to their books and good company which they should have spent on their duties and their prayers.

Young advocates in the early part of the century got their training as apprentices to writers or advocates, whose offices were rooms in their houses, up the turnpike stairs, which might be used as bedrooms at night. There, for a moderate fee, the lawyer extracted as much work in engrossing and copying briefs as he could, and imparted as much knowledge as he cared of the great Dutch jurists, whose Latin opinions were daily sonorously cited in the Court. After the young men had studied at the "lattern" (lectern or desk), they were examined for the Bar, presenting a thesis written for them maybe by Mr. Thomas Ruddiman, which compressed more Latin into twelve folio manuscript pages than their heads contained in their whole career. The richer young men, however, went off to Utrecht or Groningen or Leyden, where they casually

LORD KAMES
From the Engraving after Martin.

attended the sleepy class-rooms and yawned over the ponderous Latin lectures; and then concluded their studies by visiting Montpellier and Paris. They came home with a fine air of continental fashion, a costume from the red heels of their shoes to the curls of their wigs of latest Parisian shape, and ever after looked down on the provincial ways and speech of their home-bred countrymen.[1]

Henry Home was too poor to pursue study abroad, for he was the son of the Laird of Kames, whose acres were burdened with wadsets, whose farm-houses were in ruins, and whose fields were in nettles. Born in 1696, after a little training from the parish minister he went to Edinburgh to become apprentice to a writer; and not being sent to college, he had to educate himself by studying Latin and literature in his frugal lodgings. The struggles of his early life became bitter memories in his later years of prosperity. Often would he say that had he been assured of £50 a year, no consideration would have made him submit to the drudgery of mind and body he had then, and after joining the Bar, to undergo. His career was intended to be that of a writer, but by chance his fortunes got a new bent. One evening he had been sent by his master to Lord President Dalrymple, who was living in his suburban villa near Bristo Street. There, as he entered, was the stately old judge in his bright room over his book, the daughter singing a Scotch song to her harpsichord. When business was over, talk followed; after tea came music, and the impecunious son of the Laird of Kames, delighted with his reception, went forth into the winter's darkness to his poor lodgings emulous of a life of learned ease and dignity, which he could hope to reach only by eminence at the Bar. From that night he resolved to be an advocate, and for that purpose he worked and pinched and saved indomitably.

In 1723 he became an advocate, and then his struggles began anew in a profession where high connections were the passports to practice. The best things at the Bar were for the sons of good families like the Dalrymples and Dundases, to whose hands judgeships and lord presidentships seemed to come as by natural right. At the Bar, for instance, was

[1] Ramsay's *Scotland and Scotsmen*, i. 182.

Robert Dundas of Arniston, whose father and grandfather had been judges, and who himself, and his son after him, were to sit as Presidents of the Court. Along with Duncan Forbes of Culloden, the most eloquent advocate at the Bar, once "the plentifullest drinker of the North," were scions of the families of Grant, Ferguson, and Erskine, before whom writers grovelled. It was hard for impecunious Henry Home to pit himself against men like these. Before the august fifteen judges, however, he pleaded with good success, in spite of his lack of influence and his propensity for subtleties by which he exercised his ingenuity and considerably exercised the patience of their common-sense lordships. He had, moreover, time and taste for something besides legal ambitions. There were meetings at the inns where good drink was to be got cheap, and good talk for nothing, not merely for the legal consultation with writers, which advocates in those days always held over claret or ale in taverns. With William Hamilton of Bangour and other boon companions he was merry at Balfour's Coffee-house [1]—the "Wills" or "Buttons" of the North; he was gay at the Assembly in Bell's Wynd, to which entrance was half-a-crown, and for which he would prepare his lank person by getting his wig newly trimmed by the nimble hands of Allan Ramsay, and would carefully brush his well-used coat and waistcoat, trusting that their defects would not be detected by pretty eyes in the ball-room, ill-lighted with tallow candles. There the tall, dark-visaged advocate was a beau and a wit. Verses by Hamilton "To H. H. in the Assembly" recall the olden days:

> When Erskine leads her happy man,
> And Johnstone shakes the fluttering fan;
> When beauteous Pringle shines confest
> And gently heaves her swelling breast,
> Her raptured partner still at gaze,
> Pursuing through each winding maze:
> Say, Harry, canst thou keep secure
> Thy heart from conquering beauty's power?

The busy, eager lawyer never lost sight of his legal

[1] Hamilton's *Poems* (Life by Paterson); Tytler's *Kames*, i. 58.

prospects while dangling around fair damsels. He published reports of Decisions of the Court, which made judges look favourably on the man who could drink with wits, dance with belles, and plod with lawyers. When, in 1741, he issued in two vast folios his *Dictionary of Decisions of the Court of Session*, they were ready to bless him. For till then the decisions of judges were unclassified, unprinted; lawyers needed to ransack musty manuscripts for reports and precedents, and in despair of finding old decisions, lawyers had to quote Bartolus and Cujacius to move their lordships to an original decision.[1] The overflowing intelligence of Home sought still further outlets for its energy, and metaphysics gave scope for that subtlety at which their lordships so often winced. Philosophical discussions were the fashion for Edinburgh brains from 1720 to 1740. The speculations of Locke and of Shaftesbury, the new opinions of Berkeley, Butler, and Hutcheson of Glasgow, were keenly interesting to thinking young men. While some met at Thomas Rankin's Inn, and called themselves the Rankinian Club, Home and others were members of the Philosophical Club, and over ale, claret, and oysters discussed philosophy. His restless brain was never weary of those problems, though his victims were often weary of his questions. Irrepressibly argumentative, he corresponded with Baxter, whose treatise on the *Immateriality of the Soul* had made some noise, till "Immateriality" Baxter was worn out, broke off communications, and testily burned the letters; he corresponded with Dr. Samuel Clarke on his *Being and Attributes of God*, with Berkeley on Idealism, till the patience and politeness of these divines were sorely tried; and Dr. Joseph Butler was entangled likewise in an epistolary discussion, the great moralist hoping that each reply might be final, only to find another lengthy epistle from Scotland (postage one shilling) would arrive to prove that the persistent inquirer was not yet at rest.[2]

This exuberantly critical propensity of the advocate found scope in combating the views of his friend David Hume— then the only man of letters in Edinburgh. Henry Home, once a Jacobite and Episcopalian, had by this time abandoned

[1] Tytler's *Kames*, i. 108. [2] *Ibid.* i. 27; *Ramsay*, i. 155.

his politics and his persuasion, without adopting earnestly any other in their place, and when he became supporter of orthodoxy there was less religious ardour than speculative fussiness behind it. In Hume's denial of the law of causation, and his reduction of virtue to utility, he saw a sapping of the evidence for deity· and of the basis of morality. In 1751, therefore, appeared his *Essays on the Principles of Moral and Natural Religion*, intended to vindicate religion and confute his friend. The author soon discovered, as others have done, that it is sometimes a very dangerous thing to defend the faith; that it is possible, by a too strenuous effort to uplift an overturned faith from one side, to make it fall over on the other. To his disgust Home found that he——the champion of the faith——was charged with infidelity. An irascible, coarse-penned chaplain, Mr. George Anderson, wrote a venomous pamphlet against his dangerous principles, the Presbytery of Edinburgh was stirred up thereby against the terrible freethinking not only of David Hume but also of Henry Home, who had piously tried to confute him. The matter ended in the General Assembly issuing a solemn exhortation against pernicious infidel books that were rife, and by warning their flocks against reading them.[1]

David Hume, the heretic, was entitled to laugh at the defender of the faith being charged with the same crime as himself, in spite of the work closing with an elegant and solemn prayer which Mr. Hugh Blair had composed for his friend. Home was certainly not lucky in his argument. He granted with Hume that both moral and physical worlds are ruled by invariable laws, and that man acts from motives he cannot resist. This is alarmingly like heresy; how did he vindicate moral and human responsibility? By arguing that because man acts under the (mistaken) belief that he is a free agent, he is accountable for his actions as if he had really free will. This was the oddest way to conciliate Christians or to refute pagans. He found that it was safer to confine himself to pleadings on "multiplepoinding" and "tailzies" before their lordships and leave divinity to the care of providence.

In 1754 Home took his place on the Bench as Lord Kames,

[1] Morren's *Annals of General Assembly*, ii. 54.

for his reputation as a lawyer was high, and the expectations formed of him as a judge were great. He thought himself rich with a judge's salary of £500. Sitting beside him were men with whom he had measured wits at the Bar. Some of these were of far more polished manners than his own — Lord Minto, stately and dignified, and acquainted both with polite letters and polite manners; Lord Tinwald, most courteous of gentlemen, as he lisped out his elegant charges in dulcet tones which earned him the name of "Sweet Lips." There was Dalrymple, Lord Drummore, an elder of the kirk, who drank freely, lived loosely, and attended religious ordinances; and my Lord Grange, the unctuous Presbyterian saint, whose life and conduct were those of a Tartuffe. Beside him was my Lord Dundas, loud and rude in the bench, lively at the beard, deep in potations in the tavern, sound for orthodoxy on the floor of the General Assembly; and Lord Milton, nephew of the incorruptible Fletcher of Saltoun, who, after managing all the patronage of Scotland as henchman of the politically all-powerful Lord Islay, was in the last days of his dotage to pass the time playing with children's toys.[1] Prominent amongst his brethren was Lord Auchinleck, the plainest-spoken judge, uncouth in speech, with good sense and good law in those prolix "opinions" during which the Lord President significantly displayed the sand-glass which was kept "to time" the speeches from the bench. Such men Kames, with his keen wit, measured shrewdly, making dull brethren the butts of his jests and pleaders the helpless recipients of his sarcasms.

At that period the Parliament House, in which the law courts were held, presented a very different appearance from what it did after the great fire of 1824. The front was picturesque in its austere way, with Scottish turrets and the balustraded roofs, on which their lordships could take the air, hidden from the vulgar gaze. The Inner Court, in which sat the august "fifteen" in their robes of scarlet, was a low-ceiled room thirty or forty feet wide; its walls dark with smoke, which proceeded from the fireplace, with its broken "jambs" and its ancient grate half full of dust and ashes behind the Lord President's chair. On each side of the bench

[1] Ramsay's *Scotland and Scotsmen*, i. 40-173.

the wall was adorned with wooden frames containing the Lord's Prayer and the Commandments worked in faded gilt letters on what had originally been a black velvet ground, but now was a dingy brown. This dismal abode of justice, when evening set in, was dimly lighted by malodorous candles, which, unsnuffed, guttered in miserable tin candlesticks. The spacious hall of the Parliament House was divided by low wooden partitions. At the east end were seats and benches, whereon, in proud days, members of Scots Parliament had sat, which now were occupied by lawyers and their clients, who faced the chair against the wall on which of yore the Lord Chancellor had presided, and whereon now sat the Lord Ordinary of the Outer House. At the western end booksellers, glovers, and smiths had their stalls, and Peter Williamson set up his coffee-house, with the tiny apartments made by walls of brown paper. From behind a wooden partition on Mondays came a buzzing, often obstreperous, noise, for there a bailie tried petty offences in what was contemptuously known as the "Dirt Court"—a term most appropriate from its squalid condition and the uncleanly state of offenders and audience. In the middle of this hall, between the Outer House at one end and the "Dirt Court" and shops at the other, was the space in which advocates strolled or strutted, where briefless ones gossiped with their brethren in misfortune as they paced the *salle des pas perdus;* and men in demand walked in bland consultation with their agents till called before "my lord."[1]

Lively as was the scene within, still livelier was it outside in the Parliament Close. Beneath the piazza were to be found the pettifogging agents who took pleas in the Dirt Court—writers as damaged in character as in clothing looking out for clients on what was properly known as the "Scoundrels' Walk." On the two sides of the close, and against the walls of St. Giles', which formed the fourth side of the square, jewellers, printers, glovers, booksellers had their shops, barbers had their little dens for legal wigs to trim and legal chins to shave, and taverns were open for thirsty citizens. Mr. Thomas Ruddiman might be seen going daily out of his

[1] Chambers's *Reekiana*, p. 187; Arnot's *History of Edinburgh*, p. 293; Cockburn's *Memorials*, pp. 110-126.

printing-office to Mr. Andrew Symers, the bookseller, for his usual game of chess, and two hours after was seen to come out with flushed face and ruffled temper after the inevitable squabble. The square was full of the hubbub of life. Merchants, bankers, doctors, ministers took their morning saunter there before they had their "meridian," and exchanged greetings and snuff-boxes; lawyers and judges bustled past with their gowns flowing, their legal bob-wigs on their heads, and their cocked hats under their arms. The buzz of voices, the noise of bustling porters with their chairs, the cries of caddies on their errands, all made the place a scene of incessant liveliness, and none enjoyed it more than Lord Kames.

His life was vastly busy in his house in New Street, off the Canongate. He was up at five o'clock in the morning, and in winter two hours before daybreak, with his books to read, his papers to write on feudal law, history, on trade, on philosophy, on criticism, on drains, poetry, or sub-soil— frugally covering the backs of old letters with his extracts and notes. After early breakfast there were levées.[1] Friends came to ask his counsel, farmers and tradesmen were in the lobby to consult him about seeds or ploughing, or to crave his patronage with the Board of Trustees for some invention of marvellous efficiency, which would assuredly have secured the admission of the inventor into the asylum and of his family into the poorhouse.

The Court adjourned at mid-day for the early dinner, leaving before they resumed work little time for eating, and less for drinking, which latter operation was postponed till supper. In the evening his lordship was amongst the merriest at St. Cecilia concerts, making himself agreeable and facetious to some young lady, to whom he exclusively devoted himself. At supper he was liveliest and broadest over punch and whist.

When he achieved a practice, his first efforts were to relieve the paternal acres from their paternal burdens; and now he lived two lives—one as a judge and a man about town, the other as a farmer and a laird. If his wife had her hobby of collecting china, he had his hobby of improving land, clearing away morasses, ploughing, draining,

[1] Tytler's *Kames*, i. 205; Ramsay's *Scotland and Scotsmen*, i. 202.

planting, and enclosing. Still more scope was afforded for his rural tastes when by his wife he got the fine property of Blair Drummond near Kincardine, which brought wealth and ample opportunity for practising his husbandry. What feats he performed clearing the old wastes, removing the peat, which he floated down the Teith, introducing the best seeds and the newest implements! On arriving at night after the Court was up in Edinburgh, he would go out with the lantern to mark the growth of his saplings, and in the morning he was hurrying on his workmen with strong oaths in plain Scotch, and impatiently helping them to lift stones for a dyke. His old-fashioned farmers, who had kept the land sterile and themselves poor by old modes of agriculture, shuddered at these wild schemes, which they were certain would end in ruin. One day his lordship was boasting to one of these incredulous tenants of a manure of marvellously fertilising power, invented by Baron von Hock, a German quack. "Such, my good friend, is its power, that I should not be surprised if at some future time we might be able to carry the manure of an acre of land in our coat pockets."[1] The reply was disconcerting from the "bruit," as he would call him: "Maybe, my lord, but I suspect that you will be able to bring back the crop in your waistcoat pouch." His experiments did indeed often end in failure, hugely to the farmers' delight, but not the less he stands out as one of the most influential improvers of his time. Nothing interested him more to the end of his life than to hear of a new kind of spinning-wheel or barrow, or new modes of growing flax or turnips.[2] In the Select Society, which was energetic after 1754 encouraging industry, art, and agriculture in Scotland, no member was more active than he. He kept up correspondence with Dr. Black on the attraction of clay and water; with Professor Walker on the generation of plants; with Dr. Reid on the laws of motion or the conversion of clay into vegetable mould; with Dean Tucker on poor-laws; and with "blue-stocking" Mrs. Montagu on literary gossip.[3] One

---

[1] Kerr's *Life of William Smellie*, i. 359.
[2] Ramsay, *Scotland and Scotsmen*, i. 208; Tytler's *Kames*, ii. 27.
[3] Tytler's *Kames*, i. App.

becomes breathless in the effort to follow this versatile, indefatigable lord in his studies and his works which came from the press on antiquities, on history, on law, on belles lettres. When he asked Lord Monboddo if he had read his last book, "No, my lord," snarled his rival judge and author, "you write a great deal faster than I am able to read"[1]; and he further told his objectionable colleague that no man could write good English who did not know Greek, of which he was aware Kames knew not a word.

In 1762 appeared the fruit of long labour in his *Elements of Criticism*, in which his ceaseless interest in literature found scope, making his name as critic and man of letters spread far and wide. There he analyses beauty, taste, composition, art, gardening, showing on every subject an ingenious nature at work. All judgment on art and letters, according to him, rests on fixed principles; not feeling, but reason, is the infallible judge of taste and beauty. Unluckily for his reputation as a critic with posterity, Ossian is declared full of sublimity, Gothic art is pronounced fit only for the "rude, uncultivated" places where it was invented; the *Mourning Bride*, with its fustian sentiment, is lauded as "the most complete of English dramas." This work appeared in an age when it was the fashion to search into the origin of emotions on taste and beauty. Hutcheson in 1725 had given his inquiry on the *Original of our Ideas of Beauty and Virtue*. Hume wrote on the standard of taste; Dr. Gerard of Aberdeen had, in 1758, also issued his *Essay on Taste*; and two years before Edmund Burke had made his name in letters by his *Sublime and the Beautiful*. Meanwhile Dr. Blair, in his class at college, to his admiring audience, was laying down the canons of literary art; and on these "fixed principles" was conclusively proving Ossian to be—what it never was. These perennial efforts to answer a question on the origin of æsthetic feeling, which the plain man never puts, all leave the matter exactly where it was, and the world likes and dislikes, admires or abhors from age to age, heedless of the infallible standards or the finest principles of any theorist that ever lived.

In far-off Ferney, Voltaire, whose eager mind missed

[1] Ramsay, i. 353.

nothing, read this treatise, in which his own *Henriade* was condemned, by "Lord Makames, a Justice of the Peace in Scotland," as he called him, and he made merry over the profound critic, who begins by "proving that we have five senses, and that we are less struck by a gentle impression made on our eyes and ears by colours and sounds than by a knock on the head or a kick on the legs," and who "with mathematical precision shows that time seems long to a lady going to be married, and short to a man going to be hanged." He expressed vast astonishment that "from remote Scotland should come rules for taste on all matters from an epic to a garden."[1] But this was Voltaire's own little way. Dr. Johnson was pleased to speak of his work as "a pretty essay"; but when he was in a boisterous mood his expressions were obstreperous. Boswell one day was boasting of the advance in literature that Scotland had made. "Sir," replied the doctor, "you have learned a little from us, and you think yourself very great. Hume would never have written his history had Voltaire not written his before him [which Voltaire had not done]. He is only an echo of Voltaire." "But, sir," said Boswell gently, "we have Lord Kames." "You have Lord Kames!" cried out the great man, rolling his frame with Gargantuan mirth. "Keep him—ha! ha! ha! we don't envy you him!" His lordship did not love Johnson: most likely babbling Boswell had confided to him this pleasant remark in strictest confidence. Whatever hostile critics might irreverently say, Scotland was proud of its literary senator; to him, as to Dr. Blair, aspirants came for guidance and society bowed in homage, and in truth a very clever critic he was.

Never was there a more industrious being, and whether he knew much of the subject or whether he knew little was equally with him a reason for writing about it. When Sir Gilbert Elliot appealed to him on an obscure point of political economy, he got the advice: "Go and write a book upon it if you want to understand it."[2] So he went on writing his books and neglecting his legal duties with great assiduity, and at the ripe age of seventy-eight he sent forth from Creech's book-shop his *Sketches of the History of Man*. It is a curious, an amusing book, a strange *olla podrida* of facts and theories, of quaint

[1] *Lettres d un Journaliste.* [2] Tytler's *Kames,* i. 61.

information and acute speculation on commerce, trade, crusades, poor-laws, womankind, and a hundred more subjects drawn from his reading on history, science, and travels. It is at once shrewd and shallow, touching rather than grasping many questions on sociology, on which the old man was wonderfully alert; yet though written after Adam Smith's *Wealth of Nations*, its economic opinions are often very pre-Adamite. This, his most popular work, he called the "child of his grey hairs," and yet at the age of eighty came forth his *Gentleman Farmer*, in which, with a sharpness gained from experience and a whimsicality increased with age, he gives agricultural advice to the world. "Why should I sit with my finger in my cheek waiting till death takes me?" he sharply asked when congratulated on the activity of his old age.[1]

At the period of years when most men are dead or engaged in dying, he, with his wife, was in London, and visiting his old literary friend Mrs. Montagu at Tunbridge Wells. "At eighty-four he is as gay and as nimble as when he was twenty-five, his sight, hearing, memory perfect; he is a most entertaining companion,"[2] wrote that lively old bluestocking. To the end this nimble life continued. There were the early hours at work, the three o'clock dinner, when from fine patriotism French brandy and claret were discarded from the table for whisky-punch and port[3]; his old friends Adam Smith and Blair and Joseph Black on Mondays sharing his vigorous company. The meal ended, the party would disperse to their homes or to stroll in the Meadows or the streets, and the old man in his dressing-gown and velvet cap settled down with his clerk to law business, which occupied him very perfunctorily. He loved his walks with deferential young men of promise, who were expected to wait on him at any hour, and to listen respectfully to his peripatetic discourses. If any flagging of attention called down on them some vigorous expletive, by an adroit compliment for his farming or his books,

---

[1] Tytler and Watson's *Seamstresses of Scotland*, i. 159.
[2] Doran's *Lady of the Last Century*, p. 247.
[3] In his abhorrence of claret, he abolished it even from his circuit tables. One day at the circuit court dinner he asked Henry Erskine where he supposed D'Estaing and the French fleet in the West Indies to be. "Confined to *port*, my lord, like ourselves," was the reply.

the sardonic humour was restored to patriarchal benignity.
At evening gatherings, to which friends came when they
pleased, with the supper of Scots fare, good wine and good
talk, the veteran was the merriest, with full-flavoured stories
in broadest of speech, and cards or music till midnight.[1]

It was not on the bench he achieved most credit, able and
learned though he was. With caustic temper and flurrying
manner, he bullied dull judges out of their dignity, worried
witnesses out of their memories, and nagged pleaders out of
their arguments. "He has the obstinacy of a mule and the
levity of a harlequin," growled an over-baited counsel.[2] Yet
after all he was only one of the strangest series of adminis-
trators of justice the world ever saw—worthy, learned, shrewd
mortals, with the longest of pedigrees and the grotesquest
of manners, and it needed the stateliness of Lord Hailes and
Dundas of Arniston, and the suavity of Sir Islay Campbell, to
leaven the Court with dignity. At the end of the century
were judges whose physical strength was proved by their drinking so much and living so long. A hearty drinker was a man
to respect. That in the "daft circuit" at Ayr the legal
functionaries should be drunk all night and able to try
prisoners all next day was a source of pride. Lord Hermand,
whom all knew to be a true gentleman by birth and feeling,
regarded drinking as a cardinal virtue, and his holy wrath
during a murder case was stirred by the fact that a young
man had stabbed another under the heart-warming and conse-
crating influence of partnership over a bottle of rum. "If the
man did this when he was drunk, what would he not have done
when he was sober!" he asked in virtuous indignation. Beside
some who after him sat on the bench the peculiarities of
Kames sink into commonplace. One of the most original of
the number was Lord Hermand, clad in garments that never
fitted and never joined. His long face would light up with
emotion as he exclaimed in the course of an "opinion"—"My
laards, I feel my law—-I feel it here!" and he would smite his
bosom to point out the exact locality. In the General Assembly,
during the famous case on the orthodoxy of Professor Leslie, he
was seen dancing on the floor with pious excitement—his thin

---

[1] Ramsay's *Scotland and Scotsmen*, i. 203.   [2] *Boswelliana*, p. 275.

powdered hair in a long pig-tail waggling in kindly sympathy —protesting that he "had sucked in the being and attributes of God with his mother's milk." The preposterous Eskgrove, with his purple scurvy face, his huge nose, and protruding under-lip supported by an enormous projecting chin, would shuffle in with stealthy tread and take his place beside this worthy, and mumble his wonderful judgments in sententious mispronounced absurdities. The jury—whom he obliged respectfully to stand when he addressed them—would almost faint under his long harangues as he prosed on; "And now, gentle-men, having shown you that the pannell's argument is utterly impossibill, I shall now proceed to show you that it is extremely improbabill." The prisoner doomed to die was cheered by his farewell words: "Whatever your persuasion may be, there are plenty of reverend gentlemen who will be happy for to show you the way to yeternal life." "Esky" was the delight of the whole Bar, which had ridiculed Lord Monboddo for his whims and his hobbies, and despised Lord Strichen with his interjected "weel, weels" and his "oh dears." Stories were told, not to his moral credit, of Lord Gardenstone, who sat snuffing copiously on the bench. When Lord Kames flouted him with a scandal connected with the fair sex, he turned to his friend, whose parsimony was notorious: "Gang to the Deil, my lord; my fauts are growin' the langer the less, and your ain the langer the waur." At his country seat his love for pigs was so touching that one of them, when young, followed him like a dog, and at night slept with him in bed, till, becoming too obese, it slept on the floor, covered lovingly with his lordship's garments.[1] Contrasted with these men of whims, Lord Braxfield was powerful, with his beetle-brows, his red face, his glowering eyes, his thick lips and growling voice, which made his victims in the dock to tremble. There would come from him the coarse jokes, which in private jovial talk were seldom decent, the fleering interjections, the insolent gibes in vulgarest Scots, spoken without heart or pity. "You're a vera clever chiel, maun; but ye wad be nane the waur o' a hanging,"[2] was his reply to a prisoner

---

[1] Cockburn's *Memorials*; Boswell's "Court of Session Garland," in *Chambers's Traditions*, ii. 153; Kay's *Edinburgh Portraits*.
[2] Lockhart's *Life of Scott*, vi. 203; Kay's *Portraits*, i. 24.

who had pleaded ably for his life. Political offenders in the days of the "Friends of the People" roused his mighty wrath. "Come awa', Maister Horner," he said to Francis Horner's father, who was one of the jury, "and help us to hang some o' thae dawmned scoondrels."

The manner which was truculence in Braxfield was sardonic humour in Lord Kames, who dearly loved a "hanging circuit"; and victims were many in those days, when death was the penalty of a hundred offences. It was in 1780 that he tried a case for murder in Ayr. The prisoner was one Matthew Hay, a farmer by profession, a smuggler by practice, who had killed a man in a scramble. Kames had often played chess with this handsome, dashing, jovial fellow in taverns, and when the verdict of "guilty" was given, he turned to his old companion with a leer and said, "That's checkmate for you, Matthie!"[1] It is such little ebullitions of drollery that his amiable biographer, Lord Woodhouselee, refers to as "due to a certain humorous manner,"[2] and as "the pleasing relaxations of a great mind." One prefers the simplicity of Lord Hermand, who, when he was trying a case of theft, plaintively asked the nefarious female at the bar: "My gude woman, what garred ye steal your neebor's tub?" If only James Boswell had carried out the surely playful wish of Kames that he should write his biography,[3] what a rich picture we should have had of the versatile, ill-tongued judge and his age. But it is doubtful if Kames would have trusted his friend "Jamie." Boswell, calling on him one day, complained that he sometimes was dull. "Homer sometimes nods," graciously remarked the judge; but the instant he saw Bozzy elated at the compliment, he added with a grin: "Indeed, sir, it is the only chance you have of resembling him."[4]

One of the most remarkable figures was this Nestor of literature—the long, gaunt, stooping figure, with toothless jaws bringing nose and chin into close terms; the keen piercing eye, the mouth with Voltairian expression, between a sneer and a smile, from which came the familiar phrase of greeting to acquaintances, "How are ye, ye bruits?" Sometimes the epithet

[1] *Caldwell Papers*, ii. 129. [2] Tytler's *Kames*, ii. 211.
[3] *Boswelliana*, p. 102. [4] *Ibid.* p. 308.

was even more forcible. Each morning he was to be seen proceeding to Court from his house in the Canongate, attended by Sinkum, his favourite caddy, whose stumpy figure, with one leg shorter than the other, which caused him to duck at every step, contrasted with the tall, slouching lord, bending down to hear his companion's gossip of the day.[1] It was on a December day that he finally quitted the old Court, on whose bench he had been so notable a figure for nearly thirty years, giving his not too dignified farewell as he closed the door behind him.[2] Eight days afterwards he was dead—"of old age." He died on 27th December 1782, having his earnest hope fulfilled that he should not survive his faculties, for sight, memory, humour, shrewdness were keen to the last.

Long had he been *doyen* of Scottish literature, and while the world smiled at his oddities, laughed at his jests, doubted his law, ignored his philosophy, and deplored his lack of senatorial dignity, it honoured the old man of the energetic, versatile brain, who had lived brilliantly through a century of varied history, and won a name eminent in his day. When Adam Smith was complimented in England on the array of men of letters who threw lustre on Scotland, "Yes," he answered, "but we must every one of us acknowledge Lord Kames as our master."[3] It must, however, be owned that in that case the grateful pupils very easily surpassed their master. Never was there a more industrious mortal, a more inquisitive person than the old judge, who two days before he died told his friend Dr. Cullen that he wished earnestly to be away, because he was exceedingly curious to learn the nature and manners of the other world. "Doctor," said the indefatigable patriarch, "I never could be idle in this world, I shall willingly perform any task that may be imposed upon me."[4] Thus the restless soul, eager on everything, on drainage or philosophy, poor-laws or poetry, looked forward to heaven—we presume it was

---

[1] Chambers's *Traditions*, ii. 171.
[2] One biographer records that "a few days before his death he came to the Court of Session and addressed all the judges separately, told them he was speedily to depart, and took a solemn and affectionate farewell," (Smellie's *Life of Kames*, p. 148). The tradition is that his only farewell consisted in the touching words: "Fare ye weel, ye b—hes."
[3] Tytler's *Kames*, i. 215.
[4] Smellie's *Lives of Kames, etc.*, 1800, p. 147.

heaven—with serene complacency, ready for any seraphic job or angelic occupation which might or might not suit his mind or his manners.

Lord Monboddo

Between Lord Kames and Lord Monboddo no love was lost : they ridiculed each other's books, jeered at each other's speculations, scorned each other's law, and laughed at each other's hobbies. One night, to stop their quarrelling at Gordon Castle, the Duchess made the two judges dance a harmonious reel together.[1] Kames loved anything that was novel ; Monboddo, though twenty years younger, affected the manners and opinions of the ancients. The only thing they had in common was longevity. But then that faculty of living long seems the peculiarity of the century among men of letters and of law. We find that on these gentlemen who lived in an age when society drank hard and often, death had difficulty in laying its grim, covetous clutches. The two judges were far in their eighties when they died, so were Home and Ferguson, Carlyle and Blair, Tytler, Reid, and Mackenzie, and to be over seventy was a commonplace term of existence in these leisurely old days. Law lords held on to their posts and to life with equal tenacity, and Lord Hermand, in spite of his stupendous drinking, was vigorous till he was eighty-four. As the century was drawing to its close, the venerable form of Lord Monboddo, meagre, emaciated, plain, and toothless, deaf and near-sighted, was one of the quaintest objects in Edinburgh streets and High Street suppers ; with face still shrewd, manners delightfully courteous, and dress old-fashioned. Everybody knew his whims and his foibles, and society enjoyed his talk and his wit.

It was in 1714 that James Burnett was born in the plain, shabby, old house of Monboddo in Kincardineshire. He was educated at Aberdeen University, and Greek he imbibed from Professor Blackwell, famed in those days for his reviving classical learning in the North—an excellent Greek scholar, who fondly believed he had a fine English style. Under this

[1] Ramsay's *Scotland and Scotsmen*, i. 355.

LORD MONBODDO

From the Drawing by John Brown in the Scottish National Portrait Gallery, Edinburgh.

learned and pompous master Burnett learned that ancient Greece was the source of all science and divine philosophy, that beyond it all was darkness, that speculation not based on Aristotle or Plato was utter foolishness. All this profound misinformation the son of the Laird of Monboddo most docilely absorbed, and the belief that the "ancients" were the people, and wisdom died with them, he loyally retained to his dying day.

Being intended for the Bar, after studying in a writer's chambers in Edinburgh, he passed on to Groningen to study Roman Law, and in that sleepy little seat of erudition he remained saturating himself with feudal lore, in class-rooms resonant with the great names of Voet and Noodt, Bynkershoek and Van Eck. Throughout his life he had a profound contempt for every one—including Lord Kames—who had not learned law from Dutch jurists and had never seen the world, having only studied in an advocate's or writer's chamber in a High Street flat. It was an eventful day in 1736 on which he returned to Edinburgh. The mob had broken into the Tolbooth, had dragged the obnoxious Captain Porteous from his refuge, and the stranger was kept awake in the lodgings in the West Bow by the noise of the mob rushing down that narrow street. Going forth attired in little more than his nightgown and cap, he followed the tragic proceedings in the darkness—the surging crowd in the Grassmarket, the writhing figure of the victim in the relentless clutches of the wild mob, the gruesome hanging from the dyer's pole—all these he saw, quite forgetful of the scantiness of his habiliments.[1]

In 1737 he became an advocate, but he was for a while more familiar with social entertainments than with writer's fees. He was at the assemblies dancing minuets with the laborious steps and Batavian grace which he acquired in Groningen, to the amusement of everybody but his partners. He was assiduous in attendance at the theatre, where Gentleman Digges and the fascinating Mrs. Ward were acting; with formal gallantry handing ladies to their seats with the air of an amateur master of ceremonies.[2] At the Bar briefs came slowly to this peculiar counsel; but he had ability and he

[1] Kay's *Edinburgh Portraits*, i. 19.   [2] Ramsay, i. 353.

knew law, so, in spite of whimsicality, he made his way. In 1762 (for many years went by before he had a chance of distinguishing himself) the great Douglas cause began. The question whether Alexander Douglas was really the son of Lady Jane Douglas, and therefore he, and not the Duke of Hamilton, heir to the Douglas estates, was a matter of wildest excitement. Nothing was talked of but that momentous question in every Edinburgh flat; it was the subject of endless debate; it was the source of lifelong friendships and the cause of deadly quarrels in society; and to preserve peace it was necessary to arrange that the subject should not be mentioned in general company. The town was divided into those who were for "Douglas" or for "Hamilton."

Burnett was one of the counsel for the penniless heir, and after making visits to Paris to collect evidence, he returned under the guileless idea that he was a man of fashion. The elderly beau appeared at the Assembly clad in a white velvet suit—"like a Chancellor of France,"[1] he boasted—displaying his splendour, to the delight of spectators, in a minuet with the most grotesque steps which had ever been seen on that floor. The Queensberry influence, which was on the side of the claimant, raised him to the bench when Lord Milton retired, and his legal talents did justice to his patrons. It was while the great Case was pending that he gave a famous dinner to his brother judges. The Duchess of Queensberry had for the occasion sent wine, and also a fine haunch of venison; but the moment the dish was put on table, it assailed so vehemently the noses of the guests that the air became sanitary only when it was mercifully removed. "Monboddo, this is a pretty use to make of the Duchess' wine and venison," said a friend next day. "It is flat bribery and corruption." "Master Davidson," replied his lordship, "I confess much corruption, but no bribery."[2] Great was Monboddo's satisfaction, and wild the joy of Scotland, that day in 1769 when Islay Campbell arrived on horseback from London, and at the Cross waved his hat and shouted "Douglas for ever!" thus announcing that the House of Lords had reversed the narrow decision of the Court of Session and decided in favour of Archibald

[1] Ramsay, i. 351.   [2] Ibid. i. 355; Omond's *Lives of Lord Advocates*, ii. 66.

Douglas, giving the lad his great estates. Boswell headed the mob which smashed the windows of the adverse judges, and the question asked that night, "Douglas or Hamilton?" was put at the point of the sword to every one met on the street.

For years Burnett had been reading and thinking and writing a work more congenial to his mind than any legal business, and in 1773 there was published the first volume of *The Origin and Progress of Language*, a quarto which was the first of six volumes which were to appear in different years, till it was completed in 1792—the world having forgotten the previous tomes before the next was issued. Here were found elaborate and most learned disquisitions on the origin of ideas according to Plato and Aristotle, on the invention of language, on the art of composition,[1] on the original state of man. Society cared little for abstruse speculations, but there was something to amuse it in this formidable work. The primitive man was declared to have lived in a brute state without speech or reason, and possessed of tails like his beast contemporaries. Ingeniously the author traced how in the course of ages the human race gained intelligence and dropped their tails, and by development attained to that state of civilisation of which Greek art and philosophy form the highest point. Wits laughed aloud at him for going against common-sense; the pious mourned at his going against Holy Scripture; judges sneered at their brother on the bench for his ridiculous whims, and Lord Kames with a jeer would ask him to go before him into a room: "Just to see your tail, my lord." They little dreamt that what were the fancies of the eccentric judge were, before a century elapsed, to be the creed of the anthropologist. There is no need, however, to give the good man too much credit for originality. His picture of the primitive man is, as he owns,[2] the same as that which Rousseau had painted in his *Discourse on the Origin of Inequality*. Monboddo is original only in presenting the primitive men with tails. To "anticipate" truth is not to be a discoverer,

---

[1] Monboddo's quality as a literary critic may be judged from his opinion that "Dr. Armstrong's diction (in *The Art of Preserving Health*) is more splendid than that of Milton's *Paradise Lost*" (vol. v. p. 467).

[2] *Origin of Language*, i. 152. Kames said he wondered that Monboddo had not more pride than to swallow a Frenchman's spittle (Ramsay, i. 357).

any more than a dreamer has foresight because his dream comes true. Erasmus Darwin suggested, in his *Lives of the Plants*, that species are modified by adaptation of individuals to suit their wants, but this "anticipation" was only a fancy with him, the merit lay with his grandson Charles, when he eventually proved it a fact. In Monboddo's case, as he anticipates the modern anthropologist, he is only one of those foolish people who are wise before their time.

Among all the ingenious disquisitions of these massive tomes there is a portentous credulity and learned garrulity. Monboddo is convinced that ourang-outangs are of the human species; for he had himself seen at Versailles a specimen preserved in spirits, which, when alive, had shown all the intelligence of a man, and had quite like a rational being died of drink.[1] He upholds his pet theory that men possessed tails on the ground that 130 years before a Swedish skipper was reported to have seen a tribe of human creatures with caudal appendages in the Bay of Bengal. It is difficult to credit that so incautious a pleader in his book should have been really so able and competent a judge on the bench, a shrewd sifter of evidence on multiplepoinding and titles in the Inner House.

Yet one other great work engaged Monboddo's attention amid his legal labours—his *Ancient Metaphysics*, including a History of Mankind, which volume by volume appeared during the course of the years from 1779 to 1799—the last being published a few weeks before his death. Here ancient philosophy is maintained against David Hume—who with him is "an atheist" and a "corrupter of moral teaching"—and against the physical theories of Sir Isaac Newton. To ancient Greece we are told to look for all truth and for all physical and intellectual perfection. The origin of language and art and religion is traced chiefly to Egypt, whence they arose from a race of Dæmon Kings—dæmons being the supernatural beings described by Plato, and "the Sons of God" mentioned by Moses, who intermarried with the "daughters of men." Monboddo is really no evolutionist, for he holds that man was originally endowed with language, reason, religion, but had lost all these by the Fall, when mankind was cursed and degraded. Whether the

[1] *Origin of Language*, i. 189.

pre-Adamite men had tails or not, is left an unsettled point. Even if the ingenious judge could be said to have forestalled the modern theory of development in tracing man from almost brute state, he sadly mars any scientific reputation by whimsically insisting that since the brilliant age of Greece everything has degenerated, and mortals who originally possessed vast strength and longevity have become more and more a puny race. Monboddo prophesies that "in not many generations the race will die out, the miserable remains of the species will be destroyed by a convulsion of nature," and a new heaven and new earth will be formed for a saintly race.[1] Even from subtle disquisitions on metaphysics of the ancients he cannot exclude his darling hobby. He tells most wonderful stories of tribes with tails that exist to-day; he shows from ancient witnesses that there once lived human beings who had the feet of goats and horns on their heads. "We have the authority of a Father of the Church for a greater singularity of the human form, and that is men without feet and with eyes in their breasts."[2] That men with the paws of dogs, and monsters with the head of a man and the body of a lion, had existed, he sees no reason to doubt, because Aristotle has well said, " everything exists or did at one time exist which it is possible to exist."[3] It is unlucky for poor Monboddo that all his ingenuity and Greek learning should be forgotten and only his absurdities remembered. His books are long ago dead, if indeed they can be said ever to have lived, but we may say of them that if they wearied those who read them, they pleased their author and amused society, that never read them at all.

But let us turn from Monboddo the scholar to Monboddo in daily life. There, as in his books, he was the oddest character. In the Inner House he was never seen sitting with his brother judges on the bench, but below among the clerks, and for this a probable reason was given. It happened one time that his horse was mismanaged and died in the hands of the farrier, and he brought an action against the man.

---

[1] *Ancient Metaphysics*, v. ; viii.; vi. 138.
[2] *Ibid.* iv. 48.
[3] *Ibid.* iv. 45 ; *Origin of Language*, i. 262.

Instead of employing counsel, he descended from the bench and pleaded his own cause. After the expenditure of a vast amount of Roman law over the carcase of the quadruped, their lordships decided against their legal brother, and never forgiving the judges, especially Lord President Dundas, he never sat beside them again.[1]

He was seen at his best at Monboddo; there he was "Farmer Burnett," cultivating his acres on an estate of £300 a year; dressed in rustic garb and blue bonnet; the kindliest and absurdest of landlords to those whom he loved to call "my people,"—never removing a tenant or raising a rent, when rents everywhere were rising. "Improvers" like Lord Kames he denounced as "desolators," because they made big farms and depopulated the land of cottagers.[2] At that home and in that garb he was found when Dr. Johnson and Boswell rode from Aberdeen, through the bare, treeless country, and sent a message that they were at the gate. Johnson and he had met before, and they did not love each other. The judge afterwards wrote of the Englishman as "malignant," and sneered at him as a man who "compiled a dictionary of a barbarous language, a work which a man of genius would rather have died of hunger than have undertaken."[3] Johnson on his part laughed hugely at "Monny," as he called him, who was "as proud of his tail as a squirrel."[4] Now they met and they fraternised; the "Dictionary-Maker" grew genial under his host's courteous manner and hospitality in the long, oak-panelled dining-room, both finding grounds of sympathy in their common hatred of David Hume and Bishop Warburton. They parted pleasantly to meet elsewhere.

Topham, the English visitor to Edinburgh in 1776, remarked at the time on the love that the Scotsmen had of travelling to London. That propensity was strong in Monboddo, and after 1780 he went to England every year to meet the

---

[1] Chambers's *Traditions*, ii. 158.
[2] In his garrulous way, in his *Ancient Metaphysics*, he laments the practice of tenants having farm-servants in their houses instead of cottagers. "I could double the rent of the land by letting it to one tenant; but I would be sorry to increase my rent by depopulating any part of the country" (iii. 306).
[3] *Origin of Language*, v. 274.
[4] Ramsay's *Scotland and Scotsmen*, i. 350.

literati, and to join circles of fashion, where he gave immense entertainment by his humours and his ready wit. At Mrs. Montagu's he met Mrs. Hannah More, making her angry by upholding slavery, because Plutarch had approved of it, and by maintaining that *Douglas* was the greatest of tragedies, far excelling Shakespeare, who could never depict a king or a hero.[1] Eagerly he questioned Sir Joseph Banks, if he had during his voyage met with tribes with the primeval tails, and was disconcerted by the naturalist's negative. Old as he became, he made all his journeys on his well-known white steed Alburac—for he considered it ignominous for a man to be dragged at the tail of a horse, instead of riding upon its back; and as for riding in a chaise—a "box" he contemptuously called it—it was grossly effeminate to enter such a vehicle, which was unknown to the ancients. In Edinburgh he would not enter the modern conveyance of a sedan-chair, though, when the rain was pouring as he came out of the Parliament House, he would get his wig put into a chair and walk by its side: it was fit for a wig but not for a man.[2] George III., who knew all the gossip about everybody, was delighted with the old man, when he had him at Windsor—a veteran who, reckless of snow, rain, and stormy blast, would ride the vile roads to London. "Very odd—very odd!" exclaimed his ejaculatory Majesty; "my judges gallop to town on horseback, and my cavalry officers travel snugly in the mail-coach."[3] During one of these visits to the metropolis, the eccentric judge fell in love with that ever lovable Mrs. Garrick, and twice he offered his hand to the great actor's widow, whom everybody liked—a valuable gift which she politely declined.[4] So the widower got on the back of Alburac and placidly cantered back to his home, where truly he needed no brighter inmate than his daughter to shed sunshine.

The suppers in his house in St. John Street, off the Canongate, were memorable. There, under the most genial and courteous of hosts, the best and brightest of Edinburgh society

[1] *Memoirs of Hannah More*, i. 252.
[2] Kay's *Edinburgh Portraits*, ii. 368.
[3] Ramsay's *Scotland and Scotsmen*, i. 359.
[4] Walpole's *Letters*, viii. 297.

was to be found—men of letters, women of fashion. Dr. Gregory, Henry Erskine, Principal Robertson, and Ferguson were there; the merriest voice with broadest Scots that ever issued from lovely lips resounded in the room when the Duchess of Gordon came; blind Dr. Blacklock was present, his body swaying from side to side; and Lady Anne Lindsay sat singing "Auld Robin Gray" as she knew best how to sing it, and she alone knew who wrote it. The light of the company was the host's unmarried daughter, Elizabeth Burnett, adored for her grace, her sweetness, and her beauty. It was there that Robert Burns, in 1787, saw a brilliant company, but none so bright as she. "Well, did you admire the young lady?" asked a friend on his return from the house. "I admired God Almighty more than ever—Miss Burnett is the most heavenly of all His works!" exclaimed the enthusiastic poet. At the age of twenty-five the fragile girl died, and all Edinburgh mourned, and pitied her old father. It is pitiful to think that the one permanent effect of the scholar's devotion to antiquity was probably his daughter's death, for his Spartan regimen, which would not allow her to enter a carriage or a sedan-chair on coming from a dance or concert, was enough to injure a stronger frame than hers. In the country, in the hardest of winters, she was made to ride whatever the day might be, and Monboddo was heard to boast that he and his daughter were on horseback one wretched day, when the only traveller they met was riding with his face to the tail to avoid the blast. It is said that, after she died,[1] his son-in-law covered the portrait to spare the old man's feelings.[2] "Quite right—quite right," said the man of learning, casually looking up from his book. "Let us now go on with Herodotus." These wretched "ancients" were his model for everything. Each morning, after bathing, he must anoint himself with oil, for so the Romans had done of old. (Dr. Johnson, after he was told of that habit,[3] would speak of him with contempt as "that man of grease.") When laid down with illness, he proudly told Henry Mackenzie that it was no common fever he had—"it was a burning fever, a true Roman fever"—deriving profound satisfaction from the

[1] Ramsay, i. 354, 359.   [2] Kay's *Edinburgh Portraits*, ii. 137.
[3] Boswell's *Johnson*, 1848, p. 550.

fact.[1] Famous at his house were the fortnightly suppers, "after the manner of the ancients," the claret flagons garlanded with roses, which also bestrewed the table à la Horace, and the diet of strange fare with Spartan broth and *mulsum*. There he was glorious, pooh-poohing everybody, boasting that he "had forgotten more than most other men had ever known," discussing science with his friends, Joseph Black, the chemist, James Hutton, the geologist, and the rough, unkempt, learned printer, William Smellie, who could speak on anything and wrote on everything.[2] The decorations of the table were antique, but the talk of the guests around it was modern, and as the venerable host took his wine with most alarming frequency, it never impeded his speech, but rather gave it more copious garrulity. While he was becoming deplorably deaf, he never would own that he had lost his hearing; it was, according to him, only the degenerate generation that had lost its voice. Deaf he certainly was. His lordship, being in London, was one day attending the Court of King's Bench, when a false alarm arose that the roof was giving way, upon which judges, barristers, audience all rushed wildly to the door. With perfect composure Lord Monboddo placidly kept his seat, hearing no noise, ignorant of the cause of the tumult. When asked why he sat still, he explained that he thought it was only an annual ceremony connected with English Law Courts, and he was interested to witness this relic of antiquity.[3]

The venerable figure of Monboddo was every year seen on horseback posting off to London, to visit old friends and delight old circles. At last, however, such expeditions were too fatiguing for his shrivelled old body. He was on his way in 1799 to make his annual visit, but only got as far as Dunbar, where he was taken ill, and forced to undergo the ignominy of being conveyed home in the despised chaise. "Oh, George," he said plaintively to his nephew, "I find that I am eighty-four." A few days later, in May, the venerable humorist was dead. Then the world gossiped, according to its fashion, of stories true and false about the old man's humours — how he

---

[1] Clayden's *Early Life of Sam. Rogers*, p. 170.
[2] Kerr's *Life of Smellie*, p. 416; *Guy Mannering* (notes).
[3] Chambers's *Traditions of Edinburgh*, ii. 177.

used to fancy that the tails of babies were snipped off by midwives at their birth, and how he would watch at the bedroom door when a child was born, in order to detect the relics of a primeval ancestry.[1] Others more worthily recalled memorable nights in his society, his sayings of curious wit, his sallies which set the table in a roar, while perfect gravity reigned on his ugly old face; his pleasant ways, his courtly, old-fashioned manners. They missed the familiar form which had trotted up innumerable stairs to merry suppers—the worn-out old figure they had daily seen standing at the door of Creech's shop, or pacing the Parliament Close—the owner of a most kindly heart, the author of most unreadable books.

LORD HAILES

While Lord Kames and Lord Monboddo were sustaining the reputation of Scotland for literary ability, and the character of the Bench for grotesqueness of manners, Lord Hailes did his best to add some dignity as well as learning to the legal body, which sat on the judgment seat with ways not too suggestive of the majesty of the law. These worthies, in spite of their speech and homely habits, were all men of birth; the Bar being a profession considered proper only for a gentleman. It was by sheer dint of brain and will that Robert Macqueen, the son of a country "writer," forced himself to the front of the *noblesse de la robe*, and as Lord Braxfield, Lord Justice Clerk, dominated the Court of Justiciary with the strength of his coarse personality, bullying his brother senators on the bench and the prisoners in the dock, pleaders at the bar and witnesses in the box, with perfect impartiality.

Sir David Dalrymple in his stout little person brought to his profession the rare qualities of dignity, good manners, and a good accent. He belonged to one of those Scottish county families which seemed to supply judges to the Inner House as if by natural right. Dalrymples since the days of Lord Stair, and Dundases even after the days of Lord Melville, were prominent in good places; the best legal offices fell to their claims, the best pickings of patronage came to their hands:

[1] Kay's *Portraits*, i. 19.

LORD HAILES
From the Engraving after Seton.

> First cam' the men o' many wimples,
> In common parlance ca'd Da'rymples;
> And after them cam' the Dundasses,
> Wha raid our gude Scots land like asses.

David Dalrymple, son of Sir James, of New Hailes, was born in 1726, and was educated at Eton, unlike his contemporaries of highest birth, who were content to be taught at parish and burgh schools for 3s. 6d. a quarter. After the usual study at Utrecht, followed by a tour in France, he came home. In those days, when a young man of birth and fortune had mixed with society abroad or in London, he was apt, on his return to Scotland, to be shocked with its homely fashions, the narrowness of its interests, and the breadth of its vernacular. In such supercilious mood Gilbert Elliot of Minto arrived in Edinburgh in 1743 from his Dutch studies, his French travels, and his London visit—a spark and a fop. "Next morning," he writes,[1] "I provided myself in a huge cocked-hat, Parliament House gown, and bob-wig of very formal cut, and made my first appearance at the bar. I yawn all morning at the fore bar. The gentry are a very sensible sort of people, and some of them in their youth seem to have known the world; but by being too long in a place their notions are contracted and their faces are become solemn. The Faculty of Advocates is a very learned and very worthy body. As for the ladies, they are unexceptionable in manner, innocent and beautiful, and of an easy conversation. The staple vices of the place are censoriousness and hypocrisy. There is no allowance for levity, and none for dissipation. I do not find here that unconstrained noble way of thinking and talking which every one meets with among young fellows of plentiful fortune and good spirits who are moving in a more enlarged circle of society." A few years later the young advocate would have less reason to complain, for austerity was passing away and levity was not much restrained in the city.

David Dalrymple, who was grave and prudent, would not, like his friend Gilbert Elliot, feel the restraints of that prim life irksome. He brought with him a scholarship and a legal lore which were highly esteemed, as well as formal manners and

---

[1] *Caldwell Papers*, ii. 115.

English tones which were not esteemed at all by broad-speaking, hilarious brethren in the Parliament House. Of course he made his way at the Bar—could any of the tribe of Dalrymples fail to do so?—in spite of an awkward style and "a weak, ill-tuned voice." But he had the soul of an antiquary. From 1751 he was busy writing tractates and biographies, editing chronicles, ancient poetry, and forgotten authors, sifting chartularies, printing old documents with learned disquisitions. His reputation as a scholar and a critic was so good that modestly David Hume wished him to revise his *Inquiry into the Human Mind;* but Sir David was orthodox, and to assist a sceptic was no task for him. In 1766 he was raised to the bench, taking the title of Lord Hailes, and the ability and pains which served him well as an antiquary were displayed as a judge—with a painful proneness to insist on little points and to forget main issues, which made lawyers grumble and advocates sneer at his pedantry. "Him! he kens only the nooks o' a cause,"[1] growled Lord Braxfield. It was never forgotten that he dismissed a cause because a document had the word "justice" spelt without the final "e."[2] He sat on the bench, the most humane of judges, in days when "hanging circuits" were the delight of Kames and Braxfield; and he was the most polite and sober of law lords in hard-drinking days, when the faces of legal luminaries were as red as their robes.

Law work did not interfere with the antiquarian labours of Hailes, who studied even when riding in his coach, and went on writing and editing books which fill formidable columns of library catalogues—productions which, being of a class for which the public did not yearn, were issued at his lordship's own charges. That was an age when the literary bent of Scotsmen was towards history—such as Hume, Robertson, Ferguson, Henry, his kinsman Sir John Dalrymple, and his friend William Tytler of Woodhouselee, whose *Inquiry into the Evidence against Queen Mary,* in 1759, perturbed the serene temper of David Hume so keenly that

---

[1] Ramsay's *Scotland and Scotsmen*, i. 397.
[2] To judge of this matter I cannot pretend,
   For justice, my lord, wants an "e" at the end.
(Boswell's "Court of Session Garland," in Chambers's *Traditions of Edin.* ii. 172.)

he would leave a room if he found his little antagonist there.¹ Lord Hailes naturally followed the taste of his countrymen, and became busy over his *Annals of Scotland from the Accession of Malcolm Canmore.* Through the medium of James Boswell he transmitted, for revision of the style, the proof-sheets to Dr. Johnson, to whom Bozzy had so often praised his lordship as a "lawyer and a Christian," a scholar and a wit, that the lexicographer was moved to drink a bumper to the health of the legal paragon. We find his lordship referring to his solemn judgment the grave point whether the adjective " free " or " brave " should be used to describe the Scots—a nervous anxiety which is almost pathetic, as not one mortal could possibly care, in his excellent but not alluring diction, what epithets he used.² In 1776 the first volume appeared of a work in which early sources of Scottish history were examined and sifted with admirable acuteness and impartiality, and a connected narration was woven out of disputed documents. Many a venerable story and cherished tradition were demolished or banished to mythland. Hitherto the field had been the preserve of unconscionable pedants like Ruddiman, who warred with party animosity, and in temper as atrocious as their style, over charters and "claims" and pedigrees. Now this "restorer of Scottish History," as Sir Walter Scott has called him, lifted research into the domain of history. The *Annals* are dry, deplorably dry; but invaluable still for facts—a quarry in which later writers have dug for material out of which to build more artistic works.

In the fine library at New Hailes the judge was busy editing and compiling; composing careful pieces of elegance for the *World;* translating Church Fathers, with erudite disquisitions dedicated to Anglican bishops; writing a learned answer to Gibbon's famous Fourteenth Chapter of his *Decline and Fall,* with a learning and ability which are more than respectable. The fastidious accuracy of mind which spoiled Hailes as a lawyer and made him tedious as a judge suited him well as an antiquary.

An estimable man was this scholar; but a little less self-

---

¹ Burgon's *Life of P. F. Tytler*, p. 69.
² Boswell's *Johnson*, 1848, p. 413.

consciousness would have improved his lordship, who kept aloof from the genial society of Edinburgh lest it might impair his flawless dignity. Distant in manner, he was seldom met with even in the company of Ferguson and Blair and Adam Smith for such friendly comradeship would jar on his prim punctiliousness, and vex his due regard for what was "becoming."[1] That David Hume should so abuse his position as keeper of the Advocates' Library as to add to its spotless shelves the lewd works of La Fontaine and Crébillon called forth his condign censure; for he and Monboddo, being curators, were nervous about the morals of the Bar—for which prudery the philosopher called them "old wives." Much as Dr. Johnson respected "dear Lord Hailes," it is evident that the moralist would on this question have sided with his pet antipathy, David Hume; for when referring one day to Hailes having written of the "impure poems of Matthew Prior as worthy of eternal opprobrium, "No, sir," said Johnson to Boswell—"no, sir, Prior is a lady's book. No lady is ashamed to have it standing in her library."[2] From which we may infer that the feminine taste of that age was wondrous tolerant.

Lord Hailes preferred to live at New Hailes rather than in the Canongate, driving the five miles to Court every morning in his handsome coach. In his later years he was a short, stout person, with thick, short neck, of apoplectic appearance, fat cheeks, and pursy mouth. Self-possessed and placid,[3] he would preside at his dinner-parties, at which probably Dr. Carlyle of Inveresk was present to say grace; and he proved an admirable host to his guests, who admired his wide knowledge, listened to his excellent and decorous anecdotes, drank of his good wine, and at a seemly hour rode home unsatisfactorily sober. When Lord Hailes died of apoplexy in 1792, the country lost a great store of gentlemanly learning and the bench much good law; but the gaiety of the Scottish capital was not eclipsed.

[1] Ramsay's *Scotland and Scotsmen*, i. 410.
[2] Boswell's *Johnson*, 1848, p. 559.
[3] Kay's *Edinburgh Portraits*.

CHAPTER VIII

JAMES BOSWELL

AMID the respectable, sedate, though genial company of men of letters in Edinburgh, who had their humorous ways, their frugal means, and sober refections at dinner and supper, there bustled by day, and issued noisily from tavern by night, the pompous, fussy, self-important figure of Mr. James Boswell, advocate. His eyes goggled with a humorous twinkle which belied the air of portentous seriousness in his pursy mouth; his cheeks were baggy as half-filled wine-skins; his face was rubicund with frequent hock, and his figure paunchy from sumptuous fare. There was a curious serio-comic air about this person who was anxious to be a personage. He was at ease in all companies, and could suit himself to any society: grave with learned lords, roystering with rakish blades, ready to talk history with Principal Robertson and cock-fighting with Deacon Brodie, to discuss moral principles with Dr. Johnson and exchange badinage with neither principles nor morals with Jack Wilkes, eager to enter St. Paul's with deepest emotion on Good Friday and to come out of the Soaping Club any Friday night vocal with fatuous songs. Inquisitive as Paul Pry, no rebuff could daunt him and no reserve repress him. Nothing "put him out"; there was never anything embarrassed about him—except his affairs. He was considered by his Edinburgh friends, withal, a pleasant rattle, an entertaining companion, a clever fellow, gifted with boundless literary ambition. His early inane productions, however, did not cause any man of letters to dream that this idle, tattling, bibulous lawyer, without law, would one day produce a work destined to be immortal, when their own books, so admired, so celebrated in their day, were dead and forgotten.

Never was the law of heredity more impudently flouted than by the irrepressible, irresponsible son of a stolid Scots judge, as if he had been produced by nature in one of her most facetious moods. Lord Auchinleck was a heavy, solid character, who spoke much good sense in uncouth Scots, and much good law in very bad English. Plain-spoken, he could call a spade a spade, though, being vernacular, he called a spade a "shule." Gifted with a rough tongue and caustic humour, there was a salt in his sentences and a vigour in his contempts under which his errant son James had often cause to wince. That this clumsy, plain senator and laird had in his youth followed the pranks of fashion at which he snorted gibes in his old age, seemed so deliciously incongruous that when it was told that Auchinleck, after studying law abroad, had sported red-heeled shoes and red stockings, his son nearly fell off his chair with most irreverent laughter.[1]

One follows the career and studies the character of Mr. James Boswell with regretful amusement. Born in 1740 in Edinburgh, tutored by the worthy minister of Auchinleck, educated at the High School and Edinburgh College, he showed, before he was out of his teens, that he was "happily possessed of a facility of manners,"[2] as, to his satisfaction, Mr. Adam Smith informed him. We find him at the early age of eighteen assuming the airs of a man of letters, and describing to his friend Temple, with delightful complacency, his introduction to Mr. David Hume, "the most affable, discreet man as ever I met with, and has really a great deal of learning. We talked of genius, fine language, improving our style, etc., but I am afraid solid learning is much worn out."[3] Thus does the *blasé* youth of venerable eighteen give his verdict on literature; and yet he was at the time attending the lodging of Mr. Love the actor, humbly to learn elementary elocution and a decent pronunciation of the English tongue. The result of the instructions of the impecunious gentleman, who took his fees and borrowed his money, we can guess from Dr. Johnson's

---

[1] Ramsay's *Scotland and Scotsmen*, i. 161.   [2] *Ibid.* i. 161.
[3] *Letters between Hon. A. Erskine and James Boswell, Esq.*, 1762, p. 41.

JAMES BOSWELL
From the Portrait by Dance in the National Portrait Gallery, London.

dubious praise of his young friend's attempts at English accents : " Sir, your pronunciation is not often offensive."

Was it to keep the facile youth from the temptations of the capital, its play-actors and its taverns, that Lord Auchinleck sent his son to college in the demure city of Glasgow? If so, the result was a lamentable failure. While James Boswell was attending Adam Smith's stimulating lectures on ethics in the University, he was also attending theatres and mixing with actors, and, fascinated with popery, attending worship in the Roman Catholic chapel. His studies on moral philosophy, and interest in the drama and the chapel, ended in his running off to London with an actress of the Roman Catholic persuasion. His indignant father followed his errant son in a rage, and a post-chaise, and there was at first more difficulty in persuading him to give up his new creed than his mistress. Sir John Pringle, the eminent physician and ex-moral philosopher of Edinburgh, was engaged to reason with the youth. He pointed out that the papistry would ruin his prospects, that he would never succeed at the Bar, never be a sheriff, far less a judge. Bozzy grandiosely maintained that he cared not for his earthly prospects, but for the safety of his immortal soul. "Your immortal soul, sir!" the quondam Professor of Moral Philosophy is alleged to have exclaimed; "why, any one with the smallest spark of gentlemanly spirit would rather be damned to all eternity than give his relations and friends so much trouble as you are doing now!"[1] Whether these fine moral considerations weighed with him or not, the ailment of Catholicism passed away; and as for the nameless charmer, like Mr. Gibbon he sighed as a lover and obeyed like a son.

While he was in London he determined to see life, and found a disreputable companion in Samuel Derrick. This friend dabbled in poetry and in drink, and was not unfamiliar with a night in a gutter after an evening in a tavern—which did not disqualify him for succeeding Beau Nash as Master of Ceremonies at Bath, when, attired in the height of fashion, he would walk out attended by a man in livery, and carefully cross

[1] Grant Duff's *Notes of a Diary*, 1873-1881, i. 194 ; on J. Hill Burton's authority.

and recross the streets to show everybody that he kept a footman.[1]

Lord Eglinton rescued his young friend from such shabby company, and he was introduced to the *beau monde*, in which he naturally chose rakes that misled him, seasoned heads that out-drank him, and wild bloods at Newmarket who laughed at him. Profoundly unconscious of being a fool, he printed a fatuous doggerel piece, the "Cub of Newmarket"—of which he is the "Cub" and the hero—and dedicated it to the fiddling Duke of York. How coarse, how grossly provincial now seemed Edinburgh to the youth living in fine society! "How horrible," as he observed to the confidant of all his sillinesses, "to conform to every Scottish custom"; to hear once more the terrible, broad, familiar accents asking, "Will ye hae some jeel [the atrociously vulgar form for jelly]?" Why, consorting with such dull company was "like yoking a Newmarket winner to a dung-cart."[2]

Back, however, he must come to the parental roof and the paternal reprimands, and begin to study law. But there were still pleasures for him, to which he condescended; there were meetings of the Soaping Club, with its idiotic motto, "Every man soap his own beard"—supposed equivalent for "Every man in his own humour"—with its alluring game of "snip-snap-snorum," its jovial drinking, and its junketing at Tom Nicholson's dingy tavern at the West Bow. For this bibulous brotherhood the youthful Boswell, as worshipful laureate, wrote songs, and lustily sang them, as in these strains:

> Boswell, of Soapers the King,
> On Tuesdays at Tom's does appear,
> And when he does talk and does sing,
> To him ne'er a one can come near.
>
> He talks with such ease and such grace,
> That all charmed to attention do sit,
> And he sings with such comic a face,
> That our sides are just ready to split.

Then, after plentiful carousing, he and his comrades would walk home, rolling out Bacchanalian lays at the full pitch of their voices. Was there ever such a preposterous youth?

---

[1] Taylor's *Records of my Life*, i. 9.   [2] Boswell's *Letters*, p. 14.

His literary vanity he was meanwhile indulging by writing rigmarole "occasional verses," which he printed with puffing epistles by friends; and perpetrating an "Ode to Tragedy," which he published anonymously and dedicated "To James Boswell, Esquire"—to himself!

It was in 1763 that he set forth from Auchinleck, in Ayrshire, to London on an ever-memorable journey. He had thoughts of entering the Guards—he liked its uniform and its high society—though never of "heroic blood"; but this scheme fell through. His father had given him a growling permission and sardonic counsel, and the youth of twenty-two years departed, attired in "a cocked hat and brown wig, a brown coat made in court fashion, a red vest, corduroy small clothes, long military-looking boots, with his servant riding at most aristocratic distance behind."[1] Arriving in London, he sought out former friends and familiar haunts; but there was one great object now looming in his mind—that was to meet Mr. Samuel Johnson. Three years ago he was riding in a chaise with his father and Sir David Dalrymple (afterwards Lord Hailes), the advocate-depute, when they were on circuit. On that occasion Sir David spoke to his young friend of Mr. Johnson as a great writer in London. "This grew up," says Bozzy grandly, "in my fancy into a mysterious veneration, by feigning to myself a solemn, elevated abstraction in which I supposed him to live in the immense metropolis of London." Now the hour and the man arrived. He had made acquaintance with Mr. Thomas Davies, the old actor, now bookseller in Great Russell Street, who knew the lexicographer well, and could copy his big voice and uncouth gestures to the life. Perhaps, too, Boswell was a little attracted to the shop by the presence of Mrs. Davies, who had also been on the stage; and as he walked towards Covent Garden the lines of Churchill may have been softly murmured by him, "Upon my life, Tom Davies has a very pretty wife."

"It was on Monday, the 16th of May," he records, "when I was sitting in Mr. Davies' back parlour, after having drank tea with him and Mrs. Davies, Johnson unexpectedly came into the shop, and Mr. Davies, having perceived him through the

[1] *Edinburgh Literary Journal*, ii. 327.

glass door in the room in which we were sitting, advancing towards us, he announced his awful approach to me. . . . Mr. Davies mentioned my name, and respectfully introduced me. I was much agitated, and recollecting his prejudices against the Scotch, I said to Davies, "Don't tell where I come from." "*From Scotland,*" cried Davies roguishly. "Mr. Johnson," said I, "I do indeed come from Scotland, but I cannot help it." "That, sir, I find is what a very great many of your countrymen cannot help." At which retort the apologetic Scotsman owns he was "a good deal stunned." The interview ended in the youth—obsequious and reverential—ingratiating himself with the great man, whose friendship he was determined to cultivate. Calling at his house in the Temple, he found the illustrious man in his shabby chambers, clad in rusty brown suit, little, old, shrivelled, unpowdered wig, the shirt neck and knees of his breeches untied, his black worsted stockings half drawn up, displaying inches of his bare calves, and his feet shod in an old pair of unbuckled shoes. In this abode Boswell made himself agreeable and deferential. He flattered the great man, pleased the blind poetess, Mrs. Williams, who was sheltered under his roof; took copious dishes of tea (in each of which the lady stuck a not immaculate finger to feel if it was full) and drank them as draughts Heliconian. He was careful of Hodge, the cat that purred on the Doctor's knee; attentive to Francis Barber, the black servant that opened the Doctor's door. He stimulated his distinguished friend to talk, and when he got home, wrote down everything he had said.

These strangely assorted companions—the Scots rake of twenty-two and the English moralist of sixty—soon went everywhere together. ("Sir, I love you," the great man said to his parasite.) They met at the Mitre and the Turk's Head, where wits did congregate. Wonder arose among Johnson's friends who this new acquaintance might be. "Who is this Scots cur at Johnson's heels?" some one asked of Goldsmith. "Not a cur but a burr," answered Oliver; "Tom Davies flung him at Johnson in sport, and he has the faculty of sticking."[1]

While the young man was frequenting Johnsonian com-

[1] Forster's *Life of Goldsmith,* i. 330.

pany, Lord Auchinleck was waxing wroth at his son wasting his time instead of studying law. Nor can his stolid soul have been pacified by a preposterous publication, *Letters between the Hon. Andrew Erskine and James Boswell, Esq.*, which came forth in 1763—rollicking letters such as two silly young blades might write, and only two young fools could publish. Ominous threats came from the irate judge, and to soften his obdurate heart the son wrote pleadingly to Sir David Dalrymple to intercede. " I thank God I ever got acquainted with Mr. Johnson. He has assisted me to obtain peace of mind, and he has assisted me to become a rational Christian. I hope I shall ever remain so." His lordship, whatever his thoughts of the likelihood of Jamie being a " Christian," must have had his grim doubts of his son's chances of ever being a " rational " one. There was, however, some satisfaction that his unstable offspring had so respectable a mentor in Mr. Johnson, whose counsels regarding a project of his travelling abroad were retailed to Sir David. " He is a great enemy to a settled plan of study. He advises me to go to places where there is most to be seen and learned. He would have me perambulate (a word of his own style) Spain," and so on. Thus did Boswell write to his learned friend, with the adroit purpose of dissuading his father from sending him to a dull Dutch college. In pursuance of parental desire, however, James Boswell started forth to prosecute his law studies at Utrecht for two years, under the laborious Professor Trotz—his distinguished friend going to Harwich to see him embark ; and Bozzy tells how he kept his eyes fixed upon the sage as the ship sailed off, while " he rolled his majestic frame " on the shore.

Legal studies did not detain Boswell beyond a year in the sleepy Dutch city; he yawned as good Trotz ponderously delivered his Latin lectures on the " Pandects," wearied of Batavian-built *vrows* and their husbands, with portly forms, and " clothes which they wore as if they were luggage." So he set forth on farther travels to " perambulate " Europe on a comfortable allowance of £240 a year. We see him at the British Embassy at Berlin, where his father's friend, Sir Andrew Mitchell, was representative, mixing, in bland assurance, with diplomatists and dignitaries of all sorts and countries; then travelling in Italy with Lord Mountstuart, who admired his "noble sentiments"; at length he reached Corsica, where Paoli was fighting for the independence of his country. Bozzy's vanity was flattered by the rumour that he was a secret envoy from Great Britain, and he posed, with imperturbable composure, as a great man; had guards to attend him, and charmed the natives by wearing the Corsican costume and singing Scots ballads and Jolly Tar songs about "Hearts of Oak." He won his resistless way—with a letter of introduction from Rousseau, to whom he had ingratiated himself at Neuchâtel—into General Paoli's home and confidence; plied him with "ten thousand questions," of which the simple-hearted hero did not perceive the supreme impertinence. Years ago his play-acting, sponging friend, Mr. Love, had advised him to keep an exact diary of what he said and heard. This plan he had tried on Lord Hailes; now he practised it on the patriot, as he was doing with Dr. Johnson, and his notebook was filled nightly with his records. He left the island with great enthusiasm for the people, and with large materials for a book; and at last returned home, having visited Rousseau at Neuchâtel, where he heard his diatribes against everybody; having seen Voltaire at Ferney, where he was regaled with epigrams from the weazened old satirist.

He crossed the Channel, taking charge of Thérèse la Vasseur, who was on her way to rejoin Rousseau, whom David Hume had, to his cost, brought over to England. See him now in London, inflated by his adventures, and getting himself announced in the newspapers as "Mr. Boswell, the celebrated traveller"; and in his ridiculous Corsican attire waiting on Mr. Pitt, who received with courtesy and well-preserved gravity this the only Briton who could give news of that island, which involved political interests. The stupendous confidence of the youth was shown by his beginning a correspondence with the "Great Commoner," and begging the pleasure of "hearing from him now and then." Nothing did he talk of but his great travels and the noble Paoli, till Dr. Johnson could stand it no longer, and bade him "get Corsica out of his head."

At last the prodigal returned home, receiving a welcome not quite scriptural from his father, who further was disgusted by this fuss over a "land-loupin' chief," and growled to his friends that "Jamie has begun a toot on a new horn." However, Boswell, to Lord Auchinleck's satisfaction, settled down to study his Erskine's *Institutes* and the *Corpus Juris Civilis;* passed for the Bar—that was in 1766—and within a year made respectable fees by glib speeches before their lordships—for writers were shrewd enough to employ an advocate who was the friend of every judge and whose father sat upon the bench. He found literary company at the tables of Hume and Robertson, of Kames and Monboddo; he frequented the Select Society, and jovial company which was not select at the Soaping Club. Everybody laughed at "Paoli Boswell," as he delighted to be called, and deemed him an incorrigible ass—were they wrong? Even his father called him by that ignoble term, on which he rejoined, "No, sir, not an ass; only a colt, the foal of an ass." To be button-holed by him in Parliament Close; to listen to his pompous speeches about all he had seen and done and said; to be asked, "Have you seen my new prologue?" "Have you read my impromptu on Lord Alemore?" was a daily experience. His face was gaining already its hues of red, his figure showed a tendency to paunchiness, his confidential voice was becoming more consequential, as he revealed profound secrets to a friend's ear which would be poured into a dozen ears before an hour was over. Yet there was much that was likeable about the man; he was a "comical dog, to be sure." "Boswell is a man who I believe never left a house without leaving a wish for his return," said Johnson. "He is very good-humoured, very agreeable, and very mad," said David Hume.[1] "It is no wonder Mr. Boswell was universally well received," records old, gossipy John Taylor[2]; "he was full of anecdotes, well acquainted with the most distinguished characters, good-humoured, and ready at repartee. There was a jovial bluntness in his manner which threw off all restraint with strangers and immediately kindled social familiarity."

Unfortunately, the wholesome influence of his "revered friend" Johnson could not subdue the exuberance of Bozzy's

---

[1] Burton's *Life of Hume*, ii. 307.
[2] Taylor's *Records of my Life*, i. 216.

spirits. When the news of the decision of the House of Lords on the famous Douglas case arrived in Edinburgh the excitement was wild. Boswell, who had been one of the junior counsel in the House of Lords, headed the mob which broke the windows of the judges whose verdict was reversed, and his father, with tears in his eyes, besought the Lord President to lock up his incorrigible son in the Tolbooth Prison.[1]

In 1768 appeared *An Account of Corsica, by James Boswell, Esq.*, and the result was immediate success. Everybody read it; even the fastidious Horace Walpole praised this book " by a strange fellow, who has a rage for knowing everybody that was ever talked of." The historical part is dull, but the tour in which Paoli is Boswellised is certainly entertaining. In the fulness of notoriety the author bustled up to town, where "my book has an amazing popularity," to receive congratulations, and he took care to have his arrival heralded by paragraphs in the *Public Advertiser*. " 28th February: James Boswell, Esq., is expected in town." "24th March: James Boswell, Esq., yesterday arrived from Scotland at his lodgings at Half Moon Street, Piccadilly." Puffed up like a pouter pigeon, he went from house to house prating of his doings and his tour. " I am really a great man now," he wrote to his friend Temple. " I have David Hume in the forenoon, and Mr. Johnson in the afternoon. I give admirable dinners and good claret, and the moment I go abroad again I set up my chariot."[2] It is to Mr. Temple, an old class-mate at College, now an English clergyman, who took life and its duties very easily, that Bozzy reveals himself in the packet of letters rescued from a shop in Boulogne, where they were being used to wrap up parcels of butter. All that a man with any self-respect would keep from mortal ear he babbles forth to his friend,—his maudlin sentiments, his paternal squabbles, his moral "aberrations," his amours, his "irregularities" and his lachrymose penitence. After each lapse from virtue or sobriety he is sure to make devout promises of amendment. Just as after each carouse

---

[1] Ramsay's *Scotland and Scotsmen*, i. 170. While the case was proceeding in the House of Lords in 1767, *Dorando, A Spanish Tale*, giving the Douglas story thinly disguised, was published, for which the publisher was summoned before the Court of Session. Boswell the author escaped under his anonymity.

[2] *Letters to Temple*, p. 151.

he had his headaches, so after each irregularity he has his conscientious qualms, which are only Mr. Boswell's moral headaches that come in the morning and vanish at noon. If he gets drunk he pours out remorse in hiccoughing piety, and maunders out, "This is not worthy of Mr. Johnson." He had taken a resolution under "a solemn yew-tree"[1] to keep to his one bottle of hock; but alas, he has to own that he got wild —"not drunk, but intoxicated"—and very ill next day; and with grave reprehension on his native land, he remarks, "The drunken manners of this country are very bad." We know well that some heroic resolve is certain to be followed by some excess in liquor, and each bibulous excess, by another heroic resolve. One day he has a jovial mood, and he confesses he is really growing a "drunkard"; another day he has an altrabilious mood, and he gains sweet, but irrelevant consolation in the words, "Seek ye the Lord while He may be found." He protests that he "must not behave in a manner unworthy of Paoli's friend"; whereupon "Paoli's friend" lapses miserably. He reminds one of a man who, in his cups, cannot keep his balance, but tries to walk with preternatural erectness, deliberation, and solemnity, and then falls prone in the gutter, protesting with a dignity, slightly impaired by incoherence, that his habits are perfectly sober. He had, too, his fits of melancholy, frequent depression of spirits which should, but somehow do not, move us to sympathy; but there was considerable satisfaction to their victim in thinking that these moods were fresh points of likeness to the sage of Bolt Court.

Most characteristic of vainglorious Boswell was his appearance at the Shakespeare Jubilee at Stratford-on-Avon, that ridiculous celebration set up by Garrick, who was master of the revels. He supplied a description of himself in the *London Magazine* thus: "One of the most remarkable masks was James Boswell, Esq., in the dress of a Corsican chief. He entered the amphitheatre about twelve o'clock. He wore a short, coloured coat of coarse cloth, scarlet waistcoat and breeches, and black spatter-dashes; his cap was of black cloth, on the front of it was embroidered in gilt letters *Viva la Liberta!* on the one side of it was a blue feather and

[1] *Letters*, p. 210.

cockade, so that it had an elegant, as well as war-like appearance. He had also a cartridge pouch, in which was stuck a stiletto, and on the left side a pistol was hung upon the belt of his cartridge pouch. He had a fusil slung across his shoulders; wore no powder on his hair, but had it plaited at full length, with a knot of blue ribbon at the end of it. He had, by way of staff, a very curious vine, all of one piece, emblematical of the Sweet Bard of Avon. So soon as he entered the room he drew universal attention." And so on the egregious person proceeds, telling whom he accosted, whom he danced with, how he demeaned himself—his own verses are puffed, and his portrait in costume is inserted. Alas! the day and its mummeries were spoilt, for it poured cats and dogs—costumes were soaked, the company was drenched, the river rose in flood, and the grounds were laid in water. It was disappointing; but it had its compensations. "It was like an artichoke," philosophised Mr. Boswell, "we have a few mouthfuls, but also swallow the leaves and the hair, which are difficult of digestion. After all I was highly delighted with my artichoke." The strange creature never knew when he was making a fool of himself.

Thus for a while he went on attending taverns, waiting on Dr. Johnson, hunting out every one with a scrap of celebrity, enjoying the delicacies of the table and the indelicacies of the clubs. Everybody of note and letters he entertained in more senses than one. Reynolds, Lord Nugent, Churchill, John Wilkes met at his board, and he felt himself the equal of any. "John Wilkes and I sat together, each glass of wine produced a flash of wit like gunpowder thrown into the fire—puff —puff," he records in his Commonplace Book, where the specimens complacently treasured of his own wit are often fatuous.[1]

Never was there a more inflammable being, or one distracted by more fluctuating sentiments. Five damsels at once won his attentions. They were truly cosmopolitan—Dutch, Irish, English, and Scottish—and to these he paid his addresses, after having carefully appraised their fortunes, and toasted them with amorous inebriety at the Soaping Club. Among those who attracted this erratic amorist in later years was the

[1] *Boswelliana*, p. 322.

handsome and notorious Mrs. Rudd, whom he visited in prison, and who visited him out of it,[1] after her accomplices, the brothers Perreau, had been hanged for forgery,—an operation which Boswell, who dearly loved a hanging, did not fail to witness and greatly enjoy. Observe the fine tact and delicacy of the suitor in his directions to the Rev. Mr. Temple, how to puff his merits to the adorable Miss Blair:[2] "Praise me for my good qualities, you know them, but talk also how odd, how impetuous, how much accustomed to women of intrigue. Ask gravely, 'Don't you imagine there is something of madness in that family?' Talk of my travels—Voltaire, Rousseau." Surely there was at least one case of "madness" in "that family." No wonder his irascible parent was indignant at such an amazing son, his idleness and his folly, his debts and his vagaries. It was bad enough for the dour Presbyterian and Whig to have a son a Jacobite and an Episcopalian, without any other trials. As his lordship told Dr. Johnson, when he sat at his table, that Cromwell had "garred kings ken they had a lith (a joint) in their necks," so he did not cease to warn Jamie that there was a "lith" in the settlement of his property, which might be broken if he did not mend his ways, for it was more than flesh and blood could stand, especially from his own flesh. At last Boswell's attentions, if not his heart, were fixed, and in 1769 he married his cousin, Miss Montgomery. The same day there took place another wedding, which was duly recorded in the *Scots Magazine:* "25th November: at Edinburgh, Alexander Boswell, Esq., of Auchinleck, one of the Lords of Session, to Miss Betty Boswell, second daughter of John Boswell of Balmuto, deceased." There was a fine sardonic and malicious humour in this judge of sixty years of age. Now his son was forced for a while to settle down to practise at the bar, though with doubtful success, and to join in the simple customs of the town. Very little work did he do, and he seems to have been utterly dependent on the untender mercies of his father, whose estimable wife felt little love for her stepson. He mingled the levities of the city with sedate attendance at Dr. Black's lectures on chemistry —a study "which Dr. Johnson recommends." A flat in

[1] Fitzgerald's *Life of Boswell*, i. 221. [2] *Letters.* p. 198.

James' Court became the residence of Boswell as a married man. One entered the home by an entry on the level of the High Street, and found oneself on the fourth story of a house built on the slope of the hill looking over the tops of elm-trees across to the Fife coast. There in 1771 he was proud to entertain General Paoli, and show him all the sights and all the *literati* in the town.

We come now to the crowning glory of Bozzy's career. On various visits to London—ostensibly on law business—he had mixed with all the notabilities of the day: he had been admitted to the Literary Club by the overpowering influence of Dr. Johnson, though he was not received with effusion. "A bore," said Topham Beauclerc; "a burr," grumbled Oliver Goldsmith; "a buffoon," sneered Andrew Murphy. But once he entered the charmed circle he was found to be a most "clubable man," bringing unfailing good humour to the company. During that London visit he had successfully urged his friend and mentor to make a tour in Scotland, and travel as far as the Hebrides, a wild region unknown to English travellers, and whose attractions might seem slight to a Londoner whose ideals of scenery were houses in Fleet Street, and the "full tide of humanity" at Charing Cross.

It was in February 1773 that Dr. Johnson arrived at Boyd's White Horse Inn in the Canongate, and there the faithful Boswell found the illustrious stranger in a rage at the Scots waiter for lifting the lump of sugar with dirty fingers to sweeten his lemonade, which the Doctor flung out of the window.[1] He was conducted to Mr. Boswell's flat, with its spacious rooms, where he stayed, to Mrs. Boswell's hardly-concealed annoyance, which she conveyed to her lady friends by her emphatic verdict that "he was a great brute!" She could not endure his splutterings, his contortions, his irregular hours, his habit of turning lighted candles with the wicks downwards to make them burn the brighter, making her best carpets patchworks of grease and wax. That the sage was not a social success is very evident from information which is not furnished by Mr. Boswell. He dictated to his entertainers, bullied their guests, and laid down the law on every possible

[1] Boswell's *Johnson* (edit. Hill), v. 22.

thing. Ladies were timid, professors were silent in his overpowering presence, and all were deferential, almost obsequious, to escape his tongue. It was noted that Mr. Crosbie, the lawyer, alone "stood up" to him; while the literary and legal magnates—Robertson, Blair, Kames, and Monboddo—were meek before him. David Hume had only quitted that James' Court the year before for St. Andrew Square, having lived in the very stair in which the Boswells dwelt, else the portly bodies of the moralist and the philosopher might have come in collision in the turnpike staircase.[1] Scotsmen of fashion and men of letters thought little of his English breeding; he disgusted hosts by his manner, and hostesses by his manners. What could they say, Whigs as they were, as the Tory vociferated at the table of a Lord of Session: "Sir, George the First was a robber, George the Second was a brute, George the Third is an idiot!"[2] Yet how deferential he was at the evening party at James' Court to the old Duchess of Douglas, stupid and illiterate, whom Johnson describes as "talking broad Scots with a paralytic voice, scarce understood by her own countrymen." There he was, devoting his uncouth attention to her vulgar old Grace, whose unintelligible stupidity Boswell translated for the ear of his guest.[3]

All this was true; but what triumph was it for Bozzy to introduce his distinguished companion to the great persons in Edinburgh? to point out to his purblind vision the sights of the capital; to conduct him arm-in-arm to the Parliament Close, and pose before his brother advocates as the bosom friend of a very great man; although he was taken aback by Henry Erskine, with gross frivolity, slipping a shilling into his hand, saying it was payment "for a sight of his bear." Right glad was Mrs. Boswell when she saw the broad back of the learned rambler turned, as he set forth on his journey with her spouse, in his huge brown coat with vast capacious pockets able to contain two volumes folio, in his huge boots, and bearing his big English oak stick. The poor lady, who had

[1] Not the same flat, as was supposed by J. H. Burton, *Letters of David Hume* (edited by Hill), p. 119, note.
[2] *Jacobite Lairds of Gask*, p. 395.
[3] Topham's *Letters from Edinburgh*, p. 138; Wilson's *Memorials of Old Edinburgh*, i. 257.

no little cleverness and some sense of dignity, had been disgusted at her husband grovelling before his master. She protested that she " had often seen a bear led by a man, but never till now had she seen a man led by a bear "[1]—which sentence vexed him with its sneer, but pleased his sense of humour.

The travels in the North, are they not chronicled for all time in Johnson's *Journey to the Western Islands*, and in his friend's infinitely more lively *Tour to the Hebrides*, with those dramatic touches, so inimitable, which make it and the Biography deathless? As the strange pair perambulated the north of Scotland, in the south Lord Auchinleck was grumbling over his son's new vagary.[2] "Jamie has gaen clean gyte. What do you think, man? He's dune wi' Paoli—he's aff wi' the land-loupin' scoondrel o' a Corsican. Whae's tail do ye think he has preened himsel' tae noo? A dominie man!—an auld dominie, wha keepit a schŭle and caa'ed it an Acaademy!" After being eighty-three days in the North Bozzy brought his friend to Auchinleck, the paternal home in Ayrshire, surrounded by its fine woods, of which the laird was so proud, that he would get up at five o'clock in the morning to prune them. Here, at least, the lexicographer could not say there was not a tree to be seen. The visit was peaceful but not successful. The Scots Whig and Presbyterian judge had nothing in common with the English Tory and High Churchman. The laird, proud of his long pedigree, was not impressed by a dictionary-maker, the son of a poor country bookseller. They touched on politics and theology and churches, but there was no feud, for the visitor was evidently on his best behaviour. They were civil and respectful to each other, and parted with no desire ever to meet again. Auchinleck freely told his friends in Edinburgh his impression of his late guest: "He is only a dominie, and the worst mannered dominie I ever met."[3] "My father," bleated forth his son to his confidant, Temple, "harps upon my going over Scotland with a brute—think how shockingly erroneous!"[4] Worse than that, there were unpleasant

---

[1] *Boswelliana.* He kept notes of her smart sayings, headed *Uxoriana.*
[2] Croker's *Correspondence*, ii. 30.
[3] Ramsay's *Scotland and Scotsmen*, i. 176.
[4] *Letters to Temple*, p. 207.

menaces, and the words, "James, my estate is not entailed," would make him uneasy, and cause him to think he had better attend more to the bar in the Court of Session and a little less to the bar in the taverns. As Dr. Johnson said the father and son incessantly "divaricated," and Bozzy owned he felt under the parental treatment "like a timid boy."

Visits to London, attendances on his illustrious friend, were the triumphs of his life. Rather than join in the merriest company, where he could be glorious, or move in high society as one so proud of his ancient lineage might well have done, he would wait on Dr. Johnson in all the dirt and shabbiness of the lodgings in Bolt Court. Let this be put down fairly and fully to Boswell's credit. He left club and theatre and rout for the dingy abode with its strange menagerie of dependants on the benevolent sage, who squabbled and backbit each other from morning till night. Blind, querulous Mrs. Williams; Mrs. Desmoulins, who cooked atrocious fare, and her daughter; Polly Carmichael—"a stupid slut" his host called her; and old Richard Levett, the apothecary, whose manners were "brutal," though his heart was excellent, who earned fees from squalid patients in the form of meat, clothing, and drink, and to whom his protector would chuck bits of roll at breakfast to munch. Was there ever such a home? "Williams hates everybody," groaned the doctor to Mrs. Thrale. "Levett hates Desmoulins and does not love Williams. Desmoulins hates them both, and Polly loves none of them."[1]

Much as the life in London bulks in Boswell's career, it after all amounted to two years altogether, and the time of direct intercourse with his friend, Croker calculated, was only 267 days in all. But then, what attentive days they were! for he was the faithful companion everywhere. Bozzy would take his seat beside his friend, or place his chair immediately behind him, his mouth open, his eyes goggling with eagerness, his ear bent down close in anxiety not to miss one syllable of the Oracle's utterances [2]—"watching," as he tells us, "every dawning communication of that illuminated mind." It

[1] D'Arblay's *Diary*; Johnson's *Letters* (edited Birkbeck Hill); ii. p. 77.
[2] *Memoirs of Dr. Burney*, ii. 190.

did not disconcert him when Johnson would call out, "Bozzy!" and finding him posed at his shoulder, vociferated, "What do you there, sir? go to the table." He docilely withdrew. The notebooks were ready in his pocket to report every word, and Mrs. Thrale had some reason to complain of his "vastly spoiling conversation"; for, in the far end of Streatham drawing-room, there was the fussy, inquisitive recorder, pencil in hand. Then the endless questions he would put might well rouse the sage into passion. "Sir, I will not be put to the question. Don't you consider, sir, that these are not the manners of a gentleman? I will not be baited with what? and why? what is this? why is that? why is a cow's tail long? why is a fox's tail bushy?" One day Johnson came to Mrs. Thrale in high dudgeon.[1] "I have been so put to the question by Bozzy this morning that I am panting for breath. What sort of questions? Why, one question was: Pray, sir, can you tell me why an apple is round and a pear is pointed? Would not such talk make a man hang himself?" The insatiable note-taker, however, bore very patiently every taunt and snub. He was content to be the butt so long as he might record the hits. Some men must pocket affronts to conceal them. Boswell pocketed—and pocket-booked them—to publish them. Only did his self-respect feel wounded when he was "tossed" in company, and then the patient worm would gently turn. Under a brutal indignity Murphy had seen him leave the room in tears; but he was very, very placable, as we find in this little dialogue. BOSWELL: "I said to-day to Sir Joshua when he observed that you *tossed* me sometimes, 'I don't care how often or how high he tosses me when only friends are present, for then I fall upon soft ground; but I do not like falling on stones, which is the case when enemies are present.' I think this a pretty good image, sir." JOHNSON: "Sir, it is one of the happiest I ever heard." Whereupon Bozzy was happy once more. No rebuff could weaken his affection; no insult could lessen his esteem for his hero, whom he toadied, till the victim cried out: "Sir, you have but two topics—yourself and me: I am sick of both."

[1] *Autobiography of Mrs. Piozzi*, ii. 125.

That this garrulous, vain, wine-bibbing tattler should ally himself with the great moralist, may be explained by his love of notoriety and of notables; but that the austere, intolerant veteran of letters should like—indeed love—such a companion, is a curious problem. Yet, moralist though he was, he liked, as he said, to "frisk it" now and then,—he loved the Honourable Tom Hervey, the rake, and Topham Beauclerc, whose morals were far to seek. Boswell, though not learned, and needing his mentor's advice to "read more and drink less," knew something of letters, knew much of the world, was clever, entertaining, good-natured, and loyal.

In 1784 Dr. Johnson died while Boswell was in Scotland. The great man's death had its consolation. Mr. Boswell could now write his life. For years note-books had been filling for this set purpose; for years he had been collecting and collating, questioning friends, pestering strangers with unsnubbable pertinacity about the "great Sam," as he jocularly and familiarly called him.[1] In 1786 the inimitable *Tour to the Hebrides* was published—a foretaste of the great Biography, which came upon the world on 16th May 1791, the anniversary of the first interview in Tom Davies's back shop. For its supreme qualities the world had not been prepared by the many absurd pamphlets he had issued on politics, law, trade, and slavery, full of rhodomontade and egotism run wild. In these pages the "great man" lives as he lived in the flesh, with all his strange ways and uncouth habits, his contortions and scrofula, his appetite for fish sauce and veal pies with plums, his lurching gait as he walked, his treasuring of orange peel, his superstition and hypochondria, his brow-beating and intolerance, and withal his kindness, his honesty, his sterling virtues. Every detail of his life is there, giving marvellous vividness to the portrait, so that we know him and his friends better than we know our neighbours next door. Good Mrs. Hannah More begged the biographer to "mitigate some of his asperities," but he replied bluntly, "he would not cut off his claws to make a tiger a cat for anybody." Not a look, a gesture, an accent, seems missed by Boswell, for he was full of his subject: he was a Johnson-intoxicated man. He cared not, in his

[1] D'Arblay's *Diary,* v. 166.

effort to make a complete biography (such as he avowed had never been written before) if he offended the living in his picture of the dead. Many had indeed cause to complain of unflattering personalities—some complained because they were mentioned unkindly; others complained because, unkindly, they were not mentioned at all. He does not even spare himself, for if he meets with an insult from his "revered friend," he does not waste it; he serves it up as table talk, although he may disguise it as being addressed "to a gentleman in the company." Unconsciously he reveals himself at every turn—his toadyism, his buffoonery, his vanity, his fear of the spirits he believed in, his love of the spirits he imbibed. He tells unabashed of his maudlin piety, his intoxication at Miss Monckton's, his lowing like a cow in the theatre to the delight of the footmen. No wonder his sons could not bear to near mentioned that book about which the whole world was talking. The weaknesses of the man make the display of his literary qualities all the more surprising—the exquisite dramatic touches, the fine comedy of the "conversation pieces," the skill with which the characteristics of each person is hit off, the inevitable seizing of the salient points in every speech, the keen observation, the fine eye for effect, which have never been approached by any other biographer. Edmund Burke was right when he said Johnson was greater in Boswell's pages than in any of his own. Many essayed the great moralist's life, from Sir John Hawkins upwards or downwards, seeking to make a living out of the dead. "How many maggots have crawled out of that great body!"[1] Burke exclaimed to Hannah More; but all have vanished, as is the way of maggots, and the great work, by a small man, survives. Seven years were spent on this *magnum opus*, and no part of the author's life was spent to such excellent purpose.

The rest of his career may be shortly summed up, for it was not glorious. His father had died, old, bodily and mentally enfeebled, in 1782, and Boswell reigned in his stead at Auchinleck. He lived, however, much in London, where he took a house, and joined the English bar, believing that there a wider field could be found for his distinguished forensic

[1] *Memoirs of Hannah More.*

talents. He soon showed that he knew as little of jurisprudence, as he did of prudence; and his learning and sobriety must have been very much on a par, if we believe Lord Eldon's story. Jemmy Boswell being found drunk on the pavement when on circuit in a country town, the barristers sent him next day a guinea fee and a brief to move for a writ of *Quare adhaesit pavemento*. Boswell having in vain sought light upon the obscure legal point moved for a writ, to the delight of his brothers and the amazement of the judge, who exclaimed: "I have never heard of such a writ—what can it be that adheres to the pavement?" At last a barrister explained that it was Boswell himself who was found adhering to the pavement, and was carried to bed, and had been dreaming about it ever since.[1]

It was in 1790 that Francis Jeffrey, then a boy, had the privilege of assisting to carry the body of the distinguished biographer[2] to bed in a state of woeful intoxication, and next morning he had the honour of being patted on the head by the unabashed inebriate, who patronisingly told him he was a "promising lad," and "that if you go on as you've begun, you may live to be a Bozzy yet." This was at a time when he was promising his friends Courtenay, Malone, and Temple to preserve sobriety with the utmost fervency, and drinking with reckless frequency. Some years before, as the aged Lord Kames was getting into his sedan-chair, Boswell stopped to speak to him. On parting, his Lordship said, "Boswell, I hope to see your good father one of those days. Have you any message for him? Shall I tell him how you are going on?"[3] It is to be hoped, for the comfort of poor Auchinleck, who had been so much worried by his son in this world, that Kames held his "ill tongue" on the subject when he met him in the other.

Meanwhile his wife, a woman of sense and some wit, had much to endure—her society neglected for "good company," where he got tipsy, with the usual sequels of fits of depression and tearful sentiment. He reminds us of Sir Richard Steele

---

[1] *Life of Eldon*, by Twiss, i. 130.
[2] Cockburn's *Life of Jeffrey*, i. 34.
[3] Ramsay's *Scotland and Scotsmen*, i. 248.

with his bibulous indulgence, and protestations of affection in notelets to his much-suffering spouse: "I am, dear Prue, a little in drink, but all the time your faithful husband, Richard Steele." All his characteristics remained unchanged; his alternate hypochondria and joviality; his moods of piety and his lapses from it; his superstitions; his love of excitement—especially for a hanging, in which he was as keen a connoisseur as George Selwyn himself. He was ready to kneel down and join in the chaplain's prayers in the prison cells with the convict in profoundest devotion, and to see him turned off at Tyburn with the greatest gusto,—to witness fifteen men hanged at once filled him with the keenest pleasure and the finest moral reflections. Vain as poor Goldsmith, whose pride in his plum-coloured coat from Filbey's he laughed at, he would rush in his Court dress from a levee at St. James's to dazzle compositors at the printing-offices with his magnificence. Few figures were better known in London artistic and literary society than his—paunchy and puffy, with red face, long, cocked nose, protuberant mouth and chin, with mock solemnity of manner and voice, with slow gait and slovenly dress—the clothes being loose, the wig untidy, the gestures restless so as to resemble his great master,[1] of whom he incessantly spoke, and whose big manner and oddities he mimicked with infinite drollery, making listeners convulse with laughter at the exquisite, but irreverent copy of his "revered friend."

In his later years there was the same lack of moral ballast and self-respect; the same solemn buffoonery. One sees him in Guildhall,[2] when William Pitt is entertained by the Worshipful Company of Grocers, standing up to sing a buffoon song, preluded by a rigmarole address, till the party is convulsed with merriment, and the austere face of the statesman relaxes into an unwonted smile at the grotesquely melancholy performance; and as the vocalist, delighted at his brilliant success, retires with his friend from the Hall, he makes the streets resound with shouting again the idiotic song of the evening. He attended the English Bar, where he got no practice; wrote pamphlets which made his friends laugh and his family grave; flattered

[1] D'Arblay's *Memoirs of Dr. Burney*, ii. 190-7; D'Arblay's *Diary*, v. 306.
[2] Taylor's *Records*, i. 89.

patrons from whom he gained no posts; stood for an Ayrshire membership of Parliament, but won no seat; paid obsequious court to that social tyrant and political bully, Sir James Lowther, from whom he got a Recordership of Carlisle, and endless insults, submitting to indignities which his obtuseness never perceived.

When Mrs. Boswell was dying at Auchinleck her husband delayed in London, entertaining and carousing, and arrived to find that his ' valuable wife" was dead. Thereupon, of course, followed uxorious remorse. Not many months passed by, however, before he was seeking another wife and a fortune; writing to his friend Temple, "You must know I have had several matrimonial schemes of late."[1] So the days went by, babbling and fuddling, till the end came in 1795, and, at the age of fifty-five, this erratic, foolish, good-natured, clever creature died—a man whom no one could respect, and whom few could help liking.

[1] *Letters*, p. 342.

CHAPTER IX

JAMES MACPHERSON

THE bowling-green at Moffat about the middle of the century was a gay scene. There were present visitors from all parts of Scotland who were glad to while away the time between the intervals of drinking the sulphur waters which had gained fame for the village. Lairds and their wives from remote districts came to the wells, anxious to join the rank and fashion which every season gathered there—" nabobs " who returned from the Indies, possessed of lacs of rupees and bilious constitutions; "Tobacco lords" from Glasgow with airs of consequence as pronounced as their accents; ministers in blue, professors in black, and lawyers in scarlet coats, with ladies in their hoops and sacques of brilliant hues. On an October day in 1759, there met on the green Mr. Alexander Carlyle, the minister of Inveresk, and Mr. John Home, and Mr. George Laurie of Loudon—a young minister, who afterwards was helpful to Robert Burns. There, too, was a big stalwart youth of six feet three, standing substantially on thick-set legs, encased in old-fashioned jack-boots.[1] This was James Macpherson, tutor to young Graham of Balgowan, known afterwards to history as Lord Lynedoch, who was staying at the wells. A letter of introduction from Adam Ferguson had made the tutor known to John Home, who was always glad to make himself pleasant and useful to any one. They discussed that day many things, among them Gaelic poetry, customs, and superstitions, and the young Highlander mentioned that he had some pieces of Celtic poetry in his possession. When the

[1] Carlyle's *Autobiography*, p. 398.

JAMES MACPHERSON
From the Painting by Reynolds in the National Portrait Gallery, London.

author of *Douglas* begged to see some specimens, but owned he did not know Gaelic, "How then can I show them to you?" he was asked. "Very easily," said Home, "translate some of the poems which you think are good, and I imagine I shall be able to form an opinion of the genius and character of Gaelic poetry."[1] With reluctance he agreed, and in a few days produced a fragment called "The Death of Oscar." Some translations were also shown to Laurie. Both he and Home felt that an invaluable discovery had been made, and when they went to Edinburgh, each of them called on Dr. Hugh Blair in Riddell's Close, to show to the literary dictator these remarkable translations from an unknown Erse poet. The three friends agreed that here was indeed a literary revelation of transcendent importance, poetry of vast antiquity and rare genius. Dr. Blair became eager to see James Macpherson in Edinburgh, and, when he met him, urged him to translate still more for publication. The young man of twenty-two years was, however, a difficult youth to deal with, silent, reserved, and proud. He deprecated[2] his power to find more originals, and after he had consented he tried to avoid the task, and several times wrote begging Mr. Laurie to get him released from his engagement, urging that his Highland pride was offended at appearing to the world only as a translator. His friend, however, was insistent, and Macpherson gave way; testily swearing that the blood of Ossian would be on the young minister's head.[3]

---

[1] *High. Soc. Report*, 398, App. 68.
[2] Laing's *Dissertation on Ossian*, 1805, ii. 46, 393.
[3] *Ibid.* I. xv. Many years after, in 1788, Dr. Laurie wrote to Macpherson asking his influence with government in favour of his brother, the governor of the Mosquito Coast. Macpherson answered that he did not remember ever having met Dr. Laurie. A memorial was thereupon sent recalling their former intimacy: "The first time Mr. G. Laurie saw or conversed with Jas. Macpherson, Esq., was at Moffat. Mr. Laurie was favoured with three or four translations of ancient Irish poetry, which upon his arrival in Edinburgh he showed to Dr. Blair. He desired to see Mr. Macpherson, and that was complied with; and he took Mr. Macpherson's promise to send as many fragments as would be contained in a shilling pamphlet—about a dozen in number. Mr. Macpherson, upon his return to the north, repented his promise, and wrote several times to Mr. Laurie begging to be released from it and to use his influence with Dr. Blair. Mr. Laurie was too great an admirer of these works to undertake such a task, but rather pressed Mr. Macpherson to adhere, which he did. And Mr. Macpherson concludes his last letter with an impreca-

This unknown youth had been born in 1738, in a little thatched cottage in Ruthven, near Kingussie, where his father had a small farm. He had become a student at King's College, Aberdeen, with the intention of entering the Church, and had then gone to finish his studies at Edinburgh College. He returned to his native parish, and when barely twenty years old became the master of a charity school. An income of about £6 or £8 gave him money enough to live upon, and his scanty flock of scholars gave him leisure enough to study, for reading poetry, and writing verses beside his peat fire when the children had left for the day. Already, from the age of seventeen to twenty, he had written the portentous number of 4000 verses; and an ambitious poem called the "Highlander," in six cantos, crept into light in 1758, and at once crept back into obscurity.

While teaching at Ruthven, he amused himself by listening to the snatches of Gaelic ballads, which were recited by the people, from whose lips came verses transmitted from generation to generation.[1] A few such relics of the past had already been collected; and in 1756, in the *Scots Magazine*, a poem "Alvin, or the Daughter of Mey," with some others, had appeared, introducing English readers to unknown poetry from an unknown tongue. These translations from the Erse were by Jeremiah Stone, who had begun life when a boy as a pedlar, and ended it at the age of twenty-nine, as a learned schoolmaster at Dunkeld. Save from a few fragments, the world knew nothing of Celtic poetry till Macpherson gave his specimens.

It was when he had relinquished his school for a tutorship that literary friends discovered him, and brought him out of obscurity into the full glare of notoriety. Blair, Ferguson, and Lord Hailes, when they saw his manuscripts, were eager for their publication, and copies were sent to Horace Walpole and Shenstone, who expressed their admiration of them. Coy publishing, while his friends were urgent, he at last, swearing he would never consent, consented. Full well he knew that

tion that their blood might be on Mr. Laurie's head," etc. (from MS. of Macpherson's letter and the memorial).

[1] Dissertation prefixed to *Fingal;* Ramsay's *Scot. and Scots.*, i. 546.

he was involving himself in an enterprise which was difficult if it was honest, and perilous if it was fraudulent.

The year 1760 became eventful by the appearance in Edinburgh of an attenuated volume entitled *Fragments of Ancient Poetry collected in the Highlands of Scotland, and Translated from the Gaelic or Erse Language*, with a preface by Dr. Blair explaining that the work contained Gaelic verse of great antiquity, anterior to the clan system, and bearing no trace of Christian influence. The peculiar rhythmical prose adopted for the translation had been suggested by Home—it being that form in which Bishop Lowth had recently rendered the Psalms, which had earned the praises of Dr. Hugh Blair.

The success of these "Fragments" was immediate. All Scotsmen were delighted at being able to boast that even the most barbarous parts of their despised country had been possessed of genius before England had risen out of savagedom. Hume and Home, Ferguson and Blair, Lord Elibank, Lord Kames, Lord Hailes—in fact every one—joined in the chorus of acclaim, and were fierce at any who dared to impugn their genuineness, or to slight their beauty. Had not these verses been handed down from remote ages? Did not chiefs keep their own hereditary family bards whose themes were the feats of their clan and the wars of Fingal? Had not Adam Smith heard a piper of Argyleshire repeat some of these very poems? Did not distinguished chieftains—Mackays, Macleods, Macfarlanes—assert that they knew them well? Furthermore, were not the very names of the heroes, Fingal, Ossian, Oscar, Diarmid, still given in the Highlands to large mastiffs, as the English gave the name of Pompey and Hector, and the French gave the name of Marlborough to their dogs? So wrote, so argued David Hume, full of his usual extravagant patriotism and wild defiance of Southron suspicion.[1] Meanwhile, even in England, there was little suspicion. Shenstone and Gray were charmed, and Walpole was pleased.

This first success whetted literary appetite for more, especially as Macpherson stated that he had only given fragments of a great epic existing orally in the Highlands. We next find his admirers urging him to rescue the great poem

[1] Burton's *Life of Hume*, i. 464.

from oblivion. They offered him funds to travel in search of the nebulous epic. An enthusiastic dinner-party met in Edinburgh, over which Lord Elibank presided, and at which Robertson, Ferguson, Blair, and others gathered, their object being to gain the lad's consent to proceed in search of the missing works of Ossian.[1] He refused, he hesitated, but at last consented under such high persuasion. Before many months were over, in September 1760, he mounted his horse, fixed his saddle-bags and wallet, and set forth on his journey of discovery. How he had learned that such an epic existed he alone could, but did not, tell: the difficulty of proving his assertion may explain his reluctance to undertake the expedition. However he departed, a young man of twenty-three, with an imperfect knowledge of Gaelic and a perfect confidence in himself. Letters of introduction insured him help and hospitality in distant glens and islands with lairds and ministers from Perthshire to far-off Benbecula, where unadulterated tradition and undefiled Gaelic were likeliest to be found. Chiefs in their houses showed him dusty manuscripts hard to decipher; ministers helped him to translate Gaelic, in which he was very deficient; venerable blacksmiths, sons of bards, recited long screeds of Fingalian verse in high nasal accents, with the prospective reward of a gill of whisky or a roll of tobacco. Onwards he travelled with Macpherson, the Laird of Strathmashie, his faithful friend and kinsman, over island and mainland. Schoolhouse, croft, and manse welcomed him, and chieftains gave him the loan of treasured manuscripts containing household receipts, genealogical notes and old verse in chaotic confusion and distressful cacography—some were lent and never seen again.[2]

After four months spent on tours of discovery, the literary explorer got back to Edinburgh in 1761. His patrons were naturally anxious as to the results. Soon the precise steps of Dr. Hugh Blair with Mr. Adam Ferguson ascended the dirty turnpike stairs of his lodgings in Blackfriars Wynd, and entered the dingy flat. There was James Macpherson, "a plain-looking lad dressed like a preacher," with a manner starched and reserved. His little garret room was crowded

[1] *Highland Society Report*, App.   [2] *Ibid.* p. 31.

with books, copies of verses, manuscript books in Gaelic, some of them "stained with smoke and daubed with Scots snuff."[1] The visitors, after their interview, quitted the room highly satisfied with the assurances of Mr. James Macpherson that the great promised Ossianic epic had been found. Quickly the news ran along, and society hummed with excitement. A Celtic Homer had been brought to light after he had been dead thirteen hundred years.

In a few months Macpherson took horse with his manuscripts in his valise to seek subscribers and publishers and a patron in London. David Hume meanwhile had written to his friend William Strahan, the printer, recommending him as "a sensible, modest, young fellow, a very good scholar, and of unexceptionable morals." Lord Bute was then the Court favourite, and his favour was secured, and with a humble dedication to his lordship, who was the most patronising of patrons, there appeared in December 1761, *Fingal, an ancient Epic Poem, in six books, together with several other poems composed by Ossian, the son of Fingal, translated from the Gaelic language by James Macpherson.*

Now there was a stir in every literary circle; the poetry met, as Dr. Beattie, who was no believer, expresses it, with "a universal deluge of approbation," and it rivalled the Cock Lane ghost in the interest it excited in London. True, there were some notes of discord, the truculent Churchill had his sarcastic flings, and Wilkes had his jeers; for Scotsmen, and all who clung to Lord Bute, were the butts of every wit and witling. In Scotland, however, hardly one dissentient voice was heard. Here was an epic that cast Homer into the shade; here was a poem that shed a lustre on Scotland which England well might envy. At every Edinburgh breakfast-table it was discussed and lauded, the dinner-table resumed the talk, and every supper-party got more enthusiastic as the wine passed round. The class-room at College was crowded by the rank and fashion of the town, as Dr. Hugh Blair, with the pride of a discoverer and the pomposity of a critic, descanted in his familiar burr on the age, the style, and marvellous beauties of the blind son of

[1] *Highland Society Report*, App. p. 63; Ramsay's *Scotland and Scotsmen*, i. 549.

Fingal. When the lectures were published in 1763 his *Critical Dissertation* was hailed as a masterly and convincing performance. It was, indeed, as learned a disquisition as could be written by a man who knew nothing of his subject.

More debate, more talk arose when, shortly after these laudatory lectures appeared, the final part of the immortal work was issued—*Temora, an ancient Epic in eight books, composed by Ossian, the son of Fingal.* Here was, indeed, a surprising result of the Celt's travels for four months in the Highlands—not one, but two great epics which had survived the lapse of ages which lingered in the tenacious memories and flowed from the fluent lips of Highland crofters. By this time the translator had lost all his diffidence. He went about London with a swagger; he was vain-glorious and aggressive. Fame had spoiled his character—not that there was much to spoil—and even his old supporters winced under his manner. Good David Hume retracted alike his faith in Ossian and the good things he had said so guilelessly of the "sensible, modest fellow," and now wrote to Strahan of his "absurd pride and caprice—a mortal than whom I have never known more perverse and unamiable."[1] Three years before, he had been pleasingly diffident, and deferential to his superiors, being conscious of his poverty, his humble birth, his ignorance of the world. Now, however, that he was celebrated, patrons he owned no longer[2]; he was impatient of the advice of friends, contemptuous of the cavils of opponents. See him with his big, brawny person, dressed in ill-fitting clothes, jostling his way along the Strand; his voice strident and blustering in the coffee-houses, looking down from his height of six feet three at his acquaintances, talking English phrases in Highland tones, and assuming the grand airs of a man of the world. He was aware that society was not so loud in its praises of the great Ossian as before; that it was more sceptical of its genuineness; and this made him all the more defiant in tone. In truth, the world was weary of the melancholy monotony of the verse, of the moaning winds and "sounding shores," misty hills and "halls of shells." It found certainly more bombast in this last doubtful relic of antiquity. "Why, sir," said Dr.

[1] *Letters of D. Hume*, p. 36.   [2] *Boswelliana*, p. 213; *Report*, App. 61.

Johnson, "a man might write such stuff for ever if he would abandon his mind to it," and in spite of Boswell's patriotic protests the Literary Club would treat Ossian contemptuously.

To silence sceptics Macpherson placed in the hands of Beckett, his bookseller, certain Gaelic manuscripts; and the newspapers advertised that the "Originals of Fingal and other poems were to be seen at the shop by all who desired to examine them." "Ossian" Macpherson was not highly gifted with a sense of humour; but surely there was excellent humour of a sardonic sort in this proposal that Englishmen should satisfy themselves of the genuineness of a translation of a Gaelic epic by looking at documents without a history, manuscripts without a date, in a language of which they knew as little as a Hottentot. Is it surprising that no Englishman went to see them? For months the manuscripts lay uninspected in Beckett's back room, and then they were withdrawn in sulky triumph. Most of these documents were copies of recitals from Highland lips, with a few old papers, which sceptics like George Dempster declared were Gaelic leases from Macleod of Skye's charter chest.[1] It was possible for experts to examine Chatterton's pretended poems of Rowley and Ireland's impudent Shakespearian fraud of *Vortigern*—which Boswell knelt before and kissed with maudlin tears. But who in London could decide on those manuscripts? The translator could, however, taunt his critics by asserting that he had offered them proof which they were afraid to look at. Even in Scotland, where a year or two ago Dr. Carlyle said there were only two unbelievers, a feeling of uneasiness began to be shown, and Hume sensibly urged Dr. Blair to set on foot investigations in the Highlands among ministers and others who knew the language to make the evidence indisputable. This was not proposed from any anxiety for the translator's character, but only from jealousy for his country's honour.

A few years went by and Macpherson won his way into importance. He became an active man of affairs as well as a man of letters, a useful hack of Government, which rewarded

[1] C. Rogers, *Century of Scottish Life*, p. 60.

his services with the post of surveyor-general and secretary to Commodore Johnstone, with whom he went to Florida.[1] These two Scotsmen had tempers admirably matched—passionate, hectoring, and blustering, and they quarrelled furiously. But though the appointment was lost, Macpherson retained a pension of £200 on condition of serving the Ministry. In those days janissaries of the press abounded. For pay or posts they would malign any mortal, public or private; defend a Government in any blunder, support any job, fawn on any patron. Their stock-in-trade was an aptitude for whitewashing a Ministry and blackening an Opposition, a fine art of mendacity and misrepresentation with a copiously vituperative vocabulary. Macpherson did not descend to all this, but he descended to much, for his scruples were not of the keenest. He had time to write *An Introduction to the History of Great Britain*, in which the genius and influence of the Celtic race on the civilisation of the country are patriotically shown. In an evil hour he began to perpetrate a translation of the *Iliad* written in the familiar Ossianic prose. This work, it was said, he took only three months to write, and it was a disastrous failure. Principal Robertson loyally proclaimed it "the only translation in which Homer appears like an ancient poet and in his own simple magnificence"; but Hume more sensibly declared "he did not know whether the attempt or the execution was worse."[2]

The great questions regarding Ossian were for a while silent if not settled, but they suddenly started once more into life. Dr. Johnson made his famous journey to the Highlands in 1773, and he took with him his contemptuous incredulity to the land of the Gael. There he bullied chiefs and hectored ministers, snorted forth his contradictions and his flouts, till he reduced them to silence, and he mistook the courtesy of his hosts for the abjectness of the convicted. When the famous *Journey to the Hebrides* was about to appear, Strahan, the publisher, Macpherson's good friend and countryman, let out that some unpleasant passages and offensive charges were to appear in its pages. A civil note was written

---

[1] Saunders's *Life of James Macpherson*, p. 212.
[2] Hume's *Letters to Strahan*.

begging that any injurious statements might be omitted. No notice was taken of this appeal, and the temper of the Celt boiled over when the *Journey* was published, and a letter was despatched by him to Johnson's Court, informing his assailant that "his age and his infirmities alone protected him from the treatment due to an infamous liar and traducer." This time an answer did come, in its writer's ripest and most trenchant style. Thus it ran: "Mr. James Macpherson, I have received your foolish and impudent note. I will do my best to reply to it, and what I cannot do for myself, the law will do for me. I will not desist from detecting what I think a cheat from any fear of the menaces of a Ruffian. I thought your book an imposture. I think it an imposture still. For this opinion I have given my reasons to the public, which I dare you to confute. Your rage I defy, your abilities since your Homer, are not so formidable, and what I hear of your morals inclines me to pay regard not to what you say, but to what you shall prove. You may print this if you will.— Samuel Johnson, 20th January 1775."[1] Dr. Johnson was a very complete letter writer. As soon as this trouncing epistle was in the hands of his brawny foe, the writer bethought himself that it was prudent to buy a formidable cudgel, six feet long, headed with a knob three inches in diameter, with which to protect his aged but still sturdy person. No personal assault, however, was made. Macpherson in his tavern only spluttered forth curses, while Johnson at his club ejaculated sneers.

Busy and versatile Macpherson published *Original Papers, containing the Secret History of England,* which gave private papers revealing old political intrigues which filled Tories with rapture and Whigs with rage, and made them cry out "Impostor!" Calmly he went on writing a *History of Great Britain,* from the Restoration to the Accession of the House of Hanover, which David Hume told Strahan was "the most wretched production that ever came from his press."[2] It must be remembered that the Philosopher-historian never could bear philosophically any one who poached on his historical preserves. It produced

---

[1] Boswell's *Johnson* (Hill's edit.), ii. 279
[2] Hume's *Letters to Strahan,* p. 306.

to the author £3000 before it passed out of a second edition into oblivion.

The future career of this indomitable Scot was one of active success. He was ready with his pen to back up any ministerial policy. Did the Ministry want a writer to attack the mysterious Junius? He could write letters signed "Scævola," which supplied in venom what was lacking in strength. Did a badgered Prime Minister require a pamphlet to defend his American policy? He was ready with a pamphlet which outdid his enemy Johnson's "Taxation no Tyranny" in popularity. Did the ill-used Nabob of Arcot need an advocate to plead his claims against the East India Company? He became that potentate's advocate at a good price; and through his friend and brother Celt, Sir John Macpherson, he also became the Nabob's well-paid, highly-pensioned agent.[1] For a salary of £600,[2] the Government found in him a useful mercenary who could tune newspapers to dance to party measures, and with truculent advocacy fill columns, which Walpole called "columns of lies." Besides that he could put up friends and ministers to good things in India Stock. When in 1780 he became M.P. for Camelford, his vote was worth something, though he never made a speech. If not a great man, he now was the friend of men great in letters, art, and politics; he was rich, had his house at Putney and another in town, and drove to the City in a splendid carriage. As he was flouting one day at the English after the fashion of his countrymen, Dr. Blair expressed surprise that since he did not like John Bull he should stay in England. "Sir," he answered the precise divine, "I do not like John Bull, but I love his daughters."[3] That was perfectly true. He was not married, but he was not without children, for whom he provided well. Alas! where now was David Hume's young friend "with unexceptionable morals"? His countrymen found him arrogant, disdainful, obstinate, masterful. What had become of Hume's "modest, sensible young lad"? No longer was he deferential to Dr. Blair and others who were reigning as magnates in Scot-

---

[1] Wraxall's *Posthumous Memoirs*, i. 254.
[2] Walpole's *Journal of the Reign of George III.* ii. 57.
[3] *Boswelliana*, p. 208.

land when they saw him in London. The quondam patrons found themselves patronised in their turn by their former protégé. It seemed even to have become irksome to his vanity that he should be known only as a translator, and he grudged the blind son of Fingal reaping all the glory. Though "Jupiter" Carlyle says he was always indignant at its being suggested that he was the fabricator, yet under the unbosoming influence of wine, he seems to have more than once hinted that he was more than translator.[1] Of course in public he dared not assert this, and thereby write himself down the impostor and liar that Johnson alleged him to be. He was also shrewd enough to know that poems which gain fame and honour from their antiquity will be flung aside the moment they are discovered to be modern. The mock antique may be as exquisite as the genuine article found in Etruscan tombs or the Roman Campagna; but the instant it is known to have come from Birmingham it turns to trash. The mock pearl may seem finer than the real—but it is paste and nothing more. In an arrogant preface to the 1775 edition of Ossian he vaunted his merits: "The translator who cannot equal his original is incapable of expressing its beauties." Thus he boldly equalled Macpherson to Ossian, but he dared not say that they were synonymous.

It was in 1785 that some enthusiastic Highland gentleman subscribed £1000 to have the original Gaelic manuscripts of Ossian published, and they provokingly, but respectfully, begged the great man to undertake the task. More than twenty years had elapsed since the epic translation had appeared, and he said there were trunks in the attics, which he had not opened for years, full of manuscripts, both old and new, antique books to read, and fragments to arrange—he did not add that he had all the verse he had composed in English to turn into the supposed original Gaelic. No wonder he demurred; it was pleasanter to coax votes for my Lord North, to manipulate newspapers, to collect salaries and pensions paid quarterly, to have jovial bachelor dinners. The chests were never ransacked, the version was never issued. He proposed,

---

[1] Laing's *Ossian*, I. xx. xxi.; Pinkerton's *Correspondence*, ii. 93; *High. Soc. Report*, App. 65.

however, an absurd plan of publishing the Gaelic in Greek characters, as conveying Erse sounds better than Roman letters.

So the big burly politician lived in society, and in spite of his abominable temper with many friends, the best of them being Sir John Macpherson, son of the minister of Sleat (whose manse he had visited on his famous expedition in search of Ossian), who had made his way by his ability, his tact, his exquisite temper, to the highest office in India, succeeding Warren Hastings as Governor-General of Bengal. In the Mall were often seen these two brother Colts, who were striking, massive figures in the crowd, both men of six feet three or four—Sir John, with an expression frank and genial,[1] and his friend with aggressive expression in his keen eyes, which looked from his florid face, his handsome person dressed in a fur-edged coat.

As he grew elderly, rich, and prosperous, Macpherson's heart yearned for his old Highland district, and he turned his eyes to Badenoch; there he resolved to buy land and build a home within sight of his native mountains. Two or three small farms were bought on the banks of the Spey, and soon a villa, bearing the cockney title of "Belleville," which had been designed by his friend Adam, the architect, rose in the wilds, two miles from Kingussie. People long remembered the great man from London, who came every year, bedizened with rings and gold seals, and clad in fur-edged coat. They told stories of the grand state he kept up as a Highland chief, his splendid table, his home filled with guests; of his sallying forth in the morning and bringing bibulous lairds from houses far and near, who in the dining-room, from whose walls portraits by Sir Joshua Reynolds looked down, kept high revelry till they and the nights were far spent.[2] But good things, too, were told of Macpherson, pleasant to remember; of his refusing from a grateful Government the forfeited estate of Cluny Macpherson, which was thereupon restored to its rightful owner; his generosity to the poor, whom he employed at high wages, which no Badenoch man had ever dreamed of; his kindly remembrance of all about his native Ruthven. Now

[1] Wraxall's *Posthumous Memoirs*, ii. 6.
[2] Carruthers's *Highland Note-book*, p. 360.

that his ambition was satisfied, now that his struggle with poverty and obscurity was over he could be the pleasant, affable man, the kindly landlord, and the genial host.

It was on 17th February 1796 that Macpherson died at his Highland home, and Mrs. Grant of Laggan, who had been saddened by the quality of his morals, but was now satisfied with his penitence, describes in her old-fashioned, pious way his edifying end: "It pleased the Almighty to render his last scene most affecting and exemplary. He died last Tuesday evening, and from the minute he was confined to bed, a very little before he expired, he never ceased imploring Divine mercy in the most earnest and exemplary manner."[1] An obscure burial in a Highland kirkyard not satisfying his ambition, he left £500 to erect a monument on his land, and ordered that his important remains should be interred in Westminster Abbey. After travelling for eighteen days, the hearse arrived in London, was met at Highgate by many acquaintances, and a long range of carriages followed it to the Abbey, where the body was laid within a few feet of that of his enemy, Johnson, in the sanctuary where foes can war no more. Thus in pomp and circumstance ended the career of the poor schoolmaster of Ruthven.[2]

With him did not die out the Ossianic controversy. Englishmen forgot it, but Scotsmen were too eager for the credit of their country not to vindicate the credit of Ossian. Macpherson had left with his trustee the £1000 for the purpose of publishing Ossian in the original language, but in his chests no such documents were to be found. All the papers were modern, either in his own or his friends' writing, consisting of pieces taken down from recital, except a few unimportant manuscripts which he had borrowed and never returned.[3] But where was the Gaelic Epic? A few years later the Highland Society formed a Committee, under Henry Mackenzie, to investigate into the sources of the famous work, and information was sought from those who best knew Gaelic poetry. The result was not satisfactory. Old men who had

---

[1] Mrs. Grant's *Letters from the Mountains* (6th edit.), i. 235, ii. 203.
[2] *Gentleman's Magazine*, 1796.
[3] *Highland Society Report*, p. 80.

aided and believed in Macpherson, were ready to remember passages which they had heard in their youth, and to prove his veracity, fluently recited Gaelic verse which he had never used. Octogenarian lairds and ministers quoted many Ossianic ballads, totally forgetting that they bore no resemblance to any in Macpherson's version. The lapse of forty years does not improve the memory of men, though it may wonderfully improve their imagination.

The Report was issued in 1805, the conclusion arrived at, to the disgust of all believers, being that many memories of the Fingal legends lingered in the North, that many ballads were still recited, that many parts of Macpherson's version were formed from fragments of those songs which he had altered and interpolated at his will; but as for an epic, such as he gave it, none was to be found.[1] Later investigation led to results more destructive still to the pretensions of the famous "poems of Ossian," whom Macpherson ignorantly claimed as Highland—hopeless chronology, confused topography, wrong nationality, customs that ancient Celts never had, armour they never wore, a poetic style they never used, heroes and heroines with epithet names, which they never bore, all contained in a work which, save in a few passages, was never heard from the lips of Highland bard, far less sung by Ossian. That Macpherson—a young, raw, country lad—should have virtually manufactured this work, was a marvellous feat. As he truly told the world, "those who have doubted my veracity have paid a compliment to my genius." We find the same sombre vein in his bombastic juvenile poem, "The Highlander," as in Ossian; but he improved by practice as he provided material to meet the demands of his urgent admirers for more and more supplies of Ossian. Gray the poet was puzzled when the poems first appeared, what to believe—was it all genuine or a fraud? He found by correspondence with the young man, that his letters were "ill-wrote, ill-reasoned," which would show he was "equally unable to invent these poems or to translate them so admirably. In short, he is the

---

[1] *Highland Society Report;* M. Laing's *Ossian;* Campbell's *Tales of West Highlands;* Laing's *History of Scotland,* 1800, ii. 377; *Celtic Monthly,* Jan.-April, 1787; *Academy,* 1871.

very demon of poetry, or he has alighted upon a treasure hid for ages." The puzzle lay there. Another problem was still to be solved, which Dr. Blair urged on Hume. "Is it credible that he could bring so many thousand people into a conspiracy with him to keep the secret, or that some would not be found who would cry out, 'These are not the poems we deal in: you have forged characters and sentiments we know nothing about: you have modernised and dressed us up?'"[1] Yet Macpherson seems to have achieved the incredible.

Ossian came to English readers as a revelation, and opened up a world of sentiment of which they had never imagined. The wilds of the Highlands were then shrouded in mystery—trackless wastes which southern feet had never trod, and remote isles washed by stormy seas which their ships had seldom sailed, peopled by a barbarous race with ways uncouth and tongue unknown. This newly recovered poetry seemed to reveal the life, the feuds and loves, the genius of that people thirteen centuries before, beside the surging sea, amid the misty glens, by the lonely mountain tarns and roaring torrents, which the raven, eagle, and vulture made wilder still by their cries. The appearance of Ossian fitted in with the era of sentiment which had sprung up—sentiment which was domestic in *Clarissa Harlowe*, romantic in Walpole's *Castle of Otranto*, poetic in Percy's *Reliques*. By Macpherson sentiment was stirred for ancient life among the mountains, mists, and seas of the far North. Ossian may be no more read, yet it cannot be ignored, for it was a great force in literature. We see its influence not too happily in Gray's *Bard;* over Coleridge in his poetic immaturity of 1793; over Byron in his callow days, when he was under its glamour. One remembers how Burns, whose favourite authors were deplorably sentimental, enumerates "Ossian" as one "of the glorious models after which I endeavour to form my conduct"—how, or why, or when, he does not explain.

But abroad, still wider and more enduring was the effect. The translation of Cæsarotti initiated a new poetic school in Italy. In Germany, then going through its romantic stage, it was hailed with rapture. Klopstock wrote turgid odes

[1] Saunders's *Life of James Macpherson*, p. 208.

after its worst style; Herder gloried in it; Bürger versified it; Schiller found rare beauty and grandeur in the life of Celtic past with its background of mist; and Goethe tried his skill in translating it; and his *Werther*, to express his agonised emotions, turns to the melancholy bard of the North, and in his strains pours forth his abject woes. Voltaire laughed his dry laughter like the crackling of thorns over it, and for a while France was unthrilled. At last even it gave way to the spell, especially when Napoleon, who knew it through the Italian translation, and loved the grandiose, was moved to admiration for "Ocean," as he spelt it, carrying it with him as his favourite reading during his campaigns. French parents found baptismal names for their children in its pages, and either to please his master or his own taste, Bernadotte took a name from Ossian for his son, who became Oscar I. of Sweden, and transmitted his name to successors.[1]

The poems of Ossian are unread to-day, and will seldom be read again. They weary with their sombre monotony, their meagre sameness of sentiment and simile, their vagueness, their rhapsodies. Nevertheless they have a distinct place in literature, and with Matthew Arnold's verdict we may content ourselves: "Make the part of what is forged, modern, tawdry, spurious in the book as large as you please, there will still be left a residue with the very soul of the Celtic genius in it, and which has the proud distinction of having brought this soul of the Celtic genius into contact with the genius of the nations of modern Europe and enriched all our poetry by it. Windy Morven and echoing Sora, and Selma with its silent halls! we owe to them a debt of gratitude, and when we are unjust enough to forget it, may the Muse forget us."[2] As to the weary controversy on the origin and genuineness of this once famous work, though it may be too much to say that the last word has been written, it is pretty certain that the last word has been read.

[1] Saunders's *Life of Macpherson*, p. 19.
[2] Arnold's *Celtic Literature*, p. 153.

CHAPTER X

DR. THOMAS REID—DR. JAMES BEATTIE

AWAY in the North lived a society of which Edinburgh knew very little. With Aberdeen communication was slow, tedious, and uncomfortable; on horseback a man might spend five or six days on the road, and coaches would take as long, with the risk of axles breaking down, and the certainty of passengers being wrenched and rattled in the ruts and bogs. Aloof from the world, the people had their own ways, fashions, and manner of speech, and the University was attended only by youths from mansions and from crofts of the North. Simon Fraser, Lord Lovat, when he was at College, had as class-mate the threadbare lad, Thomas Ruddiman, who lived on oatmeal. In later years Lord Erroll competed in the classes on equal terms with sons of stocking-makers and herring-curers. In the early part of the century, when there was great poverty in the land, the colleges were sorely pinched for money. Regents had miserable pittances to live upon, although they had to teach subjects which six well-endowed professors in a modern University would hardly undertake. Colin Maclaurin, the brilliant youth, who, at nineteen, had been appointed professor of Mathematics, was glad to leave the poverty-stricken post, and become colleague to Professor James Gregory in Edinburgh, though Gregory drew the salary for seventeen years, and left his friend only the scanty fees. Depressed by penury, education was feebly fostered, and in 1709 the King's College students, in youthful irritation, audaciously pronounced their professors "useless, needless, headless, and defective." A curious light is thrown upon the impecunious state of this seat of learning by a minute of the University in 1738, in which it is stated that "the want of an accomplished gentlewoman for teaching white and coloured seams is the occasion of several gentlemen's sons being kept from college, their parents inclining to send them where they might have suitable education for their daughters also." Such a pathetic state of matters they sought to remedy by engaging a worthy woman to teach the required "white and coloured seams," lavishly advancing her for the ensuing year the sum of £12 Scots. This incident of an ancient university requiring to keep its students together and to advance learning by giving £1 sterling to settle a seamstress in the town, presents a curious picture of an impoverished age.

Dr. Thomas Reid

In the Manse of Strachan, in Aberdeenshire, Thomas Reid was born in 1710. The parish was at that time a dreary, treeless district; far and wide stretched the moorland, with patches of fields, in which grew the meagre crops of farmers, who lived in poverty. Over it swept the keen, healthy breezes of the upland, playing, or, more seriously, blustering, round the thatched manse in which dwelt Mr. Lewis Reid, the descendant of a long line of ministers. He had married the daughter of David Gregory of Kinnairdy, who was the father of twenty-nine children, three of whom became distinguished professors in Oxford, Edinburgh, and St. Andrews, and supplied through their descendants men eminent in science for over a century. The minister of Strachan lived for fifty years among a people who were keen as their east winds, and uncultivated as their thistle-filled crofts. They eyed askance the good man when he foretold weather by the aid of a barometer—an instrument unknown in rural districts—which had been given him by his brother-in-law, David Gregory, the famous Professor of Astronomy in Oxford. One summer, as the harvest was drawing to a close, he saw the mercury falling in the glass, and warned his neighbours by the river to remove their crops from the low ground. Two old ministers, who disregarded his advice and lost their crops, in the

DR. THOMAS REID
From the Painting by Raeburn in Glasgow University

Presbytery demanded that he should explain how, by honest means, he could possibly foretell a flood when there was not a cloud in the sky.[1]

Thomas Reid entered Marischal College when he was only twelve years old, and in Aberdeen he found himself among his pleasant Gregory kindred. At that period Marischal College was an ugly, dilapidated, shabby building, which through poverty and neglect had fallen into decay. In one dark room Reid joined a little group of some thirty students, who formed the class of the regent, the Rev. George Turnbull.[2] This able man, long forgotten, is yet somewhat memorable. For the modest remuneration of £40 he taught the whole range of human knowledge which was requisite for a university curriculum. He was specially notable as a metaphysician and moral philosopher, and he taught a system in which his own insistence on "common-sense" in philosophy was much in harmony with the mode to be adopted by his pupil Reid in later days. Turnbull grew tired of bad pay and of learned drudgery, and quitted Aberdeen for England, where he ultimately entered the English Church. Laboriously, voluminously, and almost annually he wrote books on philosophy and art, which the world received with provoking indifference. He was, however, to obtain an unkind immortality in an unlooked-for way. If we look at Hogarth's picture of "Beer Street," we see a porter drinking copiously from a mug to refresh his exhausted frame, after depositing on the ground a heavy load of five ponderous folios intended for the trunkmaker; and on the back of one of these we read the title: *Turnbull on Ancient Painting.* This was one of the numerous works of Reid's old Aberdeen regent. Such was not the sort of immortality poor Turnbull expected.

Years passed by, and after undergoing a six years' course of Divinity, Reid was licensed to preach in 1729, and after a further nine years at Marischal College, where he was keeper of the library, on a salary of £8 sterling, he was presented to the living of New Machar, twelve miles from Aberdeen.[3]

---

[1] M'Cosh's *Scottish Philosophy*, p. 95.
[2] Ramsay's *Scotland and Scotsmen*, i. 470.
[3] Stewart's *Life of Reid*.

The people there, being, like those of his native parish, of dour nature, were jealous of what they considered their Christian rights of choosing a minister and would not sign "the call." They had been incited to refuse by Mr. Bisset, a former minister of the parish, a notable firebrand, with big, ungainly person and huge black wig, who, preaching at the "moderation of the call," in his obstreperous voice stirred up the parishioners against cringing to the great, on the servile maxim, "I am for the man the laird is for." The presentee in consequence was received with opposition, his wig and hat were pulled off in the fray, the precentor is said to have fled before the tumult, and soldiers with drawn swords kept order in the kirk at the ordination.[1] A self-willed, austere folk were those at New Machar, who had hauled Reid's predecessor before the Presbytery on the charge of having heinously powdered his wig on the Lord's day.

The career thus inauspiciously began lasted fifteen years, during which the minister so thoroughly won the affections of his people, that when, amid tears and lamentations, he departed for the professor's chair in Aberdeen, one of them said: "We fought against Mr. Reid when he came; we would have fought for him when he left."[2] Yet he had no popular gifts to tickle the rustic ears; no hot gospelling to warm their rudimentary emotions; no muscular activity in the pulpit to excite their admiration. The affection was for the man rather than the preacher, who read "slavishly," who would treat his flock at times to the dry pulpit dialectics of Tillotson, or the moral discourses of the nonconformist Evans—which were famous in their day, but are unreadable in ours. Yet he was a man of deep feeling; and it is told that, when dispensing the Lord's Supper, in the fervour of his appeals tears would fall down his cheeks as he addressed the communicants. A private dedication of himself to God, when his wife was dangerously ill, which by some chance is still extant, gives a curious insight to his heart. He craves Divine mercy to bring his wife from the gates of death; he confesses his sins in not stirring her up to Christian

---

[1] Ramsay's *Scotland and Scotsmen*; Fraser's *Thomas Reid*; M'Cosh's *Scottish Philosophy*, p. 273.
[2] Stewart's *Life of Reid*.

virtues, in not taking sufficient pains in the upbringing of his children and servants, in being negligent in preparations for public services; and he winds up with a quaint arrangement with his Maker: "I do promise and covenant through grace to turn from my backslidings, to express my thankfulness by a vigorous discharge of my duty as a Christian minister, and master of a family, and *by an alms of ten pounds sterling to the poor in meal or money.*"[1] This is a mode of pious bargaining common in the dedications and "personal covenants" of these old times, which is indeed as old as the days of Jacob, when that Israelite indeed, who was not without guile, chaffered with Jehovah to serve Him if he would keep him in food and clothing. But, after all, we feel it is a shabby thing to spy on Mr. Reid's devout privacy, and to be an eavesdropper in his secret prayers.

Fifteen years passed by, he married, and in time the little manse became noisy and cheery with sounds of children's voices; he studied, and his bookshelves became filled with works on science and philosophy; he botanised; he gardened; he dabbled in farming, being stimulated by his friend the energetic old Sir Alexander Grant of Monymusk, who spent a lifetime in draining, enclosing, and planting his estates. It was in 1745 he first broke forth into authorship by an *Essay on Quantity*, which was read before the Royal Society of London, on the application of mathematics to moral problems, in refutation of a theory of Hutcheson's.

At length the final bent was given to his study and his life-thought. One day he read the little volume, *A Treatise on Human Nature*, by David Hume, which had come out in 1739. It was barely known in the North, but by this quiet country minister it was to be called out of unmerited obscurity and to become an epoch-making work. Reid had hitherto been captivated by Berkeley's speculations. But as he read Hume's *Treatise*, "suddenly what he thought was firm land seemed to be changed to a mirage; what to him had been a reality now seemed all a dream"; for that *enfant terrible* of twenty-five, pressing home the Bishop's arguments remorselessly to their conclusions, seemed to prove that we know as little of the

[1] M'Cosh's *Scot. Philosophy*, p. 419.

existence of mind as of matter, that we are only cognisant of a succession of ideas or impressions, affording no evidence for body or soul, for matter or spirit. After committing intellectual suicide, Hume, as we have seen, professed himself at first dismayed at the consequences to which his reasoning inexorably led him: "I am affrighted and confounded with the forlorn solitude in which I am placed by my philosophy." Similar consternation did the reading of this treatise now cause the minister of New Machar, who had hitherto seemed to be living in a well-ordered universe.[1] "I find that I have been only in an enchanted castle. I had been imposed upon by spectres and apparitions . . . I see myself and the whole frame of nature shrink into fleeting ideas, which, like Epicurus' atoms, dance about in emptiness." Dumfounded at the seemingly irresistible conclusions drawn from his once cherished Berkeleian speculations, he resolved to reconstruct the shattered faith, and to find a basis on which he could build proofs of the existence of a self, a mind, an external world, and free-will.

Leaving him to his philosophical studies, we follow him in his public life. In 1751 he was appointed regent in King's College, Aberdeen, and he and his family left the old manse amid parochial lamentations, and in a few weeks were housed in a dwelling facing the College Chapel, rented from the College, with its low thatched roof, shaded and sheltered by the trees around it. He had, as regent, to teach moral philosophy, logic, pneumatics, natural philosophy, with hydrostatics and astronomy—a course which took much out of the professor without putting much into the students. Reid did not complain—indeed, he encouraged the absurd old system of "Regenting," which was then abolished at every other University. He also persuaded the authorities to resume the old plan of students living and boarding within the college. Reid comforted anxious parents by assuring them that their sons were secure from temptation by being shut up within its safeguarding walls from nine at night till six o'clock in the morning, while the professors, watching them from the windows, could scrutinise the doings of their scholars every

[1] *Inquiry into the Human Mind* (Introduction).

hour of the day.[1] No wonder the King's Collegians soon sighed after the freedom of their brethren at Marischal College, who could live and lodge anywhere in the town. At a period when religious life was still sombre in southern counties, when worldly entertainments were regarded by "high-fliers" as morally and spiritually unwholesome, it is pleasant to find in the less austere Aberdeen that regulations were made for the encouragement of dancing among the students—to use Mr. Reid's words—"as giving graceful motions, and above all, manliness and confidence." Unfortunately, the dancing classes were robbed of all delightsomeness, by the partners not being fair damsels of the city, but rough and raw fellow-students, from farms and stocking factories, whose motions, however "manly," could not be "graceful," as they practised reel and minuet and country-dance, with steps laborious and heavy clattering of thick-nailed shoes, to the accompaniment of a fiddle.

In the Aberdeen College at that time were men of some note. Dr. Blackwell was still lecturing on Greek and writing in English, as he had done for many a year in his cockscombical way. His *Essay on Homer* and his pompous *Court of Augustus*, highly respected in their day, have gone the way of poor Turnbull's *Ancient Painting*, to the trunk-maker, without a Hogarth to immortalise their names. There were also regents of dulness profound, estimably droning out their Latin lectures, under the bland delusion that they were forming the minds of a new generation. The hard-worked, ill-paid professors had their little entertainments — their clubs, their supper-parties, their holidays in summer, when they "took the sea," and drank the waters at Peterhead Wells; or, greatly daring, went on a trip by sea to London, to see sights and celebrities; and they took horse for Edinburgh, to have their wits burnished up by the newest topics, and their wives' wardrobes supplied with the newest fashions.

Every alternate Wednesday afternoon would be seen going to the "Red Lion" five or six figures well known in Aberdeen, clad in the sedate blue cloth, bushy wigs, and full cocked hats.

---

[1] *Stat. Acct. Scot.*, "Hist. of Aberdeen University"; Dunbar's *Social Life in Morayshire*, p. 6.

The big heavy, tall figure of Dr. John Gregory, Professor of Medicine, would appear with the thick-set form of his cousin Dr. Reid; and the stout slouchy body of Dr. James Beattie, teaching Moral Philosophy at Marischal College, would walk there with Professor Campbell, a little man with benign face and catholic soul. They were on their way to the Philosophical Club. A frugal, sedate company of six or eight met at five o'clock, read and debated essays till eight o'clock, when they sat down to a modest repast, which concluded as the clock struck ten. The whole expense was never to exceed eighteenpence a head; and by written rule "any member may take a glass at the bye-table while the president is in the chair, but no health shall be drunk during that time."[1] Philosophy, science, laws, history, and religion were discussed by those gentlemen, who were more or less acquainted with such questions, seeing that, as regents, some taught their students subjects ranging from Logic to Astronomy. Each chose his special question for discussion, and the books which they published afterwards were the results of their weekly gatherings. There they propounded theories afterwards published in Professor Gerard's *Essay on Taste*, Dr. Beattie's work on *Moral Truth*, Dr. Oswald's treatise of *Common Sense in Religion*, Dr. George Campbell's *Lectures on Rhetoric*, and Dr. John Gregory's *Comparative View of Man and Animals*, in which the philosophical physician discusses everything from suckling to religion, from teething to melody.

Much they spoke of David Hume's political and philosophical essays at the meetings; and the efforts of these cautious but perplexed Aberdonians were directed to extricating morals and metaphysics from the quandary in which the audacious philosopher had laid them. Dr. Reid wrote to Hume with engaging frankness: "Your friendly adversaries, Drs. Campbell and Gerard, as well as Dr. Gregory, return their compliments to you respectfully. Your company would, although we are all good Christians, be more acceptable than that of St. Athanasius, and since we cannot have you upon the bench, you are oftener than any other man brought to the bar, accused and defended with great zeal but without bitter-

---

[1] Forbes's *Life of Beattie*, i. 31; M'Cosh's *Scot. Philosophy*, p. 227.

ness. If you write no more on morals, politics, or metaphysics, I am afraid we shall be at a loss for subjects."[1]

Besides debating Hume's opinions in his Club, Reid had now completed an *Inquiry into the Human Mind on the Principles of Common Sense*, in which he combated the theories in the sceptic's *Treatise on Human Nature*. It was no easy matter, however, as Beattie afterwards discovered, to get a work on Philosophy published. Mr. Andrew Millar, the eminent London bookseller, when visiting Aberdeen, was sounded on the matter. Of course such books were pronounced a "drug in the market," and the public naturally do not like drugs. He pronounced metaphysical works to be bad bargains for booksellers—works on which "he and his brother tradesmen had lost a vast deal of money." However, for the sake of a friend and a countryman, he was persuaded to risk it; and for the sum of £50 the author parted with his manuscript, telling his friends with charming simplicity, "I think it very well sold," although it was the fruit of twenty years' study. This manuscript, through his friend Dr. Hugh Blair, he had submitted to David Hume, in order that he might correct the style, although the work energetically attacked the heretic's own opinions. There was a fine naïveté in the proceeding. It resembled a certain sea-fight between English and Dutch ships, where the powder of the former running short, they sent a flag of truce to the enemy offering to buy more ammunition, and the commercially-minded Dutchmen struck a bargain, and the fight was forthwith renewed. Till that time the good-natured sceptic knew nothing of his opponent, and he received the parcel with natural reluctance, expecting a humdrum refutation, by a scandalised minister of the Gospel, of a treatise which he had himself discarded, and wished to be forgotten. "I wish parsons would confine themselves to their old occupation of worrying one another, and leave philosophers to argue with temper, moderation, and good manners," he peevishly remarked.[2] But the manuscript having been read, he found in the author a fit antagonist; for here was no violent assault on infidelity by a preacher of the Gospel who forgot charity in zeal for the faith; but a calm, acute

[1] Burton's *Hume*, ii. 155.   [2] *Ibid.* ii. 153.

philosophical treatise. Nothing could be finer than the courtesies exchanged between these two philosophers—divine and deist. "Your system," wrote Dr. Reid, "appears to me not only coherent in all its parts, but likewise justly deduced from the principles commonly received among philosophers—principles which I never thought of calling in question until the conclusions you drew from them made me suspect them. If the principles are solid, your system must stand; I agree with you, therefore, that if this system shall ever be abolished, you have a just claim to a great share of the praise; both because you have made a distinct and determinate work to be aimed at and have furnished proper artillery for the purpose."[1] This is admirable in tone and honesty. Very similar to these chivalrous polemics was the manner in which Principal Campbell wrote, and Hume received, the *Dissertation on Miracles*, which disputed his views, and the courtesy with which was revised Principal Leechman's *Discourse on Prayer*, which the author submitted to the prayerless philosopher.

The *Inquiry* was published in 1764. It is the work of a cautious Aberdonian, as hostile to a paradox as to a bad bargain. Reid seeks to reconstruct human knowledge against philosophical arguments on plain common-sense, or plain practical judgment. "Common-sense holds nothing of Philosophy, nor needs her aid. Let my soul dwell with commonsense."[2] Hitherto he had accepted the usual view that we have no immediate knowledge of an external world—only mediate, through our sensations. He had even once adopted the whole system of Bishop Berkeley,[3] who argued that not only have we no direct perception of a material world, but there is no material world to perceive. On reading Hume's *Treatise* he had seen with dismay how far these views, which are meant to vindicate theism, could, when logically carried out, lead to blank agnosticism. For Hume, agreeing that we are cognisant of ideas only, argued that we had as little evidence for mind as for matter, having no consciousness of the existence of either. Reid sought to confirm human convictions in the existence of an external world; and this he does, by insisting

---

[1] Burton's *Hume*, ii. 155.   [2] *Inquiry* (Introduction).
[3] *Intellectual and Active Powers*, Essay xi. ch. x.

that our common beliefs are valid, that the mind has an immediate perception that its sensations of external objects are real, that from this intuitive belief there is no appeal. All the reasonings of philosophy are considered futile against common-sense, which affirms an external world, free-will, and causation. It may not be a very subtle refutation of idealism or agnosticism, but with its vigour and acuteness it proved a good working, hard-working system. Here was a practical philosophy of which it could not be said: "It was a good horse for a stall, but a sorry jade for a journey."

It is impossible, however, for any metaphysician to be always consistent, and sometimes Reid speaks of our knowledge of outward objects as immediate, while at others he speaks of it as being due to the medium of sensations accompanied by perception or intuitive belief in real existence outside. Sir James Mackintosh remarked to that subtle thinker, Dr. Thomas Brown, that Reid and Hume really seemed to differ more in words than opinions; to which he replied acutely, "Yes, Reid bawled out, 'We must believe in an external world'; but added in a whisper, 'We can give no reason for our belief.' Hume cries out, 'We can give no reason for such a notion'; but whispers, 'I own we cannot get rid of it.'" Dr. Reid, the commonplace Dr. Oswald, author of *Common Sense in Religion*, and the forcibly feeble Dr. Beattie —Aberdonians all—became known in England as the "triumvirate of Scottish philosophy"—an incongruous trio. Acuteness and vigour of argument are the merits of his treatise; elegance and grace are not the qualities of his style. Probably he would have considered literary decoration in controversy as much out of place as the silken tackle of Cleopatra's pleasure ship on a sea-going merchantman.

The same year in which his famous *Inquiry* was published from Millar's shop, Reid was invited to fill the chair of Moral Philosophy left vacant by Adam Smith. With regret he left his old home in November 1764, parting with friends of a lifetime, with the city and colleges, which themselves were as dear as old friends, to begin a new career in a city and among a people so different in taste and manners from those of the North. For two years—until he got into his house in the Professor's Court at the College—he was to be found in a poor, narrow wynd beyond the Drygate, inhabited chiefly by weavers, whose handlooms clattered from open doors and windows all day long. "You go through a long, dark, abominably nasty entry, which leads you into a clean little close. You walk upstairs to a neat little dining-room, and find as many rooms as just accommodate my family [of five] so scantily, that my apartment is a closet of six feet by eight or nine off the dining-room." Thus does he describe his new abode to an Aberdeen friend, and he adds with an air of surprise and triumph, "The house is new and free of buggs." Besides that, "It has the best air and finest prospects in Glasgow—the privilege of a large garden, very airy to walk in"—this was the College pleasure-grounds. All these amenities—which certainly exist "beyond the Drygate" no longer—did not, however, prevent its being infested with small-pox, which dealt mortality and ugliness among the weavers, and even infected his own family.[1] Clearly his heart hankered after the old thatched home in the North, nestled among the trees, and the familiar faces in Castle Street.

He found reigning in the western city a tone of brand-new prosperity mingled with austere religiosity which were uncomfortable to him after the northern city, with old families of small incomes, who leavened society with "genteel" dignity, and with the tolerance of a region where the extremely Solemn League and Covenant principles happily had never spread. Here he found the people "without manners" or any grace (except, of course, "saving grace"), and "extremely sober." Indeed, he had to own that the only man he saw drunk was one of his brother professors. He noted that the "common people have a gloom upon their countenances," though he was not sure "whether that is due to their climate or enthusiastic piety"; and as for the clergy, "who are fanatical," "you hear from the pulpit a gospel which you know nothing about, for you never hear it."[2] It is thus the good, pious, Moderate divine described the town of his adoption to his sympathetic friend in Aberdeen, to whom he unburdened his mind.

---

[1] Reid's *Works* (Hamilton), p. 41.
[2] Correspondence in Reid's *Works* (Hamilton's edit.), pp. 40, 41.

A professor's income, as we know, was severely modest in those days; but Dr. Reid was pleased to report that he had "touched about £70 in fees, and may possibly make out £100 this session"—for which he taught classes beginning at seven o'clock in the morning, consisting of sixty students. On the benches were sons of weavers from the Drygate and of merchants from the Saltmarket, of lairds and of ministers; youths from the far-off Hebrides; and a "great number of stupid Irish teagues," who formed a third of the students, coming over thirty at a time in ships, to qualify to be teachers, doctors, and Presbyterian ministers. "I preach to them," Reid groaned in despair, "as St. Francis did to the fishes."[1] Poverty being usual among students, they came late to Glasgow in order to save their lodging. Among his brethren the new professor found congenial company. He was at home with Principal Leechman, the fine-hearted, tolerant head of the University, who, though silent and sedate, had a wife who loved romances, poetry, and fashion; with Moor, the Greek scholar, a man of infinite jest, over whose jokes he would ponder deliberately, as if they were mathematical problems, and as the meaning dawned upon him, would burst into laughter when everybody else had forgotten them. He had sympathy with John Millar, the admirable Professor of Law, whose eminent works on government and philosophy were said to be only dim reflections of the brilliant talk of a man whose boxing-matches with his pupils were not more invigorating than the intellectual training of his lectures.[2]

Reid was certainly not a brilliant expounder, but solid, plain, and clear—reading his lectures in rich Aberdonian as closely as he had done his sermons in New Machar. There was nothing in his manner to attract; but as Dugald Stewart, in his own most pompous way, remarks: "Such was the simplicity and perspicuity of his style, such the gravity and authority of his character, and such the general interest of his young hearers in the doctrine which he taught, that by the numerous audience to which his instructions were delivered he was heard uniformly with the most silent and respectful atten-

---
[1] Correspondence in Reid's *Works* (Hamilton's edit.), p. 43.
[2] Cockburn's *Life of Jeffrey*, i. 10.

tion."[1] His classes increased in size year by year, and consisted not merely of raw youths, but of old students who would come year after year (especially as no fees were charged to them), with lawyers and city ministers who came to rekindle their philosophical interest. Thus he went on for sixteen years. It was a placid life he spent, almost as uniform, as untravelled as Immanuel Kant's, who was also brooding over Hume's Philosophy. The German philosopher was as regular as the big clock of the Cathedral of Königsberg: punctual to a minute he rose from bed, drank his coffee, gave his lectures, and took his walks. Every one knew that it was half-past three when Kant, in grey coat and Spanish cane in hand, stepped out of his door to walk up and down the Linden Avenue eight times, while behind him with an umbrella, lest it should rain, followed his servant Lampe—"like a picture of Providence," as Heine says. Nearly as methodical as this were the ways of his brother philosopher in Glasgow.

There were, however, occasions when he would visit his cousin, Dr. James Gregory, in Edinburgh, and debate philosophical and mathematical points; and there were annual sojourns at Blair Drummond with Lord Kames. Were two mortals ever less alike than these two incongruous but fast friends? There was the tall, stooping figure of the Judge, with his keen, sarcastic face, and the short, thick-set Professor, with his solid, simple countenance, trudging side by side over moors and fields, on which his lordship was intent—the Judge with his broad humour, his rough jests, hurrying his workmen with his free expletives; the divine, sedate, polite, deferential, jogging along over shoe-buckles in bog. Then there was the return of the companions at dusk, hungry and weary and muddy, to supper and to his lordship's favourite port, to talk over manure and moral sentiments, potatoes and perceptions—the host plenteously sniffing up snuff, his friend putting his quid of tobacco to one side of his cheek the more articulately to discuss the questions. Then his lordship would read out parts of his manuscript of the *Sketches of Man*, containing some passages that were extremely plain-spoken, and when the decorous professor respectfully suggested, "My

[1] Stewart's *Life of Reid*.

lord, had you not better soften that passage?" the reply, "Deil a bit, Doctor—deil a bit," would silence the reverend guest.[1]

A quiet, laborious mind was his—as such impressing Dr. Samuel Johnson, when, in 1773, he arrived at the Saracen's Head in the Gallowgate, of which, "though wretchedly managed, the Glasgow folk are vastly proud." The professors paid their respects to the illustrious traveller, and he supped with them. "I am not much pleased with any of them," he informed Mrs. Thrale. They talked little and cautiously, for, as the obsequious Boswell remarks,[2] "like their brethren in Aberdeen, they did not care to expose themselves much to the battery of his cannon, which they knew might play upon them." In other words, they were courteous and did not contradict; they had some sense of dignity, and did not wish to be bullied. Of the learned fraternity, Dr. Reid was not likely to be the most loquacious or lively. "I have no pretensions to be vivacious," the worthy man acknowledged when he was aged, and he could have said the same when he was younger. Rarely did a striking sentence come from his respectable pen; never did a brilliant saying fall from his instructive lips.

Yet this man was full of active interests and keen intellectual pursuits. Soon after he came to Glasgow he was to be seen at Dr. Black's class-room, where the chemist expounded his theory on Latent Heat, as eager about experiments, as copious with his notes, as the most ardent boy-student in the class; interested in the fine types set up in his friend Alexander Wilson's foundry, excited over Dollond's telescope just arrived at the observatory, and studying optics with eager delight. We find the good man full of observation even in places where science loses a little of its dignity. Thus he records his investigations: "A nasty custom of chewing tobacco has been the reason of my observing a species of nasty little animals. I spit into a basin of sawdust, which, when it becomes to be drenched, produces a vast number of animals three or four times the size of a louse, and not very different

---

[1] Ramsay's *Scotland and Scotsmen*, i. 475.
[2] Boswell's *Johnson* (ed. Hill), v. 370.

in shape, but armed with four or five rows of pickles like a hedgehog, which seem to serve as feet."[1] As he gazes, with bent head and cauliflower wig, at these weird creatures, fit to come in a nightmare or to produce one, studying natural history in a spittoon, he presents a curious rather than an impressive figure.

In 1780 he found he was growing old, and, getting a substitute in his chair, he retired from public duties. It is characteristic of old academic ways that this successor, Dr. Arthur, was recommended by Dr. Reid because he had heard him preach excellent sermons. Sixteen years had he lectured, and for another sixteen he was to enjoy the peaceful luxury of growing gently older. He lived in the old house in the grim court, with its friendly, familiar society, pursuing his old studies, and busy with scientific experiments in more dignified quarters than a "basin of sawdust."

He was a man of seventy-eight when he published his *Essays on Intellectual and Active Powers*, which proved that his own intellectual powers were not dimmed and his active powers were not abated—giving the results of lectures of keen observation and criticism on Psychology. Commonsense there is still used as the key to truth, experience as the solvent of all problems. He ventures on no high or deep philosophical theories. As for metaphysics—strictly so called—the name of "idea" was to him a bugbear, so protean in its shapes and meanings; so difficult to define; so impossible to translate from foreign languages; so illusive to grasp in our own. "Metaphysics," said Voltaire to Dr. John Moore, when the author of *Zeluco* visited the patriarch at Ferney—"metaphysics are like minuet dancers, who, being dressed to the greatest advantage, make a couple of bows, move through the room in the finest attitudes, display all their graces, are in perpetual motion without advancing a step, and finish at the identical point from which they set out."[2] Not so neatly could Reid have expressed it; but something in this way he, like Hutcheson, his philosophical ancestor, felt towards abstruse problems of philosophy.

[1] Reid's *Works* (ed. by Hamilton), p. 49.
[2] Moore's *View of Society and Manners in France*, 1779, i. 271.

There was a fine simplicity, a sterling honesty in the old philosophical student, who in controversy was the model of courtesy, shocking thereby Dr. Beattie, who was grieved that a controversialist who professed to be a Christian should write like a gentleman. As he grew aged he became very deaf, but not less shrewd; as active at eighty-seven years as at sixty, with his short, sturdy frame, busy in his garden, keen over botany, physiology, or physics. Yet with all his energy he would plaintively say, with a kindly look on his good, plain, common-sense face, which looked like an incarnation of his own philosophy: " I am ashamed of having lived so long after having ceased to be useful." [1]

In October 1794 he died, leaving a blameless name as a gentleman, a high reputation as a teacher, and works which were to have a powerful effect in stimulating philosophical thought in Scotland—through Dugald Stewart, his own pupil, who successfully expounded his system in Edinburgh during his life; and through Sir William Hamilton, who expounded it with vastly more learning and brilliancy, long after his death. If his influence was slight in Germany, it was for a while potent in France, after Royer Collard picked up a copy of his *Inquiry* at a bookstall on the quays of Paris. Through him Reid's philosophy passed on to Jouffroy and to Cousin the prolific.

DR. JAMES BEATTIE

Social fame is not always the portion of the greatest; popularity is for those writers who support, by arguments which all can follow, opinions which all are holding; who say in verse things to which society can say "How beautiful!" and say in prose things to which society can murmur "How true!" The palm of literary celebrity in the eighteenth century was not given to the great writers of Scotland—to Hume for his brilliant philosophical essays, or Robertson for his admirable histories, or Adam Smith for his unequalled exposition of political economy, or to Reid for his acute, astute, intellectual work—but to Dr. James Beattie, author of *The Minstrel*, a

---
[1] Fraser's *Life of Thomas Reid*.

Poem, and the *Essay on the Immutability of Truth*, which "avenged insulted Christianity," and greatly insulted Mr. David Hume. To search into past literature is somewhat like excavating an old churchyard. There are bones once full of vigour, skulls in which were located brains acute and brilliant, jaw-bones on which were cheeks fresh and fair, eyeless sockets from which once darted glances of perilous fascination. These remains are found in the mould in all stages of preservation or decay—some are reduced to powder, others seem marvellously intact, yet crumble to dust when exposed to the air or touched with the spade. Similar is the pathetic experience of those who unearth dead authors, dead books, dead reputations. Some are still wonderfully preserved, some have all the semblance of life till we critically touch them—dry bones which no Ezekiel could call back into life.

When Dr. James Beattie died in the fulness of years and of fame, it was meet that a solid biography—a literary tombstone—should be erected to his memory. His friend and steadfast admirer, Sir William Forbes of Pitsligo, an excellent man, a wealthy banker, undertook the work.[1] The result is not lively reading, though not without interest, for it preserves devoutly all the traditions of the poet from the north country which we wish to learn—and a good deal more.

James Beattie was born in 1735, in the village of Laurencekirk in Kincardineshire, of parents who, the biographer informs us, "though poor were honest"—a conjunction of virtue with impecuniosity which evidently is a grave surprise to the opulent baronet. The father kept a little shop, and was tenant of a little farm. In the parish school, which had been taught in the beginning of the century by the famous grammarian Thomas Ruddiman, the boy, amid his lessons, showed precocious literary propensities; he read assiduously Ogilby's now forgotten translation of Homer; he was addicted to the disagreeable practice of getting up during the night from his chaff-bed and walking about his little chamber in airy night-shirt to think out some poetic fancy, which he feverishly wrote down to relieve his seething juvenile brain. His companions regarded him with respect, and he would go proudly to and from

[1] Forbes's Account of *Life and Writings of James Beattie*, 2 vols. 1806.

DR. JAMES BEATTIE
From an Engraving of the Painting by Reynolds in Aberdeen University.

school rejoicing in the title of "poet," with which his master had injudiciously dubbed him. At the age of fourteen he entered Marischal College, Aberdeen, where the pompous Dr. Blackwell, Professor of Greek, discovered that his pupil possessed the vague attribute of "genius." In 1752 he gave up studying for the ministry to become parish schoolmaster at Fordoun, at the foot of the Grampians, a poor occupation for a "genius," especially as for £10 he was expected also to act as session-clerk, to superintend cock-fights, and to lead the psalmody in the parish church. Lord Monboddo, who lived near Fordoun, was delighted to find in this young teacher one with whom he could converse on his beloved Greek. His biographer fondly tells how his hero would wander through the glens, nursing his poetic fancy; even strolling throughout the night, "contemplating the sky and marking the approach of day."[1] Promotion came in 1760 to the young schoolmaster, who, after becoming teacher in the Grammar School in Aberdeen, was to his natural surprise offered the chair of Natural Philosophy in Marischal College. Truly in those old academic days strange things were done. We have seen how in Edinburgh Adam Ferguson was appointed to a similar chair, the subjects of which he knew nothing about, and had to learn in three months. Here was a young country schoolmaster placed by a patron to teach a young generation matters of which he had scarcely heard since he sat as a boy listening to his regent. At his request Mr. Beattie, feeling his incapacity for the post, was immediately transferred to the chair of Moral Philosophy and Logic, of which he at least knew quite as little.

Life in Old Aberdeen was pleasant though provincial. There were the merchants making money from linen and flannel and fish; lawyers, called "advocates," who made good incomes from clients belonging to a most litigious race; county families, who in winter months resorted to the not too riotous gaiety of the little town, with its occasional balls, its frequent tea-parties and suppers. But the intellectual contribution to the society was chiefly made by the professors of King's and Marischal Colleges, enlivened by a sprinkling

[1] Forbes's *Life of Beattie*, i. 22.

of well-read lairds and ministers. Every other Wednesday the "Wise Club,"[1] as outsiders called it, met at five o'clock, and after debating till eight, partook, we are told, of a "slight and inexpensive collation" till ten, when the worthy philosophers walked soberly to their respective abodes. What a contrast this "slight collation" in Aberdeen to the many festive gatherings of the convivial philosophers in Edinburgh!

In the *Scots Magazine*—the respectable paper which weekly purveyed letters, essays, poetry, and news for Scottish society—a few verses signed "J. B." were the first product of Beattie's pen; and in 1761 a little volume crept into existence in London —*Original Poems and Translations*—which the biographer aforesaid superlatively states "stamped Dr. Beattie with the character of great and original genius, from the harmony of his numbers, the simplicity yet force and elegance of his diction, the brightness of his fancy, as well as the appropriate sentiments through it." What an old-world sound there is in all these carefully-arranged adjectives and phrases! Having better judgment than his biographer, the poet used in later years to destroy every copy he found. Genius is impatient, and decent Andrew Millar, the publisher, was blamed for his lack of energy in pushing the sale. Yet in 1766 another edition, with omissions and additions, appeared, and the success was considerable. Persons "of consequence" took the poet up. Mr. Gray, the poet, on his Highland tour was staying at Glamis Castle, and Beattie was asked to meet him. In passing through Edinburgh the English poet, with parrot-like face, all nose and no chin, had made a poor impression,[2] being reserved, silent—"a mighty fine gentleman," said the dissatisfied Principal Robertson. But with Beattie he was easy, frank, charming; for the professor had a wonderful gift, with his simple nature and his capacity of bestowing admiration, for winning friendship. "Mr. Gray," records Dr. Johnson, "naturally contracted a friendship with Dr. Beattie, whom he found a poet, a philosopher, and a good man."[3] They praised each other's poems, lauded each other's virtues, and Beattie in

---

[1] Forbes's *Beattie*, i. 31.
[2] Forbes, i. 75; Carlyle's *Autobiography*.
[3] Johnson's *Lives of the Poets*—"Gray."

the honest exuberance of his heart could drench a celebrity with compliments.

The poems of 1766 were winning praise in Scotland and in England, when Beattie, remembering that he was a Professor of Moral Philosophy, felt it his duty to defend orthodoxy against the malignant scepticism of David Hume, whose theories were a frequent subject of debate at the "Wise Club." His pious friend Dr. John Gregory, who had left his chair of Physic in Aberdeen for a more profitable chair and practice in Edinburgh, wrote to him alarming reports of the encroachments of infidelity; informing him that "materialism and atheism are the present fashion"; that "a man who expresses belief in a future state of existence is regarded as a fool or a hypocrite." "There is an insolence and daring effrontery in this which is exceedingly provoking . . . till within these thirty years the wit was generally on the side of religion. I do not remember any man of the least pretensions to genius in Britain who ever thought of subverting any principle of natural religion till of late." All this he seems to attribute to the "licentious teaching" of David Hume, who had ceased to write on philosophy many years before. The agitated Professor of Medicine indeed owns that "among Hume's disciples I do not know any one who ever read his *Treatise of Human Nature;* what was read and spoken of was anything to do with belles lettres." Who could stem the tide of infidelity?[1] "You," said Gregory, "are the best man to chastise such people as they deserve." Beattie thoroughly agreed with him. Diligently, therefore, he laboured at his work on *The Immutability of Truth,* which was to scarify wits, silence scoffers, and convince doubters, and, as his friend suggested, "warm the imagination and touch the hearts of those who are deaf to reason." The Professor was no philosopher; he knew nothing of his subject till he began to teach it, and not much even then; he disliked metaphysics, which he never could understand, and yet he essayed the task. His manuscript was read with high approval by Blacklock, Gregory, and other orthodox friends. "I want," said he, "to lay before the public in as strong a light as possible the following dilemma: our

[1] Forbes's *Beattie,* i. 104.

sceptics either believe the doctrines they publish or they do not believe them; if they believe them they are fools; if not, they are a thousand times worse." What could be more concise and compact than this? His friends hinted mildly that the language in which he sought to pulverise Hume and all his works might be more gentle—they might have said gentlemanly—but not one objectionable phrase would the good man modify, for he felt bound in conscience to speak "as a man and a Christian."

Strange to say, this famous work was launched on the world with difficulty. Booksellers refused it, but at last, under the persuasion of Beattie's friends, Mr. Andrew Millar consented to publish it, though only at the author's expense. Unwilling to hurt the author's feelings by this mortifying proposal, his admirers arranged quietly among themselves to pay the cost, and with amiable mendacity told him that it had been sold for fifty guineas, which, of course, they presented to him out of their own pockets. The Professor was delighted, yea, astonished, at so large a sum, which "does really exceed my warmest expectations."[1] The worthy man did not know—let us trust he never learned—the ironic fact, at which his adversaries would have been hugely delighted, that his great *Essay on the Origin and Immutability of Truth* was ushered into the world by the aid of a lie.

This was in 1770. The tone of the book was so peevishly bitter that the clamour in Edinburgh was like that of a startled rookery, and David Hume lost his placidity of temper and complained that he was not being treated like a gentleman. In England, however, it made a bound into favour. It was read by all who read anything beyond a romance; literary circles praised "its wit, its reason, its eloquence." Bishops were more than satisfied with its triumphant apology for truth; literary ladies were charmed with it—it was all "so clear," "so beautiful," "so convincing."[2] When, the following year (1771), appeared the first part of *The Minstrel*, in which he tuned his "Gothic lyre" to tell the vapid tale of the plaintive Edwin, the "genius" of the poet was sung in full chorus—

---

[1] Forbes's *Beattie*, i. 147.
[2] Doran's *Lady of the Last Century*, p. 286.

though to-day one sees in pretty descriptions and pleasing reflections no trace of it. Success had followed success. The poem was the subject of universal talk. "Have you read *The Minstrel?*" was the question on all sides. At Bath, at Tunbridge Wells the circulating libraries were pestered for copies by impatient inquirers; the blue-stocking Mrs. Montagu was advising friends everywhere to buy it; and Mr. Gray, the fastidious, wrote kindliest criticism and abundant laudation; in Seminaries for Young Ladies were recited the familiar lines, till every one was weary of the words:

> Young Edwin was no vulgar boy,
> Deep thought oft seemed to fix his infant eye;
> Dainties he heeded not, nor gawd, nor toy,
> Save one short pipe of rudest minstrelsy;
> Silent when glad, affectionate though shy—

and so on. In Edinburgh it was greeted with little applause, for its author had railed at its beloved infidel. "A milk and water poet," sneered the not unbiassed Hume, who spoke of him as a "silly, bigoted fellow." "A piece which could not be called a poem, without beginning, middle, or end, containing a few good lines," remarked Adam Smith.[1] But these jarring notes could not vex the complacent bard.

When his popularity was at its height Mr. Beattie and his pretty wife, in the autumn of 1771, set forth for London. An introduction from Dr. John Gregory to Mrs Montagu found him a ready welcome into literary society. In Hill Street[2] the lettered Mrs. Montagu held her "blue-stocking" assemblies. It was some years since Mr. Benjamin Stillingfleet had first trod her carpet clad in the blue stockings which gave the well-known name to the ladies who affected philosophy and polite letters in assemblies which he frequented. Up the unpaved street coaches were driven and sedan-chairs borne, at great risk from the footpads that infested the district. Not far off was Mayfair, at that period the locality for butchers' shambles, for drunkenness and riot. Near it was Tyburn Lane —now bearing the innocent appellation of Park Lane—up which the frequent carts passed carrying the victims for the

---

[1] *The Bee*, 1791, iii. p. 4.
[2] Doran's *Lady of the Last Century*, p. 286.

scaffold, while red-nosed chaplains, with characters as dirty as their cassocks, muttered their ghostly offices. The fashionable frequenters of the gay saloon could hear the shouts and revelry of the mob as they escorted the wretches to Tyburn Tree. In the "Chinese Room," with its ornaments of shaking mandarins and "fat-headed pagodas"—for it was imagined that a pagoda was Chinese for a graven image—gathered a goodly and learned company, who partook of admirable dinners, or in the evening indulged in tea and ceaseless talk. Dr. Johnson was there seated, distorting his huge body, shaking convulsively his head, spluttering over successive dishes of bohea, while around his chair clustered adoring ladies, four deep, standing on tiptoe to see and hear the great man, whose voice dominated the room with his vociferous "Why, no, sir," and his milder "Why, yes, ma'am." Sir Joshua Reynolds stood by the fireplace, with ear-trumpet alert, bearing the bland expression which the deaf always wear when they wish to look as if they heard. The esteemed but absurd person of Mr. Gibbon, in his flowered coat, was present, with the spare form of Horace Walpole. These and many more men of note—Garrick, Murphy, Richard Cumberland—were there. Among them fussed the clever, learned, and bountiful hostess, Mrs Montagu,[1] with sharp face, prominent nose, and penetrating eyes, her person bedizened with diamond necklaces and adorned in every colour of the rainbow, which gained for her the name of "Iris."[1] Other ladies in the company could fairly rival her learning and her wit—Mrs. Carter, the pretty translator of Epictetus; young Miss Hannah More, in the full flush of literary glory, whose drama of *Percy* now rivalled *Douglas*, and whose *Bas Bleu* was setting the world a-talking—for, as Dr. Johnson said solemnly to Dr. Beattie, "Sir, she is a most powerful versificatrix."

Into this brilliant world the Aberdeen poet and philosopher was introduced, and we can imagine how dazzled the plain man must have been by this galaxy of fashion and letters —now talking to the famous Sir Joshua and Garrick, now introduced to my Lord Bath, or her high Grace the Duchess of Portland. All so different this drawing-room from the humble parlours at home—these high-bred voices from the deplorable

[1] Wraxall's *Hist. Memoirs*, i. 147, 152; Taylor's *Records of my Life*, i. 92.

Aberdonian. Received with respect, even with homage, he received compliments by the bushel, till his melancholy eyes knew not where to look. In appearance he was a stout person, with a slouch in his gait, and with eyes black, piercing, and pathetic, which ladies found fascinating. Dr. Johnson was more than gracious to him, for was he not orthodox? did he not hate that rascal Hume? did he not listen with deference? In his satisfaction he forgave the professor for being a Scotsman. Beattie, writing home, told of his great doings, and reported that Johnson had been greatly misrepresented. "I have passed several entire days with him, and found him extremely agreeable. The compliments he pays me are so high that I have not the face to mention them." There was a diffident, deferential manner in the worthy poet, with a genuine simplicity of heart, that seems to have been irresistible to English people. One person, however, there was to whom the flattery of Beattie was as gall. This was Oliver Goldsmith, who became horribly jealous at the incense wafted before Dr. Beattie. Mrs. Thrale says that he went about in his foolish blabbing way saying so, so that it was no vain imagination on Beattie's part. "Goldsmith is a poor creature," the author of *The Minstrel* informed his friends at home, "eaten up with affectation and envy. He was the only person I ever knew who owned himself to be envious. In Johnson's presence he was quiet enough, but in his absence expressed great uneasiness in hearing him praised. He even envied the dead: he could not bear that Shakespeare should be so much admired as he was. ... But surely Goldsmith had no occasion to envy me," he modestly adds—" which, however, he did, for he owned it, though he was always very civil." [1]

What tales Mr. Beattie had to tell of high, brilliant society he met, when he returned, caressed and flattered, to his quiet home. Two years afterwards he is in London again. The same receptions attend him. At Bulstrode he and his wife are entertained by the Dowager Duchess of Portland; presents of money are offered by Mrs. Montagu, by the Duchess, and by the Queen; he visits bishops; he is pressed by the Archbishop of York to enter the English Church and accept an ample

[1] Forbes, ii. 267; Mrs. Piozzi's *Autobiography*, ii. 181.

living; he is received by the King, who praises his *Essay* and gives him a pension of £200 a year. When he went to Kew to present his thanks for the gracious pension, he was again complimented on such a book, which the King said he and the Queen "always kept by them"—a copy at Kew, another at Windsor. His Majesty remarked that he had heard the sale of Hume's *Essays* had fallen off since the great *Essay on Truth* had appeared, and the author modestly replied he believed that it had. His Majesty questioned his pensioner as to the length of the prayers of Scots ministers. "Sometimes a quarter or half an hour, I told him." The King, venturing on theology, profoundly stated "he could not imagine any thinking man could be an atheist unless he could bring himself to believe that he made himself." This seemed to him so weighty and original an argument that he was pleased to repeat it two or three times to the Queen. It was on a later visit that Miss Fanny Burney saw him, and then she gushes over him in the usual way. "I found him pleasant, unaffected, unassuming, full of conversable intelligence, with a round, thick, clumsy figure that promises nothing either of his works or his discourse. Yet his eye at intervals shoots forth a ray of genius that instantly lights up his whole countenance. His voice and manners are particularly and pleasantly mild, and seem to announce an urbanity of character both inviting and edifying. You would be surprised to find how soon you could forget that he is ugly and clumsy, for there is a sort of perfect good-will in his countenance and his smile that is quite captivating."[1] So records Miss Burney. "He is charming," said Mrs. Thrale, who protested if she ever had a second husband she would have Dr. Beattie. It is certainly remarkable to find the man, born and bred in poverty, who had lived in a humble position, assuming a new position in society without awkwardness, from the sheer simplicity of his nature.

We next find him at Oxford, receiving his degree of D.C.L. on the same day as Sir Joshua Reynolds—and his name was received with applause as loud as that for the great painter, the function heralded by a laudatory oration of twenty minutes. No one admired him more than Sir Joshua—whom, by the

[1] D'Arblay's *Diary*, iii. 397, 402.

way, he complimented, in his "Essay on Poetry and Music," by associating his name with that of Raphael. He stayed with the painter at his country house at Richmond, and met the best of literary company at his house in Leicester Square. As a further compliment the great artist painted an allegorical portrait of his friend clad in his doctor's hood and scarlet gown, holding a copy of his immortal *Essay* in his hand. In five hours the head was painted on the canvas, and an admirable likeness it proved. There looks out from the canvas an amiable, self-satisfied face, all signs of his slouch hidden under the doctorial garb. The picture was designed to represent the triumph of Truth over Error. A female personification of Truth is vigorously thrusting down to perdition three demons —probably Sophistry, Scepticism, and Infidelity. The face of one of the figures represents Voltaire; but was the figure which covers his face in shame from the spectator meant for Hume, as people said, and as the freethinker believed? "They may call it Hume or anybody else," Reynolds said; adding, with a smile, "It is true, it has a tolerably broad back."[1] It is this picture which has done more to immortalise the author than any book he wrote.

While he was flattered in London, and his book was being dandled into fame, his name was not fragrant in Edinburgh. When it was proposed that he should succeed Adam Ferguson on his quitting the chair of Moral Philosophy—for Lord Hailes and Gregory and the pious magistrates were eager for the defender of the faith to uphold truth in the reckless city —the clamour of the literary set was furious. He saw that if he went there he was entering a hornet's nest; but he valiantly protested he was not afraid of any Humites. "I dislike the croaking of frogs, the barking of curs, but I fear neither. Convince me of my duty to remove to Edinburgh, and you shall see me set out immediately, as regardless of the snarling of my enemies as that of the curs who might snap at my heels by the way."[2] Is the writer of this, we wonder, the man whom all in London pronounced so sweet, so amiable? Fortunately his friends did not convince him, and to the

[1] Taylor and Leslie's *Sir Joshua Reynolds*, ii. 58.
[2] Forbes's *Beattie*.

satisfaction of philosophy he remained where he was, and Dugald Stewart got the chair. He was better at Aberdeen, engaged in writing books whose names have long been forgotten, *Evidences of Christianity*, Treatises on Moral Science, Poetry, Music, and Laughter, which have long since passed into the limbo of oblivion with many of their betters. A second and inferior part of *The Minstrel* in 1774 was received with delight (there was not another English poet living at that time, we must remember), and whenever he revisited London the same welcome greeted his appearance. In 1784, when he went accompanied by his son, possessed of a sad, portentously grave countenance, he tells how he visits Drury Lane, when *Douglas* is performed; and Astley's, to see a heifer with two heads. Bishops pressed him to stay at their palaces; and Horace Walpole, who met him at Fulham, pronounced him "quiet, amiable, and cheerful."[1] Even William Pitt lost his hauteur in his little portly presence. Dr. Johnson was now old, and had not long to live, but Dr. Beattie was delighted to find that "he had contracted a gentleness of manners which pleases everybody"; while as to his appetite, "I verily believe that on Sunday last he ate as much dinner as I have done in these ten days past." Mrs. Siddons lost her stateliness in company with the elderly "Minstrel," and would listen while he played Scots airs on his 'cello—the tears starting from her majestic eyes at the plaintive tunes. He even tells that she herself sang to him "Queen Mary's Lament" to admiration, while "I had the honour to accompany her in the bass." Curiously enough, however, the great actress, when she heard this story, declared she had never sung that song in her life.[2]

These visits to London were the triumphs of his life—flattering, charming, yet, if we believe his biographer, never spoiling him. If he took all this as his due, who could blame him? Everybody called him "great," it would be foolish for him to deny it—almost impossible not to believe it. He would retire from the full glare of adulation of London to the obscurity of Aberdeen, where his pension allowed him the luxury of a chaise; and when he went to the Peterhead Wells—the resort of

[1] Walpole's *Letters*, ix. 326.
[2] Forbes's *Beattie*, ii. 139; *Aldine Poets*, Beattie, with Memoir by Dyce.

northern fashion—the poet was respectfully watched as he took his meditative walks. Above all, he was happy at Gordon Castle, where the Duchess was exuberantly attentive and he deferentially sportive, and where he read Blair's *Sermons* aloud to the household on Sunday nights. Robert Burns, who regarded *The Minstrel* as "immortal," sought his help and his compositions for Johnson's *Collection of Scots Music*, some of which do not lack the true lyric notes.

In early days the good man was under the delusion that he could write with humour. His friends to whom he showed specimens at once saw that it would be a very serious matter if he persisted in thinking he could write "droll verses," and they gave him severe discouragement; so he kept his laborious efforts to be funny for the delectation of his family. Music was his passion, and on the 'cello, flute, or organ he would play Handel or Pergolesi; and also sing his own songs to his own airs, with a voice which had survived the precentor days at Fordoun. Music seems to have been a favourite pastime of distinguished Scotsmen in those times. Even the austere seceder, the Rev. Ralph Erskine, in his little manse would play, to the dismay of his followers, on what they sadly called "a wee sinfu' fiddle." The mathematician, Dr. Robert Wallace, like Professor Wilkie, had his flute; Dr. Joseph Black also played the flute, and Dr. Blacklock had his flageolet, while Principal Campbell of Aberdeen, when his wife locked him up in his study, that her indolent spouse might be forced to write his lectures, would smuggle his violin in with him, and when he was supposed to be hard at work, the sounds of the surreptitious fiddle would issue melodiously from his room.

Let it be sorrowfully owned that the "Minstrel" drank too much, and a great deal too often. He had certainly trials enough to send a man with his constitutional melancholy almost to despair. That pretty wife whom in former years he had proudly taken to London was becoming insane, and when he entered his house he would sometimes find that china jars had been removed from the mantelpiece and placed on the top of the door, that they might fall on his devoted head.[1] With unwearied tenderness the good man waited on his

[1] *Aldine Poets*, Beattie, with Memoir by Dyce.

demented wife through anxious days and sleepless nights, till her violence necessitated her removal from the home. His eldest son, possessed of precocious ability and premature gravity enough to merit the epitaph on a pious young divine, as "a truly aged young man," had at the age of nineteen been appointed his father's colleague in the chair of Moral Philosophy, and died at the age of twenty-two, in 1790, his literary remains being afterwards fondly and foolishly published by his father.[1] A few years later the other son also died, and the father was left alone. As he looked on the body of the dead he cried, "I have done with this world!" There are few more pathetic scenes than that of the poor old man, whose memory was gone, searching every room of the house for his lost boy, saying to his man, "You may think it strange, but I must ask you if I have a son, and where he is?" He cared no more to touch his once loved 'cello, or to turn over the pages of that music which so often at evening gatherings in Aberdeen he had played with fine expression and sung with plaintive beauty. Friends saw before them a man with memory gone, with interest in the world gone, with a body racked by rheumatism and weakened by paralysis. In August 1803 he was dead—a life of prosperity darkened at its close by tragedy—while his wife, hopelessly insane, lingered out her days in the madhouse.

His fame to-day is as a tale that is told. His prose works, so lauded in their generation, are forgotten. His *Minstrel* lingers still with a slender reputation after its days of glory, and its author is stamped with that disastrous title of mediocrity—" a pleasing poet."

[1] Dr. Beattie had a contempt for the Scots tongue as "vulgar," and inculcated that feeling in his offspring. "He was early warned against the use of Scottish words and other similar improprieties . . . and after he grew up would never endure to read what was written in any of the vulgar dialects of Scotland" (*Remains of J. H. Beattie*, with Life by his father). Beattie himself published a collection of Scotticisms as a warning to his countrymen.

CHAPTER XI

SCOTTISH MEN OF LETTERS IN ENGLAND

MALLET—THOMSON—SMOLLETT

THROUGHOUT the century there was a continual stream of Scotsmen passing to London in search of fortunes which they found it impossible to win in their own impecunious land. They were found everywhere, in every trade and profession— as merchants, as authors, as physicians, as booksellers, and as pedlars. Indeed, so ubiquitous were the last class that they were said to be even found in Poland; and in England they were so common that packmen were called "Scotchmen" by the people. Mrs. Thrale remembered how in her girlhood the children would jump for joy as a pedlar came to the door, and call to their mother, "There's a Scotchman coming! a Scotchman, indeed!"[1] It was not prudent, however, for a North Briton to flaunt his thistle too openly; it was found sometimes wiser to disguise a name which pronounced his nationality too clearly, which the English could not pronounce at all. As Malloch transformed his surname to Mallet, the translator of the *Lusiad* changed Meikle to Mickle, and the great printer softened Strachan to Strahan. John MacMurray, the half-pay naval lieutenant, when he set up his book-shop in Fleet Street, altered his cognomen to Murray, as John Macmillan, the publisher of Thomson's *Winter*, had curtailed his to Millan. Maccaul, the Duke of Hamilton's valet (who had married the waiting-maid, the famous Dr. Cullen's sister), would

---

[1] Johnson's *Lives of the Poets*; Mrs. Piozzi's *Autobiography*, ii. 184.

never have prospered with his club and fashionable assembly-room if he had not transposed his to Almack.[1]

Distaste at the nation culminated when Lord Bute, the Court favourite, blossomed into Prime Minister of England, and, unpopular himself, made his country more unpopular than ever. Verses, pamphlets, lampoons made bitterly merry at the migratory race, who were vilified like Jews in Germany. Smollett, when travelling to Scotland, found "from Doncaster downwards all the windows of the inns scrawled with doggerel rhymes in abuse of the Scottish nation."[2] It was considered fine humour for a nobleman to write: "I am certainly the most unfortunate man in the world. Two Scotsmen—the only two, I am persuaded, who are out of office and employment—have plundered the house in Hanover Square. I wish the Administration had provided for them before. If I had been pillaged with the rest of the nation I could have been content, but these private preferences are very unfair."[3] The well-known taunts of Dr. Johnson were mere commonplaces of humour.[4] No abuse, no rebuff, no contumely, however, could deter an enterprising people from going wherever a livelihood could be found. Least of all were lads, stirred by literary ambition, daunted from seeking a living by letters, which none could gain at home. With no capital but youth, courage, and a stimulating poverty, Mallet, Thomson, and Smollett found their way in London. Thither went a host of adventurers —all to woo fortune, too many to wed misfortune, and become needy hacks who starved slowly and wrote desperately.

The wonder is that so many succeeded, for the capital was swarming with men trying to live by their quills and their wits. These scribblers for the press, as Henry Fielding said,

---

[1] Kerr's *Life of Smellie*, i. 437. Smiles's *Life of John Murray*, i. p. 16.

[2] *Humphrey Clinker*. John Wilkes told a friend at table, who was admiring his stewed pigeons, that he had tried to form a fine breed of them by getting them from France and other countries, but they always flew back; but at last he got them from Scotland, and they never returned to their country (Taylor's *Records of my Life*, ii. 16).

[3] *Dartmouth Papers.*

[4] Dr. Sam. Parr's commination of the Scots is the most complete of all: "I hate Scots dogs; they prowl like lurchers, they fawn like spaniels, they thieve like greyhounds; they're sad dogs, and they're mangy into the bargain, and they stink like pugs" (*Autobiography of William Jerdan*, ii. 169).

"needed no more stock-in-trade than a pen, a little ink, and a small quantity of paper." They would write omnisciently on anything and impartially against anybody for a few shillings; they would compose travels in countries they never saw, and treatises on arts they never knew, and translate from languages they never learned. They were ready at a moment's notice with reviews, pamphlets, and satires; no reputation was safe from their fulsome panegyrics or their venomous libels. It was sometimes well to appease them, as one would quiet a cur by flinging it a bone to gnaw. This was the bookseller Lintot's plan. He would invite them to supper, and feed them on beef and pudding to keep them quiet, if not grateful, lest they should scarify his publications. That able *littérateur* and rascal Gilbert Stuart showed a brother Scot, whom he met at John Murray's table, a panegyric and a lampoon on the popular idol, Alderman Beckford, both of which he intended to insert in antagonistic newspapers for a guinea a piece.[1]

Men of genius felt the pangs of hunger as well as poor witlings. There were Richard Savage, prowling through St. James's Square at night, not able to pay for a lodging; Johnson, in garments which a beggar might wear, for forty-eight hours without bread, and glad to live on fourpence halfpenny a day; Samuel Boyse, remaining in bed in his garret while his only shirt was being washed; Goldsmith, who had paid his way through France by playing his flute, afterwards working in threadbare garments in the back shop of Ralph Griffiths, the bookseller, for board and lodging—the lynx-eyed Mrs. Griffiths watching lest he ate too much and stopped writing too soon. Yet greatly daring young Scotsmen went south to join the inglorious company of writers who had their hard struggles to live, with all the ills that attended their calling:

> Debts, threats, and duns,
> Bills, bailiffs, writs, and jails.

The marvel was that so many Scotsmen succeeded so well and got on so quickly.

One of the earliest of Scotsmen to win literary success in

---

[1] Dr. Somerville's *Memoir*, p. 145.

England was Dr. John Arbuthnot, the son of an Episcopal minister in Kincardine. Having studied medicine in Aberdeen, he sought a livelihood in London in 1696—teaching mathematics and administering medicine to earn his bread. His good-luck in being at Epsom, where Prince George of Denmark took ill, led to his becoming the favourite physician of Queen Anne and all the Court. His wit and his learning and his good-nature made him the friend of Swift, Pope, and Gay, and all men of letters, and his Court favour made him the friend of Whig statesmen. He was a scholar in his work on *Ancient Coins*; a humorist in his ridicule of pedants, in the *Memoirs of Martinus Scribilerus*; a satirist in his once famous political squib, *The History of John Bull*; and a scientific writer on diseases and medicine. That easy, sluggish, slouching man was as indifferent to his fame as to his practice; would let his children make kites of his papers; would let his cleverest pieces pass by unclaimed, and let his friends alter his writings as they pleased. "The doctor has more wit than any of us, and his humanity is equal to his wit," said Dean Swift of the man whose death in 1735 was felt as a personal calamity in a brilliant circle of poets and wits.

DAVID MALLET

Among the many Scotsmen who sought and found fame in London in the first half of the century, few were more successful than that little, eager, plump-bodied man, who went by the name of Mallet, but whom Scots friends had known under the less euphonious form of Malloch. He was a familiar figure in literary circles and clubs; in green-rooms, hobnobbing with Quin, deferential to Garrick, and gay with Mesdames Pritchard and Cibber. He was to be seen at Twickenham with Mr. Pope, who would lean his fragile, deformed figure on his arm, on his way to visit James Thomson at Richmond; or in my Lord Bolingbroke's library, obsequiously listening to his talk or assiduously arranging his papers. He had much changed his condition and his manners as well as his name in the course of his career.

David Malloch was born about 1700 at Crieff, where his

father had kept an ale-house,¹ said some, or been a gardener at Abercairney, say others — for the author was naturally reticent about the period of obscurity when he carried legs of mutton from the village to the mansion. Educated by the assistance of Mr. Ker, a schoolmaster who became master in the Edinburgh High School, and afterwards Professor of Latin in the University, he is found acting as janitor in the High School at a salary of £17 Scots.² Many men long and painfully remembered having been hoisted on little David's back at the teacher's emphatic order "*tollatur*," in order to be flogged. And years after, when the ex-janitor was pompous and arrogant in London clubs, it would happen that a former sufferer, with a whisper of the mystic word "*tollatur*," unkindly reminiscent of his days of poverty, would sink him into momentary silence.³ Worthy Ker looked after the education of this clever lad, who studied at college while he acted as tutor to a gentleman's sons, on the frugal terms of "having clothes and diet, but no fixed salary." He made some local fame by poems in the *Edinburgh Miscellany*, and by the thrilling ballad, on which his slender poetic reputation rests now, "William and Margaret,"⁴ which appeared in a dusky broadside, and was sung in the streets before it found a resting-place in Allan Ramsay's *Tea-Table Miscellany*.

Edinburgh afforded no scope for a youth of literary ambition, and certainly no chance of a livelihood. One required to be a laird, a lawyer, or a minister, or, like Ramsay, a wigmaker, before he could write and live. So Malloch departed for London as tutor to the Duke of Montrose's sons, and soon he was rejoined in the metropolis by his friend and

¹ Ramsay's *Scotland and Scotsmen*, i. 24. James Malloch and Beatrix Clark, his wife, were brought before the Crieff Session in 1704 "for profanation of the Lord's Day, by some strangers drinking and fighting in the house on the Sabbath immediately following Michaelmas." In November, they "being rebuked for giving entertainment to such folk on the Sabbath Day, and promising never to do the like, were dismissed."
² Steven's *Hist. of High School of Edin.* p. 89.
³ Ramsay's *Scot. and Scots.* i. 24.
⁴ With its first verse altered from Beaumont and Fletcher's "Knight of the Burning Pestle":

'Twas at the silent, solemn hour
When night and morning meet
In glided Margaret's grimly ghost
And stood at William's feet.

class-mate, James Thomson. Before he had been a year in England, he wrote to his old patron, Professor Ker, that "my cousin would have me write my name *Mallet*, for there is not one Englishman that can pronounce it"[1]; and from that time he was called by the new name, except when the surly critic, John Dennis, dubbed him "Moloch." While he was still a tutor, he wrote verses and reviews; he made high acquaintances; produced in Drury Lane the play *Eurydice* in 1730, which had the enormous run of thirteen nights. He was assiduous in his attentions to Mr. Pope. He won the distinguished friendship of Lord Bolingbroke, and through him was introduced to Frederick, Prince of Wales, to whom he forthwith pandered in his plays and sang melodious and mendacious laudations. We find the ubiquitous man at Oxford in 1736,[2] where he had matriculated in St. Mary's Hall and taken the degree of M.A. two years before, and in the name of the University reciting with his best accents panegyric verses to His Highness the Prince of Orange, who had the form of a dwarf, the face of a baboon, and the will of a mule.[3] Proudly he sits beside Mr. Pope, when in 1739 his own play *Mustapha* is performed, while the Prince of Wales and the Court of Leicester House fill the boxes, and thunders of applause greet every political allusion meant to hit the King and his minister Walpole; and Quin is at his best and most stately as Solyman the Magnificent. Reputation grew year by year. With Thomson, he wrote the masque of *Alfred* in 1740, which with music and scenery was played in the gardens of Cliefden on the Princess Augusta's birthday. Never was he in higher favour than in 1742, when the Prince gave him the snug little berth of Under Secretary, from which he derived a salary of £200 a year for doing nothing. No one now could recognise in the pompous, vain, fat, well-dressed man-about-town, bouncing into the Smyrna Tavern, or at ease in lords' drawing-rooms, the former starve-

---

[1] Johnson's *Lives of the Poets* (edit. by Cunningham), iii. 365.
[2] There he is entered, on Nov. 1733, as Son of James Mallet, gent., of Perth, aged 28 (Foster's *Alumni Oxon.* iii. 906)—almost as many lies as words. The father's name was not Mallet, his position was not that of a "gent.," and his son was not 28, but about 33. It was impossible for Mallet to be truthful.
[3] Hervey's *Memoirs of George II.* i. 239.

ling janitor. His manners were easy, his pronunciation was fine; for Johnson, who detested him, owned that he "never caught Mallet in a Scotch accent."

Mallet unfortunately had a genius for doing shabby and shady acts. He was "ready for any dirty job," said Johnson. He first toadied Pope, and then, after betraying him to Lord Bolingbroke, wrote him down a rascal. When his noble patron died and left his papers to his useful follower to edit, he published every wretched scrap to increase his fortune. The oracle of Bolt Court denounced Bolingbroke as a scoundrel for "charging a blunderbuss against religion and morality," and as a coward "because he had not the resolution to fire it himself, but left half a crown to a beggarly Scotsman to draw the trigger after his death." Yet it was more than "half a crown" Mallet could have made, for he was offered by Millar the bookseller £3000 — which he was fool enough to refuse. He wrote pamphlets against Admiral Byng which won him a pension of £400 a year; and for the death of that victim to ministerial cowardice Mallet may claim his share of glory or of shame. Nothing was too petty for him to do, to add to his means or widen his fame, down to puffing his own plays. In 1744 Sarah, the famous old Duchess of Marlborough, had left £1000 for the compilation from family papers of a history of the great Duke, whom she henpecked during life and adored after death. She assigned the task to Mallet and Glover, the author of *Leonidas* [1] — and as Glover declined the work, the other eagerly took the money, got the documents, and accepted a pension to stimulate his industry. But not one word did he write. For years he pretended to be laboriously engaged on it; each time as he drew his pension throughout twenty years, without a blush he protested he was progressing satisfactorily.

Being anxious to get his play *Elvira* performed, Mallet took a characteristic way to attain his purpose.[2] Calling one day on David Garrick, the vainest of mortals, he told him that he was occupied night and day with his great history of the Duke. "But look you, my friend, we have found a pretty snug

---

[1] Disraeli's *Calamities and Quarrels of Authors*, 1858, p. 326.
[2] Davies's *Life of Garrick*, ii. 38.

place in it for you." "Heh! how's that? Well, faith, you *have* the art of surprising friends in the politest manner," said the delighted manager, who thereupon observed with seeming irrelevance, " Have you left off writing for the stage ? " " Well, to tell you the truth," replied Mallet, in a careless tone; " I have, when I could rob the Duke of an hour, been preparing a play." Garrick insisted on seeing it, and received *Elvira* with effusion. It was produced at Drury Lane, and he took the part of Don Pedro—the last new part in which he ever appeared. David the player was no match for David the playwright.

So swaggered through London this nefarious fellow, in his favourite suit of black velvet, " the prettiest dressed puppet about town,"—to quote Dr. Johnson again. He was to be found in all companies—literary, political, theatrical, social. His plays drew audiences, his poems gained readers, his pamphlets won money. But he was a knave and a liar—a man who wrote down reputations and traduced characters; who patronised small men and fawned on great men; too mighty to answer David Hume's request to correct his Scotticisms when he was obscure, but ready to flatter him when he was famous. An ostentatious freethinker, his voice was loud in the coffee-houses, lauding the deists and sneering at Christianity, strutting about town with his dumpy figure " round as a barrel," arrogant and self-important. At his villa at Putney was domesticated with him for a time a young man with a rotund person, an absurd little nose, puffy cheeks, and button-hole of a mouth—this was young Edward Gibbon,[1] whom his father had considered could best be cured of his popery and believing too much by boarding him with his freethinking neighbours the Mallets, who believed too little. At an assembly one evening, David Hume had his usually serene temper ruffled by Mrs. Mallet addressing him: " Sir, we deists should know each other." " Madam," he answered hotly, " I am no deist. I do not style myself so, nor do I wish to be known by that appellation."[2] Consternation, it is said, arose one day when the man-servant ran off with the silver-plate. When caught the fellow impudently told his master that he (Mr. Mallet)

---

[1] Gibbon's *Autobiography*, Hill's edit. p. 160.
[2] Hardy's *Life of Lord Charlemont*, i. 235.

was alone to blame for the theft, because his infidel talk had taken away his belief in a future judgment—a disconcerting but not quite convincing explanation.[1]

The devoted Mrs. Mallet, "a clever talking woman," who set up for a wit, and by whom the little poet got a pretty fortune, believed profoundly in her husband, though not in Christianity. "Was he not the greatest poet of the age?" she protested. Was he not the finest wit about town? Was not everybody speaking of his *Elvira*, his lovely pieces "Amyntor," and "Edwin and Emma"? In rapture she would kiss his podgy hand, saying to the amused company, "I kiss the dear hand that confers immortality."[2] She adorned his circular and abbreviated person in the height of the fashion, choosing his hat, stockings, coat, and breeches. No clothing was richer, no lace finer, no bobwig neater, no cocked hat and "clouded cane" more dapper in the Mall than his. It was quite superfluous, however, of the good lady to inform her friends that all this was supplied by herself out of her own money.[3] "Was it not annoying," she would complain, "that her Mallet should sometimes be confounded with that man Smollett?" "Ma'am," a friend suggested, "there is a short remedy for that; let your husband keep to his own name." The man lived well, and dressed fashionably,—a prosperous man with pensions and posts, with fame and fortune,—a pleasant man, too, with much ability and excellent talk, in spite of his insufferable conceit. When he died on 21st April 1765, literature lost a fourth-rate writer, the country was rid of a considerable knave, and Mrs. Mallet was deprived of a devoted spouse. According to George Steevens he was the only Scotsman of whom none of his countrymen spoke well.[4] Perhaps the best verdict on his literary character is Johnson's remark to Goldsmith: "Mallet had talents enough to keep his literary reputation alive so long as he lived." He must have had some good qualities, but if he had, they were the only gifts which he was modest enough to hide.

The fame of this "whiffler in poesy" as a contemporary styled him, is now small, though he was a considerable

---

[1] Davies's *Garrick*, ii. 47.   [2] *Autobiography of Mrs. Piozzi*, ii. 160.
[3] Davies's *Life of Garrick*, ii. 38.   [4] *Lives of the Poets*, iii. 365.

personage in his day. His plays are dead, his verses, which have some merit, are remembered no more, no one sings his once popular "Birks of Invermay," and as for his claims to the authorship of "Rule Britannia," we shall find those too are baseless.[1]

JAMES THOMSON

It was in 1725 that a college friend of Mallet's arrived in London, and sought out his countryman. He had travelled by sea in a smack from Leith—his luggage consisting, according to tradition, of a few letters of introduction, a scanty supply of raiment, and some manuscript verses. Arriving at Wapping amid strange scenes and confusing crowds, he found that his letters had been stolen—there was little else to steal. James Thomson had come, one more impecunious Scotsman, seeking a livelihood and fame in the great world of London.

Amid the uplands of Roxburghshire lies the parish of Southdean. In front of the old manse was seen the Cheviots, with the Carter Fell rising in verdant massiveness above them all. By the foot of the garden the Jed murmured in summer and rushed in winter in noisy tumult over the red sandstone rocks. It was a quiet, remote district; bleak in the wintertime when snow covered the hills and moorlands, solitary in warm summertide when the stillness was only broken by the whirr of lapwings and the shriek of curlews in the marshes, and the bleating of sheep upon the hillsides.

These were the scenes amidst which Thomson's boyhood was spent. To the manse of Southdean Mr. Thomas Thomson had removed in 1706, with his wife and nine children, from the manse of Ednam, where the poet had been born in 1700. Down to Jedburgh the boy would trudge to the

---

[1] See *post*, p. 291. Of his once famous ballad, "William and Margaret," enshrined in Percy's *Reliques*, a cruel fate tried to rob him. "Poor Mallet," writes his old boarder Gibbon in 1776, "I pity his misfortune and feel for him, probably more than he does for himself at present. His 'William and Margaret' is torn from him by the evidence of old MSS., and turns out to be the work of the celebrated Andrew Marvel, composed in the year 1680" (*Letters*, i. 284). This charge, however, is not true; he has enough to answer for without it.

JAMES THOMSON
From the Painting by Aikman in the Scottish National Portrait Gallery, Edinburgh.

Grammar School, which was held in the parish kirk—part of
the abbey, dirty, mutilated, disfigured, to make it fit for a
place of presbyterian worship. Tradition tells how the
reluctant lad was taken to Edinburgh to attend College,
riding on the family steed behind the minister's serving-man,
and obstinately returned on foot, some fifty miles, before the
servant had made his way back.

At the manse there would be few books except on theology,
for Mr. Thomson belonged to the revered "Antedeluvians"
—those who had lived before the flood of prelacy—and
had been bred in the straitest school of dogged Calvinism,
saturated besides with the superstitions of the day, credulous
of ghosts and witches, "providences" and evil spirits. In the
parish, however, there was worthy Mr. Robert Riccaltoun, a
preacher of the Gospel, who, while waiting for a kirk, lived
on a little, unfertile farm, in a poor thatched house—a man
of learning, of keen thinking, of culture, and fine poetic tastes,
who had on his scanty shelves some classics and English
literature. It was there the boy delighted to go, when college
classes were over, for congenial companionship. Already Riccaltoun had written some verses on Winter, which, as Thomson
said, contained "some masterly strokes which awakened me,"
and by the reading of Virgil's *Georgics* his appreciation and
observation of nature were fostered. At his leisure he was
wont to scribble verses incessantly, but at the end of each year
there would be a fire in the manse garden, to which with
fine discriminating severity he consigned his immature poetry.

When he was eighteen his father died. The worthy
man had been engaged in prayer, exorcising demons from a
ghost-haunted mansion in the parish; while in the midst of
his fervid exercises he was struck by illness, and died with a
mysterious suddenness, for which Satan was very severely
blamed. The widow and family now removed to Edinburgh,
where two daughters set up the highly "genteel" business of
mantua-making, at a time when there were only two of that
profession in the city.

When a student at the College, Thomson, like many others,
saw with glowing bosom his verses in the glory of print in
the *Edinburgh Miscellany*, a humble receptacle for trifles " un-

considered" by the public, though much considered by their authors—one of these productions signed "T," "On a Country Life," containing the germs of his "Winter."[1] In his college days he met the young men of letters, who were chiefly nimble versifiers, and saw good company at Newhall, where Forbes, the laird, gathered round him Allan Ramsay, Aikman the artist, and other friends who were lively and literary.[2]

Thomson was studying for the Church—then the goal aimed at by most of the clever lads of Scotland—and his studies were nearly completed, when a slight discouragement in 1724 is said to have changed his whole career. He had to deliver a discourse or exegesis on part of the 119th psalm, and this he did in so rhetorical and florid a manner that Professor Hamilton pronounced it far too poetical to be intelligible for any audience. Was such a rebuff, which every student must expect, not once but a dozen times, from a critical professor, the real reason of his renouncing his intended profession at the beginning of a session? This is doubtful, for after he had been in London some time, he thought of returning to enter the ministry. Whatever the reason was, he did depart, landing at Wapping in 1725, with the usual poor prospects and daring hopes of Scots. David Mallet, then comfortably settled as tutor to the Duke of Montrose's boys near London, and already familiar with the town, would receive him kindly; the recommendation of Lady Grisell Baillie, a remote connection of his mother's, could help him; the Elliot family, who knew his parents well at Southdean, and to whom his cousin was gardener at Minto, could befriend him; and an introduction to the Lord Advocate, Duncan Forbes of Culloden, brought him in contact with the kindliest of men. Thomson afterwards found in "Jock" the Lord President's son one of his dearest friends.[3] It is true he was sadly in need of money, but not so hard pressed as to lack a pair of shoes, according to Dr. Johnson's story. An occupation as tutor to the son of Lord Binning, Lady Grisell's grandson, only five years old, provided him with food and lodging, but no salary.

[1] Dr. Somerville's *Memoirs*, p. 130.
[2] *Gentle Shepherd, with Illustrations of the Scenery*, 1808, i. 88.
[3] Carruthers, *Highland Note-book*, p. 67.

It was in the summer of 1726 that there issued from the obscure shop of John Millan a poem in pamphlet form, " price one shilling," entitled " Winter." Millan, whose real name was Macmillan, was a young Scotsman, only twenty-two years old, who had just begun business as a bookseller, and in order to please the English taste, or to disguise his nationality, had dropped the betraying prefix of " Mac." A copy of the poem so quietly born was sent by its author to Mr. Riccaltoun, who was now minister of Hobkirk,—sorely burdened by debts he could not pay, with a big family he found it hard to rear, and with many manuscripts he found it impossible to publish. When the good man opened the little parcel from the cadger's creel, and saw the name of his boy friend on the title-page, tradition tells that he was surprised, and when he read it he dropped it in amazement. His own poem, entitled a " Winter's Day," had appeared in *Savage's Miscellany* the same year as the " Winter," of which Thomson owns his friend's verses " had put the design in his head." [1]

Some men of taste soon detected the merit of this obscure piece. Dr. Rundle, afterwards Bishop of Derry—being promoted to an Irish bishopric, because he was not orthodox enough for an English one—happened to be in the shop, picked up the poem, saw its worth, and soon sounded abroad its praises. The versatile Mr. Aaron Hill, playwright and poet, earned the poet's gratitude and adulation as " supreme in genius," by speaking well of it. That was an age of grovelling dedications, in which a great man was poetically beslavered with praise to win his favour and a present. A patron was as necessary for a book as a sponsor at a christening, and Thomson had fixed on dull-witted Compton, Speaker of the House of Commons, as a suitable protector, and he lauded his virtues and his genius mendaciously in dedicatory lines in the poem. The great man took no notice, till he was satirised by Hill and Mallet for his neglect, and then from very shame he gave the author £20 as a present. This could serve little to relieve the necessities of the poet, who was trying to raise money by selling his share of the property his mother at her death

---

[1] It had previously appeared in an Edinburgh periodical; Dr. Somerville's *Memoirs*, p. 129.

had left, who needed to borrow money from his friends in Scotland, and to get an advance of £2 from his bookseller. Dr. Cheyne, the corpulent, prosperous, wealthy physician, blandly told him that poets should be kept poor, the more to animate their genius. "That," however, the poet remarked, "is like the cruel custom of putting out birds' eyes to make them sing the sweeter. But surely they sing the sweetest amidst the luxuriant woods, with the full spring blooms around them."[1]

The merits of the new strain in Thomson's poetry could not be felt all at once. It was so new, so fresh, so natural, while the age was artificial in manners, in life, and in literature. It had sentiment, but no passion; admired prettiness, but not beauty, still less grandeur. If it read of rural life it was in a pastoral, shepherds and shepherdesses dressed as never seen save in a masquerade, who piped on "lyric reeds," to which "swains" danced gracefully on the "sward." Here, however, was a man who brought people face to face with nature. Rugged nature, too, such as the poet remembered it when "red from the hills innumerable streams tumultuous roar" down the glen at Southdean from red sandstone crags, when in winter "o'er rocks and woods in broad brown cataracts, a thousand snow-fed torrents shoot at once," as he had seen when wandering in Cheviot dale. How could English poets describe nature in its wild rough moods and aspects as did this Scotsman? Not Pope, whose scenery was that of Twickenham, and whose ideal of beauty was a fantastic grotto; not Shenstone in the pleasant woods and lawns at Leasowes; not Englishmen who mistook hills for mountains, and like White of Selborne could speak of "gazing with fresh admiration on the magnificent mountain range of the Sussex Downs." As for town poets, most of them poor as church mice, they saw no trees save in the Green Park, or water except in the Thames or Marylebone Pond, and heard no birds except sparrows twittering on the house-tops, to which their garrets were so near. When Thomson heard of an epic written by a poet who lived all his life in London, he pronounced it impossible. "Why, the man never saw a mountain!"[2]

[1] Seward's *Anecdotes*, v. 174.   [2] Moore's *Life of Smollett*, p. 104.

A poet could not live by his pen, save in Grub Street, and though he saw his poem pass into a second edition, Thomson was glad to become tutor at an Academy to a son of the Duke of Montrose, probably through the good offices of his friend Mallet, whose great genius he was ever praising in fine simplicity. In 1727 "Summer" came, and won popularity as genial as its subject; "Spring" came the next year, and then in 1730 "Autumn," his fame increasing with every fresh "Season." Each poem had a magnificent dedicatory introduction, lauding great men whom he did not know for genius and virtue they never had. All this to gain favour and money. Now the poor poet was rich in friends, if not in funds, admitted into high circles, staying with Lord and Lady Hertford at their seat; for her literary ladyship wished him to listen to her verses, and assist at what she whimsically called her "studies," though the tactless bard paid far more attention to his lordship's wine. The great Mr. Bubb Dodington, splendidly invoked as patron to a "Season," and praised for graces and talents with which providence had never favoured him, was pleased to have him at his sumptuous house at Hammersmith.

The author had changed his publisher. Young Millan was poor, and could not give terms to suit the now popular poet; but another Scotsman, Andrew Millar, became his bookseller and his friend. Millar in 1729, when only a lad of twenty-two, had established himself in the shop in which Jacob Tonson had been prosperous, known as the "Shakespeare's Head," which his successor patriotically styled the "Buchanan's Head." A kindly man, and an honest, who saw his friends in his little back shop, he modestly would go for a mug of porter to the tavern opposite. For years were to pass before he became what Johnson called him, the "Mæcenas of literature," and a man of wealth. It was from his shop, the year he set up business, that his friend Thomson sent forth his "Spring" and the "Britannia," with the magniloquent patriotic strains which made it popular when the country was excited at the prospect of war with Spain.

In those days if a poet was famous, he was almost certain to become a playwright; not that the plays were poetic, but they were heroic tragedies in blank verse. They must have rolling passages, with grandiose sentiments, fit for sonorous declamation. The stage about the middle of this century was filled with "Mustaphas," "Boadiceas," "Mahomets," "Alfreds," and "Cleones," in which each character spoke as no mortal ever spoke in flesh. Actors to suit their parts enunciated with solemn roll of voice; declaimed slowly the words of bombast, and, as Churchill said of Tom Davies, "mouthed a sentence as curs mouth a bone." As they pronounced so they dressed. There was Quin, so fine in comedy, so portentous in tragedy, acting "Coriolanus" with his fat figure stiffened out with buckram, in tunic and trunk-hose, a periwig with curls flowing in cascades over his ample shoulders; and Garrick in a Grecian part, attired in robes which blended the dress of a Venetian nobleman with the garb of a gondolier. One sees in Bell's *Theatre* of 1779 those wonderful engravings of ladies representing a Sigismunda, a Boadicea, or a Clytemnestra, with pyramidal framed hair and huge bell hoops posing in agonised attitudes before kings and tyrants, with daggers uplifted to strike the foe, or voices uplifted to pierce the ears of the dullest gods. There were dresses of heroes—Heavens! what dresses they were!—which inhabitants of no age or race ever wore; for it was assumed that anything was ancient which was not modern, and anything Oriental which never was European.

To return to Thomson. He was a successful poet. He must now become a successful dramatist. One night in February 1729 Drury Lane was full to overflowing. Her Majesty Queen Caroline was present, all London society therefore was there; gentlemen of fashion were glad to get room in the footmen's gallery, for Mr. Thomson's *Sophonisba* was to be performed by the favourites of the stage. No wonder the author was in a state of wild excitement in the orchestra. Ten nights the play was performed—an excellent run in those days. The playwright had reason to be pleased, though it was vexatious to find his drama made fun of, and his tragic line "O Sophonisba, Sophonisba O!" parodied into "O Jemmy Thomson, Jemmy Thomson O!" He changed the words afterwards to "O Sophonisba, I am wholly thine!" but what would have been his chagrin had he foreseen that posterity would remember not one scrap of all his tragedies except that unlucky line.[1]

During a tour abroad for two years as tutor to the son of Solicitor-General (afterwards Lord Chancellor) Talbot, he owns "his muse did not travel with him," he found little pleasure in nature or art, "for ruins, statues, paintings were surely not of such importance as to set the world gadding about," and he confessed "he had no taste for smelling nasty stones."[2] Nor does the poet of nature seem to have been more moved by the glories of the Alps he passed through than any of his prosaic fellow-travellers. He returned wearied of it all, with a few engravings to decorate his walls. He came back to compose his laboriously eloquent poem on "Liberty," which the author considered his best, though the world thought otherwise. "Liberty," says Dr. Johnson, with ponderous humour, "called upon her votaries to read her praises and reward her encomiasts. Her praises were condemned to harbour spiders and gather dust."[3]

In 1736 he quitted his lodging in London to settle in a small house at Richmond, for he was fairly well off, and even spoke of "hanging up his harp on the willows." He had a pension of £100 from the Prince of Wales, to whom, when questioned as to the state of his finances, he replied that "they were in a more poetical posture than formerly"—for a pleasant sinecure he had lately lost by Lord Chancellor Talbot's death, which left him hampered with debt. Some years later he got the satisfactory post of Surveyor of the Leeward Islands, with £300 a year, the minute duties of which he paid a poor friend to execute. He showed his gratitude to his patron in his plays, whose hits at Walpole and the King called forth rounds of applause from the audience who favoured the opposition.

In his country retreat he was at his ease. Though getting fat and indolent, he would walk to see Mallet in the Mall, at the Smyrna Coffee-house; at which place he announced to

---

[1] The line came from Nat. Lee's "O Sophonisba O," and was parodied by Fielding in *Tom Thumb*, "O Huncamunca, Huncamunca O!"
[2] Letters to Bubb Dodington in Seward's *Anecdotes*, v. 173.
[3] Johnson's *Lives of the Poets*, iii. 231.

the public he would take subscriptions for his poems; or call on Mr. Pope at Twickenham. He was ready to meet friends at dinner once a week at the "Bohemia Head" in London, or at the "Three Pigeons" at Richmond. His days of poverty were over, when in a sponging-house Quin came to rescue him, gave the money and regaled the distressed poet with a welcome dinner. We can see Thomson as he sat to his friend William Aikman's portrait—a night-cap on his polled head, with a face, open and frank, wide, clear eyes and full red lips, as of a man who took life with lazy enjoyment. Yet he was still obliged to work, and as plays paid better than poems, one after another came from his pen. True, his soul was too heavy to soar to tragic heights, his lazy bosom could not throb with passion, and a fat poet in heroics is never impressive.

In 1738, the year that young Smollett arrived in town, the theatre again was crowded, when *Agamemnon* was acted, with Quin and Mrs. Porter and Colley Cibber and his daughter-in-law, Mrs. Cibber, in their parts.[1] He had tried to read his piece beforehand to the actors, but as they heard him speak the heroic verse in broad Scots accents, the green-room resounded with laughter. Pope, who had revised it, was in the boxes, the Prince of Wales and his court were present; while the author in the upper gallery kept up in feverish anxiety an audible recitation of the passages as the actors played them, till the angry audience hushed him to silence. When he joined very late the friends whom he had invited to sup after the performance, he explained that his wig had been so spoiled by his perspiration in his agony of anxiety, that he had to get it retrimmed by a barber.

In 1740 the groves of Cliefden were filled with the fashion of the town, for it was the Princess Augusta's birthday, and the Masque of *Alfred* by himself and Mallet was to be acted. Quin took the principal part; the music was by Dr. Arne, who conducted the orchestra, with his ugly face, purple complexion, and goggling eyes. Whatever interest this piece possesses is due to its containing the famous ode, "Rule Britannia." As a spectacle it was good enough,

[1] Davies's *Life of Garrick*.

as a play it was bad enough. Here starts up the vexed
literary problem: who wrote that song with its stirring
refrain, "Rule Britannia, Britannia rule the waves"? which
has expressed vocal ardour of many generations of "bumper
patriots," who in moods of martial conviviality, and regardless
of the original and of syntax, persist in vociferating, "Rule
Britannia, Britannia *rules* the waves." Was it by Thomson,
or by Mallet? After Thomson's death, a revised version of
the play was performed and published by Mallet in 1751, who
in his preface says: "I am obliged to reject a great part of
what I had written in the other [version]; neither could I
retain of my friend's part more than three or four speeches
and a part of a song." Does he refer to "Rule Britannia"?
He obviously does, for out of that ode he had cut some stanzas
to substitute others by his noble patron, Lord Bolingbroke, and
he honestly, though with cunning vagueness, allows it to his
friend. Even if he did not, and meant to give the impression
that he wrote the ode himself, his word would have been worth
nothing. He had the predatory instincts of his native Highlands; he was a literary Rob Roy, only he "lifted" impartially
the goods of friends as well as of foes. Even in this preface
he cannot help lying, for he speaks of having "been obliged to
discontinue the Duke of Marlborough's history for a few
months past, till I receive from a foreign country some letters
of importance." Why, the rascal had not written one word of
it. A man who lies in one paragraph, need not be believed
in the next. Even if he had wished to claim it he dared not,
so long as Dr. Arne, the composer of the music lived to confute him. The patriotic strain, the words, the similes, find
close parallels in Thomson's "Liberty" and "Britannia"; but
none in Mallet's own work. Certain it is that, during the
poet's life, it was ascribed to Thomson, and appeared in 1756
in the *Charmer*, a favourite song-book, with Thomson's initials.[1]
There surely has been needless controversy over the matter.

Thomson never re-visited Scotland, though he kept up

---

[1] Genest's *Acct. of English Stage*, iv. 324; Aldine Poets, Tovey's *Memoir*.
On the intrinsic proof of his authorship the best and conclusive statement is
in Morel's *James Thomson, sa Vie et ses Œuvres*, p. 584. See also Churton
Collins's *Ephemera Critica*.

kindly and constant correspondence with his sisters; while his brother, John, for some time lived with him as amanuensis. Unlike Mallet, he never rid himself of his Scots speech. His hair-dresser was always addressed as "Wull." When the son of his old minister in Edinburgh, Gusthart, called on him: "Troth, sir, I canna say I ken your countenance weel," he said.

While the poet was writing plays, he could rest on his pension and his profits at Richmond, where friends came and went, and enjoyed his cellar of wine and good Scotch ale. David Mallet, whom the simple-hearted man trusted, loved, and humbly thought a better writer than himself, was a welcome guest, with his clever talk, his self-confident manner, and his self-important, podgy figure. Quin the actor, fat, jovial, and witty, would set the table in a roar. Patrick Murdoch, his old college chum, now an English parson, portly, plump, and small, celebrated in the *Castle of Indolence* as the "round-faced, oily man of God," would come full of stories and laughter. Mr. Bubb Dodington, not yet Lord Melcombe, the corpulent, pompous, over-dressed parasite of the Prince's court, would turn up from his mansion at Hammersmith in a profusion of brocade and embroidery with deep-laced ruffles and enormous periwig, and would sleep profoundly while the others talked.[1] This was the patron of Thomson's "Summer," "the youthful poet's friend," "in whom the human graces all unite." What a collection of fat friends assembled round the table of the fat poet! But there too came Mr. Pope, leaning on his cane as he walked round the garden, and he would have his misshapen, waspish little body, carefully laced in stays, placed at the table and discuss poets and dunces in his peevish voice. Dr. Armstrong, who made devoted friends by his warm heart and innumerable enemies by his hot temper, was ever welcome, both as doctor and friend; and Collins, too, the poet of the "Passions." Occasionally, the long, lank skeleton form of Lord Lyttelton—patron-in-general to poets and playwrights—came to visit, mingling gravely in the light-hearted company, saddened at signs of scepticism in his friend for whose behoof he wrote his treatise on the *Conversion of St. Paul*, to convert him to a clearer faith.

[1] Richard Cumberland's *Memoirs*, p. 124.

In this home, and with such friends, the poet grew happier and fatter and lazier. With the good nature and placidity which are the constitutional attributes of the obese, he lived a pleasant life of perfunctory virtues. He was to be seen in his garden walking in his slovenly dressing-gown and slippers, chatting with his cousin, Alexander, the gardener; according to legend, biting off the sunny sides of peaches, as they hung on the wall, with his hands in his pockets; and often found in bed at two o'clock in the day, with curtains closed, sleepily pleading to Dr. Charles Burney, in Scots accents, that he "had no mot-tive to get up,"[1] and tearing open the pages of new books with the snuffers. So egregiously sluggish was he that Quin told him he believed he would even let him chew his food for him.[2] In his later portraits he appears wearing his cumbrous night-cap, with a sleepy, torpid, double-chinned face, and a corpulent body, for he describes himself "more fat than bard beseems." At table he was dull in talk till the bottle went round, and then his big ungainly form and heavy countenance would waken up to life.[3] When engaged in composition, he could be heard walking in his library at night humming over the lines he would write out next day. But to hear him read aloud his own verses was a painful ordeal. Actors laughed as in the green-room he read to them the

[1] Prior's *Life of Malone*, p. 415.
[2] Seward's *Anecdotes of Distinguished Men*, v. 137. Thomson's *Poems: Life* by Murdoch (1802), p. 24. Yet this was the poet who had written :—

> Falsely luxurious ! Will not man awake,
> And springing from the bed of sloth enjoy
> The cool, the fragrant, and the silent hour
> To meditation due and sacred song?
> For is there ought in sleep can charm the wise ?
> To lie in dark oblivion, losing half
> The fleeting moments of too short a life,
> Total extinction of the unlighted soul !—*Summer*.

[3] As to his style of conversation, there were those who spoke of it as coarse. Boswell's *Johnson*, ii. 63, iii. 117 ; Taylor's *Records*, i. 188. George Chalmers was told by an old woman, formerly Thomson's housekeeper, that he had married an obscure woman, who lived with him as a domestic and died in London, where she was buried in old Marylebone Church. Chalmers said he found the entry in the registry: "Mary Thomson, a stranger." Later researches have, however, discovered no such entry (*Notes and Queries*, 1881, i. 46). The story seems a myth, especially in view of the poet's wooing of Amanda, and the keeping the wife as a domestic in the house—known to a garrulous housekeeper and unknown to every one else—is clearly apocryphal.

plays in Caledonian tones, without expression or decent articulation. "I can write a tragedy, but I fear I can't read one," he said good-naturedly as he handed back his *Agamemnon* to the manager. Friends winced as they listened as he spoke his poems with wretched mumbling. "You booby! you don't understand your own verses," exclaimed Bubb Dodington as he snatched the manuscript from his hand [1] and read it himself, with admirable effect, as he also did the edifying pages of *Jonathan Wild* to a company of ladies.

Even this lethargic man of letters had had an episode of romance when his dormant soul was moved to emotion. This was his love for Miss Young, a countrywoman, whom he celebrates as "Amanda" in his *Seasons* and elsewhere—who was residing with her mother at Richmond, where her brother was a surgeon. The mother, a coarse, vulgar woman, did not favour an alliance with a poet still impecunious. "What!" she said, "would you marry Thomson? He will make ballads and you will sing them!"[2] The attachment was keen, and it seemed mutual, but romance ended by Amanda marrying another man, and the poet satisfied himself with good wine and good company. A torpid and corpulent poet in love is not a romantic object. Truly an ideal place was the Richmond home wherein a man should write the *Castle of Indolence*, over which he loitered for sixteen years. In 1748 that poem appeared, and his greatest work was done. Nearly done, too, was his life, for coming one summer day from Hammersmith over-heated he went into a boat, a fever ensued, and on 27th August 1748 the poet was dead—his old friend, Dr. Armstrong, having tended him in his last hours.[3]

All loved "tried, amiable, open, honest-hearted Thomson," as his old friend Patrick Murdoch wrote of his old companion [4] —and he passed away with hosts of friends, without an enemy. The tablet set up to his memory in his garden gives a charm-

[1] Johnson's *Lives of the Poets*, iii. 238.
[2] Ramsay's *Scot. and Scots.* i. 23.
[3] Johnson's *Lives of the Poets*; Thomson's *Works*, with Life by Murdoch; Thomson's *Works*, with Memoir by Tovey (Aldine Poets).
[4] Carruthers, *Highland Note-book*, p. 68. Lord Balcarres was surprised to find his *Seasons* so good; for, as he wrote: "I lived a whole winter with him in Bath; he had nothing amiable in his conversation, and I expected little from his writings" (*Lives of Lindsays*, ii. 275).

ing estimate of the man; "The greatest pain he ever gave his fellow-creatures was that of his death." A few months later his *Coriolanus*—a horrid amalgam of Thomson and Shakespeare—was performed at Drury Lane; and Quin, who acted Coriolanus, dressed in black, spoke the prologue written by Lord Lyttelton in a voice choking with emotion, as he uttered praise of a man who had penned

> Not one immoral or corrupted thought,
> One line which dying he would wish to blot.

The poet's plays are dead, and slumber their last sleep in forgotten volumes—even *Tancred and Sigismunda*, in which Garrick was great. Robert Burns was the last to admire and to quote *Alfred* and *Edward and Eleanora*.[1] Few works, however, marked a literary era more distinctly than the *Seasons*. They were the first to awaken interest in nature—the first to describe its landscape in all its varied moods and aspects. In "Winter" and "Autumn" are pictures of its wilder phases, such as the poet had witnessed amongst the rugged mountains and barren wastes and torrents of the north; while in "Summer" and "Spring" he pictures the pleasant woodland meadows and rural life of the south. Yet there was no enthusiasm for nature: he did not feel it responding to any moods or passions of his breast—indeed, he was too sluggish to have any; he had none of the "pathetic fallacy." The very plainness of the *Seasons* made their popularity. They formed the poetry of the unpoetic; for the vivid descriptions left nothing to the imagination: the incidents interwoven with them were pleasantly vivid, and involved no mental fatigue. As Coleridge picked up a copy of the *Seasons* in a country inn, all thumbed and dog-eared, "This is fame," he remarked. Indeed, as Charles Lamb avowed, "Thomson's *Seasons* look best a little torn and dog-eared." What their influence has been is well known in literary history, over small poets as well as greater ones, like Cowper, who invested with charm the common incidents of rural life and the familiar aspects of nature.[2] In

---

[1] Chambers's *Life and Works of Robert Burns*, 1851, iii. 273.
[2] Wordsworth said that between *Paradise Lost* and Thomson there was not a single new image drawn from external nature.

France his works proved a very revelation to people who had never seen beauty beyond Versailles, any interest beyond trees all trimmed and shaped to forms fantastic, and nature laid out in parterres. It is something to a man's glory to have written words which stirred Rousseau to enthusiasm and Voltaire to admiration; verses which came from poor Madame Roland's lips in prison, as she awaited the tumbril to bear her to the scaffold.

"A born poet," is the verdict of Hazlitt, who however, asserts "he seldom writes a good line, but he makes up for it by a bad one."[1] Yes, there are many lines which living he "might wish to blot"—turgid lines and pompous phrases. In Thomson's day there was a reaction against the formal, artificial style of gardening. William Kent was laying out gentlemen's grounds with woods in careless clumps, and the better to imitate nature to perfection planted dead trees among them. In Thomson's *Seasons* there is an uncomfortable number of dry phrases and dead lines amongst the living verses, not from laziness but deliberation, for the *Seasons* were altered and enlarged in every edition. We have "gelid fount" and "gelid reign" and "gelid fleece"; we have "vegetable tubes" and "vegetable race." Poultry are the "household feathery people," and birds the "plumy races." The bee becomes a suction engine in his "Summer".

> The busy nations fly,
> Cling to the bud, and with inserted tube
> Suck its pure essence, its etherial soul.

The pebbly gravel is—

> strewed bibulous above the sands.

The poet informs the Deity in his "Spring":

> By Thee the various vegetable tubes,
> Wrapped in a filmy net and clad with leaves,
> Draw in the live ether and imbibe the dew.
> By Thee, disposed into congenial soil,
> Stands each attractive plant, and sucks and swells
> The juicy tide, a twining mass of tubes.

---

[1] Hazlitt's *English Poets*, p. 168.

And so on in a strain enough to condemn a poet to a penitentiary.

There are plenty others to quote. It would almost seem that, having come from Scotland with a limited supply of English, he had worked up his epithets with a vocabulary in his earlier days. What a change in the command and use of the language from his bombastic plays, and even from his *Seasons* and his odes, is found in the *Castle of Indolence*—begun as a few verses of jesting on his own indolence, in Spenserian measure! It strikes by its originality, it attracts by its exquisite art, and charms by its rare felicity of phrase. We find its slumbrous lines carrying us away as in a pleasant dream to the "land of Drowsyhead." The measure fits the sleepy mood, like the hum of bees on a sultry summer day murmurous among the limes. When he wrote this the 'prentice hand at English had become a passed master in his noble craft.

Tobias Smollett

It was in 1738—the year that Thomson's *Agamemnon* was played to brilliant audiences in Covent Garden—that Tobias Smollett, aged eighteen, started from Glasgow to London—his baggage consisting of a little clothing, a few surgical instruments, some letters of introduction, and the manuscript of a play. The roads were bad, conveyances were few, his funds were small; so, partly on foot, partly by waggon, partly on carriers' pack-horses, he may be supposed, like Roderick Random, to have made his way to the great Metropolis in search of fame and a livelihood, like so many of his countrymen. The year before Garrick and Samuel Johnson had also arrived, on the same errand, travelling "ride-and-tie" from Lichfield, with vague hopes in their breasts and the manuscript of a tragedy in the ex-schoolmaster's pocket.

Smollett was born in March 1721 at Dalquhurn, an old farmhouse in the vale of Leven, near Dumbarton. It had been given up by Sir James Smollett of Bonhill to his unprofitable son Archibald, who married young, never could make a living, and died leaving a wife and family dependent on his parent, the irascible old judge. When he departed this life the needy household was settled in a small farm two miles off, where the industrious widow earned enough to support her children. After Tobias had been taught and flogged at Dumbarton by that admirable Latinist and flagellator Mr. John Love—who had in the past been prosecuted by his minister for brewing on a Sunday,[1] and in the future was known by his virulent pamphleteering against the redoubtable Ruddiman—the boy was sent to Glasgow to become apprentice to Mr. John Gordon, surgeon and apothecary.

Few anecdotes are told of a man's boyhood till he becomes famous, and then, unluckily, it is too late to remember, and there is only time to invent. One story, however, in this case is veracious, though not very important.[2] It was a winter morning, the streets were thick with snow, and Tobias and his fellow-apprentices were engaged in a fight. Mr. Gordon, the little round chirurgeon, entered his shop and severely rebuked one of his assistants for neglecting his duties. The limp excuse was given that while making up a prescription a fellow had hit him with a ball, and he set forth in pursuit of him. "A likely story!" commented his master. "I wonder how long I should stand here before it would enter the head of any mortal to fling a ball at me," and as the doctor loftily reared his paunchy little person, a well-directed snowball hit him full in the face. This came from Toby, who had heard the dialogue behind the door. In spite of all his pranks, he was a favourite, and years after Dr. Gordon, when he became a physician of city renown, proud of having had the great novelist as his pupil, would say, as he gave a rap to his snuff-box: "Gie me my ain bubbly-nosed callant wi' a stane in his pooch!"[3] Tobias had a pen as forcible as his hand; he would indite verses when he should have prepared cataplasms, and made satires instead of boluses. Certainly there were many quaint aspects of society around him which appealed to any one with a sense of humour. The city, with a population of 17,000, was emerging from obscurity, merchants were

---
[1] Chalmers's *Life of Ruddiman*, p. 136.
[2] Moore's *Life of Smollett*, p. 111.   [3] *Ibid.* p. 112.

TOBIAS SMOLLETT
From the Portrait in the Hunterian Museum, Glasgow.

beginning to make fortunes from rum and tobacco, and they had a full sense of self-importance as they strutted in the streets. "Can you tell me the nearest way to a town in your country called Glasgow?" inquired Francis Osbaldistone of Andrew Fairservice, his servant. "A *toon* ca'ed Glesca!" repeated Andrew with a scornful sniff at such pitiful ignorance. "Glesca is a *ceety*, man!" It was indeed a city as pious as it was prosperous—no town had more fervid preachers, fuller kirks, more holy Sabbaths—and if the merchants could drink, they would, as they took their "meridian," doff their three-cornered hats and preface it with a grace. These were the days when the motto of the city was "May Glasgow flourish by the preaching of the Word"—leaving it for commercial bailies in another and more secular century to dock it of the sentiment "the preaching of the Word"—considering that a means of "flourishing" far inferior to cotton, shipping, soft goods, and hardware.

It was in 1738 that Smollett, tired of this abode of commerce, set forth, filled with literary ambition, having in his pocket a treasured tragedy on James I. of Scotland, which the reading of Boece's *History* had inspired when he should have been pounding his pestle and compounding his drugs. Smollett's relations, in equipping him for his journey, were sparing of their money, but as regards letters of introduction Tobias asserts, without a spark of gratitude, "their liberality was prodigious."[1] Where the youth stayed, or where he lived at first in London, is not known, but he sought sanguinely an immediate literary fame. He submitted his play, as a matter of course, to Mr. George Lyttelton—afterwards Lord Lyttelton—the great patron of letters, who had befriended Mallet and Thomson, and was to be waited upon by many another Scotsman—Home and Mickle unsuccessfully among the number. One feels compassion for this estimable man, who had an arduous reputation as a man of taste and influence to maintain. Enormous were the numbers of manuscripts submitted to him by authors in all states of obscurity and poverty and literary decrepitude. Young poets and dramatists cursed him if he did not commend their pieces, and booksellers and managers cursed

[1] Moore's *Life of Smollett*, p. 116.

him if they did not succeed. In this case he gave the apprentice-apothecary-dramatist only polite evasion, and the heart of Tobias waxed wroth within him.

As literary prospects were dim, it must have been with a heavy heart that he took the post of surgeon's mate on board the *Cumberland* man-of-war—which was sailing under Sir Challoner Ogle to reinforce Admiral Vernon in the West Indies. Never was the naval service more coarse, more brutal than at that period. Manned by the scum of the people —gaol-birds, smugglers, insolvent debtors, rascals of all shades, scoundrels of all degrees—the ships were commanded by officers whose habits and language admirably suited their crews; living in dirty cabins with canvas partitions, sleeping in squalid hammocks, and fed on coarse food set down on wooden platters on an old sail that served for a table-cloth. The lot of a surgeon and his mate was still worse in that service— bad fare and bad pay and bad language. What Smollett's impressions of sea life were we may learn from *Roderick Random*; what impressions he had of naval warfare we know from his vivid description of the incapable attack on Carthagena.

The sea life lasted about three years, and then he resided for some time in Jamaica, where he met Miss Anne Lascelles, the planter's daughter, who became his wife.

In 1744 the ex-surgeon's mate, at a time when Scots physicians swarmed in London,[1] bravely set up as a doctor in Downing Street, putting his brass plate on the door of a house where Dr. Douglas, a countryman, had had his shop and his practice. Patients being few, visits were frequent to the clubs of good Scotsmen, who met to partake of frugal suppers and punch. It was in 1746 that Dr. Carlyle of Inveresk met him and struck up a lifelong friendship[2] at the Golden Ball in Cockspur Street. The news of Culloden had just arrived; the town was in a wild state of jubilation, and mobs were swaying about in drunken triumph over the defeat of the Scots rebels, as the two Scotsmen made their way through

---

[1] Such as Clephane, Pitcairn, Macaulay, Smellie, the great accoucheur, Dickson, Armstrong, Gusthart, the two Fordyces, the Hunters, and many more.
[2] Carlyle's *Autobiography*, p. 190.

the streets—Smollett fuming at seeing John Bull in an insolent mood. His disgust at the severity of the Government and the brutality of the "Butcher" Cumberland forthwith moved him to write his "Tears of Scotland." One evening, while friends were busy at cards in a tavern, they listened to the fierce invective of his verses, and on one of the company suggesting that some were sure to give offence in great quarters, the author, to whom opposition was the surest incentive, took his pen and at a side-table wrote another stanza more defiant than all the rest.[1]

Smollett had a genius for giving as well as for taking offence—and his two satires, *Advice* and *Reproof*, which he published in 1746 and 1747, were excellent specimens of his talents in that direction. If he had desired to alienate friends, to offend patrons, to increase enemies, he could not have succeeded better, for he castigates equally ministers and gamesters, actors and usurers, poets and scoundrels. It was the same through all his splenetic career. He never could control his temper or his pen. He attacked Lord Lyttelton, and patrons saw him no more; he offended patients, and they no longer knocked at his door; he ridiculed Garrick, and Drury Lane stage was shut to his plays; he quarrelled with the old harlequin Rich, the manager of Covent Garden, for whom he had written a masque to music by Handel, which the composer afterwards adapted to Dryden's St. Cecilia's Ode, swearing, it is reported, "Dat Scot is ein tam fool; I could have made his vork immortal."

In 1747 he set up house, having married Miss Lascelles of Jamaica—the pretty, black-eyed, dark-complexioned creole—probably a year or two before. His wife's income of £300 kept poverty from the door and gave him time to write. The fruit of his leisure appeared in January 1748 in two small volumes, which were issued anonymously from the shop of Osborne, in Gray's Inn Lane—the bookseller whom Samuel Johnson had knocked down with a folio for insolence. In a letter to his friend Carlyle of Inveresk, Smollett says: "The whole was begun and finished in the compass of eight months. During which time several intervals happened of two, three,

[1] Chambers's *Life of Smollett*, p. 45.

and four weeks, wherein I did not set pen to paper."[1] At a bound the obscure surgeon rose from obscurity to fame, and ranked with the first writers of the day.

Curiosity was excited then, and conjecture has been active since, as to how much was part of his autobiography. Guesses have been busy fixing prototypes to his characters, and half-a-dozen barbers competed for the honour of having been the original Strap, his faithful attendant. Many a chin they shaved and wig they trimmed for customers who came to hear from their voluble lips the story of their imaginary acquaintance with the great novelist. A letter may set some of these guesses to rest—death has long ago put these pretended Straps to silence. In acknowledging the congratulations of his friend Carlyle he wrote: "In the midst of my satisfaction, however, I am not a little mortified to find the characters strangely misapplied to particular men whom I never had the least intention to ridicule,—by which means I have suffered very much in my moral capacity. Some persons, to whom I have been extremely obliged, being weak enough to take umbrage at many passages in the work on the supposition that I myself am the hero of the book, and they of consequence concerned in the history. I take the opportunity of declaring to you, in all the sincerity of the most unreserved friendship, that no person living is aimed at in all the first part of the book, that is, while the scene is laid in Scotland; and that (the account of the expedition to Carthagena excepted) the whole is not so much a representation of my life as of that of many other needy Scotch surgeons whom I have known either personally or by report. The character of Strap (who I find is a favourite among the ladies) is partly taken from life, but the circumstances of his attachment are entirely feigned."[2]

The modern novel was then being created. A few years before, in 1740, Mr. Samuel Richardson, in his *Pamela*, had presented the fine moral lesson that prudence in preserving virtue is the best way to win heaven and a

[1] Unpublished Letter to Dr. Carlyle of Inveresk, 7th June 1748.
[2] Unpublished Letter to Carlyle. Probably John Lewis, the bookbinder, who often sat at his Sunday dinners, may have suggested some traits of Strap (Nichols' *Lit. Anecdotes*, iii. 469). In a letter he speaks of "John Lewis, *alias* Strap."

husband of fortune. Two years after, Henry Fielding had in *Joseph Andrews* admirably mocked Squire Booby and his wife, to the disgust of the little printer, and presented to the world with inimitable humour inimitable characters. *Roderick Random* was written in a new vein. It followed the manner of *Gil Blas*—being the novel of adventure, though with a coarse colouring which Le Sage loved not.

The purpose of the book was, according to the author, to represent his hero as an " orphan of modest merit struggling with difficulties caused by his own want of experience, as well as from the selfishness, envy, malice, and base indifference of mankind." It must be owned that it is difficult to discover either the " modesty " or the " merit " of this interesting orphan—a selfish libertine without the generosity of a Tom Jones, who at least is a good-hearted animal. It is the incidents of broad humour, the grotesque figures crowding the pages, which fill our memories; above all, the delicious Strap and Lieutenant Thomas Bowling. Adventures follow in riotous profusion, and bustling scenes in town and in country, in the tavern, on the road, come in quick succession, where there is admirable farce rather than comedy, peopled with characters, who are delightful caricatures rather than portraits.

After a visit to Paris with his young friend John Moore, who became afterwards partner to his old master, Dr. Gordon, in Glasgow, *Peregrine Pickle* appeared in 1751.[1] Peregrine is even more coarse in his tastes, his ways, and his frolics than Roderick—a youth to whose hanging we would go as gladly as Mr. James Boswell ever went to see an execution on Tyburn Tree. But the comic scenes in Paris, the dinner " after the manner of the ancients," the characters that came in rich variety—Commodore Trunnion, Hatchway, and Tom Pipes, with minor figures—knaves, bullies, and "originals"— drawn with sardonic humour—all make it keenly amusing in spite of changes of time and of taste.

The success of *Peregrine Pickle* was increased by its containing the scandalous "Memoirs of a Lady of Quality " foisted into the middle of the novel. It is the autobiography of Frances

---

[1] " London, printed for the author and sold by D. Wilson, at Plato's Head, near to Round Court in the Strand, 1751."

Hawes—a lady of very bad "quality" indeed, who was at that day notorious for her intrigues and her beauty. In 1737, Lord Vane, her second husband—for she had been married to her first spouse when very young—advertised for his eloped wife, "aged twenty-two, tall, well shaped, with light brown hair, fair complexioned, her dress a red damask sacque." This dame of errant loves and mutable connections had furnished the materials, and it is said the money as well, to have her chronicles inserted in Smollett's book. An old minister in Scotland used to tell how, when he was a divinity student, he became tutor, on the recommendation of Principal Robertson, to a boy named Hawes, who lived with his mother in Bath, and how, as he walked along the streets one day, he overheard some person whispering as she passed, "That is Lady Vane." All at once it flashed across him who his employer "Mrs. Hawes" was—to whose house he had been surprised few ladies came. With prudishness or prudence he resigned his post, and told her the reason. She flushed, but said nothing. When they parted, however, as the coach was coming up, she put a ring on the young man's finger and whispered, "Had those wan cheeks been twenty years younger your Scotch pride might have been vanquished."[1] These memoirs were enough to gain a *succès de scandale* for a book. Yet they are purer than Smollett's own work—which, though coarse enough as it stands, was worse in the first edition, which he was persuaded to purge for future issues. The strange thing is that Smollett, a gentleman in mind, manners, and morals, should seem unconscious that his "heroes" are rascals, with not one touch of chivalry in their being, hardly one fine trait in their nature—fellows who mistake amorousness for love and horseplay for humour. Fielding's heroes are not chivalrous, are not high-toned, but they are at least "gentlemen of the period." Yet in spite of all their exaggerations in incident and portraiture, Smollett's pages picture the age—a gambling, drinking, duelling, rollicking age. Smollett could not in his novels refrain from carping at any who had incurred his displeasure. He ridicules them all with intense bitterness. In *Roderick Random* he satirises Garrick as Marmozet

[1] Chambers's *Smollett*, p. 59.

and Lord Lyttelton as Sheerwit, and again in *Peregrine Pickle* as Gosling Scrag, Esq. Rich, the manager at Covent Garden, Fielding and Akenside—who had displeased him by running down the Scots when he met him at Paris—are pilloried. In *Count Fathom*, in 1752, which contains vigorous and powerful scenes, Smollett professed to depict a cynical, heartless scoundrel; and he succeeded. He did not, however, succeed in interesting the world in a character who had not one redeeming feature.

He soon gave up his practice, which was very small, in spite of his engaging manner, his dignified, handsome presence, for he could as little as his friend Dr. Armstrong conceal his contempt for potions which he knew were vile, and for patients whom he thought were fools. As he testily said to an invalid lady : " If you have time to play at being ill, I have no leisure to play at curing you." Nor did his professional success increase when, having got a doctor's degree from Aberdeen for a small fee, he transferred his household and his services to Bath. In this town of fashion he found, however, a splendid field for his satiric observation of life—among a fluttering crowd of beaux and belles, of gamesters, hypochondriacs, and quacks, of youngsters who wished " to see life," and oldsters who came to defer death. Here was the centre of attraction for any one without a character or a constitution; for invalids who wished to recruit their shattered health and *roués* who wished to recruit their shattered fortune; for dyspeptics who came to pick up an appetite and adventurers who came to pick up an heiress. With his characteristic perversity Smollett published an *Essay on the External Use of Water*, in which he sneered at the miraculous effects of this English pool of Bethesda; showing that he thought its patients were simpletons and its physicians were charlatans. This was not the way to make a fortune or acquire a practice, and wisely he returned to London and devoted his pen to writing books instead of prescriptions.

In 1752 we see him settled at Monmouth House in Chelsea, a curious old Elizabethan mansion with some historical memories hovering about it. Here he entertained with lavish hospitality, and at his table were found London men of letters, Goldsmith,

Sterne, Johnson, as well as Scotsmen who were winning fame and fortune. The guests sauntered after dinner in the garden behind the house, charmed with the talk so bright, and stories so admirably told by their host. On Sundays he showed hospitality to a motley crew of literary hangers-on, whose empty stomachs he regaled with beef, pudding, and potatoes, punch and ale. These were unfortunate brothers of the quill, out at elbows and out at toes, who distributed reputations, though they never had one of their own. There were the strange guests, whom he afterwards described with little exaggeration in *Humphrey Clinker*[1]—the tutor expelled for atheism, who wrote staunchly for orthodoxy, whose labours in refuting Bolingbroke's infidelity were interrupted by a prosecution for blasphemy in an ale-house on the Lord's day; the Scotsman who gave lectures on English pronunciation; the writer on agriculture who had never seen a wheat field; the debtor who, when detained in King's Bench Prison, compiled his *Travels in Europe and Part of Asia*. Over these curiosities of Grub Street he would preside, while they gobbled and gabbled, smiling and keeping order as he sat at the head of his table. When Dr. Carlyle and Principal Robertson, in 1758, met him at Forrest's Coffee-House, they found him with a lot of his myrmidons, who had come to have their tasks of translating and reviewing assigned to them. When they were dismissed, Smollett joined the supper with two oddities whom he kept to amuse the company, while he himself delighted his friends with his charming manners and his excellent talk—much to the surprise of Robertson, who, now meeting him for the first time, instead of a well-bred, dignified gentleman, expected him to be a roystering, coarse fellow like his *Roderick Random*.[2]

On Sunday nights he was often to be seen at the laborious Dr. John Campbell's rooms, where Samuel Johnson used to go till he was driven off by his dread of being mistaken for one of the "swarm of Cawmell's" who crowded the learned Scotsman's house.[3] This prolific author was the gentleman of whom Dr. Johnson spoke, who, though he never entered a church, never passed one without taking off his hat—" which showed his

---

[1] *Humphrey Clinker* (Roscoe's edit.), p. 144.
[2] Carlyle's *Autobiography*, p. 340.   [3] *The Bee*, iii. 3.

excellent principles," said the moralist. In fact, he had hardly time to enter a church, for he was compiling books enough to fill a library, as a gentleman discovered to his cost, when having unguardedly told the doctor he should like to have a complete set of his works, he found next day a cart-load at his door, with a bill for £70. Many friends had Smollett in the Scots colony in London—physicians, authors, lawyers, and prosperous booksellers and printers like Andrew Millar and William Strahan, who knew the best terms to make. He would meet Dr. Armstrong at "Don Saltero's" at Chelsea, and utter his disgust "at a land where felicity is held to consist in stupefying port and overgrown buttocks of beef, where genius is lost and taste extinguished."[1]

But his pen was busy, leaving little time to see friends, for the income from the Jamaica estate had sadly dwindled. He had to labour, with the aid of the omniscient Dr. Campbell, at a huge compilation of "*Universal History,* projected by a band of booksellers," for which his hacks supplied raw material; to make a *Compendium of Voyages* in many volumes, with the assistance of his myrmidons; to translate *Gil Blas;* and to struggle, with the aid of a Spanish dictionary, a grammar, and Jervas's English version, at a translation of *Don Quixote*—besides preparing for the press Smellie's work on midwifery and completing a History of the German Empire.[2]

It was after a period of hard struggle and constant drudgery that he made a journey to Scotland in 1755. He had left it a stripling of eighteen, he returned at thirty-four, a man who was famous as an author, hardened by experience with the world. We may picture him as he was painted by Verelst in 1756—in full physician's costume, a stone-coloured, full-mounted coat, with hanging sleeves, a green satin waistcoat trimmed with gold lace, a tie-wig, long ruffles, a sword; a handsome face, with nothing in his open, urbane countenance to indicate those moods of melancholy and impatience which made his life miserable to himself and to others. Such was he when he arrived in Scotland. His sister was married to Mr. Alexander Telfer, a prosperous man, who had bought the small estate of Scotstown, in Peeblesshire, and old Mrs. Smollett

---

[1] So he writes in an unpublished letter to Carlyle, March 1, 1754. [2] *Ibid.*

lived with them. One day a gentleman was announced, and Mrs. Telfer, who at once recognised her long unseen brother, introduced the gentleman—tall, handsome, and grave—to her mother, who was seated in the parlour, as a stranger from the Indies. He tried to preserve his countenance, but at last relaxing into a smile, in an instant the old lady recognised her son's face. Flinging herself into his arms, she cried, "My son! I have found you at last!" "If you had continued to glower," she afterwards told him, "you might have imposed upon me for a while longer, but your roguish smile betrayed you at once."[1] This was a pleasant interlude in a hard life, and after being introduced by Carlyle to Blair, William Wilkie, Crosbie, and Robertson, and other literary friends in Edinburgh, he went to Glasgow, now rising in wealth, revisiting the scenes of his childhood in Dumbartonshire, his old haunts, and old friends — among them good Dr. Gordon, now a thriving physician and prominent citizen, and Dr. John Moore, partner to his old master. Leaving behind him pleasant impressions of grace and charm of humour, Smollett returned to his galley-slave labours and his hacks at Chelsea, to his debts and his duns.

It was in 1756 that a new and arduous venture was undertaken—no less than a *History of England from the Death of Julius Cæsar to the Treaty of Aix-la-Chapelle*, 1748. The novelist had no rival to fear, for Hume had as yet only treated of the reign of James I. and Charles I., and the productions of Rapin, Echard, Oldmixon, and other chroniclers counted for nothing as literature. He had never studied history, never accumulated materials, never made research; but he could at least write vigorously and deftly, being a master of his craft. By December 1757 the work appeared in four volumes quarto. Here, indeed, was celerity, if there was no profundity. He had taken only fourteen months to "one thousand eight hundred and three years," as he carefully states in his title-page—not one month to a century, and yet he blandly boasts that he had consulted no fewer than 300 volumes. Prodigious! He expected the world respectfully to bow before the erudition of an historian

---

[1] Chambers's *Life of Smollett*; Moore's *Smollett*, p. 136.

who had referred to about twenty volumes for each hundred years. David Hume sneered at the "great run" of this facile, pleasant narrative. What would his feelings have been had he foreseen that his own *History* and that part of his rival's which carried it on to 1762 should go down to posterity hand-in-hand, to be known as "Hume and Smollett"! By the whole work the booksellers made huge profits, the publishers increased their fortunes, but the author remained poor, though in course of time there trickled into his purse £2000, or £120 for each octavo volume.

When working for bread night and day, keeping to his house over his desk weary and ill, one glimpse of sunshine comes to him. At last he saw one of his plays produced on the stage. His luckless *Regicide*, which Lyttelton would not look at, therefore winning his contempt; which Garrick would not accept, therefore receiving his spleen; which friends read and returned in judicious silence, he had published at his own expense, after the success of *Roderick Random*, with a preface which contained a vicious commination on all his offenders. In 1757 David Garrick, the good-hearted, placable man, produced *The Reprisals, or the Tars of Old England*, a farce which for generations was received with perennial applause—for John Bull never grew tired of any ridicule of the French, and always roared at the scene of an English buttock of beef on the shoulders of four meagre Frenchmen. The irritable and impecunious author was touched by the manager's kindly reducing the usual charge for the benefit night of £80 to £60—for £20 was much to the hard-wrought man. In those days it was considered possible to pay all the expenses at Drury Lane for a night—including the cost of prompters, porters, and performers—with that modest sum. It must be remembered that the earnings of Garrick, the greatest actor of the age, were £16 a week. Mrs. Yates, Peg Woffington, Mrs. Cibber, Quin were each paid £10 a week, and many a fine actor who would be making a fortune in our day was pleased with ten shillings a night.[1] Smollett's theatrical success was a brief interlude in the endless toil. There was the poor man, translating, with the aid of his threadbare hacks, Voltaire in

[1] *Notes and Queries*, June 1885.

twenty-six volumes, editing the "*Critical Review*, by a society of gentlemen"; which had been started by Hamilton, the Scots bookseller, who, having taken part in the hanging of Captain Porteous in Edinburgh, had come south to escape being hanged himself. The wretched editor was constantly in hot water. His unsupervised hacks were hacking at Scotsmen whom he wished to praise; and at Englishmen who, in their wrath, in venomous squibs and pamphlets, enraged him by calling him "Toby," or "Smallwit," or "Smallhead," in exquisite humour.[1] "My life," moaned the poor man in his despair, "is sheer drudgery; my pen is at work from nine o'clock in the morning till one and two in the morning. I might as well be in Grub Street." In spite of his labours to make money he was worried by debts and bullied by duns.

A worse mischance befell him from this extremely "Critical Review," in a prosecution for an article in which he had pilloried Admiral Knowles as "an admiral without conduct, an officer without resolution, an engineer without knowledge, and a man without veracity." Naturally the admiral, after his blundering attack on Rochefort in 1757, did not care to be served up in neat but injurious antitheses, and the trial at the King's Bench Court resulted in a fine of £100 and three months' imprisonment in King's Bench Prison. He had already had troubles at that Court, having been heavily fined for flogging a rascally fellow-countryman. Smollett was now able to witness scenes with his own eyes which he only described from hearsay in *Peregrine Pickle*, in that retreat which had sheltered innumerable authors, who in their poverty could write anything except a cheque — some because they had libelled a statesman, others because they had defrauded their landlady. There were threadbare authors imprisoned for libel, receiving visits from booksellers, concocting another abusive pamphlet; spendthrifts, in damaged lace ruffles and wine-stained coats, with wigs awry, arranging an accommodation with Jews of villainous visage; wan wives and haggard children, who had grown familiar with those dingy bounds, knowing little of the free life that surged outside the high walls, while inside its precincts the taprooms re-

[1] Moore's *Life of Smollett*.

sounded from morning till night with drinking and merriment, obscene talk and song. While in this shady residence friends came to see him. Garrick came merrily in to see the splenetic Scot, forgetting old scores. John Wilkes appeared, talking well on everything and speaking ill of everybody; literary hacks arrived to get directions for reviews and compilations. One day bustled in honest John Newberry, bookseller in St. Paul's Churchyard—the kindly purveyor for children of the books they loved, and the agent for the James's Powders, the drugs they loathed; the rescuer of Oliver Goldsmith from the clutches of Ralph Griffiths and his harridan wife.[1] We know him in the *Vicar of Wakefield* as the "goodnatured, pimple-faced man who was always in a hurry." John Newberry had come to ask Smollett to edit his new *British Magazine*. Smollett undertook this new task, and soon side by side ran Goldsmith's delightful Essays and his own dreary imitation of *Don Quixote—Sir Launcelot Greaves*—which he wrote to beguile his leisure in prison. This was the first novel that appeared in serial form.

It is deplorable to think of this brilliant writer reduced to hateful labours, which wore out strength and health and temper. Never was a man less fitted for politics and controversy than this sensitive, morbidly irritable genius. Yet in 1762 he was editing a paper called the *Briton*, which was begun on the day that Bute became Premier, defending the administration of his lordship, which was the object of universal rancour. Thereupon John Wilkes started his paper ironically called the *North Briton* in opposition, with incessant gibes at beggarly Scotsmen and their verminous country; having in this the assistance of that swashbuckler poet Charles Churchill, whose literary bludgeon fell on any pate that stood in his way, whose huge brawny figure sitting in the front of the pit made frightened actors forget their lines. Smollett and Dr. Armstrong were stung to fury against their former friend and companion over many a bottle. While the *Briton*

[1] Knight's *Shadows of the Old Booksellers*, p. 233. With fine business instinct he puffed the powders in *Goody Two Shoes*, which Goldsmith wrote for him. We are told that the heroine's father "died miserably" because he was "seized with a fever in a place where Dr. James's powders were not to be found."

sold in its tens—only two hundred copies a week among
Buteites—the *North Briton* sold in its hundreds, for it had wit
and venom and insolence, and the people on its side. It is not to
be wondered at that in six months Smollett, writhing at every
assault, saw his paper expire, and while he was left irritated at
its death, his rival danced over its grave. This was an age of
"polite literature" and of insolent pamphlets, and no man was
fit for controversy unless he had the thickest of skins, impenetrable to the stings of literary hornets. But here was a
man whose skin was of the thinnest. His own pen was bitter
against foes real or imaginary, but every gibe on himself was
as gall and wormwood.

Amid all this worry and vexation a little glimpse we get
at the home life at Chelsea, with his good, patient wife Nancy
and beloved daughter Elizabeth. "Many a time," wrote he
pathetically to his friend, "do I stop my task and betake
myself to a game at romps with Betty, while my wife looks on
smiling, and longing in her heart to join in the sport; then back
to the cursed round of duty." But such bright scenes were soon
to close; his only child died of consumption at the age of fifteen,
and the man's heart was crushed with sorrow at home, while he
was tortured by insults out of doors. "Traduced by malice,
persecuted by faction, abandoned by false patrons, and overwhelmed by a sense of domestic calamity which it was not in
the power of fortune to repair"[1]—it is thus the poor man
describes his condition, a condition to which ailments and
debts added misery. For relief and rest he and his wife
repaired to the Continent. Before he left England his *History*
had been completed down to 1762, and in his Survey of
Literature and Art he made handsome amends, with the
courtesy of a gentleman, for all he had bitterly written
against his contemporaries. He speaks of Lyttelton no longer
as a "little great man," but speaks of his "taste, his polished
manners, and his tender feelings"; he panegyrises Garrick;
praises Akenside and Fielding; and not forgetting his countrymen, commends the plays of Home and the epic of William
Wilkie.

A weary man may travel, but unfortunately he cannot

[1] *Travels through France, etc.* Letter i.

leave his nature behind him; it follows as his persistent travelling companion to spoil his every pleasure. Smollett and his wife, two young girls committed to their charge, and a faithful old man-servant set forth. See the worn-out man of letters at Montpellier—the resort of invalids from all countries and of quacks from all provinces—writing half in sardonic humour, half in deadly earnest to a great physician of the place, a letter in Latin, describing his *systema maxime irritabile*,[1] and all the symptoms of his ill-health. He tells of his cough, accompanied with fever and difficulty in breathing; how a slight increase of coldness or dampness in the air, or putting on unused garments, or the least over-exercise in riding or shaking in a vehicle produce new ills. He details that he has the nervous system highly irritable, his fibres relaxed by a sedentary life, by the body bending over reading and writing, and his suffering from scorbutic affection neglected. He explains that "last spring a terrible misfortune brought a dreadful mental agony, leaving the patient convulsed in mind and body"; and "how after leaving his country, grief, anxiety, indignation, and savage recollection followed him." In return for this heartrending catalogue of ailments, the physician enclosed a futile prescription and a considerable bill. Naturally, with such a morbid bodily and mental constitution, Smollett looked on everything with a jaundiced eye. Though there was sunshine in the southern sky, it could not dispel the darkness within. Everything disgusted him—the land and the scenery, the hotels with their large charges and their innumerable fleas, the people with their dirt and their diet. Once or twice he was on the point of knocking a landlord down; and mobs besieged his door because of his violent temper. Sterne, in his *Sentimental Journey*, describes his meeting the distressful author. "I popped upon Smelfungus at Turin, and a sad tale of sorrowful adventures he had to tell. He had been flayed alive and bedevilled, and used worse than St. Bartholomew at every stage he had come to. 'I'll tell it to the world!' cried Smelfungus. 'You had better tell it,' said I, 'to your physician.'" Alas! he had already done so, but blue pills do not exorcise blue devils. In his

[1] *Travels through France and Italy*, Letter xi.

Travels through France and Italy, published in 1765—which are very amusing, and brimful of shrewd observation of the scholar and physician—he tells to the world his experiences, as viewed by a weary, jaded mind, never pleased by nature or art or man. He has been laughed at for comparing the Alps to "frosted sugar," the Pantheon at Rome to a huge cockpit, and for seeing neither skill nor beauty in the Venus de Medici.[1] But there is enough scholarly criticism and appreciation of art; enough acute and careful observation of places and people, to condone such whims as these.

There is something very pathetic about this man, weary and worn before old age had come, morbid and irritable, when life might yet be bright, tortured by ulcers, by rheumatism, " by coma vigil," or insomnia. Once again, in 1766, he visited Scotland, and took his wife to see his Scotch kindred.[2] The former visit had been happy, and left bright memories behind; this was one of gloom and disappointment, and left sadness in its train. His emaciated form, his wan, smileless face betokened the invalid. Mrs. Telfer was now a widow, living with her son and mother in a flat in St. John Street, off the Canongate. When Smollett and his wife left the London coach at the White Horse Inn, a few paces brought them to the house. His friends long remembered him as a tall, handsome man dressed in black, and Mrs. Tobias as a pretty, dark-complexioned woman. They were duly welcomed, and Nancy, with her handsome, dark, rather faded face, was scrutinised sharply, with her English manners and speech, by these two dames, who, like their neighbours, thought her "a fine lady, but a silly woman." In the room would sit old Mrs. Smollett, knitting her stockings and speaking broad Scots, which was unintelligible to her fine daughter-in-law; and Mrs. Telfer, with high nose and stern expression, working at her wheel and her napery, racy in speech, frugal in ways, eager for a game at cards if there was any money to be won. "Come awa', bailie, and tak' a trick at the cairds," said Mrs. Telfer, as a worthy magistrate and

[1] *Travels*, Letters xxi., xxxi. It is to be remembered, in excuse for his giving egotistical and morbid details of his troubles and grievances, that the *Travels* were originally letters to private friends. In his pages he shrewdly indicates San Remo and Nice as fit to be health resorts.
[2] Moore's *Smollett*, p. 174.

tallow-chandler came in one night. "Troth, madam, I hae nae siller." "Then let us play for a pund o' can'le," urged the importunate widow.[1] Clearly this was no congenial home for the town-bred man of letters and his well-bred wife from London. Smollett told his mother that he was ill—that he was dying. "We'll no be very lang parted onie way," the old lady is said to have rejoined with remorseless frankness. "If you gang first I'll be close on your heels. If I lead the way you'll no be far ahint me, I'm thinking." Such was the cheerful talk to beguile the weary man's cares. There followed a visit to Glasgow, where he saw his old friend Dr. John Moore, the kindest of old comrades, a man of wit and learning, with his good-humoured eyes peering out behind his shaggy eyebrows. Years after he was to earn fame by his clever novel *Zeluco* and some volumes of amusing *Travels*. There is no doubt, however, that Dr. Moore's best work was his son the hero of Corunna. While he stayed with his friends, seeing the town with its many changes, Smollett gazed and conversed without heart and brightness; he felt the visit was a failure to himself and his friends, and after he left he wrote to his friend to apologise to his kind hostess for his querulousness under her roof, bidding her know "she had only seen the wrong side of the tapestry."[2] "I am convinced," he pitifully said, "my brain was in some degree affected, for I had a coma vigil upon me from April to November without intermission." Yet the kindly attentions, the presence of old faces soothed him; the Scottish scenes to which his heart turned cheered him. A stranger to his native land, he was still a Scot at heart, and his affection speaks out in his verses in "Leven Water," the "Tears of Scotland," and his "Ode to Independence."

After a winter in Bath, with the old savagery he worked off some of his bile by writing the *Adventures of an Atom*, which appeared in 1767—a political allegory which imitates not very successfully the styles of Rabelais and Swift by turns, satirising men of all sorts, statesmen of all sides, with impartial bitterness—Pitt and Bute, Shelburne and Wilkes. All old scores are paid off in full. Lord Mansfield had been

---

[1] Chambers's *Traditions of Edinburgh*, i. 271 ; *Life of Smollett*, p. 127.
[2] Moore's *Smollett*, p. 178.

Chief Justice at his trial at the King's Bench, therefore, under the form of "Muraclami," he is gibbeted as "having a heart which is a mere membraneous sac or hollow viscus, cold and callous, the abode of sneaking malice, servile flattery, griping avarice, and treacherous deceit." To understand who are meant by the strange names in the book requires a key; yet what is the use of a key for a door no one wishes to open?

In vain had friends tried to find for Smollett a humble consulship abroad, where he might get rest for body and mind. Lord Bute took no trouble for the worn-out man, who had served him to his own cost. Lord Shelburne, to whom David Hume appealed, had given away the post at his disposal. Smollett all his life had been too independent to win favour or to ask favours. So without help, and relying on the meagre income from the fragments of his wife's property and his own labours, he set forth abroad in 1770—as he knew, "to perpetual exile." In a house which his dear friend Dr. John Armstrong had found for him in the little village of Monte Novo, on a slope of the mountain overhanging the sea, near Leghorn, Smollett and his faithful Nancy took up their abode—with lovely scenery to refresh the jaded eye, with warm sunshine to thaw his heart. Now he worked with new vigour at *Humphrey Clinker*, the old scenes at Bath, at Edinburgh and Glasgow and the roadside inns coming back to him with memories and fancies full of richest humour. There live for ever Matthew Bramble the testy, the immortal scarecrow pedant Lesmahagow, the formidable spinster Mistress Tabitha, and Winifred Jenkins with her delicious malapropisms, while the pictures of life and people in Bath and Edinburgh, and at every stage of the road form the most humorous itinerary ever composed.

The Italian sky seemed to have shone with good effect on poor Smollett, chasing for a while the clouds away, for the humour in his last book is not that of the acrid satirist, but of the kindly observer of the world moved to genial laughter. Truly has it been said his life was like music—"sweetest at its close." The close came quickly, for his strength was gone, and life was ebbing fast away. "I am already so dry and emaciated that I might pass for an Egyptian mummy, without any other preparation than some pitch and painted linen,"[1] he wrote to his friend John Hunter, the anatomist, with sad drollery. It was on 16th September 1771 that he died, worn out by worry and disease, by toil and the aches of poverty. "All is well," were his last words to his devoted wife, for whom his love never grew less warm, to whom his temper was always soothed to softness, while he was angry with the world. When on his death-bed he held in his feeble hands the volumes of his novel, fresh from the press, but he did not live to hear the chorus of praise that greeted his last and finest work.

Impetuous, impatient, splenetic, hot-passioned, with a sarcastic tongue, a corrosive pen, a temper which grew morbid through worry and work and ill-health, he was yet the most kindly and generous of souls, and the keenest of friends. As Hume said of him, "he was like a cocoa-nut, the outside was the worst." He was even more angry at wrongs done to others than to himself, indignant at anything mean or base. With dignity of nature as well as of manners, he would curry favour with no man and bow before no patron.

Fate in its irony played cruelly with this man of genius. Had he lived one year longer he would have inherited the ancestral property, with its rental of £1000, on his elder brother's death; but now it passed to his sister—that saving, money-making widow, who enjoyed her fortune and founded her bleach-fields at the village of Renton, and left her brother's widow in penury. Good neighbours at Leghorn were kind to Mrs. Smollett, ladies in Bath gave her presents, Scots ladies helped her, and in the Theatre Royal at Edinburgh a performance of *Venice Preserved* produced £360 for the widow of Scotland's great novelist.[2] Two years after his death appeared a small brochure containing his vigorous "Ode to Independence," speaking out the proud, manly spirit which had kept him poor during his life, and left his wife in poverty when he died.

When Smollett died his old friend Dr. John Armstrong was still writing essays, travels, having few patients to occupy his

---

[1] Chambers's *Life of Smollett*, p. 195.
[2] *Ibid.* p. 201.

time and exercise his temper. Son of the minister of Castleton in Roxburghshire, he had come to London to try his fortune as a physician and poet — for he wrote medical treatises as actively as he wrote verses. Setting up as a doctor, his success was slight, for he was outspoken and impatient; his success as poet was little till in 1744 appeared his didactic poem in blank verse, the *Art of Preserving Health*, which won him a reputation in which a previous nauseous piece, the *Economy of Love*, in 1735, was forgotten. The diction was admirable, some passages were powerful; but the hygienic reflections and metrical prescriptions for securing health make it dull reading to-day. His time of professional success was when he was physician to the forces in Germany. In many respects Armstrong resembled his friend Smollett — the same splenetic temper, the same hearty contempts for doctors and patients, the same fierce loyalty as a Scot, and wrath at southern maligners of his land, which made him also quarrel with John Wilkes, who abused his countrymen. The kindly man who was spluttering forth his rage at the "rascally world" could be the tender companion of Thomson on his death-bed, and the true friend of Smollett in his dying months, and the kindly brother Scot of those who met at the British Coffee-House. He died in 1779, at the age of seventy, muttering against the living and mourning over his dead comrades with a sarcastic wit and a warm heart.[1]

Yet another Scotsman out of Scotland was to attain fame — William Falconer, the author of the *Shipwreck*. Near the Netherbow in Edinburgh, always in poverty, lived a poor barber, with a small business and a large family — two of whom were deaf and dumb. Friends gave the useless barber a little money to set up a grocer's shop, but his affairs were in chronic insolvency, and his children ran in rags about the Canongate. One of these ragged brats was William, who was born in 1732. When a boy he joined a merchant ship at Leith, and afterwards became servant to Archibald Campbell, a purser in the navy, who became known by his clever satires *The Sale of Authors* and *Lexiphanes*. By this master Falconer

[1] Thomson, in a stanza of *Castle of Indolence*, depicts his friend in middle age with all his splenetic humour.

was taught to read Latin and to write English—the first fruit of his lessons being an ode, published when he was eighteen, on the death of the Prince of Wales, whom nobody lamented except in verse. It was in 1762 that he published *The Shipwreck*, on which his fame rests, for its vivid and powerful sea pictures, its unconventional freshness of style, which preserves alive a book whose lavish indulgence in nautical language makes it fatiguing to landsmen. After entering the Royal Navy as midshipman in the "Royal George," he became purser in the "Glory," and when the ship was laid up at Chatham, the captain's cabin was fitted up with a stove for the literary sailor, where he could write in peace. A slight-made man, weather-beaten and pock-marked, his manners are described as "blunt, forbidding, and awkward,"[1] with rapid, incisive utterance, but withal a good comrade and a kindly friend. His pen was busy in verse and in pamphlets, attacking Chatham and Wilkes and Churchill, patriotically defending his august countryman Lord Bute from his relentless assailants. Young John Murray, the half-pay Lieutenant of Marines, being about to set up business, at the age of twenty-two, as a bookseller in Fleet Street, opposite St. Dunstan's Church—founding the great publishing house—he asked his friend Falconer to become a partner. Unluckily the poet declined the proposal, and shortly after publishing his *Universal Marine Dictionary*, which won money and success (for it became generally used in the navy), he was appointed purser in the "Aurora" frigate, which was taking out supervisors of the East India Company. The ship sailed in September 1769, and after touching at the Cape was never heard of more, having, it is supposed, foundered in the Mozambique Channel.

In 1763 another young Scotsman started off from Edinburgh to seek his literary fortune. Having walked to Newcastle, he took passage in a collier for the Thames—two tragedies and part of an epic forming the largest and least valuable part of his baggage. This was William Julius Meikle, who had been born in 1734 in the manse of Langholm, and, under the name of Mickle, was to gain fame as

[1] Falconer's *Shipwreck* (Memoir by Clark); Irving's *Life of Falconer*.

the translator of Camoen's *Lusiad*. As a boy he kept accounts in the brewery belonging to his widowed aunt, and at eighteen he became a partner. But he had a soul above malt, and while composing tragedies the business failed, and the young bankrupt brewer took his poems to London and left his creditors in Edinburgh. Of course his poems were submitted to Lord Lyttelton, and received a tepid praise, which stirred him to wrath. But in time by poems and pamphlets against freethinkers he made a livelihood; as corrector of the Clarendon Press he found occupation; and in 1771, when his first book of the *Lusiad* was published, he won a secure reputation. The first complete edition, published in 1775, was dedicated to the Duke of Buccleugh, who did not even acknowledge it— an insolent neglect for which Adam Smith was blamed. The rest of Mickle's career was prosperous, though his tragedy, *The Siege of Marseilles*, to his rage was rejected by Garrick. He made a pretty fortune as agent for distribution of naval prize money, and paid off his creditors; he was successful as political pamphleteer, and earned a considerable name as a poet—the finest of his pieces being "Cumnor Hall," which fascinated Sir Walter Scott. The plain, commonplace-looking man was to be found in literary circles in London, though he lived chiefly at his pleasant home at Wheatley, near Oxford. On the occasion that Boswell and he visited Goldsmith's lodgings, when they saw the squalid abode, with dirty walls all scrawled over with pictures of animals—for Oliver was busy compiling his *Natural History*—he must have congratulated himself on having the thrift of a Scotsman instead of the shiftlessness of an Irishman. He died in 1788.

While these Scotsmen died out, they left many of their countrymen busied but not distinguished in literature. In that pamphleteering age, when it was said by a great man in office that "one good writer was of more importance than twenty placemen in the House of Commons,"[1] there were many eager Scots strugglers after fortune or bread; some with pens ready for any party, and arguments ready for any side; and Guthries and Gilbert Stuarts employed on travels and histories which, like their authors, have long been forgotten.

[1] Moore's *Life of Smollett*, p. 189.

CHAPTER XII

WOMEN OF LETTERS

LADY WARDLAW—LADY GRISELL BAILLIE—MRS. COCKBURN—
MISS JEAN ELLIOT—LADY ANNE BARNARD—LADY NAIRNE

IN the eighteenth century Scotswomen did not indeed take that position in literature which the more ambitious and public-minded members of their sex assumed in England. There was no learned Mrs. Carter to translate Epictetus, no blue-stocking Mrs. Montagu to write an Essay on Shakespeare, no versatile Hannah More, no didactic Mrs. Chapone. But if they wrote little—only a lyric—it had not the proverbial fate of "an old song." It lived on the lips and lingered in the ears of the people, when the works of more formidable and learned women stood forgotten on the shelves. It is remarkable how many and how good the songs were which came from ladies who were unpractised in literary art; who perhaps wrote one lyric, and ever after held their peace; who were too careless to achieve fame, or too modest to seek it, and kept their names unknown from the world. The first of these writers was Lady Wardlaw of Pitreavie. In 1719 there was printed on fine folio sheets, at the cost of Duncan Forbes of Culloden and Sir Gilbert Elliot, the Lord Justice Clerk, a fragment of a ballad, *Hardyknute,* which had come into their hands. This they accepted as a piece of poetry of great antiquity. There was indeed a fine heroic ring of the olden times in the words beginning:

> Stately stept he east the wa',
> And stately stept he west;
> Full seventy years he now had seen,
> With scarce seven years of rest.

Wider fame it won when it was included in 1724 in Allan Ramsay's *Evergreen; Scots poems wrote by the Ingenious before 1600*. How had this piece of antiquity come suddenly to light? Sir John Bruce of Kinross, on sending a copy to Lord Binning, informed him that he had "found the manuscript a few weeks ago in a vault at Dunfermline. It was written on vellum in a fair Gothic character, but so much defaced by time as you'll find that the tenth part is not legible."[1] This story deceived the very elect of the antiquaries. Then came another report that Lady Wardlaw, sister-in-law of this accomplice in deception, had found the fragmentary poem written on shreds of paper employed for the bottom of weaving clues. Finally, this lady acknowledged that she herself was the author, and confirmed her last statement by producing the two stanzas which now conclude the fragment.[2]

The truth was out at last, but only made public in 1765 by Dr. Percy in his *Reliques*. Of that clever woman unfortunately little has been discovered. We know that Elizabeth, daughter of Sir Charles Halket of Pitferran, was born in 1677, that she married in 1696 Sir Henry Wardlaw of Pitreavie, and died in 1727. Her descendants related of her that "she was a woman of elegant accomplishments, wrote other poems, practised drawing and cutting paper with scissors," and that she "had much wit and humour, with great sweetness of temper." A meagre little record of a life worth knowing. Her ballad was written at a time when a keen interest had awakened in Scotland for old songs, and a taste for writing new ones had begun among "ingenious gentlemen." In 1719 Lady Wardlaw was a woman over forty, and she must often have mingled in that gay society in Edinburgh when the lofty rooms in dingy closes resounded with Scots songs set to old tunes with the accompaniment of viol da gamba and virginal. She must have attended musical gatherings, such as in Parliament Close, where lived Lady Murray, daughter of Lady Grisell

---

[1] Ramsay's *Works* (Life by Chalmers), I. xxvi.; Wilson's *Reminiscences of Old Edinburgh*, ii. 64.

[2] This ballad set David Laing and Robert Chambers on a fool's errand to discover in her the author of most of the finest and oldest Scots ballads from "Sir Patrick Spens" downwards (Chambers's *Romantic Ballads of Scotland*).

Baillie, charming the company when she sang Lord Yester's
'Tweedside," with the dismal refrain of the mournful lover:

> Therefore I maun wander abroad
> And lay my banes far frae Tweedside.

As this doleful ditty fell from her lips we are told the audience
all fell a-sobbing.[1] Evidently there was a vein of simple
emotion in those dames beneath their brocaded stomachers,
and in those men attired in periwigs and laced coats—costumes
which we associate only with the artificial. The ballad is
certainly a clever piece of mechanism—a good imitation of the
sentiment and phrase-turns of old times. Yet it is stiff and
prolix (one wonders where the "fragment" could ever have
ended), lacking the fine simplicity and surprises of feeling that
come upon us in genuine ballads. After all, "a fine morsel of
heroic poetry," we may doubtfully own with Dr. Percy.[2]
"This," Sir Walter Scott has said, "was the first poem I ever
learned, the last I shall ever forget."

Lady Wardlaw remains but a dim, far-off figure—a
vague reminiscence of "skill in paper-cutting," "sweetness of
temper," and ladylike mendacity—scarcely visible through the
haze of nearly two hundred years. Fortunately, however,
there were others of her gentle craft of song-writing whom we
know more intimately—interesting not merely for their own
individualities, but because their lives give us light on old
Scottish characters and manners in the past.

Lady Grisell Baillie

At the dancing assemblies held in Bell's Close, Edinburgh,
any time about the "thirties," when Lady Panmure presided
over the prim and stately balls, there was sometimes to be
seen an old lady guarding as chaperon a bevy of young ladies,
blyth and winsome. On her still handsome face were the marks
of small-pox, which were not unusual on the highest-born
dames and damsels; but these were overlooked in the marks
of goodness and sweetness in the venerable lined countenance.

What a life of romance had this good Lady Grisell Baillie

[1] Chambers's *Scottish Songs*, I. lix.; Wilson's *Reminiscences*, ii. p. 65.
[2] Percy's *Reliques of Ancient English Poetry*, 1857, ii. 101.

passed through—with what strange memories her vigorous old mind was stored! There was her childhood in Redbraes, the old, four-storeyed mansion in the Merse[1] where she had been born in 1665, with its flat balustraded roof and three quaint slated turrets, the long, low-ceiled dining-room, from whose walls looked down out of black frames dour faces of ancestors of the House of Polwarth, and comely features of their wives. Then came the persecuting days, when her father, a Whig and Presbyterian, hid in the family vault at Polwarth Kirk, shivering in cold and darkness amid ancestral bones, relieving his solitude by repeating Buchanan's Psalms. In the dark, Grisell, to elude the enemy, would stealthily, like a hare, pass to the place of concealment, a mile away, to feed the fugitive, who partook voraciously of sheep's head, from the family broth, which she had concealed in her lap. Then came the escape to Utrecht, when Sir Patrick lived under the name of "Dr. Wallace," and the family of twelve children resided in the little home, on means so narrow that they had perhaps only a doit to give as charity for the poor, when the well-known bell was heard ringing in the street, intimating that the collectors were coming. If remittances were late they pawned their silver. "Dr. Wallace" taught his children English and Dutch and Latin; and in the evening members of banished Scots families would come and join the merry dancing—refreshed by modest "alabaster beer"—while the host (afterwards as Lord Marchmont to be Lord Chancellor of Scotland) accompanied the dancers with lively tunes on his flute. Mistress Grisell Home was then a handsome girl with light chestnut hair, and a fair complexion that looked charming beneath the high-crowned Dutch hat and hood. So thought especially the young exile, George Baillie of Jerviswood—whose father had been executed at the Edinburgh Cross —who, with his friend Patrick Home, was serving in the Prince of Orange's Guards. It was a frugal, but a pleasant life. The family were poor, but they were merry. There were more jokes to excuse the meagre fare than guilders to buy it. There were morning visits to market by Grisell, the prop of the household, after having counted anxiously to see

[1] Warrendon's *Marchmont and the Homes*, p. 53.

LADY GRISELL BAILLIE
From the Engraving by G. J. Stodart of the Original Painting at Mellerstain.

if there was enough to spend and to spare; there was the chaffering at the stalls in perfect humour and most imperfect Dutch; there were the clothes to mend, the house to keep with a specklessness which the most exacting *vrow* could not surpass. At last the exile ended with the landing of William of Orange in England, and the family returned to the old, sorely-desolated Scots home. They exchanged readily the excruciating cleanliness of Holland for the dirt of Scotland, with its ragged people, its filthy huts, its slatternly servant lasses, its emaciated cattle, its bogs, and the bleak moorland landscape of the Merse. All this was so different from the rich green meadows, with the sleek cattle, the spotless dwellings, and the well-clad Dutch folk. Only a few miles off, George Baillie, now restored to his estate, was living at Mellerstain—that youth whose face and manners had a gravity which dated from his father's death.

In 1692 Grisell Home married the laird of Jerviswood. Their love had been formed in Utrecht, and their union lasted for eight-and-forty years, which knew no shadow except its close. For her to miss him from her sight was dreary; he never went out but she went to the window to watch the retreating figure on horseback, till he was out of sight. So the daughter describes her parents' perfect love in one of the prettiest pictures of old Scottish life.[1]

In the new home at Mellerstain were the quiet mingling of dignity and homeliness, the simple traits of a long bygone aristocratic life of Scotland—the lady intent on her accounts, her household stores, her "jeelies" to make, her linen to spin. There would come to the stout Presbyterian's door poor "outed" Episcopal ministers seeking charity, whom Baillie treated with a courtesy his servants were unwilling to show. But life was not all spent in the Merse, for Baillie became a member of Parliament after the Union; he in time rose to be Lord of the Treasury, and much of the time was spent in London, whence the Baillies wrote home to the children of their "balls and masquerades, and parties by water, and music, and such-like." The home-comings—with their trunks to

[1] *Memoirs of the Lives and Characters of George Baillie of Jerviswood and of Lady Grisell Baillie*, by Lady Murray of Stanhope, 1824.

unpack, containing marvellous gifts from the great city—were household delights. Then there were the home parties, when in reel and minuet they danced their best, and Lord Marchmont, having driven over from Redbraes, though too old and gouty to trip it himself, would beat time with his foot, in full accord with his fourteen children and grand-children. This was the best type of Presbyterian households. All were pious, all were sedate, yet all could be merry. George Baillie, with his rigorous fasts every Wednesday, and his constant devotions beginning at daybreak, might injure his health, yet withal his gravity was softened by love of music, and by sympathy with mirth; and as for Lady Grisell—was ever Scots dame more sweet and wise than she?

Once did Lady Grisell and her husband return to the old scenes of the exile in Holland. They took their children to see the places of which they had so often spoken on winter nights by the fireside; they went to the house where Lord Marchmont, as "Dr. Wallace," had lived. But the churlish owner, on a pretext, so deliciously Dutch, that they would dirty the spotless floors with their feet, would not give admittance to the dear old rooms—no, though they offered to take off their shoes. So with mortification, tempered by a sense of humour, the little party walked away.

During the winters not spent in London, the Mellerstain family would go to Edinburgh. Lady Grisell, though getting old in years, with heart perennially young, at five o'clock would set forth in her sedan-chair, accompanied by young folk, to the Assemblies, where they were welcomed as became their rank and quality, when they ascended the dirty corkscrew staircase. At last, in 1738, George Baillie died—his death the first sorrow he caused his wife during their long companionship. Eight years after Lady Grisell also died, in London, directing her children to the black purse in the cabinet in which was found money enough to convey her body to Mellerstain—there to be laid in the vault beside her husband.

It is true that in the temple of literature this charming dame of the olden time only occupies the tiniest niche; but her little contribution to Scottish song has survived while weightier works have perished. In her girlhood at Utrecht, in her womanhood at Mellerstain, she loved to write in her room "reflections" and verses—often broken stanzas, only few lines which came in the passing mood. But amongst these was one song which gives her a small but lasting place in Scottish minstrelsy. It strikes a familiar chord, it is homely; but there is a touch of pathos in it which gives it life, especially in the recurring burden of the words, which have fallen from many lips in later generations, to express their own emotions, and at times came bitterly from the lips of Robert Burns[1]:

> Werena my heart licht I wad dee.

High-born ladies of those days did not keep aloof from the common affairs of the common people; they spoke the broad Scots tongue themselves, and the work of byre and barn, the wooings of servants and ploughmen, were of lively interest to them in their parlour and drawing-room, and did not seem themes unworthy of their verse. This we find in the fragmentary verses of Lady Grisell:

> The ewe buchtin's bonnie, baith e'ening and morn,
> When our blithe shepherds play on the bag, reed, and horn;
> While we're milking, they're lilting baith pleasant and clear,
> But my heart's like to break when I think on my dear.

The scenes of the ewe-milking in Lady Grisell's verse and in Miss Jean Elliot's "Flowers of the Forest" are reminiscent of an aspect of rural life which has long ago vanished. Up to the end of the century it was still the practice of the farmers of Ettrick forest to milk ewes for seven or eight weeks after

---

[1] When a friend asked Burns to cross the street at Dumfries and join a party of ladies and gentlemen, with whom he had lost caste, "Nay, my young friend, that is all over now," he rejoined, and he quoted Lady Grisell's verses:

> His bonnet stood aye fu' round on his brow,
> His auld ane look'd better than ony ane's new;
> And now he lets 't wear ony gait it will hing
> And casts himsel' down upon the corn-bing.
> Oh! were we young now as we ance had been,
> We would hae been gallopin' down on yon green,
> And buskin' it ower the lily-white lea;
> And werena my heart licht I wad dee.
>   Chambers's *Life and Works*, iv. 18.

the lambs were weaned.[1] In the evening were hundreds of ewes all gathered, and the voices of the peasantry would be heard "lilting" while the men "buchted" (folded) the sheep, and the women sat on their "leglans" milking. Those were days when the women as they worked sang songs which their grandmothers had sung before them, and when men as they ploughed whistled ancient tunes—so different from to-day, when old songs have died out, and whistling is heard no more in the fields.

The Duc de Simon, somewhere in his *Memoirs*, speaks of the effect on manners wrought by the introduction of hanging-bells, about the beginning of the eighteenth century. Before that day it was necessary for ladies to have within call their domestics, always near them to attend to their wants. High dames had their waiting-maids, and others their humbler servants beside them, which begot a closeness and familiarity of intercourse between them. Illustrations of that old familiarity we can see in the parts played and words spoken by servants in the plays of Molière and others of his time. In Scotland hanging-bells were long unknown—a hand-bell on the table, a stamp of the foot on the floor, or a call, would summon from behind the door the servants who were always at hand. But apart from the use or want of bells, the simple, plain fashions of the country—when mistress and daughters and maids would sit together with their rocks or distaffs and spinning-wheels—fostered a peculiar friendliness between rich and poor. That is why we find in the songs of ladies of high degree the broad Scots dialect, the intimate acquaintance with rustic life, its poverty, its courtings and weddings, which would be impossible in our days of social aloofness.[2]

[1] About 2 quarts of milk were given by a score of ewes. If out of a flock of 50 score of ewes 36 score were milked every morning and evening, the farm got 70 quarts to make into cheese. Latterly it became usual for the farmers to let the milking of the ewes at 1½d. a week or 1s. for the season (Craig-Brown's *Selkirkshire*, i. 408).

[2] It is curious to find among high ranks the same customs as those of the peasantry. In 1749 Lady Minto writes an account of the marriage of the Duke of Athole to Jean Drummond. The night before the wedding the bride's feet are washed, and after the marriage there followed the cutting of the garters and other ceremonies. There was no honeymoon. "After the supper they went to bed." The bride's trousseau consisted of "white-flowered manto," short satin sack, a night-gown, and a pair of stays (*Family of Minto*, p. 333).

MRS. COCKBURN
After the Miniature by Anne Forbes.

Mrs. Cockburn

In the stately yet simple throngs that met in Bell's Wynd, in which Lady Grisell Baillie was a picturesque figure, there was usually to be seen another whose claims to literary memory and fame also depend on one song. This was Mistress Alison Rutherford, daughter of the laird of Fairnalie. In 1730 she is numbered among the belles that graced the floor of that gay but dingy room—with her rich auburn hair, her brilliant complexion, her pronounced aquiline nose.[1]

She had been born in 1712 in the old house, half mansion, half peel tower, now gauntly standing in ruins, with quaint turrets, walls four feet thick, rooms with open fireplaces, and ingle-nooks, the lower chambers dark as cells. From its windows were seen glancing the waters of the Tweed, and the heights of Yarrow.[2] As a girl she was renowned as one of the fairest in that Assembly where beauty was so common, and she was the toast of beaux in the taverns. She had her loves—the fondest being for John Aikman, son of William Aikman, the artist. Why this did not end in marriage is not known; but when only nineteen she married Patrick Cockburn of Ormiston, an advocate, and they lived in the household of his father, the Lord Justice Clerk—an old Presbyterian of the deepest dye, who condemned cards, plays, and dancing as ungodly.[3] In deference to this austere householder, the sprightly girl eschewed worldly diversions, though none had loved dancing more or had danced better in that familiar room, to which every week she saw from her window the sedan-chairs bear their bright freights, and young men in their satin coats and powdered wigs with clinking swords hurrying along.

Bred a Whig, and married into a Whiggish family, when the Rebellion broke out her sympathies were not with Prince Charlie. Brimful of humour, her fancy took the mirthful view of things. The Prince had issued his royal proclama-

---

[1] *L'Eloge d'Ecosse et des dames Ecossaises*, par Mr. Freebairn, Edin. 1732.
[2] Craig-Brown's *Selkirkshire*, i. 553.
[3] Tytler and Watson's *Songstresses of Scotland*, i. 175.

tion, and Mrs. Cockburn wrote her smart parody thereon beginning:

> Have you any laws to mend,
>   Or have you any grievance?
> I'm a hero to my trade,
>   And truly a most leal prince.
>
> Would you have war, would you have peace?
>   Would you be free from taxes?
> Come chapping to my father's door,
>   You need not fear of access.

With this dangerous squib in her pocket, she was stopped one day as she was driving from Ravelston, by the Highland guard at the West Port, and she would have been searched had not the arms on the coach been recognised as belonging to a family who were Jacobite beyond suspicion.

When the old Judge died, she escaped from restraint, but the income was small, and on £150 a year, even in those simple days, one would not live luxuriously. Four years spent in rooms at Hamilton Palace [1] kept her still longer out of gaiety. There Patrick Cockburn with £200 a year ("rooms and coals included") acted as Commissioner to the spendthrift Duke of Hamilton, who, after squandering and gambling abroad, married one night the beautiful Elizabeth Gunning — a bed-curtain ring serving as pledge of fidelity, and £20 in his pocket as an imperfect pledge of wealth. When Mrs. Cockburn, with her husband, who was ungratefully treated by his graceless Grace, went to live at Musselburgh in poor circumstances, she would appear in Edinburgh at the balls and "consorts," and be welcomed in the flats to which up dark stairs rustled ladies in their bell-hoops, beaux in the silken coats, weighty judges not without joviality, and blue-coated divines not too unconvivial. The clever lady was an inveterate correspondent; carriers in their carts, and cadgers in their creels, bore many a bright letter from her to far-away houses. On gilt-edged paper, in cramped "hand of writ," went forth the city news of deaths and marriages and births, actual or prospective. Humour and piety jostle each other in these copious epistles with delightfully unconscious incongruity, as was the manner of

---

[1] *Mrs. Cockburn's Letters*, edit. by Craig-Brown, p. 3.

that age—high-flown sentiment and gossip about the doings of "Molly," or "Babby," or "Suffy"; recipes to "Lady Bal" for making out of bones "everlasting white" for painting on satin gauze—advice religious and medical, how to prepare for eternity before going to die, and how to take castor oil in wine before going to bed.[1] This was all extremely cheap, at ninepence for postage. In 1753 Mr. Cockburn—"her friend and lover for thirty-two years"—died, and left her a widow with a small income and one son who died in the prime of life.

She never, however, lost her liveliness, her insatiable love of mischief, mockery, and match-making. There was a vast amount of enjoyment in Edinburgh society—which was the quintessence of national life—with its close intimacies, its fine friendships, its constant visiting from flat to flat of the High Street. It was a cheery life the lady lived—welcomed at country homes like Balcarres by "Lady Bal" and Lady Anne Lindsay, and at her old home at Fairnalie, where her brother lived with his ugly and good-natured Dutch wife. At the gatherings at her little parlour, Mrs. Cockburn was to be seen attired in her striped silk saque, with her auburn hair turned back and covered with cap or lace hood, bound beneath her chin—thus clad she was portrayed by Miss Anne Forbes, whose picture certainly does not flatter her friend.

In 1764 was first printed her song, "The Flowers of the Forest," in a collection called the "Lark." It was said to have been written by her in girlhood, in her turreted room at Fairnalie. This we may well doubt, for it was surely no girl of eighteen who composed the mournful lay. Tradition [2]— which is a lying jade, never so matter-of-fact as when it is telling a matter-of-lie—gives this story its origin: a gentleman, passing through a glen in the neighbourhood, one day heard a shepherd playing on a flute an air which took his fancy, and asked Alison Rutherford to fit appropriate verses to the tune. It was that of the "Flowers of the Forest," a lament over those who had fallen on Flodden Field. Like many another song, its original words had been lost, leaving little more than

---

[1] *Lives of the Lindsays*, ii. 318.
[2] *Mrs. Cockburn's Letters*, p. 113; Stenhouse's *Illust. of Scot. Lyric Poetry*, p. 65.

the air behind it. Some lines lingered still on peasant ears of which Miss Jean Elliot of Minto could only remember [1]—

> I ride single on saddle,
> For the flowers of the forest are a' wede awa'.

According to Sir Walter Scott, the ballad was meant to bewail the pecuniary ruin in a commercial crisis of seven Border lairds; but of such a local catastrophe it is happily not too suggestive. Whatever its origin and date may be it made her fame, and in a thousand homes of Scotland, from flute and spinnet and violin, came forth the olden air, and from voices of Scots ladies in full-throated pathos came forth the familiar words:

> I've seen the smiling
> Of fortune's beguiling,
> I've felt its favours and found its decay;
> Sweet was its blessing,
> Kind its caressing,
> But now 'tis fled—fled far away.
>
> . . . . . .
>
> I've seen the morning
> With gold the hills adorning,
> And loud tempest storming before the mid-day.
> I've seen Tweed's sillar streams,
> Glittering in the sunny beams,
> Grow drumly and dark as they row'd on their way.

The strain is somewhat artificial; it lacks the simplicity of the fine old Scots lyrics; but it has its own beauty. Nimble with her pen, clever in her verses, it is on the one song Mrs. Cockburn's reputation lasts; and, strictly speaking, she cannot claim the title of a "woman of letters" except from her copious correspondence.

This woman had the kindliest of souls—"the friend of all young folk, the confidant of all love-sick hearts."[2] There were merry dancings in the tiny sitting-room of her flat in Blair Street near the Castle, led by Captain Bob Dalgleish, the king of the ball, with Jock This or Tom That with Peggy and Babby—for all familiarly were called by their Christian names

---

[1] Sir W. Scott's *Familiar Letters*, ii. 354.
[2] *Lives of the Lindsays*, ii. 312.

in homely fashion. On these nights the furniture was piled up high in the lobby, and the fiddler in the cupboard played and panted over strathspeys, or Lord Kellie's last minuet.[1]

To the end she remained the same. Friends die and she mourns to-day; some wedding is in prospect and she is gay as a venerable lark to-morrow. In her black chair she sits with her favourite tabby on her lap, reading insatiably every romance, however amazing for length of sentences and height of sentiment and depth of passion, which gratified our ancestors. She amuses herself after the mild fashions of her time. She cuts figures out of paper, she writes "sentiments" to be given at supper-tables, and "characters" in prose and verse to be recited, when the guests were intended to guess who, under the names of "Delia" and "Strephon," were described. One such "sentiment" of Mrs. Cockburn's was a dismal distich, enough to cast a company into hopeless gloom.[2]

> To the friend of affliction, the soul of affliction,
> Who may hear the last trump without fear of detection.

When old age came on her with its attendant infirmities, she became too frail to go to parties or weddings, or to cheerful funerals, for the lofty stairs fatigued her. She had her own little supper parties, when one or two were summoned to simple fare. "Four nothings on four plates of delf," as she quotes from Stella. In those days before larger incomes and bigger rents had broken in on the simple fashions of the age, when city ministers had stipends of £130 and judges lived on salaries of £500, entertainments were frugal. As Henry Mackenzie relates: "Tea was the meal of ceremony, and a supper of a very moderate number was that of a more intimate society" up the turnpike stairs. In this simple style Mrs. Cockburn could entertain on her own small income. At tea were to be met David Hume and Lord Monboddo, John Home and Adam Ferguson, Robertson and young Henry Mackenzie, who made himself useful by handing cups of tea and napkins for the ladies' laps. Among the ladies were old Lady Balcarres, with

---

[1] Tytler's and Watson's *Songstresses*, i. 110.
[2] Sir Walter Scott mistakenly thought these lines were meant for his father.—Chambers's *Scot. Songs*, p. lxii.; *Mrs. Cockburn's Letters* (edit. Craig-Brown). On "character" writing see *Lives of Lindsays*, ii. 322.

her haughty yet kindly face, and Sophy Johnston, clad in a man's greatcoat, with dark wrinkled face and hard pursed mouth, and two big feet planted well out—ejaculating "surely that's great nonsense," at anything spoken not to her mind. It was a miniature *salon*, with Scots tongues, broad, voluble, and homely. In her high black chair the hostess sat, with her Queen Elizabeth nose, her auburn hair, unsilvered by age, and untarnished by "nasty powder," surmounted by lace hood her snuff-box in hand and repartees and whimsies adroit on her lips. She hears the town news of Mrs. Siddons's wonderful performance at the theatre,[1] of the excitement of society all agog about the ploughman poet "who receives adulation with native dignity"; young Walter Scott comes to hear her old tales when she is too old to go to see her friend Mrs. Scott in George Square. Very old she becomes, but she can joke over her ailments. "I hardly know I existed last week except by the exertion of coughing and blowing my nose." On 22nd November 1794 she died at the age of eighty-two, with old friends round her bed. In her, Edinburgh lost one of its pleasantest relics of the past and society one of its most characteristic figures.

Miss Jean Elliot

With more reserve and more aristocratic exclusiveness Miss Jean Elliot, author of another famous "set" of the "Flowers of the Forest," lived in Edinburgh. A tall, slender, erect figure, attired in close cap, ruffles, and snowy broad handkerchief over her bosom, always dressed in the most correct fashion of the day. There was an expression of hauteur in her prominent nose, there was a shrewd force in her plain, sensible face. At Minto, near Hawick, her life had begun in 1727, in the clumsy old mansion near the turf-roofed kirk, with the kirkyard covered with the long grass concealing graves and tombstones, with their conventional artless art of cherub faces blowing last trumps, with cheeks in perilous state of distention, which was the rural mason's ideal of seraphic beauty, and cross-bones and weavers' shuttles

[1] *Songstresses of Scotland*, i. 180 ; *Mrs. Cockburn's Letters*, p. 113.

to represent the brevity of life. The Manse with its thatched roof overlooking the mansion was so near that the minister could watch—if he hid himself from detection—the great family in the big round room in which Sir Gilbert, the Lord Justice Clerk, presided over a circle of hungry but silent offspring. It was in the '45 that the rebels came to the house, and the judge ignominiously ran and hid himself among the Minto crags, while his daughter Jean entertained them pleasantly; the senator coming from his undignified ambush as he heard the horses ride off.[1]

One of the family, Gilbert, inheriting a literary taste from his father, who, with Forbes of Culloden, had published *Hardyknute* in 1719, had shown with other gentlemen of the time, a turn for polite letters; he could shape verses well, one song being a pastoral which was long a favourite in Scotland, played and sung to many a harpsichord and flute:

> My sheep I neglected, I broke my sheep hook,
> And all the gay haunts of my youth I forsook.

One day, records tradition, which is usually very inaccurate, Jean Elliot was riding in the family coach with her brother Gilbert. They spoke of the battle of Flodden whose memories clung to their country-side—for that historic tragedy had burned itself on the national mind. Her brother wagered her a pair of gloves or set of ribbons that she could not compose a ballad on Flodden Field. She was then about thirty, and had shown no turn for ballad-making, but she accepted the challenge. One or two lines only remained of the ancient ballad on the battle, though the famous air lingered on the ears of the people bereft of its words. Jean Elliot wrote her version, and her brother when he read it saw that he had lost his wager, and Scotland had gained a ballad which would never die. Copied out by family pens, recopied by those who saw or heard it, it went on its way to popularity. Gradually it found its way into every drawing-room, and was played at every concert, though who the writer was no one could tell. With stately reserve or maidenly modesty Miss Jean Elliot kept her secret, and her family gave no sign,

---

[1] *Life and Letters of Sir G. Elliot*, i. 22.

and never did she exert her lyrical genius in any such effort again. Hopeless uncertainty exists as to the dates and priority of the rival sets of the "Flowers of the Forest"; yet her song must have been written after that of Mrs. Cockburn, if it be true, as Dr. Somerville told Sir Walter Scott, that the song was written while he was staying at Minto House, for it was in 1767 he became minister of the parish, and lived with the Elliots as tutor.¹ A far finer work than its rival, Jean Elliot's ballad reaches near to perfection.

When old Lord Minto, the judge, died, and his son Gilbert reigned in his stead at Minto, Lady Elliot came to Edinburgh to reside in Brown Square, only five minutes' walk from the High Street, yet considered then most genteelly remote from the noise and vulgar familiarity of the town, and occupied by most "respectable persons," Henry Mackenzie, the "Man of Feeling," Lord Advocate Dundas, Islay Campbell, the Lord President, and Tytler of Woodhouselee, and Lord Justice Clerk Miller.² Clearly that elegant square, built in 1764—which has now vanished—was a fitting quarter for any people of such social pretensions as the Elliots. The high-bred Lady Elliot Murray—Miss Jean's sister-in-law—looked down on the deplorably provincial ways of the city, though condescendingly she owned that "there are many worthy, agreeable, well-principled persons, if you get over the language, manners, and address which are at first striking." "It is the misses that are the most rotten part of the society," was her emphatic opinion.³ Thus in an exclusive set these ladies spent their days.

Miss Jean lived alone after her mother's death, mixing carefully in good society. She was not a favourite with young folk. Kirkpatrick Sharpe, in his usual satiric vein, when giving his boyish memories of the old spinster, describes her face, which he calls ugly, her big open mouth, her affectation of fine speaking. "I caint" for "I can't" she would say, and

---

¹ Scott's *Familiar Letters*, ii. 354 ; Somerville's *Memoirs*, p. 120 ; *Mrs. Cockburn's Letters*, ed. by Craig-Brown, p. 113. Stenhouse gives 1755 as the date of its publication, but does not say where it appeared (*Illust. of Scot. Lyric Poetry*, p. 66).
² Chambers's *Traditions of Edinburgh*, i. 40 ; ii. 50.
³ Tytler and Watson's *Songstresses of Scotland*, i. 214.

JEAN ELLIOT
After a Miniature.

her tongue not too good-natured. He records the family terror when at tea-time Miss Elliot's sedan-chair would arrive at his aunt's door, and after a long, secret talk in the back drawing-room, she would jolt off again, leaving the aunt out of temper with everybody, accusing the young people of faults and sins—all which evil charges they laid down at the door of "The Flower," as they nicknamed the single-song lady. Did she really write that fine ballad, she who never wrote anything else, or showed gifts anywhere else? Sharpe's cousin, who knew her best, said, however, that Miss Elliot—"who never told lies"—had told her the song was her own invention.[1] The good lady's weeks were spent in stately calls, her Sabbaths were satisfyingly spent in listening to her favourite, Dr. John Erskine, in Greyfriars Kirk—a minister who had the double merits in the old maid's eyes of being both a man of God and a man of birth. She was an old woman of seventy-nine when she died in 1805. Her death made no gap in society as Mrs. Cockburn's had done. Literary fame she did not seek; she was too proud to have her name bandied about on every lip. Only by accident was it discovered who had written that superb ballad which to harp and harpsichord for many a day was sung in every house:

> I've heard the lilting at our yowe's milking,
> Lasses a' lilting before the break o' day.
> But now they are moaning on ilka green loaning,
> The Flowers o' the Forest are a' wede awa!

LADY ANNE BARNARD

Balcarres, the country seat of the Earls of Lindsay, was a solid old-fashioned château—in the style of many Scots mansions of the middle of the eighteenth century, with its large and lumbering wings, its narrow stairs, its thick walls, its turrets, and, most characteristic of all, its poverty. Facing the sea on the Fifeshire coast, it looked straight across to the

---

[1] Miss Home, afterwards wife of John Hunter, the great anatomist, wrote another set of verses on the "Flowers of the Forest." Her familiar song, "My mother bids me bind my hair," owes its vogue more to Haydn's tune than to her feeble verses (Wilson's *Reminiscences of Old Edinburgh*, i. 295).

Bass Rock, and the salt air gave intenser sharpness to that east wind which blows with such venom over the flat land of Fife. The mansion was surrounded with thick woods, where by day rooks cawed, and by night owls hooted, adding a grimness to the house, which had a little top chamber accessible only by a ladder from outside, tenanted by a "brownie" and gaped at fearsomely by the children.

Within the mansion there was a curious household. The old lord was at the ripe old age of sixty, and even looked eighty, when he had won the hand, if not the affections, of the blooming, buxom daughter of Sir Robert Dalrymple. Extremely deaf, he had no outward attractions to charm her, having a big brigadier's wig, with its three tails hanging down his shoulders, his gouty foot encased in a huge shoe, "like a little boat with a cabin at the end of it," which his impatient knife had slashed to relieve his torments: a gaunt, grim figure, with a fantastic character, which was a mixture of Mr. Shandy, Uncle Toby, and Don Quixote.[1] A family of twelve blessed—or otherwise—this union, before he died at the age of seventy-eight. He was a chivalrous gentleman, from the curl of his wig to the points of his gouty toes; a student of old books and lover of long pedigrees in his library of folios and quartos; a farmer eager on draining and turnip-sowing; a Jacobite as far as a loyal soldier to George III. could be; a gallant old man as far as adoration of the fair sex could go, regarding womankind as the ideal of perfection, and investing each with virtues she did not own, and graces she never had. There was the old gentleman riding off to Elie on an unbroken horse on his dame's commission, for he was obsequious to her every whim, never meeting a carriage on the road without gallantly asking the ladies within if he could be of service to them, while his old wig fluttered in the breeze as he swept off his three-cornered hat. One pictures the worthy "original" capturing an old woman stealing his cherished turnips—then a rare product of the fields,—rating her hotly while she curtsied duly before his choleric lordship, and after the veteran had expended his vituperations, there came the calm, audacious request, "Eh, my lord, they're unco heavy; will ye no gie me a lift?"

[1] *Lives of the Lindsays*, ii. pp. 233, 278.

The incident closed with the noble lord hoisting the sack on the back of the nefarious woman, whose parting words, "Thank ye, my lord," rang with ironic sound as he strode reflectively home.

Very different from the poor and guileless peer was the countess — a relentless disciplinarian who sought to bring up a family of four sons and eight daughters, endowed with irrepressible spirits, on the old Scots system, administering noxious drugs to their throats and incessant castigations to sensitive parts of their young persons, with a precision perfected by practice — with a sense of duty as hard as her blows. Childhood's memories in that household consisted largely of whippings, "black holes," hungry stomachs, and punitive rhubarb doses. "Woman!" protested the sturdy treble of the Honourable John to his mother when under punishment — "woman! I told you I would do it. I'll do the same thing again to-morrow." The morrow came and with it the fault, and with the fault the penalty, namely, the loss of all his playthings. As the sun shone out warm and bright, "Ah!" he cried, "my mother cannot take that from me!" The good earl's heart was wrung by all this, and he would utter his protests: "Oddsfish! madam, you will break the spirits of my young troop. I will not have it so." One day a neighbouring laird riding to Balcarres met a procession, in single file, of the children, from the largest, who bore on his back the baby, to the smallest, who toddled in the rear. This was the house of Lindsay resolved to quit their "horrious" home, and escape maternal discipline.[1] They were discovered by Robin Gray, the shepherd, who ran and cried: "My lady, all the young gentlemen, and all the young ladies, and all the dogs are gone!" As attempted-suicides, for wishing to be rid of life, are put in prison, the better to reconcile them to existence, so the rebels, for seeking to quit their home, were subjected to graduated doses of rhubarb, to attach them the more kindly to it.

Yet, in spite of all this, and although they were poor and secluded from the world, "it was a creed of our family," says Lady Anne Lindsay, "that it was impossible anybody at

[1] Hare's *Story of my Life*, vol. iii.; *Lives of the Lindsays*, ii. 306.

Balcarres could wish to be anywhere else." There was a delightful freedom and simplicity of manners—young folk riding on the sow's back, or eating raw turnips in the fields when the tutor's back was turned; the girls wading in the stream in the Den, tucking up their yellow and silver frocks, which had been made out of strips cut from their mother's wedding dress, flounced with bits of old blue gauze.

There were as familiar inmates of the establishment Mr. Small, the tutor, oblivious, guileless, and pious, and Miss Henrietta Cumming, the governess, who claimed to have descended from the Red Comyn, and who meanwhile had descended from a very small and airy Edinburgh flat, where she had painted butterflies on gauze for a livelihood. As she had indignantly refused to fare with the waiting-maid, she made her way to the dining-table, and became the most necessary member of the family, which she insisted on serving without wages. Italian and French she could teach; letters she could write, which her friend Mrs. Cockburn could liken only to Rousseau's; she sang sweetly, talked cleverly, and as for needlework, none was so deft as she at designing ruffles and painting satin, or at pleasing his lordship with waistcoats painted with figures "of the bird kind," to adorn his lank person. She was insinuating to her ladyship, she could be severe with the offspring, this tiny creature—"the least little woman to be seen for nothing"[1]—who had the figure of a sylph and the temper of a tartar.

Visitors came to Balcarres for the usual Scots period— "the rest day, the dressed day, the pressed day"—and some remained for months or years. There was Sophia Johnston, the daughter of the coarse, drunken laird of Hilton, who had come to pay a little visit and remained for thirteen years. She had grown up, according to Hilton's hideous whim, without training, or education, or religion, only furtively learning to read and write from the butler. She was able to wrestle with stable-boys, to shoe a horse like a smith, to make woodwork like a joiner, and to swear like a trooper. There she was, the strange creature, working at her forge in her room at Balcarres, playing the fiddle, singing songs with a voice like a

[1] *Lives of the Lindsays*, ii. 312.

LADY ANNE BARNARD
After a Miniature.

man's, dressed in a jockey coat, walking with masculine stride, speaking broad Scots in deepest bass, which would roll out a good round oath. The children listened with delicious awe as she sang:

> Eh, quo' the Tod, it's braw bricht nicht,
> The wind's i' the wast and the moon shines bricht.[1]

A sad "original" she was, with her lonely life, her faithless creed, her laughter, in which there was no mirth, her violent loves, and fierce hates—Miss Henny Cumming being her special aversion.

We can see the family circle in the dining-room, old as 1652, with oak walls, fine stuccoed ceiling, with "bustoes" in relief, of King David, Hector, and Alexander. There sat the old brigadier, kindly to the children, courteous to guests, though invariably his choleric temper would rise in hot dispute with any one over the virtues of Queen Mary, or the iniquities of the Union, till his face grew purple and his expletive "Oddsfish" proved quite inadequate for the occasion, while tutor and governess and family kept silent. Miss Anne Keith was there often and long, the dearest friend and cousin of Lady Balcarres, the shrewdest of women, with the warmest of hearts; and Mrs. Cockburn came by ferry and coach, full of the last news from Edinburgh, of weddings possible, probable, and certain, telling of the newest freak of Lord Monboddo, or the last joke of Harry Erskine, and discussing shapes of satin cloaks or painted ruffles.

In the household, Lady Anne, the eldest daughter, was full of fun, and the foremost in every madcap whim, yet the right hand of her old father till he died when she was eighteen— helping him with his books, his memoirs, and his old manuscripts. The monotony of her existence in Balcarres was varied by visits to Edinburgh, though there were serious difficulties to consider in the impecunious household before a young woman was rigged out for Edinburgh balls, even though Miss Henny Cumming was so nimble at making new gowns out of old frocks. In the Capital Lady Anne was welcome with her bright face, her merry humour, and her

---

[1] *Lives of the Lindsays*, ii. 316.

songs, to which she made the old spinnets musically jingle. There were visits to the Dowager Lady Balcarres, who dwelt up precipitous stairs in the Lawnmarket, subsisting on a meagre jointure, out of which, by frugal living, she contrived to save money, in order to relieve the heavy wadsets on the estates of the Lindsays. She was to be met in the street, staff in hand, dressed in the perennial black silk gown, white apron, big black silk bonnet, far jutting over a countenance stern and resolute. No wonder all made way for her as she passed along the causeway. At night in her parlour, containing a bed all neatly hid by curtains, acquaintances assembled to their tea and scones and chat, while the slenderly-waged retainer, resting against the bed-post, would rouse himself at the call, "Bring the hot water, John," and in easy colloquy with her "leddyship" would hand the kettle to "mask the tea."[1] Memorable, too, were the visits to old Lady Dalrymple—the other grandmother—most oblivious, most quaint of aristocratic souls, who would never leave her bedroom without having given health-restoring sniffs to three apples—each in turn—that stood on her toilet table. As she appeared for breakfast, with her mittens and her snuff-box in hand, Lady Anne knew for certain that she would stop on the seventeenth spot on the carpet, cough three times, come to the table, look in vain on the right hand for her key, send Anne to seek it in the bedroom, and invariably with punctual surprise discover it on the fingers of her left hand. Where, now, are originals, with their delightful oddities and characters, loved, laughed at, and respected, such as lived in the olden times?

There were also the Assemblies to go to, where Lady Anne would take her place in the "quality set," as became her rank, or in the "handsome set" at the minuet and reel, as became her face. At the many tea and supper parties, what delight it was to listen to Principal Robertson's common-sense in plain Scots, David Hume's simple fun, and the man-of-the-world talk of "Ambassador" Keith, Mistress Anne's brother, in the reunions at which many famous personages—legal, clerical, literary, fashionable, aristocratic—would meet and make the night brilliant in an atmosphere of snuff and good talk.

[1] *Thrieplands of Fingask*, by Chambers, p. 58; *Lives of the Lindsays*, ii. 320

When she was eighteen years old, Lady Margaret, possessed of rare beauty, married Mr. Alexander Fordyce—a member of a family that produced several men who were notable, but unfortunately, in his case, only to be notorious. He had gone from Aberdeen as a clerk, and achieved success in London as a banker. He was able to buy the estate of Roehampton, and was able to lose an election at the cost of £16,000. This seemed a great "catch" for a poor damsel of high degree and low fortune, but soon it came to grief. Fordyce absconded, his bank collapsed, and his fellow-bankers were ruined, involving in the crash private banks in England and in Scotland, when on "Black Monday" news came of Fordyce's disappearance and defalcations. There suffered alike lairds and farmers in Ayrshire [1] and actors in London, whose savings were lost, and for whose behoof Mrs. Abington gave a benefit. Curiously enough, Miss Henrietta Cumming, the governess, married, and lived in purring felicity with this plausible banker's brother, Rev. Dr. James Fordyce—the most popular Presbyterian preacher in London, whose *Sermons for Young Women*, full of sense for a frivolous age, were the favourite Sunday reading prescribed as a moral tonic for young ladies after the routs and balls of London, Bath, and Tunbridge Wells.

When sister Margaret, beautiful and witty, had gone, and her brothers were scattered far and wide, Lady Anne remained at home. In the little chamber, reached by a long turnpike stair, with its small window facing the sea, she would relieve her solitude by writing verses and moral reflections on the backs of old letters. Often had she heard Sophia Johnston sing, in her Amazonian voice, an old song: "The bridegroom greets when the sun goes down." [2] The words were not decorous, but the melody took her fancy, and she tried to compose new words to fit the old air. She was then twenty years old, her sister Margaret's wedding had come and gone, and left her dreary, and to while away the time she set to the work of composition. After trying to perfect her verses, she called her little sister Elizabeth to the closet: "I have been writing a ballad, my dear; I am oppressing my heroine with

---

[1] Forbes's *Hist. of a Scottish Banking House*, p. 40.
[2] *Lives of the Lindsays*, ii. 322.

misfortune. I have sent Jamie to sea, broken his father's arm, made her mother fall sick, and given her auld Robin Gray for a lover; but I wish to load her with a fifth sorrow in the four lines, poor thing! Help me, I pray." "Steal the cow, sister Annie," suggested Elizabeth; and forthwith the cow was stolen, and the song "Auld Robin Gray" completed. She never showed the ballad except to her mother, who was delighted with it. It was copied out, but none outside the inner circle knew anything of its authorship, though "Suffy" Johnston guessed full shrewdly. Lady Anne, in her rich voice, sang the tale of rural woes in Fifeshire mansions and in Edinburgh flats, and through transcripts the ballad became universally popular, and passed for an ancient song. Antique ladies, with confident but erroneous memories, professed to have heard it often when they were young; it found its way into song-books; it was sung everywhere, and even heard by the camp-fires in the American campaign; it was made subject for a play, and a clergyman honoured it by claiming it as his own. Gradually the old melody was abandoned, and the air with which we are familiar,[1] composed by an English friend of Lady Anne's, was sung in its stead.

Some years after, a sequel was written at her mother's request—for she would say, "Annie, I wish you would tell me how that unlucky business of Jeanie and Jamie ended." She remembered how the irascible old laird of Dalyell, on hearing it, had exclaimed, "O! the auld rascal, I ken wha stealt the puir lassie's coo. It was auld Robin himsel'." And such a story she makes the sequel tell. Like most sequels it is a failure, in spite of graphic touches and some happy lines. The original had told all one wished to hear. Of this song she gave no copy even to her mother who, however, could remember it all from recital, and till nearly a hundred years of age the old lady loved to repeat it, proud at feeling that she alone knew the secret of its authorship.

The old life at Balcarres at last came to an end. The eldest brother—the new earl—married, and Lady Anne went

[1] The words were given by a friend of Lady Anne's to Lieut. W. Leeves, 1st Foot Guards afterwards Rector of Wrington that he might compose an air for it. It is his tune which is now used (Hare's *Story of my Life*, iii. 27).

to reside in London with her sister, Lady Margaret Fordyce, who was now a widow, famous for her beauty, her grace, and her wit, living in the most brilliant circles of town. There she stayed till, at the age of forty-three, she married Mr. Barnard, son of the literary Bishop of Limerick, aged twenty-eight, and accompanied him to the Cape of Good Hope, where he was secretary to the Governor, Lord Maccartney—an appointment worth £2000 a year, which his energetic wife had got from her old friend Henry Dundas. She had to exchange the society of wits and men of fashion, to give up routs, masquerades, and plays for the company of half-Dutch colonists, with uncouth manners and dialect. Good-humour she carried with her, with just a touch of the condescension of the high-bred daughter of an earl and wife of an official, at the balls of the castle, where she reigned as queen. To spend the time there were journeys among the hills, picnics where every discomfort was tempered with mirth, visits to obese Dutch *vrows*, whose notions of cleanliness had suffered a sea change from Holland, and additions to collect for her hardly less cleanly menagerie. All this she described in letters full of humour and cleverness. In 1802 came the Peace of Amiens — that peace of which Sir Philip Francis said "everybody was glad and nobody was proud"—and the Colony was restored to the Dutch. Mr. Barnard's occupation was gone, and he and Lady Anne returned to England.

A few years went by and her husband died in 1808, and again she lived with her favourite sister, till after years of disappointment and of wasted love, which embittered a nature once divinely sweet, Lady Margaret married old Sir James Bland Burgess, and gained a brief space of happiness before she died. Lady Anne lived on in London, and her name often meets us in Madame d'Arblay's *Diary*, in society of the best and brightest. When she went to Paris, in drawing-rooms she heard people whispering, "*Voilà l'auteur du fameux roman de Robin Gray!*" as they looked at her, for the song had been translated. One evening she was being seen home from a party in Paris by a French nobleman, when suddenly her companion plumped down on his knees before her on the floor of the carriage. She was about to shriek out for help, when he shattered her vanity, as he dispelled her fears, by exclaiming, "*Taisez, madame! voilà le bon Dieu qui passe.*"¹ It was the Host being carried through the streets to which he devoutly knelt, and not to the lady.

Far away in Edinburgh, with the new century society was losing its old traits and quaint characters. Still, however, her mother, Lady Balcarres, was living in George Square with the cousin whom she called her "husband"—Mistress Anne Murray Keith, the little old lady, with lovely blue eyes and exquisite expression of kindliness which robbed her high nose of its air of command, with her neat cap under which were curls of ivory whiteness ranged on her forehead. Mrs. Anne's exhaustless fund of stories brought the long past days to life again as a younger generation listened—stories which Walter Scott heard with delight and served up so often in his novels² that he could not conceal his authorship from her. "Can I no ken my ain groats among ither folks' kail?" she would shrewdly ask.³ Pleasantly the old ladies dwelt together. Her venerable ladyship, whose austerity age had softened, was eager over her knitting, her cards, and her Scriptures. She returned to end her days at Balcarres, finding endless consolation in reading, with undimmed eye, the lives of Bible patriarchs, and looking to that future which was soon to her to be present; and, as she would say to her loved daughter, "then we shall all be young again, Annie." She died at the age of ninety-four. Meanwhile poor Sophy Johnston, old and haggard, lived miserly and grimly in her garret, to which every Sunday the grandchildren of her pets in Balcarres tremblingly came with a present for the forlorn old friend of their family—her skinny hands greedily held forth as her gruff voice growled out: "What hae ye brocht—what hae ye brocht?"⁴

It was only a year or two before her death that Lady Anne Barnard acknowledged the authorship of the famous song which gives her a place in literature. She said she had not

---

[1] Hare's *Story of my Life*, iii. 326; Stenhouse's *Illustrations*, p. 230.
[2] Lockhart's *Life of Scott*, v. pp. 310, 315; *Lives of the Lindsays*, ii. 322.
[3] *Lives of the Lindsays*; Cockburn's *Memorials*, p. 60.
[4] *Lives of the Lindsays*, ii. 360.

owned it because she dreaded being known as a writer, lest those who did not write should feel shy of her—a reason which is not very satisfying. Certainly the reluctance of these good Scots ladies to be known as authors is in curious contrast to the eagerness with which literary ladies in England rushed into print, rejoiced in publicity, and forced themselves into notoriety. It was partly pride on the part of highborn dames lest their name should become too familiar on common lips. It was so with Miss Jean Elliot, Lady Louisa Stuart, and Lady Nairne—partly also owing to shyness and timidity, which made Miss Ferrier shrink from publicity as from criticism. In *The Pirate*, in 1823, Sir Walter Scott quoted lines from the second part of " Auld Robin Gray," as Lady Anne Lindsay's " beautiful ballad." The secret had come forth, and now she owned it.[1] She was an old woman of seventy-five when she died in 1825, lovable and loved to the last, whose lyrical skill lives in her undying song, and whose vivid memories of her home at Balcarres enliven the pages of the *Lives of the Lindsays*.

LADY NAIRNE

The House of Gask—the "auld house" of Lady Nairne's song—in the middle of the eighteenth century stood upon a hill in the Strath of Earn, a curious, rambling house, which owed its interest to its quaintness and the picturesqueness of its situation. There lived Laurence Oliphant, the laird, descendant of an old family as proud as it was ancient, a Jacobite of the Jacobites, who loved the Stuarts with all the adoration of his absurd old soul. To win his undying favour it was only necessary for a neighbour to present him with a relic of the Royal house —a garter, a brogue, or spurs worn by His Royal Highness. To look at—but for heaven's sake not to touch—the sacred memorials, a lock of Prince Charlie's red hair, his bonnet, his cockade or crucifix, was with him almost a religious service. With indignation he bundled off Mr. Cruikshank the chaplain's gown and books by carrier when he learned that he had, on the death of Prince Charles, begun to pray for George III.;

[1] Oliphant's *Jacobite Lairds of Gask*, p. 368.

for a "nominal" prayer—that is, one in which the Hanoverian usurper was mentioned by name—was an abomination. With what care had he and his wife conveyed to Florence the piece of seed-cake which the hands of Mrs. Forbes, the nonjuring bishop's wife, had prepared for His Majesty's delectation; and with what joy he reported that when his sacred Majesty took it in his hands, he opened a drawer and graciously said: "Here you see me deposit it, and no tooth shall go upon it but my own." There was something so sturdy, so honest, so loyal in his disloyalty that King George sent him his fine message, couched in phrases to conciliate his heart: "The Elector of Hanover presents compliments to the laird of Gask, and wishes to tell him how much the Elector respects the laird for the steadiness of his principles."[1]

When Lady Gask died her last words to the children gathered round her were: "See which will be the best bairn to papa." To that household came the governess whom the aunt provided, with this recommendation: "Mr. Oliphant joyns me in thinking there is no better sign than diffidence in what one knows nothing about, therefore has no doubt Mrs. Cramond (for you know I cannot call her Miss when a governess) will make herself usefull to ye children with a little practice in many things besides ye needle, particularly as to behaviour, principles of Religion and Loyalty, a good carriage and talking tolerable English which in ye countrie is necessarie that young folks may not appear clownish when presented to company."[2] From which it would appear that Lady Henrietta's own accomplishments did not entitle her to be too exacting in the qualifications of a governess, especially as the remuneration was to be twelve guineas for the first year and ten guineas "ever after." Mr. Marconchi, the foreign fiddler, walked over from Perth once a week to teach the art of dancing and the harpsichord to the family of two sons and four daughters.

Caroline—whose baptismal name veneration for Prince Charles had once more made popular in Jacobite circles—was born in 1766, the third of the family, and she grew up reserved and dignified into a tall beauty with dark eyes and hair, the

[1] Oliphant's *Jacobite Lairds of Gask*, p. 368.   [2] *Ibid.* p. 387.

LADY NAIRNE
After the Portrait by Sir J. Watson Gordon in 1815.

toast of the country as the "Flower of Strathearn." At the
county balls she danced with so fine a grace and skill, that the
eyes of little Neil Gow, the prince of fiddlers, would gleam
with delight as he watched her threading the gladsome windings
of a strathspey. In 1792 the laird of Gask died—the soldier
of the '45 who suffered long, though he was not long-suffering,
from his aches and ails, which the abominable concoctions
prescribed as sovereign cures by his friend the laird of Thriep-
land had helped to intensify. He was true to the end to the
Stuart cause, and never forgot when proposing a toast to look
at his handsome son Charles, and to say with significant
accent: "The King—Charles." Never had he permitted any
who read the newspapers to him to mention George III. and
his queen, except as "K" and "Q." In such Jacobite
associations his sons and daughters grew up.

It was at a tenantry dinner given by the new laird
that Miss Caroline Oliphant heard sung "The Ploughman," a
coarse song with a good Scots air. Vexed at finding such
songs pleasing the people at their rustic meetings, and disgusted, as she passed through a country fair, to notice the
broadsides and ballads which were greedily bought from
barrows and pedlars' packs, she became filled with desire to
make verses more wholesome, and not less attractive, to take
their place on the people's lips. This she did in secrecy. It
was the ancestral enthusiasm for the good old cause which then
and afterwards quickened her fancy to write such songs as
"Charlie is my darling," "Will you no come back again?" "A
Hundred Pipers,"—with their romantic sentiment and martial
strain that make the pulse beat faster—songs produced
when the Jacobite cause was dead as Queen Anne, and
when no romance or song could stir it to life again. Who
imagined there could come from that stately damsel, and afterwards so proud a dame, with whom humour could scarce
venture to dwell, the lively "John Tod" and "Laird o'
Cockpen," which generations should sing with never-failing
glee; or the humble "Caller Herrin'," with its charming refrain
caught from the sound of the chimes of St. Giles' in Edinburgh?
Fond recollection of Gask she enshrined in the "Auld House,"
with its "auld laird, sae canty, kind, and crouse."

But in the "Land o' the Leal" the poet rose to her highest level, from the beginning "We're wearin' awa, John" to its close, in which the simplicity of true pathos moves with rare and tender touch.

In those days and for several years she was engaged to her cousin, Charles Nairne; but they were both poor, the young man having remote prospects of promotion in the army. "Miss Car the pretty," as she was called by the people, was no longer the beauty at every county ball, the bloom of the "Flower of Strathearn" became somewhat faded as she matured into the staid, stately, handsome lady of forty. It was then, however, when her cousin, at the mature age of fifty, became a major, that the long engagement issued in a happy marriage, and life in Edinburgh in a frugal home called "Caroline Cottage." They were poor, that high-bred couple, and they were pronouncedly proud; they belonged to the exclusive aristocratic set which was dwindling away in that city as London became the resistless centre of attraction for all who had claims to rank or position. Sydney Smith's description of Edinburgh society as "a pack of cards without honours" was becoming true.

The new century had gone on its way some years when one day there called on Mr. Purdie, the music-seller, a lady giving the name of Mrs. Bogan of Bogan, who had already corresponded with him, transmitting songs in a feigned handwriting. Mrs. Nairne appeared before the worthy tradesman in the guise of an old lady of a bygone generation—which after all was on her part no very great deception—and told him of songs she had got to publish. This was good news, because the *Scottish Minstrel* was being compiled by him; and accordingly with extraordinary mystery verses set to well-known airs by "Mrs. Bogan of Bogan" were produced.[1] For years the exquisite song, the "Land o' the Leal," had been familiar throughout the land; the pathos of Scots hearts seemed voiced by it as by no other song, and to the strains of "We're wearin' awa, John, To the Land o' the Leal," eyes had grown dim with tears. Mrs. Nairne had heard them praised and seen them bewept; and had noticed with a fret the words changed

[1] *Songstresses of Scotland*, ii. 130.

to "Wearin' awa, Jean," but she said nothing. With inexplicable reticence she even kept the secret of authorship from her own husband, spreading a newspaper over her manuscripts if he came into the room. This may have been caused by doubts as to her husband's powers of keeping a secret; but it was due also to that self-contained nature, that resolute reserve, which made her avoid with impatience the kiss which the bridegroom offered after the chaplain at Gask had married them.

In 1824 George IV. made his memorable visit to Scotland, when Sir Walter Scott worked himself up into grotesque enthusiasm in welcome of the not too respectable monarch. A memorial was prepared by Sir Walter praying His Majesty that the title forfeited by the Rebellion might be restored to Major Nairne. The petition was granted, and Major Nairne became a lord before he died in 1824.

In her later years Lady Nairne was involved in the atmosphere of pietism which began to prevail over Scotland, dating from the pious crusade of the Haldanes. Secular amusements—save painting—were no longer to her mind, the fashions of the world that pass away were no more to the taste of her who had in unregenerate days written the "Laird o' Cockpen." She had always been religious, though the humour would bubble over into fun in her songs. In later years the wave of evangelicalism went over her head, as it did over that of Susan Ferrier, who, it must with sadness be confessed, like Hannah More, degenerated as a writer as she became regenerated as a Christian. As years went on she returned to Gask, to which her nephew, the laird, had urged her to return. But it was not the "Auld House." That had been knocked down, and a more pretentious dwelling built in expectation of a fortune that never came. With the quaint old home departed associations with the olden time. In the new house, amidst her kith and kin, Baroness Nairne died, and with her the last of the band of Scots songstresses of the eighteenth century passed away.[1]

Others there were who wrote with true lyric touch, not such high-born dames as those we have described, but some

---

[1] Rogers's *Life and Poems of Lady Nairne.*

round whose memories the romance is of somewhat squalid kind. About 1771 Robert Burns heard sung in the streets the song, "There's nae luck aboot the house"; and this has been popularly ascribed to Jean Adams, who had died in the Glasgow poorhouse six years before. In girlhood she had been in service in a clergyman's manse as nurse and sewing-maid, and there pored over the manse library, its poetry and theology, to such purpose, that in a few years her verses were handed about among her friends and the society which got position and fortune from ships and fishing and sugar in the village of Greenock. To her intense joy she saw her poems collected and issued in a volume from the Saltmarket of Glasgow, with a list of subscribers, which included all the country gentry of the West. But the poems were of a ghastly type: on "Abel," on "The Method of Grace," on "Cleopatra," and the "Redemption." Now she set up as a teacher of girls, instructing her pupils about samplers, quilt frames, Bible lessons, and spelling-books, and indulged her scholars by singing to them her own verses or reading Shakespeare, over which the poor sewing mistress was so deeply affected, that when reading *Othello* she fell down in a faint at the feet of her amazed pupils. It was firmly believed she had walked all the way to London to see Mr. Richardson, the great author of *Pamela*—a domestic whose good fortunes Jean was not to follow. Meanwhile her fees were few, the forlorn volume of verse did not sell, and by advice of her publisher in the Saltmarket she shipped off to Boston by a Greenock vessel the unsold copies that were crowding the bookseller's cellar. But no money came back, and her savings were gone. So poor Jean was reduced to go about seeking for work, or money or clothing from the ladies and mothers of her late scholars, her heart bursting with shame at her ignoble resort to begging. It was the month of April 1765 that, ragged and hungry and sick, she travelled wearily to Glasgow, with sorrow in her despairing heart, and knocked at the poorhouse door. She had an order signed by two bailies of Greenock, who evidently felt there was no other resource for her, and she was admitted as "a poor woman in distress," "a stranger who had been wandering about." Next day she died and was buried by the parish.

According to local belief she was author of the song, "There's nae luck aboot the house," which Burns lavishly pronounced "one of the most beautiful in the Scots or any other language." Those who knew her had heard her sing this song as her own composition, and never doubted that the poor pauper woman had written it. On the other hand, in 1806, it was claimed for Mickle, the author of "Cumnor Hall," by his friend and biographer, who among his papers had found two copies, with alterations, and Mrs. Mickle pronounced it to be her husband's work. What a fine touch there is in the lines:

> His very foot has music in't,
> As he comes up the stairs ;

and in the sense of bewildered joy at Colin's return :

> And will I see his face again,
> And will I hear him speak ?[1]

Some years after the luckless Jean Adams was dead, there was going about Ayrshire and the southern counties, accompanying a beggarly crew of tramps, the daughter of a Kilmarnock weaver, Jean Glover by name, a handsome, wild, thieving hussy, following her light-fingered and light-hearted husband, who frequented fairs and races, as player and mountebank.[2] At quays and market-places was seen Jean in her tawdry finery and tinsel playing the tambourine and singing songs while her partner played his juggling feats and tricked the weaver lads, "the brawest woman that had ever been seen to step in leathern shoon."[3] She tramped by the weary dusty roads, or draggletailed trode the moorlands, and slept in the open on summer nights, or in sheds in evil weather, till she died on her wanderings through Ireland in 1801 at the age of forty-two. One

---

[1] Mickle's *Poems* (Life by Sim), 1806 ; Stenhouse's *Illust. of Lyric Poetry*, p. 48. On first being questioned as to the authorship, Mrs. Mickle, old and paralysed, answered with diffidence and hesitation, but on another occasion she confidently asserted that her husband had given it to her as his own composition. Dr. Beattie added the stanza with the words :

> The present moment is our ain,
> The neist we never saw—

which convey a truth more obvious than striking.
[2] Chambers's *Life and Works of Burns*, 1852, iv. 291.
[3] Stenhouse's *Lyric Poetry of Scotland*.

song she left for folk to sing when her voice was silent—a song which she, in the glee of happy vagrancy, had composed:

> Over the moor and among the heather
> Down among the blooming heather,
> By sea and sky! she shall be mine,
> The bonnie lass among the heather.

This ditty, which Robert Burns took down from her singing, is no great thing truly, yet it is a fresh voice that sings out of the sordid vagabond soul.

It is to the keeper of a poor alehouse in Ayrshire, Isabel Pagan, the song, "Ca' the yowes to the knowes," to which Burns added some verses, has been ascribed. High-born ladies did not disdain to sing to harpsichord in the best company in Scotland verses due possibly to the ugly, deformed, ill-favoured, ill-tongued, drunken keeper of a shebeen near Muirkirk, in Ayrshire, where she sold smuggled whisky to customers, who laughed at her coarse jokes as they took their illicit mutchkin.[1] The Muse kept more orderly company with clever Mrs. Grant in the Highland manse at Laggan, when she was writing her favourite "Where and O where is your Highland laddie gone"; and with another Mrs. Grant, at Carron on Spey, who wrote her brisk and spirited "Roy's Wife of Aldivalloch." When Englishwomen were writing dramas and histories and treatises, their Scottish sisters were quietly writing songs.

[1] One is sceptical as to her authorship. The collection of her verses published in 1805 is chiefly doggerel; and it is strange that Burns, who first heard the song from a clergyman, should know nothing of the claims of a woman who lived in his own county (*Contemporaries of Burns*, 1840, p. 116).

CHAPTER XIII

SONG-WRITERS—SKINNER—BRUCE—FERGUSSON

THE song-writers of the century hold a distinct place in the literature of Scotland. In our day there are writers who produce lyrics quite as good as some of theirs, which may come with one season, live on to the next, and be forgotten the third, or only sung with the singers' apology that "they have really nothing new." In Scotland in those olden times the lyrics lasted for generations. Young voices sang on to the piano what their mothers had sung to the spinnet, and their grandmothers had sung to the virginal. This permanency was often due to the charming old melodies to which they were set. As we have seen in the first half of the eighteenth century, it was chiefly gentlemen of land and fortune who wrote the songs on homely Scots subjects. In the latter half we find them coming from pens of all sorts and conditions.[1] Sir John Clerk of Penicuik, Baron of Exchequer, amused himself by writing "O merry may the maid be that married wi' the miller," which, at penny weddings and in fashionable drawing-rooms, was gaily sung. The poor, shiftless parish schoolmaster of Rathven, George Halket—who, till he was dismissed for drinking, lived with his family in a hovel which, divided by a box-bed, served in one part as school and the other as bedroom — wrote "Logie o' Buchan," which became a perennial favourite. Away in a remote district at the foot of the Grampians, another schoolmaster, Alexander Ross of

---

[1] Walker's *Bards of Bon Accord*; Buchan's *Ballads and Songs of North of Scotland*; Chambers's *Scottish Songs*; Cunningham's *Minstrelsy of Scotland*.

Lochlee, author of "Helenore, or the Fortunate Shepherdess,"
—a poem with an egregious title and a very dull story,
containing graphic pictures of northern rural life,—wrote
songs which earned him a long popularity among the people
of the North, who sang his "Woo'd and married and a',"
and his "Rock and Wee Pickle Tow" with unfailing zest.
In the Midland counties, the tall, handsome minister—wit
and *bon vivant* and saint—Dr. Alexander Webster—who,
having been engaged by a friend to urge his suit with Miss
Erskine of Alloa, did it so winningly that she offered herself
to him instead—composed his lyric, "O how could I venture
to love one like thee" to celebrate the triumph; while Dr.
Austen, the fashionable physician, who had been jilted by a
lady, revenged himself by writing "For lack of gold she
slighted me." In the manse of Crathie—then an unknown,
unvisited, dreary Highland tract—the Rev. Murdoch M'Lennan,
touched with the humour of the uneventful fight near
Dunblane, in the rising of '15, wrote his clever "Race of
Sheriffmuir," with its nimble refrain:

> And we ran and they ran,
> And they ran and we ran,
> And we ran and they ran awa', man.

The humorous Haddingtonshire farmer, Adam Skirving, found
in the surprise, defeat, and flight of Sir John Cope a splendid
theme for his "Hey! Johnnie Cope, are ye waukin' yet?"
and "Tranent Muir," which were the delights of every Jacobite
company. A former printer's compositor with the Foulises
of Glasgow, John Mayne, composed the "Sillar Gun," a graphic
picture of wapinschaws of olden days; his "Hallowe'en,"
which gave suggestions for Burns's own poem; and his
"Logan Braes," which surpasses Burns's "Logan Water." The
Aberdeen fish-merchant, John M'Ewen, touched with the
pathos of fishing life, wrote his charming "Weel may the
boatie row"—showing a consideration for seafaring folk
which he did not show to his own kin, whom he left in
poverty, to endow a hospital. The Hon. Andrew Erskine—
brother of the musical and bibulous Lord Kellie, and the
friend of Boswell—wrote songs which Burns calls "divine."

He ended his life by suicide, his body being found in the Forth with his pockets weighted with stones.

Not to be overlooked on many accounts was the author of the songs of "Erroch's Banks" and "Bonnie Brucket Lassie," set to good old airs, who was to be seen walking the High Street, as Burns describes him, "with leaky shoes and sky-lighted hat." This was James Tytler—by birth a minister's son, by education a physician, by practice a needy, drunken printer and hack of letters. On a printing-press of his own construction he composed at the same time both type and text of *Essays on Natural and Revealed Religion*, a work which no bookseller would publish. When William Smellie, the learned printer, refused to take part in the second edition of the *Encyclopædia Britannica*, he boldly undertook the task, writing copiously, and extending it from three to ten volumes. Poorly paid, the luckless editor vagrantly lived now with a washerwoman, whose tub reversed served as his desk, now in the squalid debtors' shelter at Holyrood, where, working at the articles and devouring a dinner of cold potatoes, Andrew Bell the publisher would find him—that publisher with the vastest bulbous nose that ever adorned a human countenance. Nothing came amiss to the versatile man of letters: the compiling of books on geography or surgery, schemes for bleaching linen, projects for solving the problem of perpetual motion, and experiments to rival Lunardi, the aeronaut, by a balloon with an iron stove. His first ascent was from the garden of the Debtors' Sanctuary, when he rose magnificently to the top of the wall and was deposited gracefully in a dunghill; his second and more ambitious effort was witnessed by crowds of spectators on the Calton Hill, when he rose to 530 feet and descended ignominiously. "Balloon Tytler" ended his career in this country by a seditious pamphlet as a "Friend of the People," when he absconded to America—the only wise action of his threadbare life—and died in 1801.[1] This was one of the many clever, learned, penniless hacks who formed an Edinburgh Grub Street. He belonged creditably to that fraternity of song-writers of which

---

[1] Chambers's *Eminent Scotsmen*; Kay's *Edinburgh Portraits*; Stenhouse's *Illust. of Lyric Poetry of Scotland*.

Robert Burns, who knew him well, was supreme in genius, and the Duke of Gordon, with his "Cauld Kail o' Aberdeen," was supreme in rank.

Rev. John Skinner

Among the writers of that song-writing age none take a more genial place than the author of "Tullochgorum" and the "Ewe with the crookit horn"—not a very large stock of literary wares with which to trudge to posterity. The poor, hard-working Episcopal minister at Longside is altogether a charming character, in his happy contentment with little, his exhaustless store of good humour and ready wit. In the parish of Longside, near Peterhead, is the little village of Linshart, where he lived in a mean thatched cottage, such as ploughmen nowadays would refuse to occupy—a "but and a ben," two little dark rooms with grateless fireplaces and earthen floors and open rafters, which were convenient for hanging hams, articles of raiment, and cooking utensils. Linshart was a dreary district of Aberdeenshire—"an ugly place in an ugly country." Patches of corn grew amid heather tracts, but not a tree was to be seen to relieve the weary eyes. Yet good John Skinner and his excellent wife loved the place. Buchan was to them a very paradise; its landscape, which wrought utter depression on the occasional travellers, whose bodies cowered beneath the eastern blasts that so often swept the land, was pronounced by the worthy couple "the finest on God's earth."[1] Such delightful contentments are mercifully acquired by habit if not given by providence. A Scots gentleman of that period, when visiting a friend in Surrey, was taken out one evening to hear the song of the nightingale, which was never heard in his own country. As he listened to its richest notes, given with "full-throated ease," he patriotically protested "he wadna gie the weeple o' a whaup (curlew) for a' the nightingales that ever sang."

Skinner, born in 1721, was the son of the Presbyterian schoolmaster of Birse, and in his youth was parish teacher at Kenmay, till the Episcopalian community, to the dismay

[1] Chambers's *Life and Works of Burns.* ii. 135.

of his father, snatched him as a brand from the burning, and one of its nonjuring bishops carefully rebaptized the lad, who had been only ineffectively "sprinkled in the Schism," as the Church of Scotland was contemptuously termed by the worthy men. After being a tutor in remote Shetland, he married, when barely of age, a woman who became the mother of a large family and his companion for sixty happy years.

The lot of an Episcopal minister was in those days a very hard one. Up to the Rebellion of '45 there had been in force a law forbidding a nonjuring minister to officiate in any building to a company containing more than eight persons. In 1746, when the Government regarded the Episcopal community as a nest of Jacobites, an Act prohibited any of its ministers who had not taken the oath of allegiance from preaching in any building to more than four people, and two years later the law still more stringently forbade an unqualified minister to conduct worship except in his own house, and there only before four persons. The penalties for breach of this law were six months' imprisonment for the first offence and transportation for the second. The poor shed in which Skinner preached since 1742 was ruthlessly burned by soldiers, his cottage sacked, his papers destroyed, and he only escaped under the guise of a miller. Seven years afterwards, though he had taken the oath to Government, he was cast into Aberdeen jail for preaching with orders only derived from a nonjuring bishop. Skinner evaded penalties by an expedient often adopted in those days. On Sundays gathered for worship the country folk—for Aberdeenshire was the stronghold of Episcopacy — who sat or stood outside the cottage, while the "gentles," or such as had energy to squeeze their way with much bruising of ribs and Christian temper, assembled in the little rooms of the dwelling.[1] There they could hear Mr. Skinner's voice at lessons, prayer, and discourse penetrating the thin deal board partitions, and wafted from the doorway to the humble congregation outside, who in rain or snow sat on stools or stood deep in the mire—their voices rising the old Scots psalms to old Scots tunes, which touched the hearts of Whig and Tory,

[1] Walker's *Life of Skinner*, p. 30; Pratt's *Buchan*, p. 125.

Presbyterian and Episcopalian alike, sung with long melodious drawl in Buchan tones. At times the attention would be distracted by the untimely lowing of a cow in the byre, the crowing of a regardless cock, or, as on one eventful day, by a hen, which, being injudiciously ejected from the crowded apartments, flew terrified along the little passage where the minister was stationed, and scattered wildly the detached pages of Skinner's discourse. "Never mind," remarked he calmly, " a fool [Buchanese for 'fowl'] shall never shut my mouth again." This resolve he kept, paper was discarded, and the admiration of his flock increased.[1]

When in milder days Skinner was allowed to have worship in a chapel—which was as plain as a workshop—there was no ritual in his service; in fact, many old-fashioned Episcopal ministers either did not use the English prayer-book or altered it as they pleased. A staff of twelve douce elders helped him in the pastoral work over his people, whom Skinner spoke of as his "family."[2] He could not, like St. Paul on a memorable occasion, "thank God he had baptized none of them"; rather, when he was old, he thanked God that he had christened almost all of that Episcopalian flock of lairds, farmers, and ploughmen, to whom the parson officiated in his old black gown, besprinkled and yellow with the pinches of strong rappee which he extracted from the leathern pouch in his waistcoat, to punctuate his sermons. At all social meetings in the countryside the minister was both welcome and useful—welcome from his genial humour, and useful to moderate the boisterous humours of others. His sense of fun and hatred of cant were equally irrepressible. When at an agricultural dinner a parish minister had asked a blessing of vast prolixity, while the company waxed hot as their victuals grew cold, Skinner in returning thanks repeated the general thanksgiving of the Common Prayer Book from beginning to end, to the envy of his rival, who, ignorant of the source of inspiration, surprised at such fluency, contemptuously remarked "he didna think the body had it in him."

It happened that Skinner and some of his clerical brethren were spending a day with a lady at Ellon; discussion was

[1] Walker's *Life of Skinner*, p. 49.   [2] Ramsay, i. 527.

REV. JOHN SKINNER
From an Oil Painting on Wood.

warm and tempers were ruffled between the ministers who, like Skinner, had taken the oath to Government, and the nonjurors, who despised these backsliders as renegades. To end the stormy debate the hostess expressed regret at the want of suitable words for old Scots airs, and asked the minister of Linshart to write a song to the old tune of "Tullochgorum." The hint was soon taken, and a song, which this episode of ministerial strife suggested, with its keynote, "Let Whig and Tory all agree," was the happy result. "The best Scotch song Scotland ever saw," was Robert Burns's unmeasured verdict. Here certainly was a man who could strike the right chord, who had written verses that soon were to be heard through broad Scotland singing social discord to harmony at a thousand tables.

Dr. Beattie had been asked to write a Scots pastoral song to another well-known tune, but, probably owing to his refined distaste at writing in the vulgar Scots dialect, he asked his Episcopal friend to finish the initial lines he had written—

> The ewie wi' the crookit horn,
> Sic a ewe was never born,
> Here about and far awa.

The ready pen of the pastor of Linshart soon produced the ballad, which gained immense popularity for a humour which is not exuberant or too obvious. The awkward belief prevailed that, being set to a Highland air called the "Whisky Still," it was not meant to lament a sheep, but to celebrate a shebeen.[1]

There was a charm about the quaint, homely life at Linshart. Easter hospitality was memorable in the year with his people, for after service they were entertained with ale and cakes and stories and fun by their pastor, who was living on the income of a common shepherd. As the wayfarer passed along the dreary road to Longside at night, he was sure to see a light from the cottage window to guide his dark journey, for the parson could never sleep with comfort while there was a chance of a belated Buchan man passing along the "Long gait," who might miss his way "in

[1] Walker's *Life of Skinner*, p. 99.

the mirk." He was happy in his book-closet, "five feet square," with his little stock of beloved volumes and commonplace books filled with copious extracts from works he was too poor to buy with his meagre income (for many a year) of only £15, which his efforts to increase by bad farming served sorely to diminish. Yet in that simple home there was always mirth and harmony! the daughters plaguing their father to write more songs, and singing them to him in their simple voices. In later days letters would come to him from Robert Burns, who unluckily missed seeing his brother poet when visiting in the north, begging for more verses to publish in Johnson's *Musical Museum*, to which the old man responded in admirable rhyming epistles. His lyrics appeared anonymously, and, as Burns told him, "one-half of Scotland already gives your songs to other authors," and Beattie got the credit even of "Tullochgorum."

There would often come to his house brother Episcopal parsons, who, like himself, lived in earth-floored cottages, wore threadbare unclerical attire, and managed to rear and educate families and to entertain friends on ploughman's wages, supplemented by eleemosynary supplies of eggs and hams and hens from kindly neighbours. Much were these worthy men (who were not very wise or learned) exercised over Hutchinsonian views. What these were few can tell to-day. Yet in their day they had many disciples. The able Lord President Forbes of Culloden held them as vital truths, and forsook his legal studies to study Hebrew and to give queer exegesis.[1] Mr. John Hutchinson, the founder of the system, had been land-agent to the Duke of Somerset and "riding purveyor" to George I.—a man self-taught in science and divinity, ingenious, enormously vain, who wrote worthless treatises enshrined in twelve volumes octavo. He showed to his own satisfaction that there are in Scripture certain words of the Hebrew tongue which Jehovah had revealed to Adam, containing the key to all religion and philosophy. Such radical doctrines were to be discovered in Hebrew roots; and the truths, rightly understood, could confute materialism, atheism, socinianism, and every other erroneous "ism." By manipulation of

[1] See essays in his *Works now first Collected*.

consonants and ejection of vowels as being of human invention, anything could be proved: the falsity of Newton's law of gravity could be demonstrated from Moses; the Logos could be shown to have stood on Jacob's ladder; and the Trinity could be found in the cherubim. Smitten by this alluring theory, Episcopal ministers in the North adopted the cryptogram, and pored reverently over the ex-riding purveyor's *Dissertation on the Trinity of the Gentiles*, and his *Moses Principia*. The parson of Linshart and his brethren bought grammars to study Hebrew, in order to discover mystical sense or nonsense in the divine original. They would meet over their toddy at each other's houses, and discuss in Buchanese the Hebrew tongue, losing their way and their temper in high debate over some wondrous interpretation of a divine conundrum. Worse still, on Sundays they would puzzle their humble congregations with strange exegesis, and fling Hebrew roots at their bewildered heads. To ignore the great key to Holy Writ was considered a mark of hopeless stupidity. "Have you read the works of John Hutchinson, Esquire?" or "Julius Bates?" or "Holloway's *Originals?*" an old Dean would ask a young minister, and when the answer "no" came to each question, he would gaze in pity on the unfortunate man, and say contemptuously, "Ah, ye are na far through."[1] It never struck these good souls as at all surprising that a providence, however inscrutable, should wrap up soul-saving meanings so carefully that the world could never find them, until they were discovered by the land-agent of the Duke of Somerset, and expounded by Buchan parsons. Even Mr. Skinner had his sense of humour numbed by the convincedness of this system. He studied, preached, yea, printed and published it. The fact that he and his brethren never agreed in their interpretations might spoil their tempers, but it never impaired their faith.

Skinner passed a busy life: if he was merry he wrote songs for his friends; if he was angry he wrote sarcastic verses and caustic epigrams on his enemies; if he was polemical he wrote pamphlets; when he was theological he wrote on Jacob's thrilling prophecy of the non-departure of

[1] Walker's *Life of Skinner*, p. 164.

the sceptre from Judah till Shiloh came; when he was usefully industrious he wrote his *Ecclesiastical History of Scotland*. Working in his book-closet, or visiting his people among the moorlands, he looked at seventy like a portly man of fifty, with his coal-black hair and alert blue eyes. Years passed by, and as he grew old he saw the once persecuted Episcopal body living in peace, though not in plenty; he saw the Hutchinsonian vagaries pass away from conviction and memory; he saw his big family grow up and marry, and his eldest child—his "chile," as he called him—elected a prelate, having charge of a few chapel congregations with the sounding title of "Bishop of Aberdeen," and he was proud to become a dean in his boy's diocese, with an income of £30 sterling. After a life of contented poverty he died in 1807, leaving behind him a happy memory and some admirable songs.

MICHAEL BRUCE

The merry songs of Skinner were congenial to the cheerful community he belonged to, but there was one austere religious sect to whom all verse except in devout strains was profane—that was the body of Seceders founded by Ebenezer and Ralph Erskine. The nearest approach made to poetry was the *Gospel Sonnets* by the latter divine—"sonnets" which are verily the *Marrow of Divinity* done into rhyme. Thousands of pious souls loved these lugubrious strains—which appeared in successive editions, to be thumbed out of shape and peat-reeked out of legibility.[1] At last, however, a writer of secular poetry was to arise from the midst of the Seceders in the person of Michael Bruce.

[1] Here is a pleasing sample of the "Sonnets":

>Know, then, the divine law most perfect cares
>For none of those imperfect legal wares;
>Dooms thee to vengeance for thy sinful state,
>As well as sinful actions small and great.
>If any sin can be accounted small,
>To hell it dooms thy soul for one and all;
>For sins of nature, practice, heart, and way
>Damnation-rent it summons thee to pay.
>Yet not for sin alone which is thy shame,
>But for thy boasted service too so lame,
>The law adjudges thee and hell to meet,
>Because thy righteousness is incomplete.

A little hamlet called Kinneswood, in Kinross-shire, lies at the foot of the "Lomond" hills overlooking Loch Leven—a row of thatched cottages with ash-trees. There was a quaint, old-world air about Kinneswood,—"Kinnaskit," as the people called it,—the weavers busy with their rattling looms, the wives spinning at their doors, and both men and women in the evening employed in knitting stockings at the firesides. In this village Michael Bruce was born in 1746, and there he went home to die in 1767, when he was but twenty years old. His name to-day is known as the reputed author of the "Ode to the Cuckoo," which another poet has claimed as his own. His father, who plied a weaver's loom, was a seceder of the Seceders, being an elder in the congregation of good Mr. Thomas Main of Orwell, who had been expelled from the Antiburgher body for holding that Christ died for all men— which was after all a doctrine only mildly comforting, seeing that the elect alone could be saved. The father, enriched by the bequest of £11 sterling, resolved to send his son to college that he might become a Seceder minister, for the boy's prayers when he conducted family worship, filled listeners with devout admiration. So in a garret in Edinburgh, nourished on paternal stores of oatmeal, he lived, attending classes, but reading English poetry with avidity from books friends lent him, and buying others with earnings of his teaching. In 1765, when he returned from college, he parted with his treasured books—some he sold from poverty, others —his Shakespeare and Pope—he sent secretly to a friend from fear of discovery; for to a staunch Antiburgher these were heinous works. That in the vacation he should read profane fiction like the *Faërie Queene*, as he herded the sheep on the Lomond hills, was a crime in the eyes of the covenanting folk, who mourned that the devout Rev. Ralph Erskine played on a "wee sinfu' fiddle." When college was over he taught in the summer months at a roadside school at Gairney—a hallowed spot with Seceders, for there the first Associate Presbytery was formed in a saintly ale-house. The school —which in his youth the famous seceder Mr. John Brown had taught—was but an old disused hut, a few deals on blocks of wood serving as the benches. Twenty children, offspring of strict dissenters, paid, very badly, their two shillings a quarter and their teacher had the doubtful privilege of free board and lodgings with the parents in succession.

In a room at Kinneswood, Buchan, the mason, formed his little class of village lads to practise psalm tunes for the meeting-house. In those days, both in kirk and meeting-house, Christians sang in sanctified drawl—taking their religion sadly—a stock of tunes which were known as the "old eight"—French, Dundee, York, Newton, Martyrs, Abbey, London, and Elgin[1]—consecrated by time-worn use. It was, however, considered profane by Seceders to practise music on divine psalms, especially by the aid of a human pitch-pipe. They therefore would lift their voices in solemn tunes to such doggerel as this:

> Fair London town where lives the King
> On his imperial throne,
> With all his court attending him,
> Still waiting him upon.

Or this:

> The Martyrs' tune above the rest
> Distinguished is by fame;
> On this account I'll sing this
> In honour of their name.[2]

Among the band of singers was Michael Bruce, and he was appealed to as a "scholar" to fit these old tunes to more becoming words for practice. Some of these verses, it is said, were afterwards included in the Church of Scotland collection of Paraphrases, as compositions of John Logan, to be sung with pious and monotonous ardour in all churches for generations.[3]

The ministry was still his aim, but the Antiburghers, or "Antis," as they were called, would not have him, because his father had quitted them, and he was therefore enrolled as a student with Mr. John Swanston, the Burgher minister at Kinross,

---

[1] Perhaps Dundee's wild warbling measures rise;
Or plaintive Martyrs, worthy of the name;
Or noble Elgin beats the heavenward flame,
The sweetest far of Scotia's holy lays.
— Burns, *Cottar's Saturday Night*.

[2] M'Kelvie, p. 99.

[3] These Paraphrases are those containing the well-known lines—
Few are thy days, and full of woe.
O happy is the man who hears.
The beam that shines from Sion hill.

who was professor in the humble Theological hall of his Synod, which consisted of one small room, where he delivered prolix lectures on Pike's *Cases of Conscience*, the *Marrow of Divinity*, and the *Confession of Faith*, to a poor, threadbare, earnest band, who paid as fees five shillings a session. Well-to-do adherents to the sturdy sect received these divinity students into their houses, would give them food, and occasionally old clothes. Some of these farmers could look back to bygone days, when great lights of their body, like the great Dr. John Brown or the saintly Dr. George Lawson, had got free lodging from them, and would point out proudly the "prophet's chamber," where they had burned the midnight candle. It was a curious, frugal life those old dissenting ministers lived.

Michael Bruce, when his professor concluded his lectures, found employment at Forest Mill near Tillicoultry—then a dreary moorland tract—where, beside a few cottages, stood the school, a low-roofed hut with damp earthen floor. In the hovel the delicate, ill-fed lad taught, standing on a board to keep his feet from the wet ground.[1] At this dreary abode, where he had to teach "a dozen blockheads for bread," Michael was busy with his reading, and busy writing "Loch Leven," his longest, but not very inspired, poem. When winter came he was forced to return to his father's house—trudging with weary, feeble steps the twenty miles. His poverty, his labours, his want of comforts and care had ruined a frame naturally fragile. All hope of a long life was gone; and among his family he was content to linger out the few remaining months of his short life. Not long was there to be seen in the weaver village the slender lad, with narrow chest, high shoulders, and white, pallid face and long yellow hair.[2]

The dying poet now was back in the cottage, round which his thin hands trained the honeysuckle, gazing out of the window as he thought out new verses, or copied out old ones, which he intended, if he had time and money, to publish before he died. Spring had come, the birds were singing in the hedgerows, the dour ash-trees were bursting into leaf, when

---

[1] M'Kelvie's *Loch Leven and other Poems of M. Bruce, with Life*; *Poems of M. Bruce, with Life*, by Grossart.
[2] Grossart's *Bruce's Poems, with Memoir*, p. 11.

the lad wrote his touching "Elegy" as he lay watching the
spring which he should never see again :—

> Now Spring returns, but not to me returns ;
> The vernal joy my other years have known.
> Dim in my heart life's dying taper burns,
> And all the joys of life with health are gone.
> Farewell, ye blowing fields, ye cheerful plains ;
> Enough for me the churchyard's lonely mound,
> Where melancholy with still silence reigns,
> And the rank grass waves o'er the cheerless ground.
>
> . . . . . .
>
> There let me sleep, forgotten in the clay,
> When death shall shut these weary, aching eyes,
> Rest in the hope of an eternal day,
> Till the long night is gone and the last morn arise.

On the 4th of July 1767 Michael Bruce was found dead in his bed, only twenty-one years old.

Here now begins a literary mystery. The poet had not been many months dead when one day a young man, a former college companion, came to Kinneswood to see the father. This was John Logan, tutor to Sir John Sinclair of Ulbster— a clever, uncouth young man of nineteen. When the Ulbster family were dissatisfied with the manners of the new tutor whom Dr. Blair had recommended, the divine said, "I thought it was a scholar and not a dancing-master they wanted for the young gentleman."[1] To his keeping letters and poems in a leathern-covered quarto, in which Michael had transcribed his verses, were entrusted by the father, that they might be published. Time passed and nothing was heard of them; but at last, in 1770, a little volume appeared, *Poems on Several Occasions, by Michael Bruce*. In a brief preface it was mentioned, "To make up a miscellany some poems wrote by different authors are inserted, all of them originals and none destitute of merit. The reader of taste will easily distinguish them from those by Mr. Bruce, without their being particularised by any mark." This was puzzling. How "readers of taste" were to distinguish the poems by Bruce, of whom they had never heard, or discern his style, of which they knew nothing, among the anonymous verses was a perplexing

---

[1] Sir J. Sinclair's *Correspondence*, i. 244.

question. Six copies of the meagre volume were sent to the poet's father, by whom it was looked at with dismay. The pious youth had written devotional verses, and hymns in imitation of Ralph Erskine's *Gospel Sonnets*, which had been sung in village class. They were not there. The old man burst into tears, exclaiming "Where are Michael's Gospel Sonnets?" He set forth for Edinburgh, called at Logan's rooms in Leith Wynd, and there the irate weaver was shown a few loose papers, rude draughts of verse, and when he asked for the leathern book, he was told that the servants had singed fowls with it. So matters remained till 1781, when *Poems by Mr. John Logan, one of the Ministers of Leith*, was published. The seceder farmer's son, who had been class-mate of Bruce, had blossomed into a popular preacher of the Church of Scotland. In this volume, eleven out of the seventeen pieces in *Bruce's Poems* were inserted as Logan's own—leaving only six to have been by his friend and the other "different authors" spoken of in the old preface. Folk in the poet's village, it is said, were amazed when they saw the fine "Ode to the Cuckoo" appropriated by the minister; remembering having seen it in the vanished quarto, and having heard it recited from the father's lips. One gentleman had seen a letter from Michael, saying, "You will think me ill-employed, for I am writing a poem about a gowk"[1] (cuckoo). What can be said in Logan's favour is that he claimed it; that some one had seen it in his handwriting—though not before Bruce's death; that local tradition or legend is of doubtful worth; and that village weavers would be apt to magnify a local poet's claims. One is between two straits —alike unwilling to deprive the poet of his one claim to immortality and to deprive his editor of his claim to an ode and to honesty.[2] Certainly, if Logan wrote this poem, he wrote better when he was a lad than ever he did as a man. Astonishment also arose in Kinnesswood at finding among the *Poems of John Logan* hymns which people said had been sung in their village as Michael Bruce's compositions. Did Logan play false?

[1] M'Kelvie, p. 114.
[2] On this everlasting controversy see M'Kelvie's *Life of Bruce*; papers by Shairp, Laing, and Small; Grossart's *Memoir of Bruce*, pp. 50-110. Dr. Robertson of Dalmeny said he did not see the Ode among Bruce's MSS.

John Logan, who was born in 1748, after preparing for the Burgher ministry, entered the Church of Scotland and soon became notable for literary and pulpit gifts. When minister of South Leith, he gave lectures on the "Philosophy of History" in St. Mary's Chapel, which were attended by the literary *élite* of Edinburgh. Hymns by him became favourite Paraphrases in worship. His play called *Runnymede* was played in Edinburgh, and proved a failure. When being rehearsed in Covent Theatre, it was interdicted, for dangerous political doctrines were scented in the speeches of the Barons. His poems in 1781, containing the "Ode to the Cuckoo," brought more reputation, and Edmund Burke when in Edinburgh called to see the author of the Ode he greatly admired. But soon the eloquent preacher sank into disrepute by his drinking habits, and, resigning his charge with an annuity of £40, passed on to London, warmly recommended by Adam Smith. There he became a literary hack—compiling a *View of Ancient History*, published under the name of Dr. Rutherford, who bought it from him; publishing a pamphlet on the charges against Warren Hastings, which involved the publisher Stockdale in a prosecution. He died in 1788, at the age of fifty-one—" of a broken heart," says Isaac Disraeli. Of the many manuscripts left behind him, consisting of plays, poems, essays, two volumes of his sermons were published by his friends, which have literary merit. That he had lyric gifts his popular "Braes of Yarrow" remains to prove. Was it the poor schoolmaster lad of Kinross-shire or the brilliant, dissipated clerical failure who wrote the "Ode to the Cuckoo"?—

> Sweet bird, thy bower is ever green,
> Thy sky is ever clear;
> Thou hast no sorrow in thy song,
> No winter in thy year.

Robert Fergusson

At the middle of the century, in a narrow, dirty close called the "Cap and Feathers," in the Cowgate of Edinburgh, lived William Fergusson, book-keeper to a haberdasher. His shop was then the only one of the kind in the city, situated in a flat reached by a "scale" staircase, where a few silks gave dignity to the stock consisting of "Musselburgh stuffs," "Holland checks," and "Dutch ticks." The book-keeper, on a wage of £20, by the aid of his wife, who employed herself in spinning, was able in his poor lodging, rented for thirty shillings a year, to maintain a large family. Yet Fergusson and his wife each came of a good stock; there flowed in their ill thriven veins blood—not too generous—which was of good degree; for in those days in Scotland poverty and wealth, rank and trade were brothers; and the barber could often claim kindred with the laird whose face he shaved. In the Cowgate lodging, on the 5th of September 1750, Robert Fergusson first saw the light—not that there was much to see in that dingy dwelling. The father sent his weakly son to the High School, where for three and sixpence a quarter sons of lords and shopkeepers, judges and weavers, got a sound education in Latin. The son of the draper's clerk had as schoolmates James Boswell, Tytler of Woodhouselee, Sir John Sinclair of Ulbster, Lord Rosslyn, Dugald Stewart, and many others of quality.[1] He was only eleven years old when he got a bursary allotted to the maintenance of boys of the name of Fergusson, which had as its condition that they should be educated at Dundee Grammar School and thereafter at St. Andrews University.

It was in October 1764 that Robert Fergusson presented himself at St. Andrews and was admitted as a bursar to St. Salvator College. It was a curious, thrifty life that the students spent in the shabby academic courts.[2] St. Salvator common hall was a damp vault with earthen floor and cobwebbed roof. There were dinner-tables for the students—with fare consisting of bread, eggs, and fish three times a week; beef and cabbage with ale the other four. Tables were set for students of different grades—for the "primers," sons of lords and landlords, in their fine gowns, who had paid the high fees of six guineas; the "secunders," sons

---

[1] Grossart's *Life of Fergusson*, p. 41; Campbell's *Introd. Scottish Poetry*.
[2] Rev. C. Rogers's *Autobiography*, p. 14; Grierson's *Delineations of St. Andrews*.

of ministers and smaller lairds, with robes less richly
trimmed; and the "terners," robed in poorer stuff, who paid
their humble fee of a guinea and a half. At breakfast the
boarder at the high table had "one third of a loaf and one
mutchkin of milk, to be carried to his chamber by the table-
servers"; while the bursar, by a fine distinction, had "one-third
of a scone with a mutchkin of milk or ale, for which he shall go
to the pantry himself and carry it to his own chamber and eat
it there." For dinner "half a scone and a mutchkin of ale";
and for supper half a loaf and one mutchkin and a half of
milk or ale were exactly allotted. Adjoining the common
hall were chambers in which the students lodged—rooms nine
feet square, with a little bed-closet for two bursars—but fire
there was none for poorer students, who in the winter
would try to keep out the frost by wrapping plaids round their
bodies, and by wearing Shetland gloves to protect their hands,
red with cold. The Hebdomader—the professor who took his
turn for a week to superintend the scholars—visited their
rooms at nine at night and five in the morning, to see that
order and propriety were observed; and when at six o'clock the
bell rang all must be present for prayers, and, thereafter, in
time for classes under a fine of twopence for lateness, and
sixpence (*sex assibus*) for absence, which the professor pocketed
to aid his meagre salary. On college fare and regimen Fergusson
throve much better than in his unsavoury, poverty-stricken
home. If the colleges were mean and dirty—for the scavenger,
dignified by the name of Foricarius, did his duty indifferently
—the town itself was worse. Its population of 4000 were
mostly idle and poor, its harbour was dilapidated, in its streets
side by side were straw-thatched cottages, old houses with
traces of stately days, and two-storeyed dwellings with their
"forestairs" jutting into the unpaved road, which produced
crops of grass, fertilised by the middens placed before the
doors.[1] In foul weather the people crossed the street on
stepping-stones over streams of rain and mire and gutter.
Doubtless it had even considerably improved since the beginning
of the century, when it was little more than a village, whose

---

[1] Grierson's *St. Andrews*, pp. 104, 135, 179; *Travels in Scotland*, i. 118,
by Rev. James Hall [William Thomson].

main street, according to contemporary report, was adorned with "dunghills which are exceedingly noisome and ready to infect the air, especially at those seasons when herring-guts are exposed in them."

Within the College was Dr. Robert Watson, who taught Logic, and was known afar for his *History of Philip II.*, which gained even the praise of Dr. Johnson, whom he entertained in 1773, on his memorable journey. "I take great delight in him," he was pleased to say of the historian, who had then become Principal of the University.[1] In the chair of Natural Philosophy and Mathematics was William Wilkie, that uncouth man of genius, who was the delight of his friends and an astonishment to the public. Whenever the classes were over the author of the *Epigoniad* would be off in his ploughman's dress, with his hoe over his shoulder, on his way to his fields, for he was as much interested in turnip as in Greek roots, in potatoes as in fluxions. To this kindest of souls and most eccentric of mortals Fergusson clung. The shabby, frail lad would copy out his master's lectures for him, and the grotesque professor would take him to his farm—the one full of fun and frolic, the other bubbling over with learning and ponderous poetry and humour.

Robert Fergusson early showed his gift for writing verse; he composed two acts of an inevitable tragedy on Sir William Wallace, and perpetrated satires.[2] When he was dead, legends were told of boyish pranks, over which his biographers shook their grave, dull heads. One especially. He sometimes acted

---

[1] Boswell's *Johnson* (ed. Hill), v. 59.
[2] He was only fifteen when his Elegy on Professor David Gregory, his late professor of Mathematics, was composed, in the favourite stanza of Scots elegy from Sempill to Burns:

> Now mourn ye, college masters a' !
> And frae your een a tear let fa',
> Fam'd Gregory death has ta'en awa'
>   Without remeid.
> The skaith ye've met wi's nae that sma'
>   Sin' Gregory's deid.
>
> Great 'casion hae we a' to weep,
> And cleed our skins in mourning deep ;
> For Gregory death will fairly keep,
>   To tak' his nap ;
> He'll till the Resurrection sleep
>   As sound's a tap.

as precentor in the College chapel, leading the psalmody, and it was his duty in that capacity to read out "the line" or written request for the prayers of the congregation for a person in distress, which were in those more believing days in frequent demand. One day professors were horrified to hear him utter, before the last prayer, the formula in the usual professional drawl: "Remember in prayer a young man [naming one present] of whom from the sudden effects of inebriety there appears small hopes of recovery."[1] The students tittered, the regents scowled, and the scandalised Senate severely censured the culprit. Other escapades there were which gained solemn rebukes from the grave professors, and showed the irrepressibility of the young scamp, whose exuberant spirits strait-laced biographers deplore with portentous gravity.[2]

While at College he was about to study for the Church—of which two of his great-grandfathers had been ministers—but, fortunately for the kirk if not for himself, that intention was ended by the death of his father. The boy went home to his widowed mother, who in dark, malodorous Jamieson's Land eked out a livelihood by keeping lodgers in the spare —very spare—room. An experimental visit which he paid to a prosperous uncle, a farmer and factor in Aberdeenshire, ended in failure. What availed his knack at writing verses? or his pious addresses when he assembled the farm servants who could not get to the kirk on Sunday, and preached to them from a peat-stack till he brought tears to their eyes? He was useless on the farm; he wore out both his clothes and his uncle's patience; and one day when, being called in to see my Lord Deskford, he was not fit to appear, he was dismissed from the house. In high dudgeon he went off to a neighbouring ale-house and wrote a strenuous epistle to his uncle. A sovereign was sent out to him as answer, and with his pride and his money in his pocket he walked footsore and indignant to Edinburgh. Thus ended a second intended career.

We next find him—appointed by the aid of his father's friends—a clerk in the Commissary Clerk's office, where he had

---

[1] Fergusson's *Poems*, 1801, with Life of Author, p. 18.
[2] Irving's *Life of Fergusson*.

ROBERT FERGUSSON
By permission of Miss Raeburn, from the Painting by Runciman.

to copy deeds, wills, decreets, and declarators of marriages for so much—or so little—a page. Of old it had been at "one plack a page"; in his time it was still small, for there are farthings mentioned in his memoranda of earnings, such as a deed at elevenpence farthing. The office was in Parliament Close, consisting of a little room about ten feet square, which was reached by a dark winding stair, at the risk of falling at every step. There the Commissaries—one of them a cousin of Tobias Smollett—sat, deciding on wills, decreets, and declarations.[1] The lad stuck to his work, and so punctual was he, that it was said his coming round the corner on the way to the office was a mark of time surer than the Tron clock. The pay being miserable, the lad tried to earn a little more money by teaching sword-play to a few pupils—he boasts of having eight.[2] In his garret, as he sat over Pope and Shenstone or Somerville's *Chase*, he forgot his troubles, poverty, and cold, for reading poetry was his chief pleasure. There were other pleasures, too, in the evening hours, when shops were shut, and men were gathering in the taverns, and over oysters, rizzared haddocks, and ale, merriment was loud and songs were jovial. There the threadbare clerk was often seen. He was poor—miserably poor—but the entertainment was cheap; convivial cronies were kind—unkindly kind—to the lad who would amply repay their hospitality by jests, over which they roared, and staves, to which they clattered their tankards in thunderous chorus.[3] At Lucky Middlemist's in the Cowgate, or in the little room of John Dowie's tavern, nicknamed the "Coffin," the drudgery of the day was forgotten in the festivity of the night. The thin, pale-faced lad would stay with his friends, and often outstay them to join other relays of convivialists; and he would sing with his rich voice Mallet's "Birks of Invermay," to charm a toping crew to maudlin sentiment. Up to every prank, having wagered one evening that he would sell a bundle of ballads in two hours, he set forth from Dowie's inn (whose guests made riotous at night Liberton's Close, where the "Man of Feeling" was born), wrapped in an

---

[1] Topham's *Letters from Edinburgh*, p. 299.
[2] Fergusson's *Poems, with Life*, p. 49.
[3] Irving's *Life of Fergusson*; Grossart's *Robert Fergusson*.

old greatcoat, a scratch wig, down the High Street, singing his ballads, parleying with the crowd that followed him, selling his wares by dozens, and rejoining his comrades to drink the wager and the proceeds.

All the musicians in St. Cecilia's Hall were his devoted friends, and long years after the famous Tenducci—first favourite in Edinburgh—would burst into tears, in his emotional way, as he spoke of the lovable, luckless genius. Eager for the play and a favourite with the actors, he was to be seen in the "Shakespeare's box," to which he was allowed free access—his face alive with enthusiasm, banging the front of the box in his exuberant delight; especially that evening when, in the Theatre Royal, Arne's *Artaxerxes* was performed, with three songs by himself. Naturally the lad imagined the applause came forth not as a tribute to the music or the singing of the great Tenducci, but to his own poor words.[1]

In February 1771, in the *Weekly Magazine*—that not very robust rival to the old *Scots Magazine*—published by Walter Ruddiman, the son of the famous old grammarian, a paragraph appeared: "We have been favoured with three pastorals under the titles of 'Morning,' 'Noon,' and 'Night,' written by a young gentleman of this place, the style of which appears as natural and picturesque as that of any modern ones hitherto published." They appeared, but in them there was as little trace of nature as of art. The "young gentleman," in fact, seemed a failure. But in January 1772 appeared verses called "Daft Days," and three months later "Elegy on the Death of Scots Music," which showed that one had arrived possessing the craft and humour of Allan Ramsay. That generation had seen nothing like these—not great, but racy with humour, nimble in rhyme, vivid in speech, Scots at every turn. Successive numbers of the stupid old magazine were enlivened by other poems from this unknown hand— "Caller Oysters," "Braid Claith," "The Farmer's Ingle." The numbers sold rapidly, to the surprise of the printers, accustomed to a frigid reception from the public. The verses were discussed in every tavern and club and supper-table, and

[1] Grosart's *Robert Fergusson*, p. 87 ; Harris's *St. Cecilia's Hall*, p. 112.

won a wider fame when a little volume, "*Poems by Robert Fergusson*, price two shillings and sixpence," was published by subscription, with a dedication—without permission—to Sir William Forbes, the banker. That gentleman was the admirer of Dr. Beattie's whiffling *Minstrel*, but he never acknowledged by a word or a guinea this far brighter genius who had craved his patronage. Fifty pounds, however, were gained by the book (more than double what Burns was to get for his Kilmarnock edition), and as the money jingled in his pocket the young author said, "My poor mother shall have her full share of this"; and she had, for her love was first with him. Fools flattered him, and as they pronounced him far superior to Ramsay, he would exclaim, "This is not praise, it is folly!" "Mr. Robert"—old Miss Ruddiman would say long afterwards —"was a dear, gentle, modest creature; his pale cheeks would flush with girlish pink at a compliment."

From 1771 to 1772, from month to month, verses appeared in the Magazine, and the poet got gifts of suits of clothes—one for week-days, another for Sunday wear—which reveals more of the poverty of the poet than the munificence of the publisher. After all, his was but a thriftless, aimless life. There seemed no prospect of rising above his humble post; for he had no steady ambition for anything higher. With fame and flattery and foolish patrons, with a sociable nature, a fragile constitution, and a facile temperament, temptations proved too strong for that weak will of his. By day Edinburgh citizens had their "meridians," and their "whets" at night; they had their tavern meetings in festive gangs, when merchants, clerks, thriftless lawyers, and rakish writers were glad of the company of the good-natured, clever fellow who sang at a word, and could turn a smart verse more easily than they at night could turn a corner. It was delightful for himself, when "deeds" and "decreets," over which his fingers ached, were laid aside for the day, to leave his squalid home and set forth as dusk fell, hearing friendly greetings of "Weel, Rab!" and to meet thirsty admirers in a cosy tavern; to join jovial souls at the Pandemonium Club, in a subterranean oyster cellar, or at the Cape Club, at the Isle of Man Arms, in the narrow Craig's Close, where, with his friend Woods the actor, Alexander Runciman the painter, and other boon companions, the night flew swiftly by; for

> while noisy ten-hours drum
> Gars a' your trades gae danderin' hame,
> Now mony a club jocose and free
> Gie a' to merriment and glee.
> Wi' sang and glass they fley the power
> O' care, that wad harass the hour . . .
> Now some in Pandemonium's shade
> Resume the gormandisin' trade. . . .
> But chief, O Cape, we crave thy aid
> To get our cares and poortith laid.[1]

Thither would pass the lad, with narrow shoulders, long nose, eyes blue-black and piercing, and high forehead, his fair brown hair, with a curl at each cheek, tied behind in a queue with silk ribbon. A pretty youth he seemed at that time, with a pleasant countenance and strong, clear, frank voice. After he was dead he was described by one who had often seen him in homely terms as "very small and delicate, a little in-kneed, and waigling in his walk." His dress bore marks of penury in the faded, threadbare coat, the soiled white stockings in his shabby shoes.

A posthumous reputation has been given Fergusson as being utterly dissipated and drunken.[2] If such had been his real character, it is unlikely he would have retained his post in the Commissary's office to the end. If he was foolish, he was young; if he was unsteady, temptations were strong in that convivial city. When counselled by friendly voices to be prudent, he would cover his face with his hand, and sobbing say, "Oh, sir, anything to forget my poor mother and these aching fingers"—a poor enough excuse for forgetting himself, but it tells much. Once he was busy at a county election, exposed to cold and the riotous excesses of electioneering conviviality, and after that there came a reaction of melancholy. Probably it was at this time an incident occurred of which much has been unnecessarily made. One day Mr. John Brown, the old seceder minister, found this unknown lad disconsolate in the churchyard at Haddington. They spoke for a few minutes together, and

[1] Fergusson's "Auld Reekie." [2] David Irving's *Life of Fergusson*.

the minister, surrounded by suggestive tombstones, made a
few remarks on mortality—for he had a professional propensity
for improving the occasion. He remarked that soon they
should be laid in the dust, and that it were well in time to
prepare for eternity. If any impression at all was made on
Fergusson by the little incident, he returned to town and to
the old mirth again. Yet this interview with a most genial
old divine, which took place in 1772, has been represented
as the cause of the poet's final despair and madness, and the
"damnatory creed" of Calvin has been damned as the incitement to his religious melancholy two years after—quite a
gratuitous indignation.[1]

It was not till July 1774 that a paragraph appeared in
the *Caledonian Mercury*: "Many lovers of poetry will feel
regret to know that Mr. Robert Fergusson, the author of some
of the most natural and humorous poems that have appeared
of late years, has been seized with a dangerous illness." It
was too true. Insanity had begun to dim the brilliant brain,
and heavy depression fell upon the light heart. In despair
he flung his manuscripts into the flames; and he was heard
to mutter: "There is one thing I am glad of: I have never
written a line against religion." The Bible which his mother
had given him on his going to school in Dundee was his
companion from morning till night; but it brought no light to
his darkness, and the words of his paraphrase of the third
chapter of Job, which was quoted in a time of gloom by
Robert Burns, expressed his mood:

> Say, wherefore has an o'er-bounteous Heaven
> Light to the comfortless and wretched given?

Occasionally the old buoyancy would show itself, and he
would visit his old haunts and his friends the Ruddimans;
but the melancholy quickly returned. Delusions tortured
him that he was the perpetrator of a murder which had
recently been committed, of which the town was talking; and
that he was one of the reprobates who had crucified the Lord.
Two months before the end he had spent one lucid evening with
a few friends; but as he left the house his feet caught in the

[1] Fergusson's *Poems, with Life*, 1807.

carpet and he fell down the steep staircase, and was carried home insensible. Next day his consciousness returned, but not his reason. His mother was occupied with her lodgers, and it was necessary that he should be removed to the madhouse, to which he was conveyed in a sedan-chair—to that building adjoining the old Darien House in Bristo Port, grimly called the "Schelles" (or Cells). In the dismal chamber, with stone floor and straw beds, as he found himself entrapped he uttered one great cry, which was answered by the wretched fellow-inmates of the place. Days passed by—now he was walking gloomily round the cell, plaiting a crown with the straws from his bed, proclaiming himself a king; now he was telling his keeper with glowing eyes that he should be one day a "bright minister of Christ." Sometimes his friends found him stretched on his bed of loose straw, and he would beseech them to set him free. When he was alone the cell would resound with melody, as, with rare pathos, he sang his "Birks of Invermay" and other favourite songs. The weary days and nights dragged on. It was October, early winter had set in, and one evening, when his mother was sitting by him, he asked her to heap his clothes together upon him, murmuring that his feet were "cold — cold." He asked his sister, "Might you not often come and sit by me? You cannot imagine how comfortable it would be; you might fetch your seam and sew beside me." And as his mother sobbed silently before him, "What ails you?" the poor youth said; "I am well cared for, I want for nothing; but it is cold—it is very cold." The keeper whispered it was time to leave, and as they were about to go, "Oh! do not go, mother—oh! do not leave me!" he cried, and with this distracted appeal ringing in her ears they parted never to meet again. In the solitude of that night—the 10th of October 1774—the poor poet died, only twenty-four years old.

Three days later "a large company" gathered at the West Bow, and followed to the Canongate churchyard the coffin of Robert Fergusson, "writer"—as by courtesy he was called, not in reference to his being an author, but clerk to a lawyer. Shortly before or just after his death his mother had a letter from her sailor son beyond the seas, enclosing some money, which would have enabled her to bring her afflicted boy to her own fireside; and soon after the poet was dead a draft for £100 came from a gentleman for Fergusson, and an urgent invitation that he would join him in India.[1] Such is one of life's bitter ironies; one of destiny's many fantastic tricks.

The Scots poems[2] of Robert Fergusson—vivid, humorous pictures of town life and characters and manners, and also of rural ways—gain further interest from the powerful influence they exercised over his great successor, Robert Burns. It was in 1784 they seem to have first stimulated his admirer to the production of his masterpieces—suggesting style and subjects and form of stanza. Robert Fergusson, when he died at the age of twenty-four, had written better than Burns wrote at the same age; but whether Fergusson would ever have risen to any much higher level as a poet had he lived, it is idle to conjecture, it is fruitless to inquire: as a Scots proverb says, "It's ill work chappin' at a deid man's yett."[3]

[1] Grossart's *Robert Fergusson*, p. 130.
[2] Fergusson's poems in English are utterly without character or life.
[3] Which may be Englished: "There is no use knocking at a dead man's door."

CHAPTER XIV

ROBERT BURNS

BEFORE there appeared in Kilmarnock, in 1786, *Poems, chiefly in the Scots Dialect, by Robert Burns*, vernacular literature seemed to have become a thing of the past. Society had ceased to care for Allan Ramsay's poems, and left his *Gentle Shepherd* chiefly for the delectation of peasants; poor Robert Fergusson, dead only twelve years, was little spoken of in literary circles; his poems, full of Scots town life and humour, were neglected like his tangled grave in the Canongate kirkyard; only ballads, sung to old native melodies, preserved the Scots tongue in fashion, and ladies of birth deigned—though in secret—to compose them with fine lyric grace. That excellent man, but very mediocre poet, Dr. Beattie, whose taste had been over-refined by intercourse with well-bred society in London, in 1771 ventured to affirm that "to write in vulgar broad Scotch and yet to write seriously is now impossible. For more than half a century it has even by the Scots been considered as the dialect of the vulgar." It is true that the higher ranks, all with any pretension to social position and fashion, were learning assiduously to speak English, to free their talk of Scots phrases and their tongues of Scots tones, leaving the vernacular writing for the taste and the vernacular speech for the voices of the common people. When Burns's poems, therefore, came out, they gave a startling revelation of the power of expression which lay in the despised "vulgar dialect"—its picturesqueness of word and epithet, its capacity to give language to pathos, satire, and humour, its power to utter any mood and feeling with verve and vividness when wielded by one who was at once a master of his native speech and a poet. Very soon it was felt that what had fast been becoming a provincial patois had again become a great written language.

Robert Burns was born on the 25th of January 1759, in a clay cottage near Alloway Kirk, in Ayrshire, that crazy tenement built by his father William Burness, which fell before the winter's blast a week after the poet's birth. William Burness was gardener and overseer to a small laird, and also farmed on his own account a few acres of meagre soil. As time passed on and the family increased—Robert was the eldest of seven children—there was difficulty in paying for education out of a miserable livelihood, but the services of John Murdoch could be got cheap, and he was employed by several small farmers, with board and lodging in their houses by rotation, to teach their families. From this clever youth, full of literary interest, Robert and Gilbert, young as they were, learned much; Robert gaining from his teacher a skill in grammar and writing, and a taste for letters; learning scraps of Thomson and Mallet and Gray and Shakespeare from the school-books. When the father removed to the little farm Mount Oliphant, with "the poorest land in Ayrshire," they still attended the stimulating Murdoch's class at Alloway, and when he went away the education was undertaken by the impecunious father—a hard-headed, stern-voiced, keen-thinking, and much-reading man, whose tuition by the light of peat fire or candle at nights was, owing to a very irascible temper, more strenuous than delightsome. Home life was poor in the little two-roomed cottage, and toil hard on the farm, on which the family did all the work. Robert and Gilbert, as each reached the age of thirteen, would weed the furrows and thresh the corn; at fifteen they would act as ploughman and shearers, working from daybreak till late evening, when they were ready to go weary to their chaff beds. The fare, like the home life, was mean and monotonous—sowans and kail and milk, with little variation at the meals; no meat appearing on the board except when a cow or sheep died of old age or infirmity. They had few neighbours, and lived much aloof, but there was a keen life of intelligent interests among themselves.

Acquaintances would find the lads at the simple food, busy reading with books spread before them. The father, with his serious face and scanty grey hairs, for he was aged beyond his years, would raise discussions over books, on geography, or science, or history—not omitting theology, though he was no Calvinist. Not able to buy books, they read with avidity all that were lent, and a curiously incongruous lot came into Robert's hands: a volume or two of Shakespeare, Taylor's *On Original Sin*, a *British Gardener's Directory*, Tooke's *Pantheon*, and Hervey's lugubrious *Meditations*, Stackhouse's *History of the Bible*, and Ramsay's *Poems*, Locke *On the Human Understanding*, and a *Collection of English Songs*. It was the last which, says Burns, "was my *vade mecum*. I pored over them driving my cart or walking to labour; song by song, verse by verse, carefully noting the tender or sublime from affectation and fustian. I am convinced I owe to this practice much of my critic craft, such as it is." Then there were happy weeks when he studied Latin grammar and French under the helpful Murdoch at Ayr, returning with an inevitable *Télémaque* and a dictionary to acquire those set French phrases which he loved to air with painful frequency in his most studied letters and conversation. At home there was an austere existence, for the house was dominated by the presence of the father, who, with all respect for his many qualities, was somewhat feared, and by violent gusts of temper would reduce the household to silence. There was over that peasant dwelling a burdensome air, an atmosphere of care, debt, and depression.

In 1777 the father was deeper than usual in his chronic poverty and debt; his landlord had died, and the factor, exacting of rent and arrears, seemed to the indignant family a hateful Shylock, and as such was afterwards immortalised in "The Twa Dogs." But another farm was found at Lochlea, in Tarbolton parish, of 130 acres, with the fated meagre and reluctant soil. Here Robert and Gilbert became regular servants to their father, at the usual ploughman's wage of £7 a year, and they had work enough to try harder constitutions than theirs. No wonder the poet bore marks of hard toil in his slouching shoulders, and the results of that dull, drudging life in his moody, melancholy fits of temper.

Yet life had its relaxations. There was the dancing
class at Tarbolton, to which, in spite of his father's stern
antipathy, Robert went when he was seventeen, to improve his
manners and acquaintance with young folk; there were visits
to neighbours' houses, at which he was welcome, and, young as
he was, he was always enslaved by some young woman
— sometimes indeed by two or three at a time, for his
heart was as tinder when the sparks alighted from the eyes of
a goddess of the byre. His first apprenticeship in love and in
verse had begun when only fifteen years old, with the girl
with whom he worked in the harvest-field, whose charms he
celebrated in youthful strains. With more strength he now
made songs for and about his favourites—not too subtle for the
hearts or too refined for the heads of damsels who were
more able to enjoy the delicate humour of their select songs
"She rose and let me in," or "The Kirk will not let me be"
than the laborious efforts of his Muse, when it was speaking
English, "I dreamed I lay where flowers were springing
gaily in the sunny beam." Courtships occupied an important
place in rustic life. While older folk were snoring the snores
of the weary in their box-beds, youths, carrying their shoes in
their hands, would creep stealthily out, and hie off to the
abodes of their charmers. Then there would come the well-
known inviting whistle, the tap on the window-pane, and the
damsel, hastily attired, would step forth cautiously at the
"chappin' oot," and among the sheaves in the harvest-field,
or in the less romantic, more odorous shelter of a byre,
the swains cooed their rural loves. Young as he was, Rob
was an adept at wooing, especially after he went to Kirkoswald
village to learn mensuration and dialling from the schoolmaster; for in that place, notorious for its smuggling and
attendant devil-may-care vices, there were youths of freer ways
than about his home.

A greater change came over his life when, in 1781,
he went to learn flax-dressing at Irvine. Under the belief
that he might improve his condition and be sooner able to
marry by becoming a "heckler" or flax-dresser, he began
to learn that business under a relation of his mother's,
whom he compactly describes as "a scoundrel of the first

water." He lodged in a poor room at a modest shilling a week, and lived chiefly on the supply of oatmeal sent by his father. Like Kirkoswald, the sea-port was given over to smuggling or "fair trading" and free living; there were "scenes of swaggering and riotous dissipation," and the lad got in with wild spirits, who could not cope with him in wit, but could outdo him in drinking. He learned more lax principles than flax-dressing, as he owns. On New Year's Day his master's shop was burned during a customary carousal, and the apprentice was left without work and without a sixpence. So back he came to Lochlea, finding home restraints more irksome after his free and tumultuous life. More eagerly than ever he found his way to Tarbolton when the day's work was over—to the masonic meetings, to whose jovial mysteries he was initiated; to the Bachelors' Club, at which young fellows met once a month for mental improvement and bodily regalement at the frugal charge of threepence. There it was easy for Burns to out-talk, out-argue, and out-shine them all. Then there were the "rockings," when neighbours met at each others' houses, each girl bringing her spinning-wheel, as her mother in older days had brought her distaff or "rock" (from which these meetings still kept their name); and there they talked and sang and laughed and flirted as the wheels whirled round; and all was brought to a close by the delicious convoying home, youths carrying gallantly the wheel of the favourite of the time through the fields when "corn rigs were bonnie" in the moonlight. There were the merry Hallowe'ens and the joyous penny weddings, which relieved the monotony of rural existence. Such were the scenes of the poet's life, of his pleasures and his songs. On Sundays Burns was at the kirk, the handsomest and gayest of all, with the only tied hair in the parish, his plaid round his shoulders in a manner of his own, discussing in the kirkyard theology with his acquaintances, sometimes from sheer perversity taking up the Calvinists' side; at other times flaunting his wilder notions, which were hissed by his hearers. "Between sermons," while seniors went to the inn, he and his companions went with the lassies to stroll in the fields. In such rural life he loved to reign supreme; he was "ever panting for distinction," we are told. He was proud of his power of talk, as he was proud of his letter-writing, and he could make love, he tells, out of vanity of showing his parts in courtship. His tongue so plausible could speak more seductively than his pen could write, and he could make the damsels follow his lure as rats and children followed the Piper of Hamelin.[1]

The sentimental was a mood dear to him as to Sterne. If we can imagine a Charles Surface having really in his heart the noble sentiments which his brother Joseph had so copiously on his lips, we should have the composite character of Burns —Rab the Ranter one day, with the emotions of a Mr. Harley, the "Man of Feeling," the next. "My favourite authors," he told Murdoch in 1782, "are of the sentimental kind—such as Shenstone, particularly his elegies; *The Man of Feeling*— a book I prize next to the Bible; Sterne, especially his *Sentimental Journey*; Macpherson's *Ossian*, etc. These are the glorious models after which I endeavour to form my conduct." To model a character on *Ossian* and the *Sentimental Journey* was surely the oddest plan on which any mortal ever tried to fashion a life.[2]

The intellectual side of Burns, however, was never suppressed by the amorous. He read with avidity books of every sort, especially the poets of his day, for many of whom he preserved a persistently exaggerated esteem; for Shenstone, "whose divine elegies do honour to our language, our nature, and our species"; for the "immortal *Minstrel*" of Beattie, and for Thomson's turgid tragedies,[3] from which he was addicted to quoting fine utterances which are woefully vapid.

---

[1] Beware a tongue that's smoothly hung,
A heart that warmly seems to feel;
That feeling heart but acts a part—
'Tis rakish art in Rob Mossgeil.
Works, edit. by W. Wallace, i. 114.

[2] Chambers's *Burns*, i. 64.

[3] *Ibid.* (ed. by Wallace), vii. 22, 63, 66. He quotes from *Alfred* commonplace lines, which we trust were Mallet's, that he "repeated 10,000 times," to "nerve his manhood and steel his resolution":

Hear, Alfred, hero of the state,
Thy genius heaven's high will declare—
The triumph of the truly great,
Is never, never to despair,
Is never to despair!

This literary taste made him live in two worlds—one the rough, squalid life of the ploughman, with the rude tone and taste of his class; the other the higher intellectual life of the poet, with the finer companionship of his books. The blending, or rather the conflicting, of these two opposite lives accounts for much of the complexity of Burns's character and career.

In the Lochlea days Burns wrote little which gave evidence of his high gifts except his "Poor Mailie" and his exquisite "Mary Morison." When using English models it was natural that he should give an echo instead of a voice. Rarely, if ever, at his best when writing in English, he felt to the last it was a hard exercise rather than a real gift. "These English songs gravel me to death," he wrote to George Thomson in his latest years. "I have not that command over the language as I have over my native language." That was true, but the moment he touched his native earth, used his own speech, he gained strength. From the day in 1784 that he read Robert Fergusson's poems, he saw where his true field lay. He says somewhat grandiloquently that Fergusson caused him "to string anew his wildly sounding rustic lyre with emulating vigour"; and, as results showed, did so to good effect.

Troubles came anew on the luckless father. He quarrelled with his landlord, to whom he was hopelessly in debt, and before the time came for the goods to be sold off and the household turned adrift, Robert and Gilbert had taken a small farm, Mossgiel, where they could afford shelter and a livelihood for the family. Worn out by care and worry and consumption, William Burness died in 1784. As he lay on his death-bed, he had said there was only one for whose future he had any fear. "Oh, father, is it me you mean?" said Robert, and as the old man said "Yes," his son turned to the window with tears streaming down his cheeks. His impulsive nature, his passionate will, his reckless love of pleasure, with all his powers of wild humour, made life for him a perilous game. It was fortunate that the worthy man died before a scandal arose about his son, who towards the end of the year had to do penance in the kirk. A little more reticence would have become the culprit; a little less of the bravado with which he brazened it out in his "Welcome to the Love-begotten"—which is certainly admirable as verse —where he snaps his fingers with immoral courage before decorum's face:

> The mair they talk I'm kenned the better—
> E'en let them clash.

Burns's attitude towards propriety was that of his brothers of the plough. What he wrote for his friends' delectation was what hinds were saying at the farm. They would appear demurely before the minister and congregation to express their penitence and to receive rebuke, and then go back to the farmyard and laugh over it all; men and women joining in loud guffaws over the elders, the minister, and the offenders. Burns had the average morals of his peasant class, with more than the average success and variety in his conquests. "Rab the Ranter," as he called himself jovially, was a rural Tom Jones, with all the good-nature which was supposed to cover a multitude of sins with that class of heroes, under the convenient but vague ethical code·

> The heart's aye the part aye
> That maks us richt or wrang.

Now settled at Mossgiel, one mile from Mauchline, where the whole family lived and worked, Burns proposed to begin a new and sedater life. "Come, go to, I will be wise!" was his brave resolution, though Mauchline was dangerously near, with cronies, gossips, and taverns to entice him on long dull nights from home. Seriously he bent himself to the difficult task, gravely he studied *Wight on Husbandry*, carefully he attended markets and fairs, punctiliously he began to keep account-books. But soon these were scribbled over with more snatches of verse and song than entries of barter and sale of grain and stock. While he was working in the fields he was also composing in his mind. Verses satiric or plaintive came according to his vagrant fancy. At Lochlea he had written little; now he was discovering his true gifts and his true speech, and was becoming sensible of his real powers, though not to their full extent. At Mauchline, with the local gossip ringing in his ears, he found themes for his satire in the ecclesiastical polemics of the district. In Ayrshire, more than in almost any other quarter, both people and clergy were divided into two hostile classes—the "old lights" or the evangelicals, and the "new lights" or the moderates. Old light ministers were orthodox, austerely Calvinistic; their sermons were full of soul-searching doctrines of original sin, total corruption, election and reprobation and free grace, with a strong flavour of brimstone from the bottomless pit seasoning the whole. Their oratory was unctuous and fervid, awakening to soul and body, though in prolix discourses, "three-mile prayers and half-mile graces." For these attractive pulpit qualities the people loved them, in spite of the stern discipline of the sessions over their morals and their manners. Yet these ministers usually had better claims to esteem from their earnestness and piety. The moderates, on the other hand, left dogma aside, and therefore were dubbed generally by the bigots "Arians" and "Socinians"; they preached everyday duties, and therefore were nicknamed "legalists" and "moralists"; they were tolerant and genial, and were therefore called "lax." While an evangelical preached "without paper," the moderate read his discourses, which the people pronounced "dreich" and "caudrife"; and sometimes no doubt their pulpit essays were, in De Quincey's phrase, like "cold water over slabs of marble." There can be no doubt that the moderate clergy were, whatever their defects, more educated and cultured than their rivals; they humanised divinity, softened hard dogmas, brought an air of tolerance into religion, and broke down the tyranny of the kirk, being men of the world without being therefore worldly men. It was with that class—favoured by the lairds and lawyers—Burns had most sympathy. Democratic though the poet was, he thought too little of the judgment of the people to believe that they should choose their own ministers. That the "sheep" should elect their "herds" was to him a paradox.

It so happened that Mr. Gavin Hamilton, the lawyer at Mauchline, from whom Mossgiel was leased, had been brought before the kirk-session on the charge of being irregular in attendance at church and negligent of family worship—by Mr.

Auld, the minister, most austere of disciplinarians, and his docile elders. Later he was accused of the heinous crime of directing his gardener to dig potatoes on the Lord's Day. He was even heard to whistle on a Fast Day, and to say "damn it" before the minister's very face. Mr. Hamilton appealed against his censure to the Presbytery, which, being largely composed of moderates, acquitted him. Naturally, Burns took the side of his friend and landlord: he liked the moderates for their common-sense, having no love for an austerity from which he himself had suffered at Tarbolton, when doing penance for his fault. When two coarse "old light" ministers, named Russell and Moodie, fell out, quarrelled in the public road, and vilified each other about a parish boundary before a delighted audience in the Presbytery, with full strength of lung and language, Burns satirised the event in his "Holy Tuilzie, or the Twa Herds,"[1] and his verses passed from hand to hand, to the delight of the people and the scandal of the godly. Similar success attended "Holy Willie's Prayer"—a daring travesty of high Calvinistic prayers, with deprecations, imprecations, and execrations—put into the mouth of a canting elder who had been one of Mr. Hamilton's judges in the Mauchline session. Local reputation was spreading, his verses circulated in the countryside, were roared over in every farmer's house and tavern, and chuckled over in laird's mansions and every moderate minister's manse. Such notoriety he naturally loved; indeed, it was his delight to shine, to be talked of, be it at markets or clubs, at kirk doors, weddings, or funerals.

Hamilton, a man of good position, social qualities, and ability, and Robert Aiken, the clever, glib-tongued lawyer of Ayr, now praised his verses to the skies. "I never knew there was any merit in my poems till Mr. Aiken read them into repute," said Burns. In rapid succession came from his pen yet more stinging satires, in which the squabbles of the clergy and the morose preaching of the

---

[1] Sic twa—O, do I live to see't,
Sic famous twa should disagree t,
An' names like villain, hypocrite,
Ilk ither gi'en,
While new light herds, wi' laughin' spite,
Say neither's leein'!

evangelicals are touched with trenchant humour; and the "Holy Fair," that "joyful solemnity" in which the scandals attending the open-air communions are painted with vivid power and merciless veracity. In these satires there is not *saeva indignatio* at evils he hated, but wild humour over scandals he laughed at. In them he was merely voicing the feelings of the educated classes, and echoing the teaching of the moderate clergy in two-thirds of the Lowland pulpits of Scotland. To say that Burns, by his drastic lines, broke down the despotism of the Church, overthrew the spirit of Puritanism, and dispelled religious gloom in the country, is to speak in ignorance of the real part he played. That work had been begun effectively by others before him, and was to be carried on by others who never felt his influence.

During the winter of 1785-86 the full strength of his genius shone forth as at no other time—producing with marvellous prodigality masterpieces of humour and fancy which shaped themselves in his mind as he worked at his farm. As he follows the plough, he intercedes with the gadsman who runs to kill the little field-mouse which the ploughshare had startled, and forthwith he composes the lines on the "wee sleekit timorous beastie." As he returns from a bibulous masonic meeting at Tarbolton, his eye catches the words, "Advice will be given on common disorders at the shop gratis," in the window of the impecunious schoolmaster, who kept a shop and dabbled in physic to increase his meagre earnings. Thereupon the brilliant fancy strikes him of an apparition of Death to the unconscious friend of his craft, and the "Death and Dr. Hornbook" is composed as he proceeds homewards. One Sunday evening, as they were walking, Robert repeated to Gilbert the "Cottar's Saturday Night"—a picture of his old home, of his father before the assembled household, beginning worship with his solemn phrase, "Let us worship God," and reading "the portion of the Word of God." The whole poem, owing to its attractive sentiment rather than genius, has done more than any other of his works to endear the poet to the masses of what used to be called "Bible-loving" Scotland. This winter of 1785-86 at Mossgiel was the most prolific and most brilliant period of his life. It was then he wrote "The Ordination," "Hallowe'en," "The Cottar's Saturday Night," "The Vision," the "Jolly Beggars," "To a Mouse," "The Twa Dogs," "Address to the Deil," and others, any one of which would have brought a poet fame. Now in the fulness of his powers, according to his varying moods he could write in any strain, without effort, with marvellous spontaneity, with rich enjoyment in the doing. "All my poetry," he told Mrs. Dunlop, "is the result of easy composition, but of laborious correction." His mastery over his dialect was like that of a great musician over his violin, which he makes to speak in every variety of expression —now with a merry lilt and now with mournful strain: by one movement making the feet to dance and by another the eyes to fill. It is strange to think that his finest works were not intended for the public eye, but merely pleasure-works made for the nonce, which might, for all he knew, be never heard of beyond his countryside, and might wear out of memory, as the manuscript copies wore out by use. In spite of his vast gifts of originality, he too modestly leant on others to give him a hoist on to his Pegasus, though once up none rode more superbly than he. He often needed the lead to a theme or a strain from some other writer before he began. The "Death and Dying Words of Poor Mailie," the mare, would never have been written if Hamilton of Gilbertfield had not written the "Death and Dying of Bonnie Heck," his greyhound; the "Elegy on Poor Mailie" would never have been written if a century before Sempill of Beltrees had not composed his "Habbie Simson, the Piper of Kilbarchan," and Ramsay or Fergusson had not copied it; his epistles "To Davie" and to Lapraik would not have been written if Hamilton of Gilbertfield and Ramsay had not exchanged rhyming letters before him. From Fergusson came further hints and helps. "Scotch Drink" follows on his predecessor's "Caller Water," the "Brigs o' Ayr" come after "Planestanes and Causey," the "Saturday Night" got suggestions from the "Farmer's Ingle," the influence of "Leith Races" is seen in his "Holy Fair," and other debts were due to a poet he called his "model." But then the distance from the suggestion to the masterpiece was worlds wide—and those pieces, like

"Tam o' Shanter," which came without any literary progenitor, showed how independent and original his genius could be, surpassing all whenever he chose.

While engaged on the farm, which did not pay much, and composing poems, which paid still less, he had time for his favourite wooing, which paid worst of all. His relations with the "sex" were many and migratory. He was no sooner off with the old love than he was on with the new, and even for that he often did not wait. In his tastes he was not fastidious as to the position, quality, or even looks of his entrancer. "He had always a particular jealousy of people who were richer than himself, or had more consequence," says his brother Gilbert. "His love therefore seldom settled on persons of this description." A buxom barn-door beauty, a servant girl was enough, although she was as devoid of romance as of stockings. He must be the superior. A "fine woman," especially among his humble acquaintance, he could not resist; and seldom could she resist the masterful wooer, with his winning ways, his bewitching talk, his eyes that "glowed like coals of fire." Not long after he came to Mossgiel he had met Jean Armour, a Mauchline mason's daughter, at a penny ball. She was handsome and sprightly—wooing began, courtship proceeded, and it was in time apparent that a child would follow. What should he do? marry or fly? To his crony confidants of all his amours he protests that he is fixed as fate against staying at home and owning her as his wife. "The first by heaven I will not do—the last by hell that I will never do." He did relent, from kindness if not from honour, and gave her a paper acknowledging her as his wife—a legal Scots compact. What was his dismay when the indignant "auld licht" mason forced the girl to give up the paper and packed her off to Paisley, rather than make her an "honest woman" by marrying her to a poor farmer and scapegrace poet. That he, the irresistible, should be discarded; that he, who had intended to desert Jean, should by Jean be shamefully deserted; that he, who had out of mere good pleasure and munificence of heart promised her marriage, should himself be rejected was indeed galling to his pride. To his boon companions, with whom he had no reticence, he denounced the girl's perjury and ingratitude when rumours reached him that she was going to marry somebody else—" for never man loved more than I do her. I have often tried to forget her, I have run into all kinds of dissipation and riot to drive her out of my head." He enjoyed himself with his companions in the Whiteford Arms, holding the free-spoken " Court of Equity." A failure as a farmer, he had no career before him, his life was "without an aim," and he was arranging to become overseer of a plantation in Jamaica, as a fit exile for a love-lorn man. But while protesting that his heart was wrung for lack of Jean Armour, he solaced himself with other wooings. There is one " Eliza " about whom he philanders, and to whom he sings in fine English strains, stating that " oceans roaring wide never can divide my heart and soul from thee."[1] Two months after the marriage lines were destroyed there occurred the episode of a meeting by the banks of a river, when two lovers—one being the distracted adorer of perfidious Jean—stand on either bank of a murmuring stream, lave their hands in the running water, hold a Bible between them and swear perpetual love, and exchange copies of the Holy Scriptures. To her as to Eliza songs are made, in which he asserts, that though he " cross the raging sea," while " his crimson currents flow he'll love his Highland lassie." There is something vague about this romantic story, on which the hero was unusually reticent. Some even dare to doubt if this " Mary in Heaven "— afterwards immortalised in exquisite lines—ever was a Mary on earth. But she seems to have been a domestic servant quite of earth—Gavin Hamilton's nursery maid or a dairymaid,[2] who died of fever in the west country the year after this scene. It is to be hoped that Jean and Eliza and Mary—the rivals—never met to compare their soft experiences and the rapturous songs of the versatile wooer.

For the scandal connected with the lost Armour, Burns had to make three several appearances before the congregation at Mauchline, with all demureness—Mr. Auld leniently letting the culprit stand in his pew instead of in the ignominious place of repentance, on condition that he should remember

[1] Chambers's *Life and Works*, i. 252.
[2] *Works of Burns*, edit. Scott Douglas, i. 255-57.

the poor. What could Burns now do? He was poor, his farming was a failure, he was without permanent occupation Jean Armour presented him with twins; old Armour threatened him with pains and penalties for aliment for his daughter and the surreptitious offspring, which he could not pay. In dread of jail he skulked off to Kilmarnock, seeking shelter in the house of his aunt, with his chest ready for him to sail for the Indies. But he had no money to pay his passage. Evidently his companions and brother confessors in every amorous scrape could not; certainly his richer friends, Hamilton and Aiken, did not offer the requisite money—only nine guineas. They, however, urged him to make money by publishing his poems, and this idea he readily caught up—the wonder is they had never urged it before. "I weighed my productions as impartially as in my power," says Burns: "I thought they had merit, and it was a delicious idea that I should be called a clever fellow, even though it should never reach my ears—a poor negro-driver—gone to the world of spirits perhaps, a victim to that inhospitable clime. I was pretty sure my poems would meet with some applause; but at the worst, the roar of the Atlantic would deafen the voice of censure, and the novelty of West India scenes make me forget my neglect." Never, surely, was poet more modest.[1] He was overawed by the genius of a Dr. Beattie, bowed before the pre-eminence of Allan Ramsay, praised lavishly the verse of other people, and his own matchless work he threw out as unconsidered trifles, to please a mood, to praise a girl, to amuse a friend, and enliven a tavern supper.

Soon Wilson's little printing press at Kilmarnock was wheezing out 600 copies of his poems. Friends and patrons had subscribed for 350, and quickly the rest were sold, and the poet was ultimately richer by a poor £20. Success was immediate; his book was received with acclaim in farm and cottage, in mansion and manse in the whole south country, and copies were thumbed out of existence. The local reputation of a "clever fellow," who paid little regard to farming or to morals, the frequenter of taverns, with a knack of verse-

[1] Even when in his full glory in Edinburgh he talked modestly of Ramsay and Fergusson as his models (Lockhart's *Scott*, i. 187).

making, changed in a month. His poems were a revelation of
the man, for range of motive and subject, for sentiment and
satire, such as had not been seen in Scots before. In Catrine
House Professor Dugald Stewart had him as his guest, full of
kindly attentions to the new poet; Mrs. Dunlop of Dunlop,
whose heart was touched by the "Cottar's Saturday Night," sent
post haste to Mossgiel for six copies of the volume, with a
request that the author would call upon her; and from that
time began the intercourse and correspondence of long years
—the clever lady somewhat didactic, prolix, and exacting; the
poet respectful, circumspect, yet independent, for he would do
much because he was obliging, though nothing because he felt
obliged. Others of rank and consequence recognised him and
brought him into their society—strange to a man whose highest
associates had been chiefly young drapers, teachers, farmers,
clerks, and shoemakers. His new acquaintances scanned him
critically. His manners were "simple, manly, and independent,
but without anything that indicated forwardness, arrogance,
or vanity. If there had been a little more of gentleness and
accommodation in his temper he would, I think, have been
more interesting; but he had been accustomed to give law in
the circle of his ordinary acquaintance, and his dread of anything approaching to meanness or servility rendered his
manner somewhat decided and hard"—such was the impression made on Dr. Stewart, the urbanest of gentlemen. There
was about him the boldness of a shy man, anxious to seem at
his ease; but it was difficult for a man brought up in the social
familiarity of the rustic and village coteries to know how far
to go in that more fashionable and formal company.

The gathering fame might elate him, but it could not
satisfy a man with an aimless life. He had failed as a farmer,
he could not live as a poet. The bookseller would not print
another edition because the author had no money to supply
him with paper. He protested that he had to endure "pangs
of disappointment, the sting of pride, with some pangs of
remorse, which never fail to settle on my vitals like vultures
when attention is not called away by the calls of society or
the vagaries of the Muse. Even in the hour of social mirth
my gaiety is the madness of an intoxicated criminal under the

hands of the executioner." In these moods exile seemed the only resource, and with his money he took out a passage for the Indies. Then occurred the event that changed his destiny.

Not far from Mossgiel, in the manse of Loudoun, lived Mr. George Laurie, one of the most genial and cultivated of the moderate clergy; intimate with men of letters in Edinburgh, and numbering among his friends Principal Robertson, Dr. Blair, and Dr. Blacklock. He had nineteen years before brought "Ossian" Macpherson to the notice of Dr. Blair. He had a family consisting of several daughters, accomplished and beautiful, a son, afterwards his assistant and successor in the living, who, with the minister's benign wife, all made a charming household. In the evenings the sons and daughters of neighbouring lairds would often come over in coach or on horseback, and after supper there was the dance, when the minister, little and fat and paunchy, his kindly face surmounted by a cauliflower wig, would join in the country dance, his nimble, short, silk-stockinged legs twinkling like expert black knitting-kneedles to the music of the spinnet. Gavin Hamilton and Burns would sometimes ride over to dinner, join the dancing, and occasionally stay all night. Burns had paid his last visit to the manse previous to his departure for the Indies; he had bid farewell, leaving in the bedroom the lines beginning, "O thou Dread power," and as he strode over the moor in the sultry, darkening autumn evening, with pelting showers, he composed what he expected would be "the last song he should ever measure in Caledonia," "The gloomy night is gathering fast."[1] His box was on the way to Greenock, when a letter was handed to him from Dr. Blacklock— the blind poet — to Mr. Laurie, who had sent to him a copy of the poems, to get his opinion of them—for though a poor poet himself, he was a literary arbiter in Scotland. It was full of enthusiasm, urging that a second edition should be published. The opinion of one of the literati, who seemed to the Mossgiel farmer as gods of Olympus, too high to hear, too great to approach, was with Burns decisive. "Dr. Blacklock belonged to a set of critics for whose applause I had not

[1] Chambers, i. 302.

dared to hope. His opinion that I could merit encouragement in Edinburgh[1] fired me so much that I posted off for that city without a single acquaintance, or a single letter of introduction."

In December, he set off on a borrowed pony, entering the city with strange interest—the crowded High Street, the dark, densely-peopled wynds, the tumultuous taverns. He shared a bed in Baxter's Close with an old Mauchline acquaintance, Richmond, who had a lodging at three shillings a week. He found some Ayrshire acquaintances—gentlemen whom he had met in his neighbourhood—and he was introduced to Lord Glencairn, whose handsome form and exquisite face were matched by a noble and charming nature. Through this nobleman the members of the Caledonian Hunt subscribed liberally for the new edition, which that sleek and learned bookseller, Mr. William Creech, who had formerly been tutor to his lordship, had undertaken to publish. Henry Erskine, full of wit and good-nature, took him under his wing. Dr. Blacklock welcomed him to his little breakfast-room with gentle effusiveness. Dr. Blair was gracious and patronising, admiring his sentimental poems, and conscientiously trying to appreciate his humorous verse, though the prosaic critic had not a notion of humour. The kindly "Man of Feeling," Henry Mackenzie, received the admirer who had worn out two copies of his book by devoted use, and praised his poems in the *Lounger*, that weekly paper formed after the model of the *Spectator*—or rather the more ponderous *Rambler* —with snatches of poetry, criticism, mild romance, and character-painting by literary lawyers, who aimed at originality and always missed it. The masonic body received Brother Burns with acclaim, and the Grand Master gave the toast "Caledonia and the Caledonian Bard" amid vociferous enthusiasm. The doors of aristocratic flats and mansions were open to receive the poetical ploughman; the tables of literati had a place for him; ladies were entranced by his manner, his deferential address, his grave face, that dark eye of his, which we are told literally *glowed*. "I never saw such another in a human head," said Walter Scott, who as a boy had seen him one

[1] Dr. Blacklock in his letter says nothing about that. Chambers's *Burns*, i. 305.

memorable evening at Dr. Adam Ferguson's.[1] The Duchess of Gordon, from whose pretty lips came Scots as broad and words as free as his own, protested that "this man carried her off her feet." The Ayrshire poet was the theme of universal conversation. There was the man, tall, strong, gainly, without clumsiness, though his shoulders had the slouch of a man who had followed the plough, dressed like a farmer in his Sunday best, in his top-boots and buckskins, blue coat and waistcoat, striped with blue and buff, the costume of Charles Fox and the livery of his admirers; his black hair without powder, tied behind and spread over his forehead; his dark eyes, with a gleam of melancholy in them, kindling up with wonderful animation; his talk vigorous and full of intelligence, expressed in strong Scots accents, but in good English words, with a voice "sonorous and replete with the finest modulations." The manner was manly, and the opinions were spoken with self-confidence by this young peasant-farmer before gentry whom he had never met on terms of equality before; before literary patriarchs and legal magnates. He was no "illiterate ploughman" but a well-read man. The dignified Principal Robertson owned he scarcely ever met any man whose conversation displayed more intellectual vigour.

Had Burns been born forty years earlier, when town and country manners were more alike, when classes high and low had less difference in living, when laird and merchant, lawyer and shopkeeper were of kindred blood, all speaking broad Scots, all with frugal incomes and simple ways—had Burns lived in Allan Ramsay's time, the disparity of rank and manners between the Ayrshire farmer and the Edinburgh citizen would have been less marked. By 1786 a wide

[1] Lockhart's *Scott*, i. 185. "Nothing in the literary way has occupied Edinburgh for some weeks past so much as the poems of Robert Burns, an illiterate ploughman of Ayrshire. His poems are many of them extremely good, both those in Scots dialect and in the English. He is thought to be equal, if not superior to Ramsay in original genius and humour. I am not certain of that. But he surpasses him in sensibility. We, you may believe, with the prejudices of the Scotch, are ready to believe that the productions of the milkwoman of Bristol are mere whey compared to Burns; and that the poems of Stephen Duck, the thresher, are but like chaff in comparison. Lord Glencairn is his patron. A new edition of his poems is printing. But I hear he has not been so advisable as to suppress some things that he was advised to suppress" (MS. letter of Dr. Carlyle to Duchess of Buccleugh).

ROBERT BURNS
From the Painting by Alexander Nasmyth in the Scottish National Portrait Gallery, Edinburgh.

distinction had arisen between classes, and side by side with remains of quaint Scots simplicity there was a modern air of fashion as different from the ancient ways as the fine New Town was from the squalid Old Town. When the poet appeared, therefore, he found manners, talk, interests in which he had no part, and that though in society he was not of it. It was not so long since he had been for the first time in a room with a carpet, at John Rankin's at Adamhill, when he went gingerly round it, afraid to put his hobnails on a covering so dainty. He had lived in a "but and a ben," and a few years before had lived on a ploughman's wage of £7 a year. That he should now bear himself with dignity and fine self-possession in the highest society in Scotland was in itself a great achievement. Regarded with interest, treated with courtesy, he yet felt that there was an air of condescension in it all, and that gentlemen raised their eyebrows under their capacious wigs or powdered hair when he ventured to hold his own. He imagined, as weeks went by and curiosity was sated, that some who had caressed him passed him by, and he writhed when he saw persons of rank or wealth preferred to himself. It galled him to see Lord Glencairn pay deference to a man of higher station, and he wrote in his commonplace book: "He showed so much engrossing attention to the only blockhead at table that I was within half a point of throwing down my gage of contemptuous defiance!" It was mortifying to him "to see a fellow, whose abilities would scarcely have made an eightpenny tailor, and whose heart is not worth three farthings, meet with attention and notice that are withheld from the son of genius and poverty." It was no doubt pleasant to be taken by the hand in friendly grasp as an equal; it was hateful to him to be "taken by the hand" as an interesting protégé. The men of letters, who in the distance had seemed so great, whom since a boy he had read of with awe, seemed small men when he met them at table, separated only by a few feet of mahogany—their talk, their wit, their humour he no doubt thought inferior to that of Willie Nicol the teacher, and William Smellie the printer, in Dowie's tavern. The literati were ready with their advice, but he cared little for it. As he said to Ramsay of Ochtertyre, who asked him if they had mended his poems by their criticism: "Sir, these gentlemen remind me of some spinsters in my country, who spin the thread so fine that it is neither fit for weft nor woof."[1]

So the months passed, with dinners in society, meetings at taverns at night with congenial bottle-companions, the writing of songs for the engraver Johnson's *Musical Museum*. At Smellie's printing-office he would turn up, pacing the compositors' room, cracking his long whip, as his pages passed through the press.[2]

In May 1787 he left Edinburgh, the scene of his triumphs. The second edition of his poems, consisting of 2800 copies, was published by Creech, enriched by "The Ordination," "Death and Dr. Hornbook," the "Brigs o' Ayr," and the "Address to the Unco' Guid." It became a problem among his admirers what should be done for this poet, who had neither money nor a career. A commission in the army was spoken of. Adam Smith, who was one of the first to acknowledge his genius when the poems appeared, suggested he might become a "salt officer." When the Chair of Agriculture in Edinburgh University was founded, Mrs. Dunlop and others thought that post would fit him — for that a man should fail as a practical farmer has never disqualified him for teaching with confidence the theory of farming.[3]

After an excursion in the southern counties with his new friend, Robert Ainslie, the law-clerk, he returned to Mossgiel, after six months of flattering enough to turn the head of a man less assured of his rightful place. He had left home skulking from a sheriff's warrant for a bastard's aliment, he went back with his fortunes raised, his fame established. People, who a few months before had despised him in his obscurity, looked up to him now in the hour of his glory.

---

[1] The only advice he adopted from Dr. Blair was to alter the words in the "Holy Fair" from "tidings of salvation" to "tidings of damnation." Dr. James Gregory, to whom he submitted his "Wounded Hare," wrote plain-spoken, pedantic, niggling criticism, which must have proved as nauseous to the poet as his critic's own "Gregory's mixture." With infinitely more courtesy and kindness Burns wrote his suggestions to Helen Maria Williams on her flimsy verses, praising generously wherever he could (Chambers's *Burns*, i. 266, iii. 44).

[2] Kerr's *Life of W. Smellie*, ii. 256-59.

[3] *Correspondence between Robert Burns and Mrs. Dunlop* (edit. by W. Wallace), pp. 15, 16, 167.

Bitterly he wrote to William Nicol, that hard-drinking, cross-grained, High School teacher: "The stateliness of the patricians of Edinburgh, and the civility of my plebeian brethren since I returned home, have nearly put me out of conceit of my species." Equally he felt the "mean and disgusting compliance" of the Armour family, who, having despised him as a bad farmer, with a character as dilapidated as his fortunes, were complacent when he came back a great man. It would have been well if Jean had proved less "compliant" and Burns with her been less persuasive.

Evidently his part in farming Mossgiel was given up. For the next few months were taken up with visits to the Highlands — now with the humorous, ill-conditioned Nicol, now with Dr. Adair, brother of Mrs. Archibald Laurie of Loudoun, and a relation of Mrs. Dunlop of Dunlop—and he was received with honour at Gordon Castle, and Blair Castle, and Ochtertyre, taking his place with dignity among dukes and gentry, with what Mrs. Riddell described as the almost "sorcery of his fascinating conversation," to which the brightness of his eyes gave power.

In December he is found again in Edinburgh, staying with his friend William Cruickshank, the High School teacher. Mr. Creech is slow of paying the money, about £500, for his poems. He had many an interview with that courteous bookseller, so carefully dressed in powdered hair and his velvet breeches, at his Luckenbooth shop. But though he lingered out the winter months, this second visit, like most literary sequels, was a failure. It lacked the freshness, it had none of the glory of the former. Where now were the caressing flattery of ladies of rank and fashion, the suppers with literati, the dinners with the great, the many gilt-edged invitations that shed a splendour in the poor lodging in Baxter's Close? These now were few and far between. Instead, there were meetings in the taverns, where drink was copious, songs were merry, jokes were as broad as the nights were long; the gatherings of the Crochallan Club, with its wild, free mirth, where Burns and rough-tongued Smellie bickered jovially. It is true, the coarse humour of Nicol and Smellie and Robert Heron, the toping literary man-of-all-work, over a collop, a rizzared haddock, and whisky in John Dowie's or Douglas's tavern was vastly more amusing than Lord Monboddo's whims or Dr. Blair's platitudes. Here, at least, Burns met no superiors: he could be king of the company, say what he liked, and drink as much as he pleased. It was better to reign in a tavern than to serve in a drawing-room.

Then came the flirtations with the angelic, though portly Clarinda. Burns had met at a friend's house Mrs. M'Lehose, whose incompatible husband was abroad, leaving his wife and his children to live in a poor flat at General's Entry, in Potterrow. She was a "gloriously amiable, fine woman," as he told her, and the poet was ever enamoured of a "fine woman." He was charmed at the first interview with the sumptuous, sentimental dame, and she with the poet, with the dark glowing eyes and seductive manners. By the overturning of a hackney coach, Burns was disabled by a bruised limb from calling on her for "six horrible weeks"; during which time he was attended by his friend Dr. James Gregory, whose opinion was considered equally valuable on poetry and physic. He beguiled the weary days by writing songs for Johnson's *Museum*, and with a rapturous correspondence with the grass widow—he taking the name of Sylvander, she that of Clarinda. Marvellous letters they are—love and piety, passion and theology, devout apostrophes to heaven, violent protestations of devotion to Clarinda jostle each other in oddest incongruity in those voluptuous letters, sent from his lodgings in St. James' Square, all written in his best English and finest falsetto sentiment—the most pious of them being penned "at midnight," probably after a merry evening with his friends. She was a gushing, warm-hearted soul, with religious scruples, which were safeguards for affections which might go beyond the Platonic with a too ardent, and not too refined, lover. When she is troubled by rumours of his ridiculing religion, for Calvinistic theology was her "darling topic," he can assure her that "devotion is the favourite employment of his heart." When she has qualms at loving another while she is a married woman, he can pacify his "dearest angel" by showing she owes the faithless M'Lehose nothing. How can she distrust herself or him, when her adorer can beautifully write, in a sweet conjunction of piety and passion:

"I love you and will love you, and will with joyous confidence approach the throne of the Almighty with your dear idea." What rapture to read: "I admire you, I love you as a woman beyond any one in all the circle of creation"! And the interviews, which required to be stealthy as friends were ill-naturedly talking, confirmed the ardour of the daily letters. Amazing reading are these adoring epistles of the two amorists: Clarinda's ring true though foolish; Burns's, we have an uncomfortable feeling, often ring false and foolish.

The time for leaving Edinburgh arrived; he had settled terms with the slow-paced Creech, his parting with solemn vows from Clarinda was over, and he returned to Mauchline.

> He deceiving,
> She believing,
> What can lovers wish for more?

Jean Armour was again in trouble. In winter she had been driven out of her home by the enraged father. She got shelter with a female friend of Burns in Kilmarnock; but he now brought her to a lodging in Mauchline as the time drew near when she should be confined of twins—for her misfortunes did not come single. In a letter to a friend, not all printable, he narrates coarsely his sordid arrangements with and for Jean [1]; and in similar style, also unquotable, he wrote to another friend ungallantly concerning his wife by law. In February Clarinda is informed: "I am disgusted with her. I cannot endure her." To compare her to his angel is profanity: "*Here* is tasteless insipidity, vulgarity of soul, and mercenary fawning. *There* polished soul, good-sense, heaven-born genius," and so on. "I have done with her," he protests; and the letter ends in subtle humouring of the pietistic Clarinda: "At eight o'clock I shall be with the Father of Mercies, at that hour on your own account," for he made assignations in prayer as in passion.[2] This mixture of devotion to God and to Clarinda is disconcerting—some may use a stronger word.

---

[1] "I have taken her to my arms, I have given her a mahogany bed, I have given her a guinea. . . . I swore her never to attempt to claim me as her husband. She did all this like a good girl." *Works of R. Burns* (edit. Scott Douglas), iv. 95.

[2] *Ibid.* iv. 114.

Life has its surprises. One day in March Sylvander writes to the angelic Clarinda, promising "to love her to death, through death and for ever," and devoutly winding up by saying: "I am going to remember you in my prayers." A fortnight later Robert Burns and Jean Armour met in Gavin Hamilton's chambers and were made formally man and wife! The poet was honestly paying a debt of honour. Poor Clarinda! When aged, wrinkled, and plain, she would speak of those old days when she was a "gloriously fine woman"; she treasured the letters, yellow with years, full of rhodomontade which she took for passion, and pietistic phrases she took for piety; and the old eyes would light up with venerable love and pride for the faithless, unromantic, unchivalrous Sylvander—dead in his grave those many years. When, in 1793, they resumed their correspondence and interviews, the sentiment of that song "Ae fond kiss and then we sever" must have consoled her:

> Had we never lov'd sae kindly,
> Had we never lov'd sae blindly,
> Never met—or never parted,
> We had ne'er been broken-hearted.

Was he making love or was he only making a song? The next year they finally parted. Clarinda died fifty years after.

There are foolish persons who will not allow one depreciatory word spoken of any thing or being that they admire: fond parents who are indignant at a flaw suggested in their offspring; devoted citizens who get hot at any aspersion on their town— its skies never rain too much, its streets are never dirty, its people have the warmest of hearts and the purest of accents; infatuated patriots will not hear a word spoken against their native land, its climate, or its history, or its inhabitants—all are the finest. To such persons it is a sin and shame to say anything against a national bard. If he had faults—"we all have"—we are referred from his personal acts to his brilliant productions. We are bade to think what beautiful poems he wrote, what fine lines he penned, what noble sentiments he uttered; and he is justified by his works—which are literary. A poet's faults are condoned because he wrote beautiful poems; though a preacher's faults are not usually condoned though he writes beautiful sermons. Enthusiasts are like Théophile

Gautier, who said that if he had the bad taste to find any verse of Victor Hugo's poor, he would not dare to confess the fact to himself even quite alone in a cellar without a candle. We can imagine how vastly amused, though terribly bored, Robert Burns would be if he heard the magniloquent eulogies and festive oratory of adorers, and their laudations of his being "so human"; for he had an exceedingly keen sense of humour.

Before leaving Edinburgh Burns had got a commission as officer of excise, which he retained in case of emergency, for he had also arranged to take the farm of Ellisland, near Dumfries, which Mr. Miller of Dalswinton had leased to him on favourable terms. It was in May that he settled on the farm and the dilapidated house was put to rights. Mrs. Burns arrived with her surviving pre-nuptial twin (the others had died), to whom were afterwards to be added two children by his wife, and a child by somebody else, whom the good-natured, not too fastidious Jean nursed with her own. Before her arrival at Ellisland the poet had written in her praise the charming "Of a' the airts the wind can blaw," and it is perhaps true that she was then "the lassie he lo'ed best," —though where was Clarinda? Yet there were several second "bests," as we know—each of them in scholastic phrase *proxime accessit*. But, after all, as Matt Prior says: "Odds life! must one swear to the truth of a song!" He describes her genially as possessing "a warm heart, gratefully devoted to me, with all its powers to love me; vigorous health, sprightly cheerfulness, set off to the best advantage by a more than commonly handsome figure"—thus he appraises her to Mrs. Dunlop. And to Miss Chalmers—to whom, too, he had boldly made love—he owns "this marriage was not perhaps in consequence of the attachment of romance. I have no cause to repent it. If I have not got polite tattle, modish manners, and fashionable dress, I am not sickened and disgusted with the multiform curse of boarding-school affectation; and I have got the handsomest figure, the soundest constitution, and the kindest heart in the county." And then she could sing and did sing his songs, "for she has the finest wood notes wild I ever heard." This, of course, was very true, though it is not usual in more refined circles to describe the "points" of a spouse. Clearly he had made a suitable marriage. He had wedded a kindly soul, a thrifty wife, with a "handsome figure"—qualities in a young woman which, however, mature prosaically into a " decent body." Refinement would have been irksome to him—too much delicacy of feeling would have been galled by his peasant nature and tastes. Much sympathy has been expended on his fate in passing his life among his own people—that he got no lucrative post, where he could have lived in a higher social sphere. If he had, Jean Armour would have kept him fatally down : her antecedents, her homely nature would have made her socially impossible; and her husband must have left her behind when he entered society—like Thomas Moore's much loved, much deserted " Bessy," to whom the little poet of fashion wrote so copiously of the brilliant company he met which she could never share.

Ellisland is beautifully situated on the banks of the Nith, about six miles from Dumfries, opposite to the woods of Dalswinton, which clothe the opposite side of the river. Probably the happiest months of Burns's life were spent here. He was busy with his farm and his markets; friends came in, and there was jovial talk; gentry asked him to their houses and he was genial with lairds, whom he could fascinate with his brilliant, lively talk over their claret and their punch. But from the gay, noisy companionship, however, he would often return ill satisfied with it all. There would follow a reaction and moody depression, and then he would vent his feelings in verse, which gave him unfailing relief. He loved to walk by the river-bank, along the Scaur, where the rocks descend precipitately into the water, both in the sunshine and in the storm, when the winds were beating furiously and rain swelled the current below. The aspects of Nature touched him as responsive to his own moods. " I never heard the loud solitary whistle of the swallow on a summer's morn, or the wild noisy cadence of a troop of grey plovers on an autumn evening, without feeling an elevation of soul like the enthusiasm of devotion or poetry." It was so he wrote to Mrs. Dunlop, to whom he oftenest revealed the better side of his character. It is to ladies of pure tone and sympathetic soul—like Mrs. Dunlop and Miss Chalmers—that he writes with feeling, and evidently with sincerity—uttering what was highest and deepest in a nature possessed of fine impulses. At other times and in other moods, and to men of his class, Smiths, Browns, Rankins, he cast restraints away, and showed himself a master, in epistles and verse, of that style we may call "the unquotable." He could pass from one note to another with curious rapidity in harmony with his correspondent. Ever since his uncle bought him at Ayr a collection of "Letters by Eminent Hands" when he was a boy, he tried to "excel in letter-writing," and there are many we read with a strain, for the trail of the "Complete Letter Writer" is over them all. Yet no man had more skill than he, when he was natural, in writing letters, with masculine, vigorous, admirable English—and his brother Gilbert was not far behind him.

With strange transition of temperament, as the mood fell on him, he wrote, now rollicking in humour, now in deepest feeling, to-day words which made Dowie's tavern roar with laughter, to-morrow songs and lines which made Mrs. Dunlop's eyes fill with tears. One day his wife heard him crooning to himself, then breaking out into wild gesticulations and joyous excitement, tears rolling down his cheeks as he spoke out the words as they came to his mind:

> Now, Tam, O Tam, had thae been queans
> A' plump and strappin', in their teens,—

"Tam o' Shanter" was being made. Another day—it was a September evening in 1789, the anniversary of Mary Campbell's death—he walked up and down the farmyard looking to the clear starry sky, and then lying down on the straw, Mrs. Burns found him with his eyes fixed upwards, and on coming indoors he sat down and wrote that exquisite lyric to Mary in Heaven—"Thou ling'ring star, with less'ning ray"—immortalising an episode which time had idealised so much that there was no need for jealousy in his wife's capacious bosom.

At Ellisland some golden months were spent, but they were doomed to be few. At home he lived for a while a douce quiet life; he was a kind husband, a devoted father, a genial neighbour, and a generous master. He worked in the fields with his stalwart form among his men; he conducted worship with his family and his servants; he was to be seen on Sundays at Dunscore kirk, listening wearily to Calvinistic discourses. But farming schemes were failing, difficulties were increasing, his spending was lavish, his returns were meagre, and when autumn came he was forced to apply to Graham of Fintry to get him employment as an exciseman. Now were conjoined the two occupations of farmer and of gauger. "I am now a poor rascally gauger, with a salary of £35, condemned to gallop 200 miles every week, to inspect dirty yards and yeasty barrels," he wrote bitterly. When he came to a village the "good fellow" rose above the Government official, and a hint to the alewife as he entered her tavern would give her time to remove beyond reach her nefarious casks. As he reached an inn, however late at night, the servants would get up to listen to his wondrous talk. There were convivial temptations in that life of his, for as he passed from house to house in all weathers he must go through prolonged refreshments; for the punch-bowl was full, the company were thirsty, and they acted on the jovial motto of bibulous days: "Be ours this night, who knows what comes to-morrow?" That way, however, lay bankruptcy. Money went out, bills came in, harvests were poor, and workers lagged at home when the master excised abroad.

By December 1791 the stock was sold; Burns removed to Dumfries, to which district he was attached as gauger; the household and its gear were carted off from the lovely land of Ellisland to the narrow Wee Vennel. Burns had been anxious to get the post of port officer at Greenock or Port Glasgow, but had to content himself with a "foot-walk," which was a district where no horse was required.[1] Dumfries in those days was an ideal residence for a man who wished to indulge convivial tendencies—it was then the worst place for a man who wished to overcome them. Diligently as the poet did his work, carefully as he kept his books, there were temptations in that society of young clerks, small lawyers, drouthy shopkeepers, who met at the King's Arms at night, and jovial farmers who went to "wet" their bargains at the Globe on market-day. Among them Burns went too often and stayed too

[1] *Corresp. between Robert Burns and Mrs. Dunlop* (ed. Wallace), p. 245.

long, wasting his glorious company on inglorious comrades, over whom he reigned as king. If he was gay, he went to indulge his humour; if he was in a black mood, he went to drive dull care away. Topers sent for him to entertain their friends, who were eager to see the famous poet; and sometimes it may be feared that he made sport for the philistines, though a proud flash of the eyes, a keen stroke of the tongue, would warn them that to take a liberty was a dangerous thing.

There were friends of a higher order, and if he lost them it was his own fault. He could have no warmer friends than the Riddells at Friars' Carse—at whose house he met the corpulent antiquary Captain Grose, for whose pages he wrote "Tam o' Shanter." At Woodley Park lived Mrs. Walter Riddell, a clever and charming woman; but she had a refinement which Burns forgot when on leaving the dinner-table with a company half-drunk like himself, he took a liberty she never forgot, and was slow to forgive. When, in spite of his apology, the friendship stopped, his wounded pride stirred his coarser nature, and in rancid lampoons and epigrams, vulgar, brutal, and unpardonable, he insulted the lady and her husband, who were his loyalest friends.[1] This cost him other friendships in the class which could best have raised him, and he consorted more with a poor herd. It is true, all his follies were exaggerated by local gossip—all that was done was seen, all that was seen was retailed, and much that neither was seen nor done was told by scandal, which never sees a man make a false step, but it reports that he has fallen down a whole flight of stairs. For the proud man to be ignored and eyed askance by others; for the man conscious of rare intellectual powers to be despised by those, be they rich or noble, whom he felt his inferiors, was galling. Republicanism was then in the air—the spirit of democracy which had sprung up with the revolt of America had become stronger with the revolution in France; the political

---

[1] Burns's *Works* (ed. Scott Douglas), iii. 178. Among them are lines "Pinned to Mrs. Walter Riddell's carriage":

> If you rattle along like your Mistress's tongue,
> Your speed will outrival the dart :
> But a fly for your load, you'll break down on the road,
> If your stuff be as rotten as her heart.

These rival in coarseness the lines on the dead Mrs. Oswald.

trinity—"liberty, equality, fraternity"—was welcomed by great numbers in Scotland who read Tom Paine's *Rights of Man*, by weavers at their looms, tailors cross-legged on their benches, cobblers at their lasts, and ploughmen loitering round the smithy when the horses were being shod, talking wildly, incoherently of the "rights of man." Burns had fallen in, as he winced under social inequality, with this fashion. Years before Dr. Blair had, with unusual shrewdness, said "his politics smelt of the smithy." His democratic spirit, though chiefly due to a generous feeling of philanthropy, had something in it of personal grievance that he himself should give way before "yon birky ca'ed a lord." "A man's a man for a' that" was not entirely a cheap maxim to voice the equality of man —it was also an assertion of jealous revolt against the empty rank and fortune which society honoured. In this mood his good sense and prudence sometimes failed him. His sympathies with the French Revolution and political reform were too pronounced, and his opinions were too outspoken not to come to the ears of authorities, and the Excise Board began inquiries into his conduct as of one disaffected to the Government. Dreading lest he should be dismissed, and his wife and family left destitute, in full alarm he besought his patron Graham of Fintry, who was one of the Commissioners of the Excise, to intercede "to save me from that misery which threatens me, and which—with my latest breath—I will say I have not deserved."[1] This was a humiliating position for such a man. Fortunately, with a rebuke and a warning, the storm blew by, and the poet-turned-politician, the exciseman-turned-democrat had cause for thankfulness that he escaped so easily, seeing that those were days when "Friends of the People" received drastic treatment at the hands of Tory judges. Yet even after this trouble his feelings in hot moods were shown, to the scandal of quiet citizens. When at a large dinner, after the toast of William Pitt was drunk, he left in high dudgeon because he was not allowed to give his toast: "To George Washington, a better man." When at another, he proposed the sentiment: "May our success in the present war be equal to the justice of our cause"—which brought upon him an

[1] Chambers, iii. 274.

affront which he would have challenged had he not feared to risk the peace and welfare of his wife and family on a drunken squabble. Not yet was forgotten his act of fatuous braggadocio a year before, when, after seizing a smuggling vessel as exciseman, he bought four carronades as politician, and packed them off to the National Convention as a mark of his sympathy—which gift, with his letter, was intercepted at the Dover Custom-House. This action of presenting four guns valued at £3 from a gauger to a foreign state was chiefly faulty for displaying a curious lack of humour. All these escapades were forgotten and forgiven when, after war with France broke out, none proved more loyal and enthusiastically patriotic than he.

It is a sad truth that the last years of his life showed a woeful declension in social esteem and self-respect. Friends looked doubtfully askance at him, great folk, lairds and ladies, no longer welcomed him as of old. When a gentleman, meeting him one day in Dumfries, proposed that he should cross the street to join a group of ladies and gentlemen, " Nay, nay," he bitterly replied, " my young friend, that is all over now," and he quoted the lines of Lady Grisell Baillie with the pathetic refrain : " And werena my heart licht I wad dee."

The best proof, however, that the stories of his dissipation and drunkenness in these last years must have been exaggerated consists in the wealth of lyrics he contributed to literature. His power for composing great works was either dead or dormant, but his lyric gifts were still splendid in these last days. To the volumes of Johnson's *Scots Musical Museum*, of which he had been virtual editor, he had contributed one hundred and eighty-four songs since 1787 ; for George Thomson's collection he contributed sixty-four, original or adapted —all sent without money and without price. Devoted to Scots music and minstrelsy, he had a patriotic enthusiasm for their preservation ; and he refused payment for any one of those songs which he lavished with bewildering prodigality on Johnson and Thomson. He was even full of gratitude at Thomson's munificence in sending a shawl for his wife, and a little picture by Allan to himself. Never was there a less mercenary soul than he, having nothing in common with Dr. Johnson, who said a man was a blockhead who did not write

for money. To many old airs there were only snatches
of the original songs surviving — if any part was good,
he would retain a verse or a line; if they were coarse or
poor, new words were written. With unerring touch and tact
he would change some poor catch into a lyric, which for light
grace, pathos, or humour was matchless. A phrase changed
here, a verse transposed there, and, as if by magic, the crudity,
the grossness vanished, and a work of perfect art was
made.[1] He was not thinking of fame, still less of gain, when
he wrote; it was only to give new life to old music, new
beauty to old songs. It is true that closer research has shown
that many lyrics which were supposed to be entirely original
were really founded on ancient words, which had a lively
originality of their own—like "Whistle, and I'll come to you
my lad," whose initial verse he takes from old work. It is
true that "Auld Lang Syne," like many others, is but
a mosaic of his own and some long dead singers; but so
far from seeking credit for making it, he even pretended
to George Thomson that he had heard it from an old
man's lips. All this may diminish the claim made for
him—not by him—to marvellous originality. But it is worse
than foolish to speak of these fragments he wove into his verse
as "pilferings."[2] A man cannot be said to steal verses and
phrases from others, when he is really giving to them his own
infinitely finer skill and art, to inform them with fresh life and
to shape them to perfect form. Long before his poems were
published, he had been composing songs, rhyming epistles, satires
which he never dreamt would meet the public eye. Even the
"Jolly Beggars," that splendid achievement, he never printed,
even forgetting what he had written in it after that night John

---

[1] Literary taste is a capricious thing, as is exemplified in a story by Aubrey
de Vere : "'Read the exquisite songs of Burns,' Tennyson exclaimed, 'in shape
each of them has the perfection of the berry ; in light the radiance of a dew-
drop ! You forget for its sake those stupid things, his serious pieces ' The
same day I met Wordsworth and named Burns to him. Wordsworth
praised him even more vehemently than Tennyson had done, as the great
genius who had brought poetry back to Nature, but ended : 'Of course I refer
to his serious efforts, such as the "Cottar's Saturday Night"; these follow little
songs of his one has to forget.' I told the tale to Henry Taylor that evening ;
but his answer was : 'Burns's exquisite songs and Burns's serious efforts are to
me alike tedious and disagreeable reading'" (*Memoir of Tennyson*, i. 211).

[2] Henley's *Essay on Burns, passim.*

Richmond and he looked into the boosing-ken of Poosie Nansie, with its tramps, tinkers, and scoundrels. Yet this, which was almost the best work of his genius, he cast aside, to be surreptitiously published after his death. If in these works, as well as in his songs, there are forms of verse and words which he had met with in the course of his reading, it was due to a curious carelessness. It was not to deceive the world by decking himself in borrowed plumes, for they are poorer feathers than his own, and he never thought the world would see his lines or know his name. He invented no new measure, but used the traditional forms of stanza, and that was natural. It does not matter who made a mould, it is only of importance what metal is put into it—others had run in lead, Burns poured in pure gold.

Step by step came the inevitable end. Troubles had increased in 1795; his only daughter, to whom he was devotedly attached, died; his melancholy, which came through all his life in fitful moods, hovered over him; he was troubled with debt,[1] burdened with rheumatism, and his careless living made his ailments worse. Hardly had he recovered from a fever, when, on coming home drunk from a jovial party at the Globe Tavern, at three o'clock in the morning, he fell asleep in the snow, and all his troubles came back redoubled—at every debauch he knew he parted with a "slice of his constitution." With shattered health he was taken to Brow, a village on the Solway, emaciated and worn, and there Mrs. Walter Riddell, who also had come there for her health, met the poet, to whom she was reconciled. As he called on her his salutation was, with a sad smile upon the wan face: "Well, madam, have you any commands for the other world?" She saw "the stamp of death impressed on his features, seeming already on the brink of eternity." He spoke as a doomed man, with regrets for the past, with anxiety for his family, with fears for the letters and papers written with unguarded freedom, which might be unearthed after his death

---

[1] Chambers estimated that Burns's income, including his salary of £50, which was usually increased by extra allowances to £70, would, with perquisites, be equal to about £90 (iv. 124). Though he could have made money by publishing poems that were passing from friend to friend in manuscript, he would not consent, fearing to lessen his reputation.

to damage his name. Worry and anxiety vexed his dying months. A lawyer, demanding payment to a client of a wretched £7, price of his volunteer's uniform, put him in dread of being sent to jail, and in agony of mind he for the first time sent for £5 to Thomson in Edinburgh, to whom he had been sending packets of priceless song for which he would accept no return. "Do, for God's sake, send me that sum, and that by return of post. Forgive this earnestness, but the horrors of jail have made me half-distracted. I do not ask all this gratuitously, for upon returning health I hereby promise to furnish you with five pounds worth of the neatest song-genius you have seen."

In July the dying poet was back at Dumfries, worse than when he left it. Tended by the daughter of a friend, he died on 21st July 1796, while his wife was on child-bed in another room—his last thought being the bitterness of the fear of prison.[1] When the company was attending the funeral, his wife was giving birth to a child.

The tragic close came with all the inevitableness of fate. Only one end was possible to the broken career of that genius, with generous heart, independent spirit, strong passions, and a faulty life. Death to him was not the "last enemy," but now his best friend.

[1] Chambers's *Life and Works*, iv. 205.

CHAPTER XV

HENRY MACKENZIE—DUGALD STEWART—CLOSE OF THE CENTURY

In 1771 a small volume appeared anonymously called *The Man of Feeling*. Soaked with sentiment, it gives the story of a man sensitive to his finger-tips to every form of emotion, who passes through a succession of harrowing scenes, by which he is wrung with agonised compassion. At once it gained popularity. The libraries of Tunbridge Wells, Bath, and Cheltenham were besieged by ladies demanding to be the first to read it; it lay on the drawing-room tables of every one pretending to fashion, who, jaded with routs and gaming-tables, wept till their rouged and powdered cheeks presented runnels of tears, like cracks on old china, over " dear, good Mr. Harley," who would not let a beggar pass without a shilling and a sigh, though the reader herself would not cross a puddle to save a life. This novel appeared at a period when the tide of sentiment had been set flowing by *Clarissa Harlowe*, which was then affecting "feeling hearts" in England, to whom Sterne's *Sentimental Journey* appealed adroitly with its falsetto pathos.

The author, whose name the public did not know, was a kindly, lively, hard-headed man of business. Born in August 1747, in Libberton's Wynd, Henry Mackenzie from his earliest days was familiar with the brightest, liveliest literary company in Edinburgh. As a boy he heard the best talk in High Street flats, when up the dark stairs ladies and men of note picked their steps carefully over the dirt to reach them. As they drank their tea he was proud to hand round cups and napkins for their laps, and listened wonderingly to great literati's talk. Destined for the legal profession, he studied

Exchequer business in London, and married and settled as a lawyer in his native town.

In a lofty tenement in M'Lelland's Land, where the Cowgate joins the Grassmarket, for years lived old Dr. Mackenzie, his second wife and family, with Henry Mackenzie, his wife and children—all forming a harmonious and genial household. On the third floor Mrs. Sym, Principal Robertson's sister, kept boarders—one of them being young Mr. Brougham of Brougham Hall, who was to marry the daughter, Eleanor, and become father of Lord Brougham. From the windows they looked down on the twenty carriers' carts which came from and departed to all parts of Scotland from Candlemaker Row.

He was at the age of twenty-six when he turned from his writs and his law cases to write the book on the fame of which his memory and his familiar title the "Man of Feeling" rest. As no one claimed this anonymous work, a Mr. John Eccles, an Irish clergyman living in Bath, thought it a pity that its authorship should go a-begging, so he carefully transcribed the whole book, made appropriate blots and pseudo corrections to give his papers a plausible appearance of being an original manuscript, and fatuously proclaimed it to be his own. The publishers denied the claims of this poor creature, whose death in trying to save a boy from drowning in the Avon may be allowed to atone for his mendacity. Evidently in Bath his imposture was not known, for in the *Gentleman's Magazine* of 1777 there are verses "by an invalid" "on seeing the turfless grave" of the Rev. Mr. Eccles, winding up with a proposed epitaph which begins:

> Beneath this stone "The Man of Feeling" lies:
> Humanity had marked him for his own,
> His virtues raised him to his native skies,
> Ere half his merit to the world was known.[1]

The phrase "beneath this stone 'The Man of Feeling' *lies*" is excellently appropriate.

In the tale the Man of Feeling sets forth for London, on his journey encountering characters that touch his "sensible

---

[1] *Gentleman's Magazine*, May 1777, pp. 404, 452; Boswell's *Johnson* (ed. Hill), i. 423.

HENRY MACKENZIE
From the Painting by W. Staveley in the Scottish National Portrait Gallery, Edinburgh.

heart"—for "sensible" was not the prosaic cold-blooded quality of to-day. Beggars on the road who steal hens and tell fortunes win his charity and his tears; humorists in inns impose on his infantine simplicity; he visits Bedlam— then one of the favourite sights of London for pleasure-parties —where he witnesses with anguish the lunatics, on straw and in fetters, who moved the visitors to merriment. From scene to scene he passes, his good-nature imposed on by rogues and his heart touched by the misery of unfortunates whom he restores to peace. At last, after a quaint love episode, Mr. Harley dies. The book is moist with weeping. The hero is always ready with "the tribute of a tear." An old cobbler turns out to be a friend of his youth. "'Edwards,' cried Mr. Harley, 'O Heavens!' and he sprang to embrace him, 'let me clasp thy knees on which I have sat so often'"; and after hearing his tale he "gave vent to the fulness of his heart by a shower of tears." "'Edwards, let me hold thee to my bosom, let me imprint the virtues of thy suffering on my soul,'" etc. A shepherd blows his horn. "The romantic melancholy quite overcame him, he dropped a tear." The lachrymal ducts are in excessive working order in all the characters, and Mr. Harley is an inveterate sobber. There is in the novel a gentle humour which reminds us of Goldsmith's, a pathos that recalls that of Richardson, and a lack of strength which is the author's very own. Yet here is a tale which in a few years Burns was to prize—of course "next to the Bible"—which he bore about his person as he ploughed, and fingered till two copies were worn out; one of the books of sentiment on which he says he "endeavoured to form his conduct," and which he loved incessantly to quote.[1] Samuel Rogers in his youth went to Edinburgh, anxious to see—not Dr. Robertson or Adam Smith, but the author of *The Man of Feeling*.[2]

The success of his story stimulated Mackenzie to write *The Man of the World*, a contrast to the tearful Mr. Harley. Here

---

[1] Chambers's *Life and Works of Burns*, i. 64: "In the charming words of my favourite author, 'May the Great Spirit bear up the weight of thy grey hairs and blunt the arrows that bring them rest'" (Chambers's *Burns*, iv. 180).
[2] Clayden's *Early Days of Rogers*, p. 112.

is a man who rushes into selfish pleasures, and consequent misery and ruin. Even here the sentimentalist plies his business—good persons in the pages are strongly addicted to tears. Though it tries to be vivacious, it is dull reading to-day. In fact, the only things not dry in the novel are the eyes of its personages. In *Julie de Roubigné*, his next work, he strikes a more tender chord, and works out a finer theme, though not too powerfully. There is, however, pathos in this epistolary romance. Sir Walter Scott called it "one of the most heart-wringing histories that has ever been written"; but "heart-wringing" is not the sensation one feels to-day as we take it from the highest shelf, blow the top and bang the boards together to dispel the dust of years that has fallen undisturbed upon it. Allan Cunningham said it was too melancholy to read; Christopher North pronounced it of all Mackenzie's works the "most delightful."

It is sad destiny which makes the fine thoughts of yesterday the platitudes of to-day, and the pathos of one age the maudlin sentiment of the next. We cannot weep over what our fathers, and especially our mothers, cried half a century ago. One day at a country-house the company wanted something to be read aloud. *The Man of Feeling* was selected, though some were afraid it might prove too affecting. Lady Louisa Stuart tells the result: "I, who was the reader, had not seen it for many years [this was in 1826]. The rest did not know it at all. I am afraid I perceived a sad change in it, or myself, which was worse, and the effect altogether failed. Nobody cried, and at some passages, the touches that I used to think so exquisite—oh dear! they laughed. I thought we never should get over Harley's walking down to breakfast with his shoe-buckles in his hand. Yet I remember so well its first publication, my mother and sisters crying over it, dwelling on it with rapture."[1]

While writing touchingly, and with a gentle humour too, books to which he never put his name, the author was passing an active, prosaic legal existence in Edinburgh. No pathetic lachrymose Mr. Harley was he, but Henry Mackenzie, Writer to the Signet, keen as a hawk over a title-deed, shrewd

[1] *Lady Louisa Stuart*, edit. by Home, p. 235.

as a ferret over a pleading — indifferent to the tears of
defendants in his insistence on the claims of his clients. He
had his sentiment under perfect control. See him at a cock-
fight in a Canongate slum, among an eager throng of beaux,
burglars, and bullies, in the dirty, ill-smelling, ill-lighted cockpit, his kindly face all alert, and his heart palpitating with
excitement as he watches the "mains" and the mangled bodies
of disfeathered, bleeding combatants, which would have made
Mr. Harley sob his heart out. After the fight of fowls was
over, up the turnpike stair to his house jubilant he would go,
proclaiming that he had had "a glorious night." "Where had
he been?" "Why, at a splendid fight!" "Oh, Harry,
Harry," his wife would plaintively exclaim, "you have only
feeling on paper!"[1]

The "Man of Feeling," by which name the literary lawyer
became and remains known, was incessantly busy with
literature. There were plays which managers declined to
take; plays, such as the *Prince of Tunis*, which the public
declined to see; there were essays in the *Mirror* and the
Lounger, which were published weekly in Edinburgh, modelled
after the *Spectator* or the *Adventurer*, containing contributions
from lawyers addicted to polite letters, like Lord Craig and Lord
Hailes, by not very humorous humorists, mildly facetious,
politely moralising, with literary reviews which were sensibly
critical. The best papers were by Mackenzie — such as his
"La Roche," in which he delineates delicately David Hume,
and his warm appreciations of the new poet, Robert Burns, in
1787. Characteristically the amiable literary sentimentalist
singles out for special praise the addresses "To a Mouse" and
"To a Mountain Daisy." His novels, his essays, his abortive
plays, with his biographies of John Home and Blacklock, form
the staple of works which he consigned to posterity in eight
volumes octavo.

It is really the character of the man rather than his writings
which retains our interest in the patriarch of letters, who died
in 1831, the last survivor of a brilliant age. In his young days
he had danced in the Old Assembly rooms in Bell's Close, and
danced attendance at the concerts of St. Cecilia's Hall in Niddry

[1] Burgon's *Life of Patrick F. Tytler*, p. 25.

Wynd. He had been a welcome guest and pleasant entertainer of Hume and Blair, and of Adam Smith and Lord Kames. He was the gentlest visitor in the little parlour of Dr. Blacklock, where the blind poet would stand to recite his verses with his strangely swaying body, and there he had seen great Dr. Johnson talk loudly and swallow slobberingly the nineteen cups of tea which caused such dismay to good Mrs. Blacklock. He had seen, as time passed on, the men who had shed lustre on Scottish literature grow old and feeble, attired still in the cocked hats and trim wigs, each bearing the long staff, which were old-world fashions to a new century—surviving as toothless shadows of their olden selves. He saw them die one by one, leaving fragrant memories behind them, as link after link was broken with the quaint past when literature was styled "Belles Lettres."

As he grew old his memory was stored with curious recollections of the past, to which persons of another century loved to listen, when the modern political air was filled with talk of a Reform Bill. He could remember when the ground covered by the New Town was fields and meadows; and cattle browsed where Princes Street now stands; he had caught eels in the Nor' Loch when Princes Street Gardens were not even a dream of the future; he had shot snipe and coursed hares where George Street now runs; and got curds and cream at the remote inn called "Peace and Plenty," on the place where Heriot Row, in which he was living, was built.[1] The High Street when he was young had been thronged with the finest of Scottish fashion and learning and wealth, who dwelt in those miserable flats which, when he was middle-aged, he saw abandoned to the poor and the squalid. In his old age he looked back on that poor and dingy past with romantic affection.

When he was past eighty, visitors at Heriot Row found the lively little patriarch in his study,[2] seated in the highbacked chair, with his black velvet cap, his brown wig, his face with innumerable wrinkles, his blue eyes shrewd beneath his white eyebrows, munching out his words with mouth sans

---

[1] Scott's *Works*, iv. 178.
[2] *Peter's Letters to his Kinsfolk*, i. pp. 106-9.

teeth, while his wife, the graceful old lady, sat in black silk gown, high cap, fixed with lace beneath her chin; and as each visitor came in there was the eager talk of all that was going on that day. Sir Walter Scott describes[1] the old gentleman on his visit to Abbotsford setting forth on a shooting expedition attired in white hat turned up with green, green jacket, green spectacles, brown leather gaiters, a dog whistle round his wrinkled neck, like a venerable Mr. Winkle—a juvenile of eighty years of age, as eager after a hare as after a law deed, sharp as a needle on politics or trout. The attenuated figure was to be seen on days when hardly any mortal could venture out, as the wind blew hurricanes, tottering across the North Bridge before the blast, his big surtout clinging close to his fragile figure.[2] On such a tempestuous day he would pass eagerly and panting into the printing-office of John Ballantyne—the clever, lively, and bibulous printer receiving him with profound obeisance, as he came to look over some proofs for his friend Walter Scott. At last the familiar face was seen no more—thin, shrivelled, yellow, and "kiln-dried," with its profile like that of an amiable Voltaire.[3]

When he died on the 14th of January 1831 the new generation had almost forgotten the writings of the "Man of Feeling," though the old remembered in their youth having read with moist eyes the once famous books of which Lockhart speaks with unwonted gentleness: "The very names of the heroes and heroines sounded in my ears like the echoes of some old romantic melody, too simple, too beautiful to have been framed in those degenerate, over-scientific days. Harley, La Roche, Montalban, Julie de Roubigné, what graceful mellow music is in the well-remembered cadences!"[4] Where are they now? Where are the roses of last summer?

Dugald Stewart

When society was still sentimental over Julie de Roubigné, more robust intellects were interested by the

[1] Lockhart's *Scott*, vi. 240; iii. 140.
[2] R. P. Gillies's *Memoirs of a Literary Veteran*, iii. 51.
[3] Cockburn's *Memorials*, p. 265.
[4] *Peter's Letters to his Kinsfolk*, i. 109.

lectures at the College of Dugald Stewart, who was teaching with eloquence the philosophy of Thomas Reid. When the views and arguments of the old master were expounded to enthusiastic students in the classroom of the new College, never had philosophy been so agreeable, so intelligible. As it came from the lips of the urbane teacher, psychology seemed almost an intellectual pastime. One remembers Sydney Smith's jokes about the Scots' love for "metapheesics," and of his overhearing at a ball a young lady remark to her partner in the dance, "What you say, my lord, is very true of love in the *aibstract*———" the rest of the sentence being unfortunately drowned by the tumult of the fiddles. In truth, Stewart did make mental philosophy a pleasant theme even for drawing-rooms. There was something fascinating in this professor, with broad, bald head, bushy eyebrows, and eyes of alert intelligence, standing at his desk[1] prelecting on mental powers and moral qualities with only notes before him, uttering with pleasing soft voice his mellifluous sentences and sonorous periods "possessed of cathedral pomp."

He was born in 1751 in the precincts of the College, where his father, Matthew Stewart, the Professor of Mathematics, resided—that lively little geometer who had made a very brilliant scientific reputation after quitting his quiet manse of Roseneath. After studying in the College at Edinburgh, young Stewart went to Glasgow, where he lodged along with his friend Archibald Alison, who was to become known as an admired preacher of the Scottish Episcopal Church, and to be esteemed as the author of an *Essay on Taste*—the last of that century's many futile theories concerning the "Beautiful." Doubtless the attraction to the western university was the teaching of Professor Reid, and he eagerly imbibed from those plain and ponderous lectures the principles of "common-sense philosophy" which he himself was to expound in after years with an eloquence to which philosophy was quite unaccustomed.

When his father was laid aside by illness, Stewart, though only nineteen years old, acted as his substitute, and when Adam Ferguson went to America on the futile Peace Com-

[1] Cockburn's *Memorials*, p. 25.

DUGALD STEWART
From the Mezzotint Engraving after Raeburn.

mission, he also undertook to lecture for his friend on Moral Philosophy, with the easy versatility peculiar to those perfunctory days. It was on a Thursday he was asked if he would teach ethics, and he was ready to begin on the Monday, daily working up his lectures with infinite zest as he paced up and down the College gardens. No wonder when the session was done the young man was so exhausted that he required to be lifted into a carriage. Relying on Stewart's varied accomplishments, whenever a professor was ill or abroad he would ask him to take his duty, and Stewart was ready at once to teach Rhetoric or Logic or Greek.

On his father's death [1] he succeeded to the chair of Mathematics, but he was glad to exchange that post for the chair of Moral Philosophy ten years after, on Ferguson's retiral, in 1785—for he owns he was "groaning at teaching Euclid for the thirteenth time." Now he was in his element. With no great capacity for intellectual subtleties, no love for metaphysical problems, he studied the powers and faculties of the mind, the passions and emotions of the heart, with the minuteness of an observant naturalist. His opinions and his system were substantially those of his master Thomas Reid. He broke no new ground, indulged in no original speculation. He had a cautious and astute way of evading difficulties, and when his students were expectant as he approached some fine problem, he usually deferred the solution to another day which never arrived.[2] But then his literary grace none disputed; his exquisite elocution bore off the fine-sounding sentences and added beauty to his poetical quotations; his art of putting things was admirable, the speculations of others became clear and attractive, set forth with his copious—too copious—illustrations and fluent periods, too diffuse and ornate. Of German philosophers, since they had given up writing in

---

[1] Stewart's *Works*, ix.; Memoir by Veitch.
[2] Cockburn, p. 26; *Memoir of Sydney Smith*, ii. p. 134. Sydney Smith writes characteristically of his timid old friend. "We have had Dugald Stewart and his family here for a few days. We spoke much of the weather and other harmless subjects. He became once, however, a little elevated, and in the gaiety of his soul let out some opinions which will doubtless make him writhe with remorse. He went so far as to say he considered the King's recovery as very problematical' (*Memoir of Sydney Smith*, ii. p. 90).

Latin, he knew nothing, for he was ignorant of their language, and of Kant he owned he could make nothing.[1]

For many a year—ever since Blair and Ferguson began to teach—it had been the fashion for members of English families of rank and fortune to be sent to Scottish Universities, to attend lectures of professors whose fame was far spread, and they were welcomed like godsends as boarders by those teachers who were glad to have additions to their humble incomes. Towards the end of the century, when the war hindered travelling and studying abroad, high-born youths in greater numbers came north, either with their tutors or to live with professors, who could look after their morals and their studies. Noblemen did not grudge £400 for the privilege of their son being admitted to Professor Stewart's charming home. On the benches in the College sat Lord Henry Petty, afterwards Lord Lansdowne, and lads to be afterwards notable as Lord Palmerston, Lord John Russell, Lord Dudley and Ward, who had as class-mates Henry Brougham, Francis Horner, Henry Cockburn, and Francis Jeffrey. These men looked fondly back in their older years to those delightful days of plain living and high thinking in Edinburgh, "amidst odious smells, barbarous sounds, bad suppers, excellent hearts, and most enlightened and cultivated understandings,"[2] where they studied under Playfair and Robison and Dalziel. But it was Dugald Stewart whom they regarded as their master, as he set forth fine moral aims and ideals—especially when discussing the application of ethics to the principles of government and the conduct of citizens in political life. He was liberal in politics, and when the French Revolution came, with its rage of democracy, Whig views were regarded with dismay. The very phrase "*political* economy" had to the ears of parents a suspicious sound, unaware that it concerned itself with such innocuous affairs as duties on corn and malt, free trade and exchange. Dreading all dangerous sentiments Francis Jeffrey's father kept his son out of that classroom[3] lest his mind should be contaminated with demo-

---

[1] This is apparent enough in his *Dissertation on the Progress of Metaphysical Philosophy.*
[2] *Memoir of Sydney Smith*, i. 22.   [3] Cockburn's *Life of Jeffrey*, i. 52.

cratic heresies. Never, however, was there a man less revolutionary than that mild, polished, most prudent gentleman. As Henry Cockburn listened in his boyhood to the persuasive eloquence, he felt his whole nature changed by his teacher: "his noble views unfolded in glorious sentences elevated me into a higher world."[1] Francis Horner was touched and moved to admiration; and it was the inculcating of high moral purpose on men and citizens which influenced young men who had a public career before them. As Sir James Mackintosh said, his disciples were his best works. He was, in fact, an eloquent philosophic preacher. This position he retained till he retired in 1811, when Thomas Brown succeeded him, and dismayed him by teaching doctrines he vehemently rejected.

In the class and out of it he was the same—the courteous, kindly gentleman. No gatherings were more delightful than those at his house every fortnight—at the old house in Horse Wynd and at Ainslie Place, with his accomplished, clever, plain-faced wife as hostess. His rooms were the resort of all persons of position and culture in the city. The same attention was paid to the awkward student, who trod the carpet shrinking at every squeak his new pumps made on the floor, as to the judge or peer, to whom the company was deferential. There Whig and Tory both agreed, political and ecclesiastical differences were laid aside for the evening. Not being gifted with much humour, it was all the more delightful to catch the eminent philosopher in some playful mood, as at Woodhouselee, when, on opening the drawing-room door, the old professor was discovered playing with little Patrick Tytler, his host's son, the future historian of Scotland—both prancing on the floor, seeing which should longest maintain the peacock's feathers poised on their respective noses.[2] In his country house at Catrine and in Edinburgh he entertained Robert Burns, not with the pompous patronage of old Dr. Blair, not with the peddling criticism of Dr. Gregory, but with the easy frankness of a friend. All these social and intellectual graces he bore finely to his death in 1829.[3] No great

---
[1] Cockburn's *Memorials*, p. 26.   [2] Burgon's *Life of Patrick F. Tytler*.
[3] When Stewart's death was announced at a large dinner-party in England,

thinker, no founder of any new school of speculation, he was an acute exponent, a stimulating teacher of an accepted philosophy; according to Lord Cockburn, "one of the greatest didactic orators."

CLOSE OF THE CENTURY

As the century drew to its close the men of the old generation were passing away one by one. Venerable, picturesque figures they were, who had contributed so long to the social and intellectual life of the country. In 1790 died the historian, Dr. Robert Henry, minister of the Old Kirk of Edinburgh—who should not pass without notice—a man of whom we hear little in literary and convivial circles, though respected as a worthy member of them. It was in 1771 the first volume of his *History of Scotland* was published—a history formed on an original plan, each period having its political, military, literary, social, ecclesiastical affairs treated in separate departments. The writer appreciated better than other men the importance of studying the social movements of a nation as essential parts of its real history, and in his wake later historians were led to follow. It was a work novel in design, showing ability and industry, if not great literary skill, which met with praise both from men of letters and from his Church, which elected him Moderator of the General Assembly. Published at his own cost, though afterwards he sold it for £3000, it came out in successive quartos from 1771 to 1785. As on fine sunny days the wasps abound, so when prosperity is shining on an author literary wasps are sure to come forth. That clever but consummate rascal Gilbert Stuart, who was venomous whether he was drunk or sober, attacked Henry and his works with untiring pertinacity. In 1773 he had tried his utmost to vent his spleen on men of letters as editor of the *Edinburgh Magazine*—on Monboddo, Kames, Robertson, Henry —and when all this became intolerable in Edinburgh, he sought

---

the news was received with levity by a lady of rank. Sydney Smith, who sat beside her, turned round and cuttingly said: "Madam, when we are told of the death of so great a man as Mr. Dugald Stewart, it is usual in civilised society to be grave for at least the space of five minutes" (*Memoir*, i. 319).

an outlet for his malice in London newspapers and reviews.[1] Dr. Henry was his special victim; he "vowed to crush his work." On every opportunity this amiable divine was attacked — his sermons, his speeches, his book — till the sale of his *History* was stopped, and the work to which he had devoted his many years and his few savings seemed ruined. Stuart would spy out when he was going to London to look after the sale of his work, and then in hot haste would write to his satellites in London to have damaging paragraphs in the *Chronicle* or elsewhere to scathe him on his arrival. In 1775 the scoundrel gloated over rumours that his victim was dying, and jubilantly he writes: "Poor Henry is on the point of death, and his friends declare that I have killed him. I have received this information as a compliment."[2] However, the reverend doctor survived the malice of his assailant, and the assailant himself, who, after making a considerable name as an able, florid writer on history, died of intemperance. Of the rascal's habits many stories were flying. Smellie, the printer, would relate how the man, when intoxicated, staggered into the ash-pit of a great steam-engine which stood by the roadside, and, awakening from drunken sleep, as he saw the furnace opened and grimy black figures stoking the fire and raking the bars of the enormous grate, while the machinery clanked furiously with its beams and chains, he thought that this was hell, and in horror exclaimed, "Good God, is it come to this at last!"[3]

Dr. Henry was one of those characteristic Moderates of the old school who were genial in society, humorous at table, and deplorably dry—and deliciously conscious of being dry —in the pulpit. He belonged to that class of ministers who, according to Lord Robertson, of facetious memory, "are better in bottle than in wood." His colleague was Dr. James MacKnight, an estimable and learned divine, whose *Harmony of the Gospels* was regarded in its day as a marvel of criticism, though simple folk wondered that the doctor should write a

---
[1] Hume's *Letters to Strahan*, p. 158 ; Kerr's *Life of Smellie*, i.
[2] Disraeli's *Quarrels and Calamities of Authors*, 1858, p. 135.
[3] Kerr's *Life of W. Smellie*, i. 304.

book to " make four men agree who never cast oot."[1] Like the historian he was deeply dull as a preacher, so that the Old Kirk pews were sparsely attended by a slumbrous congregation. Dr. Henry would quietly observe to his friend that it was a blessing they were ministers of the same church, for otherwise " there would be two toom (empty) kirks instead of one." One pouring Sabbath Dr. MacKnight came into the vestry drenched. Carefully the beadle wiped him down, as the bells were "ringing in," and the harmonist anxiously exclaimed, " Oh! I wush I was dry—I wush I was dry; do you think I'm dry noo?" " Never mind, doctor," the historian consolingly remarked, " when ye get to the pulpit ye'll be dry eneuch." It was in 1790 that one day a summons came to the Rev. Sir Henry Moncreiff to come and see Dr. Henry at Stirling. " Come out directly, I have got something to do this week—I have got to die." He found his friend sinking fast, but cheerful and chatty; and as they were talking a neighbouring minister was announced. " That wearisome body!" sighed Mrs. Henry. " Keep him oot—keep him oot; dinna let the cratur in!" exclaimed the moribund divine. But in he came, and the sick man, with a meaning wink at his attendants, closed his eyes as if fast asleep. The visitor sat motionless, waiting for the invalid to awake, and if he ventured to whisper, a motion of Mrs. Henry's finger to her lips reduced him to silence. At last he slipped out on tiptoe, and as the door was closed the dying man opened his eyes and broke into a merry laugh.[2] That night the old man was dead, at the age of seventy-two.

In the same year passed away Dr. Cullen, eminent as a physician, a lecturer on physiology, a reformer in medicine a brilliant teacher in his chair of Theory of Physic, and

---

[1] "I think I see his large, square, bony visage, his enormous white wig, girdled by many tiers of curls, his old, snuffy black clothes, his broad, flat felt, and his threadbare blue greatcoat. He rarely walked without reading. His elbows were stuck immovably to his haunches, on which they rested as brackets and enabled him to form a desk for his book. In this attitude he shuffled forward [in the Meadows] at the rate of half an inch a step, moving his rigid, angular bulk forward without giving place to any person or thing, or being aware there was anything in the world except himself and his volume. He died in 1800" (Cockburn's *Memorials*, p. 53).

[2] Cockburn's *Memorials*, p. 51.

ROBERT HENRY
From the Painting by David Martin in the Scottish National Portrait Gallery, Edinburgh.

Edinburgh missed that tall, slouching man, with his massive wig and cocked hat, huge arched nose and pendulous lips, who used to walk contemplatively up the street with his hand in the bosom of his coat, or be borne in a sedan-chair to patients. Dr. Joseph Black, the brilliant chemist, was to be seen till 1799—the year Lord Monboddo died—tall, cadaverously pale, with face of sweetest expression, and dark, clear, benignant eyes, the sparse hair carefully powdered and gathered into a long, thin queue, and his body clad in speckless black coat and silk stockings and silvered buckles, carrying a green silk umbrella. Everybody honoured and loved him. Rough boys and impudent caddies made way respectfully for him on the pavement. One day in March he was found dead in his study—before him his simple fare of bread and a few prunes, and carefully measured quantity of milk and water, his cup set on his knees, held by his hand, as if he had just ceased to speak.[1]

Others of an illustrious brotherhood survived. Dr. Carlyle lived on, active, vivacious, full of social and literary interests, and wondrous handsome, with that figure which age had not bent when he died in 1805. "He was one of the noblest-looking old gentlemen I almost ever beheld," says Lord Cockburn. Dr. Adam Ferguson was hale and rosy in silvered old age; and John Home, pleasant, good-humoured, but mentally enfeebled. These old friends had stood at the grave of their old companion Dr. Robertson in 1793 and of Dr. Blair in 1800.

In the College were professors well sustaining the fame of the venerable university. In the chair of Medicine was Dr. James Gregory, successor to his father, one of a family which had sent into the world many men of science throughout a century—one of the most able of lecturers, acute, bluff, and caustic, constantly in professional disputes, when his opinions were generally right, and engaged in feuds, when his ways were always wrong—maintaining his cause both by his ferocious pamphlets, which he hurled forth in huge quartos, and by his stick, which mauled his opponent Dr. Hamilton—though he avowed, as he paid the fine of £100, that he would will-

[1] Black's *Lectures*, i.; Memoir by Robison, p. 74.

ingly pay double to do it again. His appearance conformed
to his militant character—a large figure, bold and stalwart,
walking with his cane suggestively over his shoulder like a
weapon.[1] A fine Latinist, in frequent request to concoct
epitaphs and dedications, he knew a good deal of literature and
a great deal of physic. His kindliness and virtues were to
remain long fragrant in the memories of the people, while his
famed and infamous "Gregory's mixture" was to stink in their
nostrils. Professor Playfair was lecturing to full classrooms
on mathematics, with a European fame as a scientific writer;
adored by students, liked by all men and loved by all women,
of whom this "philanderer of the needles," as Jeffrey called
him, was a devoted champion. He was growing more youthful
in soul as he grew old in body, with a florid face of beaming
good-nature. As his fellow-professor he had Dr. John Robison in the chair of Natural Philosophy, who was to continue
till 1805 his distinguished career in mechanical philosophy.
Quaint in character as in appearance, this philosopher was a
lively, humorous man in spite of bouts of hypochondria—unconventional in dress as in opinion, with his long pigtail, thin and
curled, hanging down his back; his enormous head surmounted
by a huge cocked hat when walking the High Street, and by a
capacious nightcap when in his study; having the legs of his vast
frame covered up to the thighs with white worsted hose.[2]

By the close of the century the clergy had almost
ceased to contribute to science, learning, and letters, though
many were admirable writers on agriculture.[3] The wonderful
crop of able men who were born between 1718 and 1724,
and entered the Church when it was freeing itself from the
fanaticism of the "wild party" and the domination of the
people, had few successors. At the middle of the century,
and on to about 1770, the clergy held a higher social
position than they did at any other time. "With the advantages always of a classical, and sometimes of a polite,
education, their knowledge," says Henry Mackenzie, "was

[1] Kay's *Edinburgh Portraits*, i. 450; and as in Raeburn's portrait
[2] Cockburn's *Memorials*, p. 264; Raeburn's portrait of Robison.
[3] The best county surveys of agriculture issued by the Board of Agriculture
were written by shrewd moderate clergymen who farmed their land

equal or superior to that of any man in their parish. When the value of land was low, and when proprietors lived more at home, the clergyman stood high in the scale of rank among his parishioners, and, as I can well remember, was able to maintain a certain style of plain and cordial hospitality which gave him all the advantages of rational, gentleman-like society. The clergy of Edinburgh mixed more than I think they have done at any subsequent period with the first and most distinguished persons of the place—distinguished whether for science, literature, and polite manners—and even as far as the clerical character might allow with men of fashion conspicuous for wit and gaiety."[1] The most notable specimen of the accomplished country clergyman was Dr. Carlyle of Inveresk, the companion of all men of letters, who, being born in 1722, appeared at the time which, by some strange coincidence, produced most of the famous Scots literati. By right of good lineage, of culture and talent, he took his place with the best of them, and he was more adapted to shine in society than perhaps any one of them. Tall, strikingly handsome in form, with noble features that won for him the name of "Jupiter" Carlyle, with dignity of manners, humour, and vivacity in talk, he was a notable figure in his day. There was he living in his manse on a stipend of about £100 a year, yet entertaining at times Lord Elibank, and the Hon. Charles Townshend, and Sir William Pulteney, with his friends Hume, Ferguson, and Robertson. He was an able man of affairs in the Church, the brilliant associate of people of fashion, as welcome at Dalkeith Palace as in an Edinburgh tavern, the trusted friend of politicians like Townshend, Dundas, and Sir Gilbert Elliot, the favourite companion of men of letters and law in Edinburgh and of Smollett in London, and yet a popular pastor to his people. A cool, shrewd man, he was a moderate of the most distinct type; very apt to mistake enthusiasm for cant and zeal for fanaticism, and disposed to look with contempt on men of a narrower type. It was indeed difficult to hide that contempt for dull-witted brethren in his Presbytery who had libelled and censured him for "contravening the laws of God, of this kingdom, and the Church," in

[1] Mackenzie's *Life of Home*, p. 10.

witnessing *Douglas* performed—a play which they averred
" contained tremendous oaths and woeful exclamations." These
brethren complained that the culprit "did not feel humble."[1]
It is not as a man of letters that Carlyle can rank, for with all
his keen taste for literature he made but slight contributions
to it. When he appeared in later years at St. James's, being
in London on Church affairs, we are told he impressed
courtiers with his striking appearance, "his portly form, his fine
expressive countenance, with aquiline nose, and the freshness
of his face"[2]; while he impressed politicians with his sound
sense, his honourable principles, and social qualities, in which
he never forgot his character as a clergyman. Living on in
vigorous old age, he deplored the departure of learning and
culture and high breeding from the Church before the end of
the century. Owing to several causes had this great change
taken place. Other professions, more lucrative employments,
had allured able and ambitious minds from a profession which
remained poor in days when the ways of living had become
less frugal. While cheap education brought into the ministry
men of humble birth, the meagreness of the livings kept
the best intellects out. The moderates who were then chosen
by Tory patrons had seldom a taste for letters, while
evangelical ministers devoted themselves exclusively to their
pastoral work.[3]

[1] In the Presbytery trial, one dull-pated minister condemned with holy horror such impious expressions as "despiteful Fate," where he protested: "Fate must signify God, and consequently 'despiteful God' was blasphemy; also the following were quite impious, such as 'Mighty God, what have I done to merit this affliction?' and in like manner, speaking of Matilda's death, 'Her white hands to heaven seeming to say, Why am I forced to this?' But, above all, the monstrous and unnatural crime of suicide was represented in such a manner as to render it more familiar to these kingdoms, which are already branded with that very crime above all the rest of the globe. Whereas the author might have represented Matilda bearing her misfortunes, and thereby showing the excellency of the Christian religion, saying, 'The Lord gave and the Lord taketh away, blessed be the name of the Lord,' which would support her under her calamities." Another co-presbyter quoted words from the tragedy, "which," he cried, "Moderator, appeared to me so horrid- they shocked me so much, that I freely own to you, Moderator, I threw the book from me on the ground!" (from Carlyle's MS. account of the proceedings of the Presbytery of Dalkeith, April 19, 1757). Home withdrew from his play some expressions that had given offence.

[2] Description by Chief Commissioner Adams. Carlyle's *Autobiography*, p. 567.
[3] Cockburn, p. 236; Mackenzie's *Home*, p. 10.

When the century came to an end, those who were to be famous in the next were scarcely known. Scott, after translating German poetry, which Henry Mackenzie had first brought to knowledge, had settled down as Sheriff-Substitute of Selkirkshire, amusing his leisure time with collecting Border minstrelsy. Francis Jeffrey was making his nimble way at the Bar, not dreaming of his future career as critic and reviewer, as dispenser and demolisher of reputations. James Hogg, while herding sheep in Ettrick, was composing ballads sung by the lasses in the district—who called him "Jamie the poeter"—and on the hillsides was scribbling verses on scraps of paper in uncouth printed letters, with a phial full of ink hanging to his button-hole. With delicious self-confidence even then he was sure that he could equal his brother peasant Robert Burns. John Leyden, who in Teviotdale had also herded his father's sheep, was acting as tutor during intervals of study at college, yet already possessed of vast stores of reading in most European and Eastern languages. He was often to be found in that favourite resort of book collectors, the little shop in the High Street newly set up by young Archibald Constable, who put over his door the legend "Scarce Old Books," which sarcastic brothers of the trade persistently read "Scarce o' Books."[1] There, amid the frequenters (including old Dr. Blair, who would often come in for some novel or romance), Leyden would prowl among the shelves—a sandy-haired youth with staring eyes, talking with "saw tones," screech voice, and excited gestures on Icelandic or Arabic. Quite satisfied that his multifarious knowledge could issue in solid work, "Dash it, man," he would say, "if you have the scaffolding ready, you can run up the masonry when you please." He was to die at Batavia at the age of thirty-six, great as an Orientalist and of repute as a poet. Susan Ferrier, the future novelist, a tall, dark, and handsome girl of twenty, was keeping house for her father, the Writer to the Signet. Joanna Baillie, the poetess, living at Hampstead, among a pleasant, tea-drinking literary coterie, was to be seen at the gatherings at Mr. Barbauld's, demurely sitting as they praised her *Plays of the Passions*, quite unaware that she

[1] *Archibald Constable and his Literary Correspondents*, i. 20.

ever had written a line in her life; for, as Miss Aikin expressed it, "she lay snug in the asylum of her taciturnity."[1] Encouraged by the liberal teaching of Dugald Stewart, his pupils, Henry Brougham and Sydney Smith (then taking charge of his pupil in Edinburgh), with Francis Jeffrey, were concocting the *Edinburgh Review*, which was to startle the world by its youthful audacity when it appeared in 1802, clad in the buff and blue colours of the Whigs, which they copied from the hues of their idol Charles Fox's capacious coat and waistcoat. Men like Dugald Stewart, Adam Ferguson, and Henry Mackenzie, who had seen much of the famous old days, saw that the venerable generation had finished its task. They could not yet, however, foresee whence were to come those literary forces in Scotland which should make the new century as brilliant as the last.

[1] Clayden's *Early Life of Rogers*, p. 80.

INDEX

Aberdeen University, 243, 248
Adair, Dr. James, 401
Adam, Robert, architect, 56
Adams, Jean, 302
Aiken, Robert, 391
Aikman, William, painter, 14; paints Thomson's portrait, 290
Ainslie, Robert, 400
Anderson, James, antiquary, 8
Arbuthnot, Dr. John, 276
Armour, Jean, 394, 403, 405, 407
Armstrong, Dr. John, 294, 316, 317
Assemblies, dancing, in Edinburgh, 23, 29, 323, 342
Auchinleck, Lord, 177, 209 et seq.
Auld, Rev. William, 391, 395, 403

Baillie, Lady Grisell, 323-326
  „ George, of Jerviswood, 324, 325, 326
Baillie, Joanna, 435
Balcarres, Lord, 338
  „ Lady, 338
  „ Dowager Lady, 342
Barnard, Lady Anne, 337-346
  „ A., 345
Barry, Spranger, acts in *Douglas*, 66
  „ Mrs., as Lady Randolph, 74
Bath, Hume at, 57; Smollett at, 305
Beattie, Dr. James, 359-372; Burns's admiration for, 387; on Scots dialect, 382
Berkeley, Bishop, 38, 247
Black, Dr. Joseph, 116, 167, 171, 431
Blacklock, Dr. Thomas, 139-147; and Beattie, 268; letter to Mr. G. Laurie, 145
Blackwell, Professor Thomas, 188, 249
Blair, Dr. Hugh, 57, 121-132, 227, 230, 236, 251, 399
Blair, Robert, author of *The Grave*, 28-30
Bolingbroke, Lord, 279, 291

Boswell, James, on Hamilton of Bangour, 26; at David Hume's, 54; at theatre with Dr. Blair, 128; and Kames, 186; account of, 203-225
Boswell, Mrs., 216
Braxfield, Lord, 185, 200
British Coffee-House, 52, 70, 89
Brown, Rev. John, 365, 378
  „ Thomas, on Reid's Philosophy, 25
Bruce, Michael, 364-370
Buccleugh, Duke of, 159
Burnett, Elizabeth, 198
Burns, Robert, on Dr. Hugh Blair, 130; account of, 383-410; at Mount Oliphant, 383; at Lochlea, 384; at Mossgiel, 388; visit to Edinburgh, 399; second visit to Edinburgh, 405; at Ellisland, 407; at Dumfries, 410; death, 416

Campbell, Principal, 250
  „ Dr. John, 306
Campvere, 71
Carlyle, Dr. Alexander, 53, 68, 81, 92, 106, 109, 163, 300, 433
Carmichael, Professor Gershom, 32, 33
Charlemont, Lord, descriptions of Hume, 46
Chesterfield, third Lord, Adam Ferguson companion to, 113
Cheyne, Dr., advice to James Thomson, 256
Churchill, Charles, 270
Clergy, Scots, in 1750, 82; towards end of century, 99, 432; "Old Lights" and "New Lights," 390; Episcopalian, 3, 359; Burghers, 366
Clerk, Sir John, 13, 355
Cockburn, Lord, on Dr. Robertson, 101; on Adam Ferguson, 119; on

Dugald Stewart, 427; on Dr. Henry, 430; on Dr. Black, 431
Cockburn, Mrs., 329-334, 341
Collection of Scottish Poems, 1706-11, Watson's, 11
Club, Philosophical, in Aberdeen, 262
" Anderston, at Glasgow, 156
Clubs, Edinburgh, Athenian, 8; Rankinian, 175; Philosophical, 175; Easy, 12; Poker, or Militia, 53, 112; Oyster, 167; Soaping, 206; Pandemonium, 378; Cape, 378; Crochallan, 105
Coleridge, S. T., on Thomson's *Seasons*, 295
Concerts, Edinburgh, 23
Constable, Archibald, 430
Conway, General, 51
Crawford, Robert, song-writer, 8, 16
Creech, William, 105, 399, 403
Crosbie, Andrew, 83, 110, 217
Cumming, Henrietta, 340, 342
Cuckoo, Ode to, authorship of, 316
Cullen, Dr., 58, 171, 187, 430
" Lord, 93

Dalrymple, Lady, 342
" Sir David, *see* Hailes
D'Arblay, Madame, on Dr. Beattie, 267
Davies, Thomas, introduces Boswell to Johnson, 207
Derrick, Samuel, 205
Defoe, Daniel, 4
D'Holbach, Baron, 47
Digges, West, 65, 67
Dissenters, Episcopalians, penal laws against, 359; Seceders, 85; increase of, 86; Burghers and Antiburghers, 366
Dodd, Dr., 113
Doddridge, Dr., 28
Dodington, Bubb, 292, 294
Douglas cause, 190
Douglas, Tragedy of, 65-66, 74
Du Deffand, Madame, 48, 161
Dumfries in 1790, 410
Dundas, Lord President, 83
Dunlop, Mrs., 397, 407

Eccles, Rev. John, pretends authorship of *Man of Feeling*, 418
Edinburgh Review, begun, 436
Edinburgh, social life in, 22, 377, 422; literary society, 104, 106, 109; St. Giles' Church, 123; University, 99; foundation of new College, 101; Parliament House, 177; Parliament Square, 179
Elegiacs, writers of, 8

Elibank, Lord, 64, 95, 112
Elliot, Sir Gilbert, Lord of Session, 335, 336
Elliot, Sir Gilbert, 83, 131, 199, 290
" Jean, author of "Flowers of the Forest," 334-337
Encyclopædia Britannica, 105, 357
Erskine, Henry, 138, 217
" Andrew, 209, 356
" Dr. John, 81, 99, 337
" Rev. Ralph, his *Gospel Sonnets*, 312
Eskgrove, Lord, 185
Evangelical clergy, or "Wild" party, 81

Falconer, William, 318
Ferguson, Adam, 91, 107-121, 171
Fergusson, Robert, on Dr. Wilkie, 139, 370-381; Burns's indebtedness to, 381, 391
Ferrier, Susan, 430
Forbes, Sir William, his *Life* of Beattie, 260; neglect of R. Fergusson, 377
Forbes, Duncan, of Culloden, 284, 321, 362
Fordyce, Alexander, 343
" Lady Margaret, 342, 345
" Dr. James, 343
Foulis, Robert and Andrew, 155
Freebairn, Robert, printer, 11

Gardenstone, Lord, 185
Garrick, David, rejects Hume's *Agis*, 62; rejects *Douglas*, 68; accepts *Agis*, 280; and Smollett, 363
Gay, John, 19
General Assembly, meetings of, 80; parties in, 82-87; condemns works of Hume and Lord Kames, 176; royal letter to, composed by Hume, 50; character of, in 1780, 87
Geoffrin, Madame, 47, 161
George III. praises Blair's *Sermons*, 128; on Beattie's *Essay*, 268; and Lord Monboddo, 195
Gibbon, Edward, 97, 163, 280
Gillespie, Rev. Thos., deposed, 84
Glasgow University, 151, 257; society, 154, 254, 299
Glencairn, Lord, 399, 401
Glover, Jean, 353
Goldsmith, Oliver, reviews *Epigoniad*, 136; jealous of Dr. Beattie, 267
Goodall, Walter, 88
Gordon, Duchess of, 188, 271, 400
" Dr. John, 298
"Grand Tour," 159
Grant, Mrs., of Laggan, 239, 304, 354
Gray, Thomas, 68, 262

INDEX

Gregory, Dr. John, 250, 263
" Dr. James, 404, 431
Griffiths, Ralph, 136, 335

Hailes, Lord, 198-202, 207, 209
Halket, George, 355
Hamilton, Gavin, 390
" William, of Gilbertfield, 8, 392
Hamilton, William, of Bangour, 16, 22-26, 174
Henry, Dr. Robert, 402-430
Hermand, Lord, 184
Heron, Robert, 140
Hertford, Lord, ambassador at Paris, 44
Hogg, James, Ettrick shepherd, 435
Home, John, 54, 60-76, 84, 88, 165; on Blacklock, 143
Hume, David, 35-60, 111, 142, 157, 176; on Ossian, 229, 231; and Dr. Reid, 252; anger at Dr. Beattie, 266; and Mrs. Mallet, 280
Hunter, Dr. John, 275, 317
" Mrs., 296
Hutcheson, Professor Francis, 31-34, 151
Hutchinsonianism, doctrines, 362
Hutton, Dr. James, 167

Islay, Lord, 81

Jardine, Dr. John, 43, 82, 87
Jeffrey, Francis, and Boswell, 223
Johnson, Samuel, on Hamilton of Bangour, 26; on *Douglas*, 67; on Robertson, 96; on Presbyterian churches, 124; on Blair, 129; visits Blacklock, 139, 146; altercation with Adam Smith, 162; at Monboddo, 194; intercourse with Boswell, 207; visit to Scotland, 216; on James Macpherson, 235; and Beattie, 265; on Mallet, 279, 284
Johnson's *Scots Musical Museum*, 362, 402, 413
Johnston, Sophia, 143, 340, 346

Kames, Lord, 24, 171-188; and Monboddo, 191; and Reid, 256; and Boswell, 223
Kant, Immanuel, 256
Keith, Miss Anne Murray, 341, 346
Ker, Professor, befriends D. Mallet, 336
King's Bench prison, Smollett in, 318
Kirkcaldy, 148
Knowles, Admiral, 310

Laurie, Dr. George, 226, 398

Leechman, Principal, 34, 252
Leyden, John, 435
Lindsay, Lady Anne, see Barnard
Literary Club, Adam Smith admitted member, 163; Boswell becomes member, 216
Lockhart, J. G., on Mackenzie's novels, 423
Logan, Rev. John, 369, 370
Loughborough, Lord, Alex. Wedderburn, 82, 88
Love, William, actor, 64, 83, 204, 211
Lyttelton, Lord, 292, 295, 299; satirised by Smollett, 312

M'Ewan, John, song-writer, 356
Mackenzie, Henry, author of *Man of Feeling*, 417-423; on Blacklock, 143, 333; on Scots clergy, 435
Mackintosh, Sir James, on Robertson's style, 98; on Reid's philosophy, 253; on Stewart's teaching, 427
Macklin, Charles, as Macbeth, 70
Macknight, Dr. James, 429
Maclaurin, Colin, 31, 99, 423
M'Lehose, Mrs., Burns's "Clarinda," 404-407
Macpherson, James, 226-252
" Sir John, 114, 230, 238
Mallet, David, 276-282; and "Rule Britannia," 291
Marchmont, Lord, Sir Patrick Home, 324, 326
Marchmont, Lord, in General Assembly, 88
Mayne, John, song-writer, 356
Meston, William, 27
Mickle, William, J., 319
Millan, John, publishes Thomson's *Winter*, 287
Millar, Andrew, bookseller, 43, 91; and Dr. Reid, 251; and Dr. Beattie, 264; publishes Thomson's *Seasons*, 287
Millar, Professor John, 256
Milton, Lord, 177
Moderates in the Church, 34, 87, 122, 390, 432; intellectual influence, 86, 430
Monboddo, Lord, 181; life and works, 188-198
Moncreiff, Sir Henry, 430
Monro, Alexander, 31
Montagu, Mrs., on Kames, 183; her parties, 265
Moor, Prof. James, 156, 255
Moore, Dr. John, 307, 315
More, Hannah, 221, 266
Murdoch, Rev. Patrick, 292, 294
Murray, John, bookseller, change of

name, 274 ; offers partnership to W.
  Falconer, 313
Nairne, Lady, 347-352
  „   Lord, 350
Newberry, John, bookseller, 311
North Briton started in opposition to
  Smollett's *Briton*, 310

Oliphant, Caroline, *see* Lady Nairne
  „   Laurence, of Gask, 347, 349
Ossian, poems of, Blair on, 126 ; publication of, 223, 231 ; literary influence, 241 ; influence on Burns, 387
Oswald, Dr., 253
Oxford, University of, 149

Pagan, Isabel, 354
Parliament House, Edinburgh, 177
Patronage, Act of, effect of, on literature, 86
Pennecuik, Dr. Alex., 14
  „   Alexander, 6
Percy, Bishop, 114
Pitcairn, Dr. Archibald, 9, 10
Pitt, William, 170, 224
Playfair, Professor, 117, 432
Poker Club, 53, 112
Pope, Alex., 276, 288, 292
Porteous Riot, Monboddo present at, 189
Prince of Wales, Frederick, patronises Mallet, 278 ; pensions Thomson, 289
Pringle, Sir John, 41, 115 ; and Boswell, 205

Queensberry, Duchess of, 190
Quesnai, Dr., 160
Quin, James, 288, 293, 295

Ramsay, Allan, 12-21
  „   „   painter, 68, 111
Rebellion of "'45," the volunteers, 60, 79, 141
Reid, Dr. Thomas, 242-259
Reynolds, Sir Joshua, 266 ; paints Beattie's portrait, 269
Riccaltoun, Rev. Robert, 283, 285
Rich, John, manager of Covent Garden Theatre, produces *Douglas*, 66 ; quarrels with Smollett, 301
Riddell, Mrs. Walter, 411, 415
Robertson, Principal, 77-103, 127 ; Dr. Carlyle's character of, 93, 127, 132, 306, 400
Robertson, Rev. William, 78
Robison, Professor John, 432
Ross, Alexander, song-writer, 356
Rousseau, J. J., brought to England by Hume, 47 ; quarrel with Hume, 50 ; visited by Boswell, 210
Rudd, Mrs., 215

Ruddiman, Thomas, 10-12, 177
  „   Walter, 328
"Rule Britannia," authorship of, 291

St. Andrews, university, 371 ; town, 272
"Schism Overture," 86
Scotsmen and Englishmen, antipathy between, 51, 70, 273, 310
Scott, Sir Walter, at Adam Ferguson's, 119 ; visits Black Dwarf, 120 ; on Miss Murray Keith, 296 ; meets Burns, 368 ; on Henry Mackenzie, 420
Seasons, Thomson's, 354
Select Society, 54, 111, 154, 180
Selkirk, Alexander, 4
Sempill, Francis, of Beltrees, 8, 393
Sharpe, Chas. Kirkpatrick, on Jean Elliot, 336
Sheridan, Thomas, presents medal to John Home, 67
Siddons, Mrs., as Lady Randolph, 75 ; and Dr. Beattie, 270
Simson, Professor Robert, 31, 34, 155
Skinner, Rev. John, 303-367
Skirving, Adam, song-writer, 356
Smellie, William, printer and author, 105, 112, 401
Smith, Adam, 58, 117, 125, 148-171 ; on Lord Kames, 187 ; on *Minstrel*, 263
Smith, Sydney, on D. Stewart, 425, 427
Smollett, Tobias, 90, 104, 297
Snell Scholarship, 149
Songs, Scots, Ramsay's *Tea-Table Miscellany*, song-writers, 7, 321, 352, 355 ; Burns's contributions to, 413
Spence, Joseph, edits Blacklock's poems, 142
Sterne, Laurence, on Smollett, 313
Stevenson, Professor John, 78, 100
Stewart, Professor Dugald, on Robertson, 92, 94 ; takes Ferguson's class, 116 ; on Reid, 255 ; on Burns, 397, 423-428
Stewart, Professor Matthew, 221, 424
Strahan, William, printer, 91, 128, 162, 231
St. Simon, Duc de, on social effect of hanging bells, 328
Stuart, Gilbert, 275 ; assails Dr. Henry's History, 428, 429
Stuart, Lady Louisa, 420

Taverns, in Edinburgh—Crosskeys, 21 ; Rankin's, 175 ; Fortune's, 81 ; Diversorium or Carrier's Inn, 83, 112 ; White Horse, 216 ; Dowie's,

53; in London—British Coffee-House, 51, 70; Mitre, 208; Smyrna, 289; in Glasgow—Saracen's Head, 257
Telfer, Miss, 308, 314, 317
Temple, Rev. William, Boswell's letters to, 215
Theatres, popular plays, 62, 69; costumes, 69, 288; salaries, 309
Thomson, James, 278, 289-297
„ George, 413, 415
Thrale, Mrs., on Beattie, 332
Turnbull, Professor George, 245
Tytler, James, song-writer, author, and projector, 357
Tytler, William, 200

Union, effect of, on literature, 3

Vane, Lady, Lady of Quality, 304
Voltaire, 106; on Lord Kames, 182; visited by Boswell, 210; describes metaphysics, 258

Walker, Rev. Robert, 123
Wallace, Dr. Robert, 82, 123
Walpole, Horace, on Hume's plays, 74; on Robertson's History, 91; on Beattie, 270
Ward, Mrs., actress, 65, 189
Wardlaw, Lady, author of *Hardyknute*, 321-323
Watt, James, 154
Wealth of Nations published, 163
Webster, Dr. Alex., 82, 94, 123; song by, 356
Wedderburn, Alex., afterwards Lord Loughborough, 83, 89
Wilkie, Professor William, 80, 132-139
Wilkes, John, 214, 270
Wilson, Professor Alex., typefounder, 154
Wodrow, Robert, on Dr. Pitcairn, 9
Woffington, Margaret, as Lady Randolph, 66

THE END

Printed by R. & R. CLARK, LIMITED, Edinburgh.

Lightning Source UK Ltd.
Milton Keynes UK
174692UK00001B/177/P